The Universe That Is God

An insight into the Thousand Names of Lord Viṣṇu

I. Panduranga Rao

With a Foreword by
Karan Singh

JÑĀNA - PRAVĀHA
Centre for Cultural Studies
Varanasi 221 005

D.K. Printworld (P) Ltd.
An Intercontinental Publishing Enterprise
New Delhi - 110 015

Cataloging in Publication Data — DK

Panduranga Rao, I. (Ilapavuluri), 1930 –
The universe that is God.

1. Viṣṇusahasranāma — Commentaries. 2. Vishnu (Hindu deity) — Names. 3. Hindu hymns, Sanskrit — Criticism, interpretation, etc. 4. Philosophy, Hindu.
I. Title.

Published by:

JÑĀNA - PRAVĀHA

Centre for Cultural Studies
Samne Ghat, Garhwa Ghat, Ashram Road, Bhagawanpur,
Varanasi 221 005, INDIA,
Phone : (0542) 366326, *Fax* : (0542) 366971
E-mail: jppvns@vsnl.com

and

D.K. Printworld (P) Ltd.

An Intercontinental Publishing Enterprise
Regd. office : '*Sri Kunj*', F-52, Bali Nagar
New Delhi - 110 015
Phones : (011) 545-3975, 546-6019; *Fax* : (011) 546-5926
E-mail: dkprint@4mis.com

First Edition: 1999
ISBN 81-246-0153-4

Phototype setting: Vardhan Computer Graphics

Printed by: Display Printers Pvt. Ltd., Culcutta - 700019

पुरुष एवेदꣳसर्वम् यद्भूतं यच्च भव्यम्
puruṣa eveda ꣳ sarvam yadbhūtaṁ yacca bhavyam

All that has been and is going to be is All that
He is — the *Puruṣa* of thousands of heads,
thousands of eyes and thousands of feet

सहस्रशीर्षा पुरुषः सहस्राक्षः सहस्रपात्
saharaśīrṣā puruṣaḥ sahasrākṣaḥ sahasrapāt

Publisher's Note

In our daily prayers we chant many hymns, but seldom try to understand the inner meaning and its effects. In an endeavour to unfold the petals of our scriptural lotus, we offer this book - 'The Universe That Is God' explaining the divine synonyms of ' Sri Vishnu Sahasranama Stotram'. Dr. I. Panduranga Rao an erudite scholar and devotee deserves our rich compliments and admiration. Our heartfelt gratitude is due to Dr. Karan Singh, a great philosopher, scholar par excellence and Rajarshi in true sense, for his learned forwarding note. We also thank all our colleagues and friends with whose help this publication has taken shape. We humbly present it to readers with a hope that it will help in arousing the quest to go into the depth of our scriptures.

श्रीमता पाण्डुरंगेण सूक्ष्मबुद्ध्या समीक्षितम्
विष्णोर्नाम सहस्रं नो भातु भूति विवर्धनम्

śrīmatā pāṇḍuraṅgeṇa sūkṣmabuddhyā samīkṣitaṁ
viṣṇornāma sahasraṁ no bhātu bhūti vivardhakaṁ

Varanasi
Makara Saṅkrāntī
January 14, 1999

Bimla Poddar
(Managing Trustee)

Foreword

Apart from the great Shastras in the Hindu tradition - the Vedas, the Upanishads, the Puranas, the Epics and so on - hymnology has also played a significant role in the development of India's religious and spiritual life down through the ages. Indeed, these Stotras represent a bridge between the highly sophisticated texts and the common people who worship various deities such as Shiva & Vishnu, Lakshmi & Durga, Ganesha & Hanuman, Rama & Krishna. The hymns usually contain 108 (Ashtottara) or 1000 (Sahasranama) appelations of the worshipped deity. Regular prayers are performed in many temples established in South India, and this practice flourishes down to the present day.

Indeed so important are these texts, that many great Acharyas have written commentaries upon them, mainly in Sanskrit. Sri Vishnu Sahasranama and Sri Lalita Sahasranama are among the most popular of these great hymns, the former having been recited by Bhishma while lying upon his bed of arrows after the terrible battle of Mahabharata. Adi Shankaracharya wrote erudite commentaries upon both these hymns.

Dr. I. Panduranga Rao, whom I have known for many years, is an outstanding Sanskrit scholar with numerous publications to his credit in Hindi, Telugu and English. He is a great devotee of Lord Vishnu, and has in this book - 'The Universe That Is God' given us an excellent commentary on the Vishnu Sahasranama, one of the most important hymns in the great corpus of Hindu literature. This hymn consists of 107 verses, and Dr. Rao has explained the significance of the thousand names of Lord Vishnu by devoting one chapter each to every verse. He has also given them separate names, so that their purport is more easily comprehensible to the general reader. Dr. Panduranga Rao has brought all his devotional equipment as well as scholastic talent to presenting what will be a widely read commentary on Sri Vishnu Sahasranama.

While congratulating the author on his achievement, I would also like to commend a comparatively new institution, JÑĀNA - PRAVĀHA set up recently in the sacred city of Varanasi by Smt. Bimla Poddar and Sri Suresh Neotia. This will be their first major publication, and I am sure many more will follow in due course. Living as we are in an age of great tumult and turmoil, strengthening our spiritual awareness has become a prime necessity if we are successful to overcome the challenges that face us. In the present Kaliyuga, devotion to a personal deity and repetition of His/Her name is considered to be the simplest and most effective path of salvation. It is in this broader context that I have great pleasure in presenting this Volume - **The Universe That Is God** by Sri I Panduranga Rao to interested readers in India and around the world.

New Delhi
January 1, 1999

(KARAN SINGH)

ॐ

Mine, but Not Mine

Śrimad-Bhagavadgītā and Śri Viṣṇu Sahasranāma have been looking after me and my welfare - both secular and spiritual - with parental affection right from my childhood. My mother used to recite the lyrical rendering of Gītā in our mother-tongue Telugu in the early hours just to wake us up. My father used to perform Sahasranāmārcanā daily and I used to assist him in reading out the thousand names of the Lord. This routine initiated me into the two sacred texts in a tender age of hardly seven years. One Sadhu presented a copy of Gītā to me more or less at this time and asked me to read it daily and then have anything to eat. I took it as a divine sanction for the service I was rendering to my parents. Thus the two texts have become an integral part of all my thoughts and actions.

I never imagined that I would, one day, be commissioned to say something about these monumental works in Telugu, my mother tongue Hindi, the link-language for the cultural interaction in India and now in English, the most effective medium for the dissemination of spiritual and cultural wisdom promoted by the sages and the seers of this country. It has been my sincere feeling that I was only instrumental in offering this service to humanity at large and I drew the whole inspiration and insight from the generosity of the Great Grand Father of the Universe. I, therefore confess sincerely that this work of mine is just supposed to be mine, but not mine in the real sense.

I shall consider it a great blessing to me in life if what I have attempted to say in this exposition helps the discerning readers feel even for a split of a second that thiswhole universe is the eternal abode of the Self within ourselves, the soul of all souls and the essence of all existence which we worship as God. He is present in every atom of this 'atmic' habitat. We see with His eyes, hear with His ears, think with His mind and share with Him His blissful moments and movements as His unspelt but inbuilt and in-felt blessings.

I am grateful to the management of JÑĀNA-PRAVĀHA for having taken up the noble cause of spreading the message of our sages through such publications and I feel it a great privilege that they have chosen my humble contribution to inaugurate this programme of publication which, I am sure, will have an endless flow like the perennial one of the holy river Gaṅgā, the symbol of creativity.

I do not know how to express my gratitude to Dr. Karan Singh, a spiritual statesman of our times who has introduced this work to the readers' community with a great heart.

I am indebted to Smt. Bimla Devi Poddar and Smt. Kalyani Khaitan who have organized this publication with great devotion. May the Lord bless them and also all those who have contributed to this cause.

In the end, I pay my homage to the primordial sound OM, the fountain-head of all voice, vision and wisdom.

OM NAMA ITI

ॐ नम इति

I Panduranga Rao

New Delhi

January 1, 1999

(I. Panduranga Rao)

Sequence

The Text And The Context

Is there any Supreme Spirit responsible for the creation, sustenance and dissolution of this phenomenal world called Universe? If so, who or what is that? Is He or She or It an individual soul like any other living being or a Universal Soul *Viśvātmā*? How to realize and visualize that Cosmic existence, excellence and exuberance transcending the limits of time and space? What is the ultimate goal of this life temporal obviously marching towards something eternal, everlasting and inexplicable? What is it that one can and should do to get a glimpse or at least a feel of that Omnipresent, Omnipotent and Omniscient force that directs and controls all the other forces - both terrestrial and celestial?

These are some of the basic issues which have been engaging the attention of the most enlightened minds and even some of the realized souls of this world since time immemorial. Such questions become all the more pronounced in times of cultural crisis and spiritual degeneration. This happens because of the imbalance between matter and spirit, voice and vision and wealth and wisdom.

More or less a similar situation prevailed at the time of the great war of *Mahābhārata*. This battle was fought mainly to restore human values and dignity to their virtual status and re-establish *dharma* (righteousness) under the guidance and leadership of Lord *Kṛṣṇa*, the Man, the Divine. As a Spiritual Statesman, though *Kṛṣṇa* assumed the role of a charioteer for *Arjuna*, He was the key person and the cynosure of the entire scenario exercising full control over all the events and eventualities of the great battle. It was He who tried His best to avoid the battle as a messenger of peace. But when all His efforts failed, it was again He who set the battle in motion and placed it on a straight and strong footing. When *Arjuna* was almost mentally withdrawing from the strong will to fight the battle, it was again He who energized him and made him realize his duty not only from the secular and the strategic point of view, but also from the socio-political and spiritual angle. This message addressed to *Arjuna* at a personal level in a critical juncture later became a spiritual sermon for the vast mass of humanity in the form of the most celebrated text known as *Bhagavadgītā*.

Again, on the conclusion of the battle with the desired end achieved, it was Lord *Kṛṣṇa*, the same Spiritual Statesman, who advised *Yudhiṣṭhira*, the eldest of the five *Pāṇḍavas*, to approach *Bhīṣma*, the greatest political philosopher of his times for his wise counsel as to the re-establishment of law and order in the chaotic conditions created by evil forces. It should be remembered that it was this same *Kṛṣṇa*, the mysterious master of the universe, who used all his diplomacy to manage the self-surrender of *Bhīṣma* whom even death cannot win over unless he himself volunteers. *Bhīṣma* readily agrees, at the mere sight of *Kṛṣṇa* leading this delegation, to address *Yudhiṣṭhira* and answer all his queries. But *Bhīṣma*, a rare combination of spiritual radiance and strategic innovation conveys his soul-elevating message in the form of glorious tributes to the Lord of the Universe.This message of the *Ācārya,* almost towards the conclusion of war, like the one delivered by *Kṛṣṇa* just before the war, took the form of another sacred text known as *Śrī Viṣṇu Sahasranāma Stotra*, a popular hymn containing thousand names of the Lord.

Whatever be the context in which these two sacred texts--*Gītā* and *Sahasranāma*--emerged, the spiritual world is blessed with these two monumental works which are almost universal in their appeal. These two texts-- *Gītā* and *Sahasranāma*--are so popular among the scholars and students of Indian philosophy and more so among the devotees of the Lord that these short titles hardly need any expansion. Though there are several texts like *Pāṇḍava Gītā, Brahmā Gītā, Śiva Gītā* etc., the word *Gītā* is readily understood as *Śrīmad Bhagavadgītā.* Similarly there are number of texts under the titles ending with the word *Sahasranāma* like *Śrī Lalitā Sahasranāma, Śrī Śiva Sahasranāma, Śrī Subrahmaṇya Sahasranāma etc.* But if we simply say *Sahasranāma,* it denotes *Śrī Viṣṇu Sahasranāma.*

The placement of these two texts is also significant. Both the texts are integral parts of the celebrated epic *Mahābhārata*. There are 18 *parvas* or thematical sections in the *Mahābhārata. Gītā* figures in the sixth one named *Bhīṣma Parva* where the great war of *Mahābhārata* starts and *Sahasranāma* comes in the thirteenth *Parva* called *ānuśāsanika parva* where the battle almost comes to an end. Thus *Gītā* finds its place in the last among the first six *Parvas* and *Sahasranāma* in the first among the last six. Thereby these two texts not only trisect the whole epic into three phases-- pre-war, war and post-war - but also serve as an introductory key-note to the Great War by the Key person *Kṛṣṇa* and as a solemnified summing up by *Bhīṣma* the learned *Ācārya* and Stateman combined in one when the whole struggle came to a peaceful end.

Apart from the placement, which could be just a coincidence, there is a more stimulating and scintillating concordance in the purport of the two texts. One paves the way for war and prepares the warrior for a poised and purposeful participation in the battle fought for the establishment of righteousness, while the other one--*Sahasranāma* -- sums up the good and the bad effects of an inevitable encounter and prepares an outline, or so to say, a blue print for the establishment of peace amidst chaos and confusion. Thus the two time-honoured texts serve as prologue and epilogue for the major event of *Mahābhārata*-- the battle between virtue and vice, expectation and exploitation, consideration and conceit and in short, between the right and the wrong. The diction and style adopted by the two preceptors (Lord *Kṛṣṇa* in case of *Gītā* and *Ācārya Bhīṣma* in case of *Sahasranāma*) are so appropriate to the context that they serve as complementary to each other.

Gītā is in the form of a dialogue and the message and is in complete sentences making full meaning even to the average reader though the subtleties require a discerning mind to grasp. But *Bhīṣmācārya* chose to convey his thoughts in the form of a sacred hymn glorifying the splendid attributes and excellences of *Viṣṇu*, the Lord of the Universe. Thus the text consists of isolated and highly significant names (trying to qualify the undefinable qualities of the Cosmic Being) in an enchanting and exhilarating diction. The names sing for themselves and the aspirant chanting the names feels so much absorbed in the exercise that it ceases to be mechanical and rapidly transforms itself into a metaphysical experience. What *Gītā* tells us in 700 verses covering full 18 chapters each devoted to a specific theme, *Sahasranāma* tries to communicate the same in a short and sweet paean consisting of just thousand names of the Lord covered in 107 verses reverberating with Vedic vibrations.

Despite this difference in the diction, the two texts have many points of similarity in substance. For instance, the thousand names of the Lord start with the name *Viśvam* which means the Universe. The most significant phenomenon in *Gītā* is the manifestation of the Cosmic Form *Viśvarūpa* by *Śrī Kṛṣṇa* to *Arjuna*. There are several names of the Lord enumerated in *Sahasranāma* which describe this cosmic form like *Viśvātmā* (225), *Viśvabhūk* (239), *Viśvabāhuḥ* (316), *Viśvadakṣiṇaḥ* (425), *Viśvamūrti* (717) and so on besides the very first word *Viśvam*. Similarly, *dharma* (righteousness), the main thrust of *Gītā* finds frequent references in the names like *Dharmādhyakṣaḥ* (135), *Dharmaḥ* (403), *Dharmaviduttamaḥ* (404) and *Dharmī* (477). The references to *Atman* and *Brahman* are also common to both the texts. The only difference is that *Gītā* explains the significance of all these concepts while *Sahasranāma* leaves it to the imagination and receptivity of the devotee who recites.

One more example is perhaps worth our attention to appreciate this point better. When we come across the names *Karaṇaṁ* (378), *Kāraṇaṁ* (379), *Kartā* (380), *Vikartā* (381), *Gahanaḥ* (382) and *Guhaḥ* (383) occuring in quick succession in *Sahasranāma*, our attention is instantly drawn towards the parallel references in *Gītā* discussing *karma*, *akarma* and *vikarma* with the concluding observation - *gahanā karmaṇo gatiḥ*. The full text of the relevant verse in *Gītā* is as follows :

कर्मणो ह्यपि बोद्धव्यं बोद्धव्यं च विकर्मणः ।
अकर्मणश्च बोद्धव्यं गहना कर्मणो गतिः ॥

karmaṇo hyapi boddhavyaṁ
boddhavyaṁ ca vikarmaṇaḥ I
akarmaṇaśca boddhavyaṁ
gahanā karmaṇo gatiḥ II [*Gītā:* 4-17]

As pointed out earlier, it is easier to grasp the message of *Gītā* expressed in clear terms compared to the assimilation of ideas hidden in the isolated words (names) of *Sahasranāma*. But the beauty about this garland of names *nāmamālikā* is the blissful blend of sound and sense if only the aspirant is blessed with an imaginative insight to visualize the world of message behind these words that blossom. One excellent example for this type of expression is a line consisting of six names which is as follows:

सुव्रतः सुमुखः सूक्ष्मः सुघोषः सुखदः सुहृत् ।

suvrataḥ sumukhaḥ sūkṣmaḥ sughoṣaḥ sukhadaḥ suhṛt I

The six names enumerated in this line are supposed to be the attributes of the Lord of the Universe, the presiding deity of the paean. But if we carefully examine the qualities projected in these words and follow the sequence in which they are arranged, we find the basic principles of public administration applicable to anyone in charge of man-management. The names *Suvrataḥ* (strong determination), *Sumukhaḥ* (proper motivation), *Sūkṣmaḥ* (careful consideration of various implications and subtleties involved), *Sughoṣaḥ* (communicative skill), *Sukhadaḥ* (positive approach to see that what is contemplated ultimately leads to general welfare and happiness) and finally *Suhṛt* (being good at heart) give us a comprehensive picture of a sound administrative pattern to follow. Naturally, the Lord of the Universe ruling the vast mass of humanity and countless creatures He has created is the source of inspiration for cultivating these qualities.

Such examples can be multiplied and in fact, the whole text is full of such words of wisdom which will enable the aspirants to purify themselves and come closer and closer to the cynosure of spiritual radiance projected in each and every name of the Lord. As *Bhīṣma* points out in the introductory verses, these are the names cited and recited by the great seers *ṛṣibhiḥ parigītāni*. Sound *nāda* for these seers is not something merely to be heard,but it has to be seen, visualized and realized in its potential form. *Gītā* too supports this view by saying that the absolute knowledge ,as different form the conditioned one, is based on the direct experience of the sages who sang its glory in several tunes and notes, words and vibrations, metres and mantric modes *ṛṣibhir bahudhā gītaṁ chandobhirvividhaiḥ pṛthak* [*Gītā*: 13-5].

But one has to remember that it is unqualified devotion that helps in the proper assimilation of the content of this simple and beautiful garland of names. Even if one does not know the real meaning, the mere chanting of these names with correct articulation and intonation coupled with undivided attention produces vibrations in the body, mind and spirit which go a long way not only in the purification of the soul, but also in the visualization of divinity potentially present in all living beings.Thus the *Nāmasahasraṁ* caters to the needs of both the scholar and the common man. Even hearing somebody chanting these names elevates the soul. There is no elaborate equipment necessary to do the recitation part of it. There is no time-restriction either . One can do it at any time and in any place convenient to him. It can be done at home or in the working place at leisure-time or even while relaxing just before going to bed. If one has got the text by heart, it can be an excellent exercise to contemplate on the names and their meaning. The more we concentrate or meditate on the deep meaning of the names, the more we feel refreshed, enlightened and accomplished. It promotes physical health, mental relief and spiritual awareness. If it is sung in chorus, it becomes *Nāma-Saṅkīrtana* (collective chanting) which adds to the social harmony of the group of devotees.

How the mere chanting of the names either orally or mentally can be so effective as to bring about an electronic change in the physical and metaphysical status of an individual is a matter which finds its key in a dialogue between *Nārada* and *Sanatkumāra* as presented in *Chāndogya Upaniṣad* [Ch. VI].

Once, in a moment of trance and tranquility, *Nārada* started contemplating on all the knowledge he acquired and felt that inspite of his learning in various fields, he could not make himself a full man, let alone a perfect one. He, then, approached the young but matured scholar *Sanatkumāra* for advice and guidance. *Sanatkumāra* wanted to know what *Nārada* had already learnt. *Nārada* mentioned almost all the disciplines he had mastered. But the long list including *Veda, Vedāṅgas,* mythology, astrology, logic, philosophy, grammar, archery and so on could not impress the realized soul *Sanatkumāra*. He simply smiled and said that what *Nārada* had learnt so far was just a name or a group of names and nothing beyond that. He further remarked that even the Name he had learnt would not take him to the highest stage of learning unless he cultivates an insight into it and visualize the absolute reality hidden in it.

Then *Nārada* wanted to know the various faculties of learning more rewarding than Name. *Sanatkumāra* says, 'Yes. Speech *vāk* is higher than name. Then the dialogue continues for a long time leading to the identification of higher and higher faculties of learning. Name, speech, mind, determination, contemplation, cognition, competence, food, water, light, space, memory, aspiration, respiration and so on find a place in the list. The order in which these faculties are arranged is mainly due to the fact that one leads to the other and the former forms the basis for the latter. *Nārada* stops his further queries when *Sanatkumāra* comes to *prāṇa* (life-breath). This is because *Bṛhadāraṇyaka* equates *prāṇa* with *Satyam* (truth). *Prāṇa vai satyam.* This observation had, of course, a special connotation for *Nārada* as he had all the time been worshipping his deity *Nārāyaṇa* chanting His name with devotion and playing it on his *Vīṇā Mahati.* Now he suddenly realizes that the *Nāda* (the sound) is the real essence of *Nāma* which, in fact, is the manifestation of *Prāṇa.*

On a careful analysis of the entire discussion, one can easily conclude that all names disappear, but the *nāda* (the primal sound) remains just as *prāṇa* remains after the body gets dissolved. Another subtle difference between name and sound is that the former is dependent on some object or concept while the latter is totally independent. But it is the name that takes the aspirant to the primal sound, *nāda.* According to *Patañjali*, the primordial sound, *Praṇava* or *Om* is the code syllable for the Lord of the Universe *tasya vācakaḥ praṇavaḥ*. Thus the simple name can rise to the level of universal sound with the help of deep meditation, concentration, contemplation and devotion. This is what this episode tries to bring home to the aspirants of *Nāma-saṅkīrtana* (chanting the name of the Lord).

Śaṅkara makes this point clear in his commentary on *Chāndogya Upaniṣad* by saying that this chapter VI of the *Upaniṣad* is devoted to deliberate and dwell upon the highest truth and the ultimate goal of life. *paramārtha tattvopadeśa pradhāna paraḥ ṣaṣṭhodhyāyaḥ*. It is this background that makes *Śaṅkara* suggest in his famous lyric *Bhaja Govindam* that one should sing the glory of the Lord in thousand names as they resound in *Gītā* (*Geyaṁ Gītā Nāma Sahasraṁ*). It looks as if he is saying, 'Name Him, the song is sung'.

There are a few points to be remembered while reading or reciting the *Sahasranāma*. Firstly, correct pronunciation is very important as it is the Sound *nāda* that matters more than the meaning or the substance of the word or the name. The vibrations produced while uttering the names are very effective and powerful. These vibrations are designed in a well thought out sequence to produce the desired result by the sages who had visualized the voice. It is a voice of vision that we find in this sacred text.

Secondly, one does not notice any thought-sequence in the names as we recite them. But there is a sequence of vibrations which should be noted and cultivated by practice. These vibrations have nothing to do with the meaning normally found in the dictionaries. For instance, the names like *Nyagrodhaḥ, Udumbaraḥ, Aśvatthaḥ, Śikhaṇḍī, Nahuṣaḥ, Vṛṣaḥ, Kapiḥ* have entirely different meaning in the sacred hymn. One has to depend upon the scholarly interpretation and divine grace to catch the spirit behind these names.

Thirdly there are certain names which are not found in common usage like *Śipiviṣṭha, Svāsya, Apyayaḥ, Vaikhānaḥ*. One has to make special efforts to understand them and such efforts are always awarding.

Fourthly, there are certain names which look like antonyms like *arthaḥ* and *anarthaḥ*. Both are the attributes of the Lord. But an average person stops for a minute and struggles for proper understanding. In this case, the name *artha* means 'that which is aspired for'. As everybody aspires for the Lord, He is called *arthaḥ*. He is, in the same breath, called *anarthaḥ* too which is just contrary to the preceding name *artha*. One wonders what it means? *Anarthaḥ,* here, means that there is nothing else to be aspired for once the Lord has granted His divine grace.

There is yet another illustration of this tendency to bring together two opposite concepts and attribute both of them as tributes to the Lord. A line consisting of seven names including three pairs of antonyms is as follows :

अणुर्बृहत्कृशः स्थूलो गुणभृन्निर्गुणो महान्।

aṇur-bṛhat-kṛśaḥ sthūlo guṇabhṛn-nirguṇo mahān I

> The minute and the majestic, the slender and the strong, the container of all the three *guṇas*, yet transcending all the three and hence very great.

The last point worth noting is the repetition of cretain names with different shades of meaning in different contexts. Out of the thousand names, there are 75 names repeated twice, 11 names thrice, and only 2 names are repeated 4 times. This repetition is not to be taken as a matter of chance or overlook. It is deliberately done with a purpose of highlighting the significance of the multifarious shades of a certain name. The name *Viṣṇu* itself is repeated thrice (2, 258 and 657). The meaning is different in different contexts. Therefore special attention has to be paid to understand the various nuances of these words. As if, to highlight the significance of such repetition, the word *Vasupradaḥ* is repeated without any gap. The following is the verse in which this repetition occurs:

मनोजवस्तीर्थकरो वसुरेता वसुप्रदः ।
वसुप्रदो वासुदेवो वसुर्वसुमना हविः ॥

manojavas-tīrthakaro vasuretā vasupradaḥ |
vasuprado vāsudevo vasur-vasumanā haviḥ ||

It can be seen that the word *Vasupradaḥ* appears here as the last word of the first line followed immediately as the first word of the next line. One can also notice the frequency of the sound *vasu* in various names occuring in this verse. This tendency to repeat the same sound in different names in the same verse is also very common in this sacred text. This is a clear indication that sound is as much important, if not more, as the meaning of the word. The best example to illustrate this point is the following verse:

ब्रह्मण्यो ब्रह्मकृद्ब्रह्मा ब्रह्म ब्रह्मविवर्धनः ।
ब्रह्मविद् ब्राह्मणो ब्रह्मी ब्रह्मज्ञो ब्राह्मणप्रियः ॥

brahmaṇyo brahmakṛd-brahmā brahma brahma-vivardhanaḥ |
brahmavid-brāhmaṇo brahmī brahmajño brāhmaṇa-priyaḥ ||

There are abundant instances of this type in the entire paean. Incidentally, this promotes the generation of pleasant vibrations while reciting the names.

In fact, the whole text is a feast not merely for the ears but also for the heart, mind and soul. One has to experience it and realize how enchanting the chanting of these names could be.

The Prologue

The main text of the sacred hymn, *Śrī Viṣṇu Sahasranāma Stotraṁ* consists of 107 verses forming the central portion of ch. 149 of the *Ānuśāsanika prava* of *Mahābhārata.* The chapter, however, contains 142 verses of which the first 13 verses form the prologue and the last 22 verses highlighting the efficacy of the prayer form the epilogue. Most of the devotees recite the whole text including the introductory and the concluding verses though for religious and ritualistic purpose, the main text covering the thosand names of the Lord should suffice. While performing *arcanā* (worshipping the deity with flowers or sanctified rice), only the names are uttered adding *Om* as prefix and *namaḥ* (salutation) as suffix. Some devotees use the text for meditation, chanting the names mentally. In that case they have improvised their own preliminary prayer consisting of sacred expressions like *dhyānam* (invocative verse) and *nyāsa* (an analytical appraisal of the various components of the sacred text as *mahāmantram* - each name treated as a *mantra* by itself).

For a comprehensive assimilation of the significance of the whole text, it is worth going through the introductory and the concluding verses as well. The first 13 verses forming the prologue contain a dialogue between the King *Yudhiṣṭhira* and *Ācārya Bhīṣma* where the King wants to know from the learned *Ācārya* as to who exactly is the Supreme Deity among various deities worshipped for solace and salvation and which *dharma* or ritual or code of conduct among all *dharmas* is of utmost purport and significance. In fact this is not the first question that the King has put to the *Ācārya*. He already made several enquiries about many spiritual matters and received valuable guidance and instruction from *Bhīṣma*. That is what *Vaiśampāyana* informs us as an introduction to the dialogue. He tells *Janamejaya*:

श्रुत्वा धर्मानशेषेण पावनानि च सर्वशः ।
युधिष्ठिरः शान्तनवं पुनरेवाभ्यभाषत ।।

śrutvā dharmānaśeṣeṇa pāvanāni ca sarvaśaḥ /
yudhiṣṭhiraḥ śāntanavaṁ punarevābhyabhāṣata //

> Having heard exhaustively about the various intricacies of *dharma,* the ethical code of conduct from a great soul like *Bhīṣma*, the son of *Śāntanu, Yudhiṣṭhira*, the eldest of the five *Paṇḍavas* once again approaches the *Ācārya* with some more queries to get his doubts clarified and make his mind more and more purified.

It can easily by noticed by any sincere reader of this soul-searching dialogue between the inquisitive disciple *Yudhiṣṭhira* and the condescending mentor like *Bhīṣma* that the learner is trying to derive the maximum benefit out of the kindhearted Master of all learning who was in the most matured moments of his life.

Dharmarāja too appropriately referred to here as *Yudhiṣṭhira*, strong in his determination to win his cause in churning the milky ocean of knowledge, addresses the *Ācārya* in a polite language expressing his doubts as follows :

किमेकं दैवतं लोके किं वाप्येकं परायणम् ।
स्तुवन्तः कं कमर्चन्तः प्राप्नुयुर्मानवाः शुभम् ॥

kimekaṁ daivataṁ loke kiṁ vāpyekaṁ parāyaṇam |
stuvantaḥ kaṁ kamarcantaḥ prāpnuyurmānavāḥ śubhaṁ ||

Who is the One Supreme Lord of this entire universe and who, indeed, is the final refuge for all the living beings? By singing whose glory, grandeur and grace or worshipping whom wholeheartedly, the people inhabiting this phenomenal world can attain the highest bliss and benevolence?

को धर्मः सर्वधर्माणां भवतः परमो मतः ।
किं जपन्मुच्यते जन्तुर्जन्मसंसारबन्धनात् ॥

ko dharmaḥ sarvadharmāṇāṁ bavataḥ paramo mataḥ |
kiṁ japanmucyate janturjanma-saṁsārabandhanāt ||

What, according to your most esteemed opinion, is the highest form of righteousness or the most sacred duty one can and should cultivate? By chanting which reverberating and sanctified assemblage of soul-stirring sounds can any living being be liberated from the bondage of birth and rebirth?

According to *Ādi Śaṅkara,* the great commentator of this sacred text, there are six points raised by *Yudhiṣṭhira* in this query. But the *Ācārya* hardly takes any time to respond to the query or series of queries made by the King and presents a lasting and standing solution to the whole problem with a synthetic approach and scintillating articulation of the sacred names of the Lord. He starts abruptly with reciting four names of the Lord of his heart presenting Him as the Lord of the Universe *Jagatprabhu,* the most celestial among all celestial deities *devadeva,* the Infinite *anantam* and an Embodiment of Excellence *puruṣottama.* These four names of the Lord form the first line of the ten verses in which he responds to the queries made by his disciple. Then he proceeds to advise him that an aspirant who seeks the grace of the Lord has to recite or chant His thousand names with alertness that knows no punctuation.

जगत्प्रभुं देवदेवमनन्तं पुरुषोत्तमम् ।
स्तुवन्नामसहस्रेण पुरुषः सततोत्थितः ।।

jagatprabhuṁ devadevamanantaṁ puruṣottamaṁ I
stuvannāmasahasreṇa puruṣaḥ satatotthitaḥ II

Without giving any mark of full-stop or even a semicolon, the *Ācārya* goes on to reiterate his advice saying -

तमेव चार्चयन्नित्यं भक्त्या पुरुषमव्ययम् ।
ध्यायन्स्तुवन्नमस्यंश्च यजमानस्तमेव च ।।

tameva cārcayannityaṁ bhaktyā puruṣamavyayaṁ I
dhyāyanstuvannamasyaṁśca yajamānastameva ca II

> It is He that has to be worshipped daily with a devoted heart. It is the same Eternal Soul of all souls that has to be meditated upon, hymned and prostrated with an undivided attention.

In this second verse of his message, the *Ācārya* imperceptibly introduces another name of the Lord, the Imperishable *puruṣa-avyaya* indicating thereby that all forms of worship ultimately reach Him as He is beyond all that is perishable and also what is imperishable.

In the next verse, the *Ācārya* resumes his method of conveying his content through concording the attributes of the Lord saying -

अनादिनिधनं विष्णुं सर्वलोकमहेश्वरम् ।
लोकाध्यक्षं स्तुवन्नित्यं सर्वदुःखातिगो भवेत् ॥

anādinidhanaṁ viṣṇuṁ sarvalokamaheśvaraṁ |
lokādhyakṣaṁ stuvannityaṁ sarvaduḥkhātigo bhavet ||

> One who worships the Lord of Eternal Existence without a beginning or an end, the Omnipresent *Viṣṇu*, the Supreme Command controlling all the worlds and the Presiding Deity of the entire cosmos with sustained attention and devotion will transcend all sorrows of this transient world.

Here again we find more names of the Lord - *Anādinidhana, Viṣṇu, Sarvalokamaheśvara* and *Lokādhyakṣa.* When the *Ācārya* completes the sentence towards the end of the verse, we feel that he is summing up his observations. But in the next verse, he springs up with six more significant names in quick succession which complete the first spell of his reply. The whole verse is full of these names leaving no space for any other part of speech. The scintillating names in the verse are:

ब्रह्मण्यं सर्वधर्मज्ञं लोकानां कीर्तिवर्धनम् ।
लोकनाथं महद्भूतं सर्वभूतभवोद्भवम् ॥

brahmaṇyaṁ sarvadharmajñaṁ lokānāṁ kīrtivardhanaṁ |
lokanāthaṁ mahadbhūtaṁ sarvabhūtabhavodbhavaṁ ||

He is the promoter of all learning leading to the realization of the Absolute Reality. He is fully aware of what is right and what is wrong. He is behind the progress and prosperity of the wide expanse of all the worlds. He is the driving force behind the Universe, He is a magnificient measure of all existence and He Himself is the Being behind the being of all living beings.

These four verses comprise the first spell of the *Ācārya's* sermon delivered from the spiritual bed of arrows. There is only one verb *bhavet* in the whole quartet and that too is in the form of blessing. There are 15 names in this quarto which serve as a splendid specimen of the whole hymn that is going to follow. In these four verses, the *Ācārya* has answered most of the queries raised by King *Yudhiṣṭhira*. Now he takes up the case of *dharma,* the righteousness. The question was what is the highest *dharma.* The *Ācārya's* reply is very short, simple and straight. He says:

एष मे सर्वधर्माणां धर्मोऽधिकतमो मत: ।
यद्भक्त्या पुण्डरीकाक्षं स्तवैरर्चेन्नर: सदा ॥

eṣa me sarvadharmāṇāṁ dharmo'dhikatamo mataḥ |
yadbhaktyā puṇḍarīkākṣaṁ stavairarcennaraḥ sadā ||

Well, the highest and the most comprehensive *dharma* or the righteous act, in my opinion, is to sing His glory and thus worship Him always with devotion thinking of Him as your Charming and Cherished Guardian looking after your well being like a well-blossomed flower spreading fragrance in your heart. This is all that one can and should do to be meritorious in this mundane world.

This single verse, a self-contained answer to the question relating to *dharma,* also adds one more name - *Puṇḍarīkākṣa* (the lotus eyed) to the list of names of the Lord chosen by the *Ācārya* for his prologue. The verbal instruction in this second spell of the message is *arcet* (worship one should, to merit the grace of the Lord).

Ācārya has so far given us 16 names of the Lord-the Sweet Sixteen, sweeter than the sweetest. He then proceeds to the third spell of the sermon which too starts with the words that blossom themselves into the sacred names. The continuity in the flow of thought is evident in the inherent music in the composition of another quartet that follows. These four verses are:

परमं यो महत्तेजः परमं यो महत्तपः ।
परमं यो महद्ब्रह्म परमं यः परायणम् ॥

paramaṁ yo mahattejaḥ paramaṁ yo mahattapaḥ I
paramaṁ yo mahadbrahma paramaṁ yaḥ parāyaṇaṁ II

पवित्राणां पवित्रं यो मङ्गलानां च मङ्गलम् ।
दैवतं देवतानां च भूतानां योऽव्ययः पिता ॥

pavitrāṇāṁ pavitraṁ yo maṅgalānāṁ ca maṅgalaṁ I
daivataṁ devatānāṁ ca bhūtānāṁ yo' vyayaḥ pitā II

यतः सर्वाणि भूतानि भवन्त्यादियुगागमे ।
यस्मिंश्च प्रलयं यान्ति पुनरेव युगक्षये ॥

yataḥ sarvāṇi bhūtāni bhavantyādiyugāgame I
yasminśca pralayaṁ yānti punareva yugakṣaye II

तस्य लोकप्रधानस्य जगन्नाथस्य भूपते।
विष्णोर्नामसहस्रं मे शृणु पापभयापहम्॥

tasya lokapradhānasya jagannāthasya bhūpate |
viṣṇornāmasahsraṁ me śṛṇu pāpabhayāpahaṁ ||

All the four verses are so well-knit that they make one single sentence with the verb *śṛuṇu* (listen). The paraphrase of the four verses broadly is as follows:

> Now listen to me, oh ruler of the Kingdom, chanting the thousand names of *Viṣṇu* that destory the sin and dispel the consequent fear as He is resplendent with the Supreme Splendour, Matchless power of surpassing penance, the Creative source of all creation, the ultimate abode of all the resorts, the purest of the pure, the most auspicious of all that is auspicious, the most divine of all the forms of divinity and the eternal Father of all living beings from where the whole creation germinates when the *yuga* (aeon) starts and into whom the whole creation merges at the final dissolution of the aeon. These are the names of that All-pervading *Viṣṇu,* the Chief controller of the Universe and the Guardian of the phenomenal world-both dynamic and static.

The last verse in this prologue contains the announcement of the *Ācārya* that he is now going to present the citation of the thousand names of the Lord, the Great Grand Guardian of the Universe:

यानि नामानि गौणानि विख्यातानि महात्मनः ।
ऋषिभिः परिगीतानि तानि वक्ष्यामि भूतये ॥

yāni nāmāni gauṇāni vikhyātāni mahātmanaḥ I
ṛṣibhiḥ parigītāni tāni vakṣyāmi bhūtaye II

He says, he is uttering these names for the benefit and beatitude of the vast mass of humanity. He also says that these are not ordinary names; these are the attributes of the Almighty and are well-known to the sages and seers who have been singing and resinging them since hoary past.

Of the 13 verses in this prologue, the first one goes to *Vaiśampāyana,* the prime composer of the whole episode and the next two cover the query made by the King *Yudhiṣṭhira.* Then follow the words of wisdom articulated by the *Ācārya* in ten verses which constitute a comprehensive key-note to the sacred hymn containing the thousand names of the Lord of the Universe. These ten verses reveal the vision the *Ācārya* had before he actually enumerated the names endowed with sagacious sanctity and intrinsic divinity. Like the *Maheśvara Sūtras* of *Pāṇini* which form the basic network for his celebrated work *Aṣṭādhyāyī,* these ten verses of *Bhīṣma* lay the foundation for the sacred text of *Nāma Sahasraṁ* and present a microscopic vision of the voice that follows like a spontaneous spring of devotional ecstasy.

There seems to be a self-designed symmetry in these ten verses and their composition. There are 24 names of the Lord covered in this prologue. This number represents the basic syllables of the *Gāyatrī mantra.* Number ten (the number of verses) also represents the number of words in *Gāyatrī.* The names chosen by the *Ācārya* are in different case-endings. It looks as if the *Ācārya* was initiating *Yudhiṣṭhira* into a sacred *Mahāmantra* in an informal way. He hints at this in the last verse when he says that these are the names sung and resung by the sages of different ages and hence have a special significance. The first four names represent the *Mahā Vyāhritis Bhuḥ, Bhuvaḥ, Suvaḥ*- preceded by the primordial sound *Om*. These are supposed to be words uttered by *Brahmā* during creation. This makes the prologue, an authentic precis of the *Sahasranāma* as it is done by the author himself.

The Nascent Nine

The sacred hymn *Śrī Viṣṇu Sahasranāma* starts with the articulation of the primordial sound *Om* usually denoted by the word *praṇava*. In fact, it is neither a word nor a name - not even a syllable, but a code conceived by the experts and exponents of the 'calculus of speech and sound' which serves as a link between the visible and the invisible, the ephemeral and the eternal, the individual and the universal, and, in the present context, the human and the divine. The mere utterance of *Om*, either verbally or mentally, makes the divine presence felt by the humankind and the dialogue starts in a language intelligible more to the soul than to the mind. Once this link is established, the man or the human being transcends the limits of muscle and mind and becomes unmindful of all that surrounds him as he is face-to-face with the supreme and sovereign reality - existence, excellence and ecstasy, all combined into one.

The nearest and the most accurate expression that can describe *Om* is *akṣara,* an entity which does not accept any end, an okay which knows no decay. That is why the seers and the sages equated this mystic manifestation of the most magnificent master of this mysterious universe with the Absolute Reality *akṣaraṁ brahma paramam*. The single syllable (*akṣara,* to be more precise) *Om* stands for the entire universe - its creation, preservation and dissolution. It covers the past, the present and the future and also any other dimension of time beyond these three.

The presence of this primordial sound can always be felt by all human beings and, to a large extent, by all living beings whether they are awake, asleep, fast asleep or unconscious of the distinction between these three stages. In short, the utterance of *Om* motivates the individual soul towards realization of the potential divinity within him and elevate him to the cosmic heights where time and space merge into eternal existence of the everlasting soul - the Supreme Self.

It is significant to note that the celebrated hymn *Śrī Viṣṇu Sahasranāma* not only starts with *om*, but also concludes with the same utterance *óm nama iti*. All the thousand names of the nameless trying to give a form to the formless are inserted between these two utterances implying thereby that the entire universe with its myriad forms and names, beings and becomings, longings and belongings is but an intelligent insertion between two absolute points of silence. But this silence is so eloquent that it can silence all the eloquence of life. There cannot be a more appropriate start for the soul-elevating *stotra* (hymn) dedicated to Lord *Viṣṇu*, the Lord of the universe, *Viśvam*.

The first *śloka* of the text containing nine names of the Lord reads as follows :

ॐ विश्वं विष्णुर्वषट्कारो भूतभव्यभवत्प्रभुः ।
भूतकृद्भूतभृद्भावो भूतात्मा भूतभावनः ॥

om viśvaṁ viṣṇurvaṣaṭkāro bhūta-bhavya-bhavatprabhuḥ |
bhūtakṛd-bhūtabhṛd-bhāvo bhūtātmā bhūtabhāvanaḥ ||

The first among the thousand names of the Lord incorporated in the text happens to be *Viśvam* and not *Viṣṇu* though the entire hymn is named after Him. It cannot be an arbitrary choice, but a well-conceiv ed and well-designed beginning. Well-begun is normally half-done and in this case, it is definitely more than half - both meaningful and fruitful. The *Ācārya* has, in his characteristic way, chosen to introduce his exposition on the Lord of the universe with the word 'universe' itself. The word *viśvam* is as universal in meaning as the universe itself. It covers everything in space - both outer and inner. In the Upanishadic language, *brahman,* the absolute, is identified with *viśvam* His creation *brahmaivedaṁ viśvamidaṁ variṣṭham.* The creation and the creator are one and the same because the creator resides in the creation and presides over it. He is present in every particle of the universe as the omnipresent. He is seated in the heart of hearts of all human (and living) beings, guiding them, goading them and driving them ultimately to the blissful abode of life - both herein and hereafter. The word *viśvam* in the *saṁskṛt* language is of the neuter gender. This denotes that the Supreme Self identified with *viśvam* is also neuter and neutral. He, she or it is neither male nor female nor animate nor inanimate. It can take the form of a plant, a mountain or a river. All forms present the unpresentable and similarly all names can define the undefinable. In fact, all that we see or aspire to see, hear or try to overhear, feel or tend to feel, admire or absorb is essentially divine because it is a part of life and life is potentially divine.

The second name *Viṣṇu* literally means all-pervading. While the first name *Viśvam* prepares the ground for entrance, extension and expansion in all directions and dimensions, the second name *Viṣṇu* introduces the architect of the vast expansion named *Viśvam* which provides shelter not only for the entire creation, but also for the creator himself. The wonderful thing is that the Lord, while creating the universe makes sure that there is adequate scope for sustenance of the endless creation. The creator assumes the role of sustainer. *Viśvam* becomes *Viṣṇu.* In fact, the creation, the creator and the sustainer combine themselves into one. Thus the process of 'many' converging into 'one' and 'one' assuming the role of 'many' starts even in the initial stages of the voyage of words sponsored by the author of *Śrī Viṣṇu Sahasranāma.*

The third name *Vaṣaṭkāraḥ* is more mysterious than the first two in the sense that it denotes neither an object nor a person. It stands for a mere utterance, an invocatory word uttered by the meditator to call on the Lord. The word *vaṣaṭkāraḥ* literally means to say *vaṣaṭ* addressing the deity of meditation like *indrāya vaṣaṭ*. Thus the utterance of this third name by the practitioner of *Viṣṇu Sahasranāma* indicates that he is invocating the presence of the Lord. The Lord appears before him and the devotee merges with the deity thus completing the process of creation, occupation and identification. In other words, these three names - *Viśvam Viṣṇu* and *Vaṣaṭkāraḥ* - denote creation, preservation and dissolution of the universe. They also represent the form, the name and the formulation which form the three basic components of all the names that follow. The third name *Vaṣaṭkāraḥ* strikes the key-note for the entire exposition of the inexplicable. It also sums up the substance of its two preceding names - *Viśvam* and *Viṣṇu*.

Another interesting thing worth noticing in this context is that once a name is uttered, its impression does not end in itself, but is carried forward to all the names that follow. Thus *Viṣṇu* combines *Viśvam* and *Vaṣaṭkāraḥ* combines both *Viśvam* and *Viṣṇu*. Thus the first three names put together make the third one with its potency, in terms of efficacy of name, work out to six. Similarly, when we come to the thousandth (the concluding) name, its potency will not be one or thousand but the sum of all numbers from one to thousand i.e., five million and five hundred. In fact, the names of the nameless are infinite as they go on multiplying indefinitely with the process of recitation.

In the light of the foregoing observation, the name *Vaṣaṭkāraḥ* gains a special significance. The word *ṣaṭ* (meaning six) has a world of significance. The sound *va* is the most auspicious one as it is generated by the combination of *u* and *a* (उ and अ). By making it sixfold, the author (or the seer, to be more appropriate) of this sacred text presents the whole universe consisting of *bhūḥ* , *bhuvaḥ, suvaḥ, mahaḥ, janaḥ and tapaḥ* leading to the highest plane of consciousness namely *satyam* . All these six planes are both within and without. The six psychic centres of the body regulating the three dimensional dynamism namely *mūlādhāra, svādhiṣṭhāna, maṇīpūra, anāhata, viśuddhiḥ* and *ājñā* are all covered in the most significant name *Vaṣaṭkāraḥ* of the Lord and these six centres lead to the *sahasrāra* of the body which is again what is implied in the word *sahasranāma*, the caption chosen by the creator or the generator of this powerful passage. In fact, the *Ācārya* hints at the significance of the name *Sahasranāma* after concluding the entire text by saying '*sahasranāmāya namaḥ śivāya sahasra rūpāya janārdanāya*'. The compassionate creator assumes thousands of names to perpetuate peace in the universe and takes innumerable forms to inculcate humanity in mankind as a continuous process.

In common parlance, however the name *Vaṣaṭkāraḥ* simply means the act of offering to the Lord. But as the Lord to whom this offering is made is after all seated in the heart, there is no difference between the person who makes the offer and the deity who receives it. In fact, the very act of offering is divine and is therefore equated with the deity. In the *Nārāyaṇa Upaniṣad* the deity is identified with devotion. He is the *yajña* (the ritual) and He is the *Vaṣaṭkāra* (the utterances that attract the attention of the Almighty).

In this respect the third name *Vaṣaṭkāraḥ* of the Lord establishes perfect identity between devotion, devotee and deity. It is also significant to note that the first name *Viśvam* is in third person, the second name *Viṣṇu* is in the second person and the third name *Vaṣaṭkāraḥ* is in the first person, thus completing the process of propitiation. 'That thou art' is the key-note of the entire hymn and these three stages are covered in the first three names.

Thus covering the three major aspects of the three-dimensional world, both within and without, in the first three names, the preceptor proceeds to present a picturesque description of the Lord in terms of time which again has three dimensions - past, present and future. The fourth name *bhūta bhavya bhavat prabhuḥ* glorifies the deity as the controller of the time that was, that is and that will be. It is worth noting that the first three names cover the formation and the transformation of life through three consecutive stages - creation, preservation and dissolution- while the fourth name, in one spell, spells out the passage of time both in the relative and also in the absolute sense of the term. Whatever has happened, whatever is going to happen and whatever is happening at the moment are all relative. What is present now was future just a minute ago and will become past a minute later. This transitoriness of time makes it relative while the governance of time by an invisible but tangible force makes sure that the rhythm of rotation and transition is maintained with perfect harmony and surpassing symmetry elevates the status of time to the highest level of comprehension making it absolutely obscure - intelligible only to the intelligence beyond the intellect. This is what *Māṇḍūkya* describes as *trikālātītam* (beyond the three tenses). The word *prabhu* (meaning the generator or the governor) occurring towards the end of this lengthy name explains how the Lord exercises a remote control over time-both relative and absolute.

This name consists of four words - *bhūta, bhavya, bhavat and prabhu.* All the four are derived from the root *bhū* meaning 'to be'. The root *bhū* basically denotes 'existence' *bhū sattāyāṁ.* Keeping this in view *Śrī Śaṅkara Bhagavatpāda* significantly qualifies the supremacy *aiśvarya* of the Lord over the three tenses or divisions of time as *sanmātrā.* In fact, the whole of the first stanza consisting of nine names concentrates on the *sat* existence aspect of the Lord. The five names that follow in the second line - *bhūtakṛt, bhūtabhṛt, bhāva, bhūtātmā* and *bhūtabhāvana* - are also derived from the root *bhū*. Another striking feature about the nine names occurring in the first stanza of this sacred hymn is that two syllables *bhū* and *vā* (भू and वा) are predominant in them. These two syllables stand respectively for existence and expansion. *bhū* means 'to exist' and *va* means 'to spread, flow, blow or pervade'. These two roots are incidentally the ones cited by *Pāṇini* in his aphorism *bhūvādayo dhātavaḥ* defining the characteristic feature of a verbal root. The choice of the two roots is significant as they represent the two basic states of life - static and dynamic. It is in this light that the pronounced usage of the syllables *bhū* and *va* in the inaugural stanza of the sacred hymn should be understood and absorbed by the discerning devotee.

The first name in the second line is *Bhūtakṛt* which means the creator of all creatures ranging from the lowest insects to the highly evolved souls. It also means One who dissolves all creatures. The process of creation has, in it, the seed of dissolution as well. This is inherent in the nature of the universe. Whatever is created is bound to be destroyed. The consumer gets consumed automatically in the process of consumption. This law of nature is well-illustrated in the illustrious name *bhūtakṛt.*

But the Lord who is responsible for both creation and dissolution takes full care of its proper maintenance and sustenance. He is therefore, called *Bhūtabhṛt.* He supports all that He creates because it is all His creation. The three basic traits or *guṇas* as they are technically called, namely, *sattva* (existence), *rajas* (exuberance) and *tamas* (engrossment) are manifest in their subtle as well as gross forms in the three functions - creation, sustenance and dissolution.

The next name *Bhāva* summarises the three functions and transcends them assuming no form, no function and no trait at the culminating point of all evolution. The word *bhāva* (being) is the most appropriate term to describe this state of existence. It is just Being and nothing else. It is not even non-being. The eternal conflict between 'to be or not to be' comes to an end at this blissful point and it is just there to be there forever, just to promote the well-being of all living beings. He is just a *bhāva* (भाव) present in every particle of this universe *bhava* (भव) . He is the feeling behind this being and fills the hearts of all living beings with infinite variety of feelings. In short, He is *Bhāva-Nārāyaṇa Nārāyaṇa* in *Bhāva.* Otherwise, He is just *bhava*, a feeling, and nothing else. This is the state of existence which the Lord describes as *sat* (existence) beyond what is consumed *kṣara* and also beyond what cannot be consumed *akṣara.*

Having said this in two-and-a-half syllables - *bhāva* - the seer of *Sahasranāma* feels thoroughly satisfied that his spell-bound mind has spelt out the absolute reality in absolute terms.

But still, he has something more to say by way of conclusion. So he adds two more names - *Bhūtātmā* and *Bhūtabhāvanaḥ. Ātman* means something to be obtained, acquired, assimilated and identified with. It is not visible because it is not divisible. It is beyond the symmetrical shape of the human organism and the sophisticated software of the human mind. It can neither be visualized nor imagined and is, therefore, beyond all definition. It is indefinite, infinite and hence all-pervading. The eighth name following the supreme seven eminently puts it as *Bhūtātmā.* All souls are His as He is present in all beings in the form of soul-within-the-soul. He is the soul of all souls, being of all beings and existence of all existence. In short, He is.

He, the universal soul, is not merely all that is, but also all that becomes. The last and the ninth name in the first verse of this sacred hymn glorifying the grace and grandeur of the Lord of the universe connects the Being of the phenomenal world with the immense potentialities of its Becoming. Hence, the name *Bhūtabhāvanaḥ.* He becomes all that is, was and is going to be. He is both being and becoming for all time to come. In fact, He knows neither past nor future. He is ever-present making His presence a pleasant surprise for all that is present.

Thus the nine names of the nameless occurring in the introductory verse of this fascinating manifesto of the magnanimous master of this mysterious universe presents a picturesque account of the absolute reality, existence and bliss in a graphic language adopting a photographic style of its own. These nine names can be appropriately termed *Nāma Navamī.*

The Eminent Eight

How the existence present in various forms in the world of relativity rises to the highest plane of absolute existence is effectively illustrated in the eight names that follow in the second verse of this Song of the Universe *Viśva Gītam*:

पूतात्मा परमात्मा च मुक्तानां परमा गतिः ।
अव्ययः पुरुषः साक्षी क्षेत्रज्ञोऽक्षर एव च ॥

pūtātmā paramātmā ca muktānāṁ paramā gatiḥ I
avyayaḥ puruṣaḥ sākṣī kṣetrajño 'kṣara eva ca II

The first step is that *bhūtātmā* (the physical or the biological entity) should get purified gradually elevating itself to the status of *paramātmā,* the supreme soul. With the unfolding of divinity by constant effort, the individual becomes universal, the relative becomes absolute, the imminent becomes eminent, the impure becomes pure and the imperfect becomes perfect. This process of perfection through purification may take a long, long time spread over endless (though rapid) cycle of births and deaths. But the ultimate goal of Absolute Good is sure to be attained once the attempt is on and the goal is set right. This assurance is given by *Paramātmā,* the second name occurring in the verse and it becomes explicit in the third name *Muktānāṁ paramā gatiḥ. Paramātmā* grants *Paramā gati,* the ultimate good that can be cherished not only by the souls bound by the fetters of body and mind, but also by the highly developed souls who have realized the futility of the passions and fashions of the phenomenal world and have succeeded in releasing themselves from these self imposed bonds. Purification and liberation, thus, go hand-in-hand. The former is the cause and the latter the effect. The agent that brings about this transformation is the all-pervading or the universal soul, *paramātmā*. When *ātman* transcends the level of *bhūta* and attains the status of *parama*, the *bhūtātmā* becomes *paramātmā* with the intervening stage of *pūtātmā*. Thus the three names - *Pūtātmā, Paramātmā* and *Muktānāṁ paramā gatiḥ* - forming the first line of the second stanza are not only interlinked but also connected with the penultimate name *Bhūtātmā* occurring in the previous stanza. This shows that the various names listed in the illustrious text are not isolated nor are they to be construed by their semantic significance. They are to be understood and assimilated in the context of the names that precede and succeed them.

A casual comparison of these names with their counterparts occurring in a similar context in the same *Parava* of *Mahābhārata* (popularly known as *Śiva Sahasranāma*) reveals a close co-ordination between the two. The name *Pūtātmā* here becomes *Prītātmā* there and the name *Muktānāṁ paramā gatiḥ* gets slightly modified as *Bhaktānāṁ paramā gatiḥ*. *Pūta* (purified) and *mukti* (liberation) take the form of *prīti* (love) and *bhakti* (devotion) when *Śiva* is the deity. *Bhakti* or devotion is generally defined as the highest form of love *parama prema rūpā*. That is why *Śiva* grants His devotees the highest form of love and unqualified affection so that they can derive anything they desire out of it.

A note of continuity in the names that sound similar in the *Sahasranāma* can also be noticed if the particle *ca* following the name

Paramātmā is properly understood. The immediate use of this particle here is to connect the three names - *Bhūtātmā, Pūtātmā and Paramātmā* - all ending with the word *ātmā*. The state of identification with the soul enables the individual to transcend the limits of body and mind. Body-consciousness differentiates one from his fellow-beings. Physically, there is diversity in creation, but mentally or intellectually this diversification gradually diminishes ultimately touching almost a vanishing point at the atomic or atmic or the spiritual level. These three levels are indicated in the three names - *Bhūtātmā, Pūtātmā and Paramātmā*. There is divinity in each of these levels but in varying degree depending upon the measure of its disclosure. When this process of revelation of divinity in humankind reaches its perfection, *Bhūtātmā* becomes *Paramātmā*. By attributing all the three names to the absolute existence or reality, the sacred hymn illustrates and establishes the intrinsic universality of Man, the Divine, as different from Man, the Body, and Man, the Mind.

It is human to apprehend diversity, but it is divine to visualize the unity behind it. Broadly speaking, there are three stages through which the individual soul passes before it attains the status of the universal soul. There are, however, many more intermediate stages which the individual has to experience. These stages also find expression in the *Sahasranāma* at appropriate places. For instance, names like *Samātmā, Caturātmā, Dhṛtātmā, Ameyātmā, Viśrutātmā, Viśvātmā, Nivṛttātmā, Anivṛttātmā, Prasannātmā, Aprameyātmā, Prakāśātmā, Vṛddhātmā, Vimuktātmā, Naikātmā, Anantātmā, Vijitātmā, Vidheyātmā, Viśuddhātmā, Trilokātmā, Gabhīrātmā, Ekātmā and Ātmavān* are only suggestive of the various stages through which the *atman* passes and not the various forms. *Ātman* is one whether it is manifest in *Jīvātmā* or *Viśvātmā*. It is One Single Self *ekātmā* which appears to be *naikātmā* (nominee) for secular purposes. These names glorifying the nameless and the formless *ātman* present a thought-provoking and soul-searching account of the soul of all souls. In a way, it is a comprehensive biography of the soul ranging from *Bhūtātmā* (8) to *Ekātmā* (965). The particle *ca* immediately following the eleventh name *Paramātmā* thus presents a key-note to this great exposition of the garland of names glorifying the universal soul.

The gradual and well-programmed unfolding of divinity in man as depicted here reminds one of the three stages - *nara* (man), *narottama* (the perfect man) and *nārāyaṇa* (godhead) - portrayed in the majestic composition of the *Mahābhārata*. The same phraseology is explained here in a concise form by using the three 'atmic' names *Bhūtātmā, Pūtātmā and Paramātmā.*

Paramātmā (the supreme self) grants *paramagati* (supreme status) not only to *muktas* (the liberated) and *bhaktas* (the devoted) but also to *unmuktas* (the forsaken). All souls - good or bad, devoted or deviated - have ultimately to seek shelter under His eternal abode. Once the individual soul finds entry into this blissful abode of the Lord, there is no fear of reversion, retreat or retrenchment. The pathway to God is the path of no return. That is why it is called *Paramāgati* (the ultimate goal of life).

The indeclinable and imperishable nature of the soul withiṇ souls, the eternal spirit enshrined in the ephemeral bodies of all living beings and the immortal essence of the mortal frame is explained in the five names that follow. The first among them is *Avyayaḥ* The word *avyaya* has also a grammatical connotation wherein it implies a word that does not change with number, gender or case. It does not accept any suffix or prefix. It is fixed once and for all and no ecology can change its cosmology. What a superb expression the author of *Viṣṇu Sahasranāma* has chosen to explain the inexplicable! It may be recalled that in the eleventh chapter of *Gītā*, the sincere aspirant, *Arjuna*, uses the word *avyaya darśayātmanamavyayam* while referring to the cosmic vision which he is eager to see if he is considered eligible. Again, at the very first sight of the celestial splendour to which he is exposed, he exclaims.

त्वमक्षरं परमं वेदितव्यं त्वमस्य विश्वस्य परं निधानम्।
त्वमव्ययः शाश्वतधर्मगोप्ता सनातनस्त्वं पुरुषो मतो मे ॥

[*Gītā* 11-18]

tvam-akṣaraṁ paramaṁ veditavyaṁ
tvamasya viśvasya paraṁ nidhānaṁ ।
tvamavyayaḥ śāśvata-dharma-goptā
sanātanas-tvaṁ puruṣo mato me ॥

> You are the eternal one, the imperishable one, the only one that needs to be known, the only treasure that one can cherish, the indeclinable one, the one who protects the law that protects all, the everlasting one, the one and the only one that can be termed *Puruṣa,* the first inhabitant of this cosmos.

One can easily see how these lines resemble the five names that strat with *Avyaya.* Incidentally, the name *Avyaya* is the first among the names which start with *a* (अ)which is considered to be the primordial sound identified with the originator of this creation. 'Of all the syllables *akṣaras*', says the Lord, 'I am *a-kāra*'. It is significant to note in this context for an analytical appreciation of this scared hymn that there are exactly 108 names beginning with the syllable *a* in the entire text and these start with *avyayaḥ* the unchangeable, and end with *akṣobhyaḥ* (the unshakeable). Moreover, the word *avyayaḥ,* it should be noted, has not been used here in the grammatical sense of the word. This is deliberately done so that it can serve as a qualifying name for the one that follows, namely, *Puruṣa*. In fact, the word *Avyaya* later occurs on two more occassions as a part of a name-*Nidhiravyayaḥ* (30) and *Bījamavyayam* (429). In the former case, where it means inexhaustible treasure, it is in the masculine gender, whereas in the latter case, it is in the neuter gender and means the undying seed. In any case, it is never used in the grammatical sense of the term.

It is, therefore, clear that the word *avyaya* qualifies the name *Puruṣa*. Thus the whole expression *avyayaḥ puruṣaḥ* stands for The Man (not a man). It is exactly in this context and connotation that *Kaṭhopaniṣad* uses the word *puruṣa*, who is of the size of a human thumb, seated in the heart of hearts of all human beings shining like a smokeless flame. It is about this *Puruṣa* that the *Upaniṣad* declares : He is the master of the present and the future, He is present both in the present and in the future, He is there today and He will be there tomorrow. [*Kaṭha* 2-1-13]

The word *puruṣa* is so suggestive and expressive that its etymology explains the location of the *puruṣa* in the cosmic language of the seers and the sages. The word literally means one who dwells in a cosy corner of the cosmic city. This city may perhaps, be the human body itself when it refers to the individual soul and the same expression may refer to the entire globe - both celestial and terrestrial - when it refers to the universal soul. One is 'micro' and the other one 'macro'. Both refer to the cosmic form of the formless. When there is no form there is nothing to fade out. What does fade out is the mortal frame and not the immortal *puruṣa,* seated inside the human body. He cannot have a specific form because He has to accomodate Himself in all the forms simultaneously and continuously. He has to be consistent, too. This accounts for His formless uniformity and flexible inflexion. This is the same person *puruṣa* depicted in the *Puruṣa-sūkta,* perhaps, the only hymn common to all the four

Vedas. The *puruṣa* referred to here, is the Supreme Being pervading the entire cosmos from all sides and transcending the ten directions with His thousands of heads, thousands of eyes and thousands of feet. He is all that has been *yad-bhūtam* and all that will be *yatca-bhavyam*. One can easily see the vedic vision highlighting this name *Puruṣa*. In fact, all the thousand names have these vedic vibrations behind them as they are sung and sanctified by the seers and the sages *ṛṣibhiḥ parigītāni*. The *Kaṭha-Upaniṣad* places this *Puruṣa* at a level that excels all *sā kāṣṭhā* and depicts it as a goal beyond which there is nothing else to scale *sā parā gatiḥ*.

These characteristics of the *Puruṣa* make him a witness to all that occurs both within and without. He is, therefore, termed *sākṣī*, an eye-witness to the entire cosmos. He sees everything, but nothing can see Him. He is the seer who cannot be seen *adṛṣṭo draṣṭā*. The word *sākṣī* is again a favourite term for the vedic seers who visualize a harmony between sound and sense. It is only when the eyes are able to hear and the ears are able to see that the audio-visual mechanism, inbuilt in the human body and mind, can feel the absolute touch of the all-pervading and all-perceiving soul. Even the feeling of the presence of this universal perceiver within can purify the body and make it a temple of understanding.

This invisible eye-witness, seated in all living beings is the real knower of the purpose and the potentialities of the mortal frame and it is He who keeps a constant and cautious watch over the minute-to-minute development of the potential divinity in them. That is why He is called *kṣetrajña* (one who knows the *kṣetra* or the living organism). The whole of the thirteenth chapter in *Gītā* is dedicated to the delineation of the distinction between *kṣetra* (body) and *kṣetrajña* (its knower). The mere possession of the body does not enable one to know it. It requires a positive and persistent enquiry into the internal mechanism and the spirit behind its well-designed and well-devised dynamism to understand it thoroughly. Only such elevated and gifted souls can realize it. The Lord of the universe present in all living beings as *sākṣī* (observer) is, perhaps, the only *kṣetrajña* who not only knows the purpose behind the possession of the body but also controls it from within. It is a universal mechanism which works without any intervention once it is well-set. The setter is the *sākṣī-puruṣa* (the umpire) who is *avyaya* (indeclinable) and *akṣra* (imperishable).

The last name in the verse is *Akṣara. Gītā* defines *akṣara* as the immortal soul seated at the key position in the mortal frame *kuṭasthokṣara ucyate.* All the five names - *Avyayaḥ, Puruṣaḥ, Sākṣī, Ksetrajña* and *Akṣaraḥ* attempt to describe the nature of the immortal soul controlling the entire cosmos with compassion and concordance. But the author of *Viṣṇu Sahasranāma* does not seem to be satisfied with this description and, therefore, adds two more words *eva* and *ca.* Both are particles which do not change with any grammatical modifications. They are, therefore, the most appropriate appraisers of the absoulte nature of the *puruṣa* who has hitherto been described as *avyaya* and *akṣara.* Of the two particles, the first one - *eva* - means 'only' or 'alone' and the second one - *ca* - means 'and' or 'much more'. Thus the two expressions suggest that the *puruṣa* who is being spoken of in the present context is not merely an *avyaya* or an *akṣara,* but something more. This 'something more' will come to light in the next verse where the *puruṣa* becomes *puruṣottama.* For the time being, however, the *puruṣa* is *akṣara* because He is above the mortal nature of the body though closely associated with it. But the *puruṣottama* (the supreme soul) who figures towards the end of the following verse transcends both *kṣara* and *akṣara* and there is none superior to Him. In short, *puruṣa* plays a significant role in the ephemeral world in effecting close co-ordination between the temporal and the eternal while *puruṣottama* excels them both.

In the first verse containing nine names of the Lord, we have witnessed how the Lord indentifies Himself with the universe which is His own creation. In the present one, the Lord is trying to establish that He is not different from *jīva* (the living organism) through He has a distinct role to play in elevating *jīva* to the level of *brahma*. That is why this verse concludes with the name *akṣara* but strikes a note in the end that there is much more to add to make the equation tangible for an intelligible solution by using the particle *ca*.

It is with this optimistic note that we proceed to the next verse of the text.

The Supreme Seven

Where there is unity, there is divinity. There is one Supreme Soul which has given rise to many. It is, therefore, logical that the supremacy of one single soul can be realized only when one can visualize one in many. This is the sum and substance of all scientific investigation into the supremacy of the soul which is best expressed by the term *Yoga*. The word *yoga.* literally means adding up, summing up, rejoining or, in short, effecting a reunion of diverse looking objects through unified vision. As long as our vision is narrowed down to body and body alone, we are many and the world around us looks as diverse as we are. But the moment we are aware of the soul-spirit within us and directing us, we realize that we are one. This transition from the physical consciousness to the spiritual awareness effected by the mediator is what is called *Yoga*. It is the shifting of the human mind gradually from the 'Body' to the 'Soul' resulting in the permanent union (or quasi-permanent for the time being) of the mind and the soul *ātma-manaḥ saṁyogo yogaḥ*. Once the human mind attains this state of union with the soul, the *yogī* becomes *Yoga* and finds himself face to face with *Yogeśvara*. In other words, the *Puruṣa* becomes *Puruṣottama*. The self becomes Supreme. The individual becomes universal. This spiritual attainment called *Yoga* is the subject matter of the third verse which starts with the name *Yoga*.

योगो योगविदां नेता प्रधानपुरुषेश्वरः ।
नारसिंहवपुः श्रीमान् केशवः पुरुषोत्तमः ॥

yogo yogavidāṁ netā pradhāna-puruṣeśvaraḥ ।
nārasiṁhavapuḥ śrīmān keśavaḥ puruṣottamaḥ ॥

One who knows a little knows not what knowledge is though he is knowledgeable. It is only the Omniscient who knows what knowing is because he is one with it, in it, beside and beyond it. He is knowledge personified. So is the case with *yoga.*, the knowledge of the self. The ultimate goal of *yoga.* is to realize the self - the universal self. This self-realisation is God-realisation. That is why God is named *Yoga.* here.

As the Supreme Self is the embodiment of *yoga.*, He is the best guide for its practitioners. He is, therefore, called the leader of *yogīs* (or the experts in *yoga*). He not only guides the aspirants but also looks after their safety, security and prosperity as promised in *Gītā yogakṣemaṁ vahāmyaham.* He directs not only the developed souls but also the beginners - the developing and even the undeveloped and the underdeveloped ones. This He does in the form of *yoga.* He assumes this form so that the new entrants who step into the field for the first time may feel the divinity in and around them. Then they are led into the sanctum sanctorum step by step by the considerate and compassionate Master who is appropriately named *Yogavidāṁ netā.*

Having said so much about *yoga,* the *Ācārya* who is preaching divinity through its attributes proceeds to discuss about the two major components of this cosmic creation, namely, *Prakṛti* and *Puruṣa.* They are technically called *Pradhāna and Puruṣa.* That is why the *Ācārya* depicts the Lord of the Universe as *Pradhāna-Puruṣeśvaraḥ* the controller of both *pradhāna* (or *prakṛti*)and *puruṣa.* He is above *vyakta and avyakta* - manifest and unmanifest. *Pradhāna or Prakṛti* in its subtle form is unmanifest and it is *puruṣa* or *jīva* who manifests himself with the help of the unmanifest nature or *prakṛti* within him. The Lord is the master of both. This name introduces the aspirant or *sādhaka to Sāṅkhya* philosophy at a very appropriate time and in the most appropriate language. The *Sāṅkhya-Darśana* is the right vision or appreciation of the perfect correlation between *vyakta and avyakta.* It is also appropriate that the *Ācārya* has introduced this philosphy immediately after discussing *yoga. Sāṅkhya* and *yoga* go together. They try to visualze the absolute from two different angles. Viewed from any angle, the substance is the same. In order to underline this basic unity in all systems of philosophy, the *Sahasranāma* presents the Lord in a form which can be human when viewed from one angle and can even be an animal from a different angle. This is done in the next name *Nārasiṁha-vapuḥ.*

When questioned by the notorious demon-King *Hiraṇyakaśipu* whether Lord exists in all forms and at all places, his devoted son *Prahlāda* replies in an emphatic affirmative. In order to substantiate this 'yes', the Lord manifests Himself in a form which is half-man and half-lion. The manifestation takes place at the time of sun-set i.e. when it is neither day nor night nor both. The form of the Lord was enchanting to the devoted son and dreadful to the arrogant father. The sword-like nails of the Lord which are neither animate nor inanimate pierce through the abdomen of the demon separating his mortal frame from the immortal self. The event takes place just at the threshold of the royal palace which is neither interior nor exterior to the edifice. There can not be more appropriate form for the Lord to manifest Himself to uphold the right and uproot the worng. This is the great efficacy of the name *Nārasiṁha vapuḥ,* which not only brings out the eminence of the Omnipotent but also speaks out how the opposites unite themselves in the presence of the Lord. He is an antidote for all antonymns in the world.

Enchanted by the excellence of this highly suggestive and expressive name, the *Ācārya* tries to qualify it with an apt epithet - *Śrīmān.*

Śrīmān is the most favourite name for the author of *Śrī Viṣṇu Sahasranāma.* This occurs in four places in the whole text - with different connotation on each occasion. This being the first occasion brings with it all the grace that the word can command and contribute to the uncomparable splendour of the Lord of the Universe. It is a universal splendour and *Śrīmān* is also a universal title for all dignitaries in the world. The word *Śrī* means many things. It means radiance, splendour, lustre, loveliness, grace, glory, beauty, plenty, prosperity, dignity, majesty, magnanimity and all these things put together. More significant than all these things, it means *Lakṣmī,* the goddess of prosperity and, of course, the consort of Lord *Viṣṇu.* So the presiding deity of the celebrated text *Śrī Viṣṇu Sahasranāma* is most appropriately named *Śrīmān* here. He is the real *Śrīmān* while others borrow the epithet only to invoke His blessings. In fact, the *Śrī* that adorns the flourescent forehead and the blossoming breast of the Lord is the universal grace that glitters in every inch of this vast span of space - not only in men and women, but also in brids and animals, flowers and forests, wind and water, earth and ether and even in the stellar univese. Thus the name *Śrīmān* summarizes all splendour that the universe can command and, therefore, the Lord of the universe is called *Śrīmān.*

This *Śrīmān* is not only a combination of all conflicting forces but also a resultant spirit of all such forces governing creation, preservation and dissolution of the vast universe. He is, therefore, given the name *Keśava.* The word *keśava* consists of three components - *ka, a* and *īśa* - representing *Brahmā,* the creator, *Viṣṇu,* the protector or the preserver and *Śiva,* the dissolver respectively. He oversees the three cosmic forces as the supreme Lord who maintains cosmic equilibrium. That is why he is called *Keśavaḥ*. The final syllable va is an auspicious ending for the glorious name of the gracious Lord.

There are other derivations for the name *Keśava*. They will be discussed at appropriate places when the name is repeated to express different attributes of the Omnipotent. It suffices here to understand the significance of this name in the context of cosmic creation and its purpose.

The last word in this verse is *puruṣottamaḥ* which, incidentally, is the twenty-fourth name of *Viśvātmā,* the universal soul. It may be recalled that a devoted Hindu starts any religious ritual by taking three spoons of water in succession and uttering three names of the Lord - *Keśava, Nārāyaṇa* and *Mādhava. Keśava* is the first of the three names which initiate the devotee into the act of devotion and these names are followed by twenty one more, making a total of twenty four. The number 24 is again very significant as it indicates the composition of the human body - consisting of 5 *karmendriyas*, 5 *jnanendriyas*, 5 elements (earth, water, fire, air and ether), 5 sense-objects (sound, touch, form, taste and smell) and the 4 *antaḥkaraṇs*. All the twenty four elements originate from the union of *prakṛti and puruṣa* at the cosmic level. This was already spelt out in the last name in the previous line - *Pradhāna Puruṣeśvaraḥ.* The last name in the present line - *Puruṣottamaḥ* is only an affirmation of the same formula.

The name *Puruṣottamaḥ* also sums up the entire discussion about the Universe that is God spread over the twenty three names that precede. The terminology used has close relationship with *Sāṅkhya* philosophy and also the *Puruṣhottama yoga* preached by Lord *Kṛṣṇa* in His song Celestial. According to *Gītā*, all living beings are destined to meet death sometime or other and are, therefore, classified under the *kṣara* (perishable) category, while the soul-person located in the human body technically called *kūṭastha* is the *akṣara* (indestructible or imperishable). Both *kṣara* and *akṣara* - parts of the living organism - come under the substance called *Puruṣa,* while the *Puruṣottama* named here is beyond the two levels. *Kṛṣṇa Paramātamā,* the preceptor of *Gītā,* asserts that He is termed *Puruṣottama* in the secular as well as the spiritual sense *atosmi loke vede ca prathitaḥ puruṣottamaḥ.*

Thus the name *Puruṣottama* strikes a significant note equating *Viśvam* (the universe) with *Viśvātmā* (the universal soul) through various intermediate stages like *Bhūtāmā, Pūtātmā, Paramātmā* and ultimately the supreme status of *Puruṣottama. Ātman* is one though the manifestation can be manifold. This is the essence of the entire preaching of the *Ācārya* who is trying to impress upon his audience consisting of the five *Pāṇḍavas* and their divine companion and guide *Kṛṣṇa* that the Supreme Self is essentially the same as in the individual or the isolated self and in order to visualize this oneness in many, one has to surrender his little self and identify himself with the Supreme Self.

The twenty-four names occurring in the first three verses of the sacred hymn *Śrī Viṣṇu Sahasranāma* thus strike the key note to the process of unfolding the divinity in man. This is the purport of this sacred hymn, a garland of thousand names of the Lord of the universe glorifying His qualities that attempt to qualify the unqualified.

All In All

In the 24 names of the Lord of the Universe enumerated so far, we have travelled from *Viśvam* (the Universe) to *Puruṣottama* (the Supreme Self). We shall now proceed to the next verse starting from the attribute *Sarva* (all) and ending with the visualization of *Īśvara* (the mightiest of all the masters of this mysterious universe). The verse reads as follows:

सर्वः शर्वः शिवः स्थाणुर्भूतादिर्निधिरव्ययः ।
संभवो भावनो भर्ता प्रभवः प्रभुरीश्वरः ॥

sarvaḥ śarvaḥ śivaḥ sthāṇur-bhūtādir-nidhir-avyayaḥ |
saṁbhavo bhāvano bhartā prabhavaḥ prabhur-īśvaraḥ ||

He is all in all, anything and everything that one can conceive of. He exists in all and all that exists exists in Him. As observed in the *Mahābhārata* elsewhere, He is worshipped as *Sarva* (all in all) as He is fully aware of what exists and also what may not exist. He resides in everything and everything resides in Him.

He is not only the perennial source of all existence, but the ultimate resort to the entire creation. Hence He is called *'Ś'arva* (शर्व) one who withdraws all beings unto Himself at the time of deluge or dissolution. The two names *Sarva* and *Śarva* are so close in sound that one cannot imagine that a minute difference in the syllable *sa* changing to *śa* can make so much of difference in their meaning. The dental soft sound *sa* is all-inclusive while the palatal counterpart of it *śa* becomes all-absorbing.

But the Almighty exercises His right to promote existence or resort to extinction at His sweet will only for the betterment of the world He has created. He is 'All in All', but is good at heart. He is Good personified. So He is called *Śiva.* God is where good is.

But whatever He does, He does it with strong conviction. He is firm, sticks to His stand. So He is called *Sthāṇuḥ* immovable, unchangeable and irresistible.

He is also *Bhūtādiḥ*, the first and the foremost of all that has come into being. He is the prime cause of all existence. He exists prior to all existence and also after the whole existence comes to an end merging in Him. At that point, He serves as the undiminishing and never-failing resort to the entire creation. The whole existence emerges from Him and merges into Him. That is why He is called not only *Bhūtādiḥ* but also *Nidhiravyayaḥ*, a treasure that knows no diminishing. He is there forever, for all eventualities and for all living beings.

He is also called *Sambhavaḥ* (the originator of life). He causes birth and also takes it back at His will and on His own. In His incarnation as *Kṛṣṇa*, He revealed His intention to descend on Earth or to be born from time to time in order to uphold *Dharma* (righteousness) and root out *Adharma* (evil). He also clarified the difference between His birth *janma* and actions *karma* and those of others. He also asserted that those who realize the real nature of His advent and action which are basically divine merge into Him and do not have to be born again. This special feature of His advent and absorption makes Him *Sambhava* (self-born) and He effects this with His intrinsic ingenuity *ātmāmaya* . One can realize this through self-discipline *ātmayoga.*

As He has full control over His own entry into and exit from the *Saṁsāra* (nescience), He exercises the same power to grant the fruits of action to all on the merit of their penance and perseverance. Hence the name *Bhāvanaḥ*, the effector or the benefactor of the good *puṇya* and evil *pāpa* of all living beings.

This is the way He runs this chain of birth and nescience in this mortal world leading to the ultimate immortality. He is the Head and Sustainer of this phenomenon. So He is called *Bhartā*. Thus He is responsible not only for His own Manifestation but also for the Dispensation and Protection of His creation. In fact He is the source of all this divine sport *līlā* . Hence, the name *Prabhavaḥ* (the birth-place). He is also the *Prabhu* (the power house) of this phenomenal world. Hence, He is depicted and worshipped by His devotees who identify themselves with His innate power as *Īśvaraḥ* the Lord of all, the Master of all, the Ultimate State of all that is universal.

The twelve names in this verse starting from the name *Sarvaḥ* up to the last one *Īśvaraḥ* attempt to understand and assimilate the Supreme Command of the Lord of all Lords *Sarveśvaraḥ* who is all in all and above all. It is this supremacy that is extolled in the *Māṇḍūkya* by saying *eśa sarveśvaraḥ* this state of Supreme Lordship is what is to be realized transcending the three states of awakening, dreaming and deep and intense identification with one's own real self. The first and the last names *Sarvaḥ and Īśvaraḥ* combined give rise to this concept of *Sarveśvaraḥ* which summarizes this wonderful verse with scintillating words and vibrations.

The Best Of All

The next nine names that follow present the Lord as self-born, self-radiant, self-vibrant, self-fluorescent and the eternal exchequer of all the best that exists and excels all other forms of creation and preservation in this ephemeral world. The verse reads:

स्वयंभूः शंभुरादित्यः पुष्कराक्षो महास्वनः ।
अनादिनिधनो धाता विधाता धातुरुत्तमः ॥

svayaṁbhūḥ śaṁbhur-ādityaḥ puṣkarākṣo mahā-svanaḥ /
anādi-nidhano dhātā vidhātā dhātur-uttamaḥ //

The attribute *Svayambhu* (self-born) figures in several scriptures. *Īśāvāsya* mentions this along with similar attributes like *Kavi* (the innovator), *Manīṣī* (the intelligent) and *Paribhūḥ* the encircling excellence.

That the Self-born is so born with a specific purpose is brought out in the next name *Śambhuḥ*. *Śam* means anything that is good. He is born to promote this universal Good. So He is called *Śambhuḥ*.

The next word *Āditya* is a broad-based epithet for the Almighty. In common parlance, it means Sun. But as an adjective, it can denote anything connected with the solar origin. There are 12 forms of *āditya*, *Viṣṇu* being one of them. In *Gītā*, the Lord identifies Himself with the most significant form of the 12 *Ādityas (ādityānāṁ ahaṁ Viṣṇuḥ)*. As the son of *Aditi*, the fifth *Vāmana* incarnation of the Lord is also called

Āditya. The seventh constellation *punarvasu* in which the Lord assumed the form of *Rāma* is also called *Āditya*. *Vālmīki* refers to this in his expression, *nakṣatre-aditi-daivatye*. Etymologically, the word *āditya* can be interpreted as that which does not entertain any form or type of depression. So, in all these respects and multiple shades of the term, the attribute *Āditya* presents the Lord in His .Excellence at its best.

The Lord looks like a 'blue lotus', a beautiful lake and sometimes like a fiérce-looking but fascinating cloud. All these phases of the appearance of the Lord make Him *Puṣkarākṣaḥ*, the lotus-eyed as placid as a lake and as composed and compassionate as an unpredictable cloud.

He is called *Mahāsvanaḥ,* as any utterance that comes out of His vocal chord or even the life-wind that comes out of His nostrils has a world of significance and appeal to those well-versed in the divine diction of the voice of vision. He is the originator of all holy scriptures. Anything that He spells out becomes sacred and spreads throughout the Universe making the nature-animate and inanimate-spell-bound. He dins into our ears day and night all sacred sounds which we can hear if only we have the ears sanctified by His sound, the mighty sound of the Almighty.

The second line of the verse present the Lord who has neither a beginning nor an end. He is *Anādinidhanaḥ*. Nothing existed before Him nor can anything survive Him. He survives all and supports all, creates all and controls all, protects all and promotes all.

He is a maker of all that makes some sense. He creates all that can re-create and transcreate. He is the author *ādhātā*, the originator *dhātā* and the ordainer *vidhātā* of this magnificient manifestation of His marvellous Master-Mind. Being an *ādhātā*, *dhātā* and *vidhātā*--all in one, He is extolled as *Dhāturuttamaḥ* the innovator of the best of all. Everything emerged and emanated from Him. He is, therefore, not merely All in All, but the Best of All.

The Master Mind

Even though the Lord is seated in our hearts, it is very difficult to comprehend Him as we can not see Him in flesh and blood nor can we speak to Him face to face. We have to reach the innermost layers of our consciousness with pure heart and clear conscience. The following verse with ten attributes of the Lord will tell us how we can reach Him though He appears to be immeasurable, inaccessible and firm.

अप्रमेयो हृषीकेशः पद्मनाभोऽमरप्रभुः ।
विश्वकर्मा मनुस्त्वष्टा स्थविष्ठः स्थविरो ध्रुवः ॥

aprameyo hṛṣīkeśaḥ padma-nābho'mara-prabhuḥ |
viśva-karmā manus-tvaṣṭā sthaviṣṭhaḥ sthaviro dhruvaḥ ||

We cannot see our Lord with our naked eyes unless they are charged with some divine power to see things beyond time and space. It was with such a vision that *Arjuna* could see the Cosmic image of the Lord. One cannot even imagine or contemplate on such a cosmic vision without divine grace. That is why He is called immeasurable, *Aprameyaḥ*.

But as the Lord Himself says that one can have this vision if he starts imagining the presence of the Lord in the various senses and sense-perceptions of the body with a strong desire and devotion. This is what is explained in the second name in this verse, *Hṛṣīkeśaḥ*. He is the Lord of all the senses and it is with His grace that we derive pleasure out of these senses. Our senses are called *hṛṣika* as they give us pleasure though momentary in their nature. As these are operated and controlled by the supreme Self seated within the self of all living beings, He can transform this momentary pleasures into monumental and memorable experience that blossoms into a blissful blessing.

The Lord is called *Padmanābhaḥ* because there is supposed to be a Lotus *padṁa* symbolising the source of all the Cosmic vision in His navel. In fact, every limb of the Lord looks like a lotus. He is lotus-eyed, His face resembles a lotus, His feet are like the lotus flowers and His heart, the heart of hearts of all individual souls where the Lord resides and presides over his movements and moments is the most enchanting lotus because that is the source of the eternal bliss that the whole universe cherishes. The word *padma* literally means the key which opens up the whole grandeur of this marvellous creation of the master.

He is the Lord of both mortals and immortals. It is His grace that grants immortality to all the mortals. Hence, He is called *Amaraprabhuḥ*, the Lord of the immortals.

He has made this universe assuming the role of *Viśvakarmā*, the divine architect. Hence the name *Viśvakarmā* . He also assumes the role of *manu* the thinker. He is also *Tvaṣṭā*, who is also supposed to be a celestial architect. All these three names come one after another to show that it was He who lent His divine hand in creating this universe, making it marvellous and mysterious and also shaping it from time to time so that its elegance is maintained.

He is the biggest architect as the universe He has made transgresses all limits of time and space. Hence He is *Sthaviṣṭhaḥ*. He is the most ancient, hence He is called *Sthaviraḥ*. He is also *Dhruvaḥ* as He is firm.

The Most Auspicious

No doubt, it is extremely difficult to comprehend and catch the height of divinity the Lord manifests in His unique way. But He is the most pious, compassionate and auspicious master who condescends to the common level on His own and blesses the choiced few who deserve His grace by virtue of their intrinsic and acquired merit. This point is focussed in the verse that follows:

अग्राह्यः शाश्वतः कृष्णो लोहिताक्षः प्रतर्दनः ।
प्रभूतस्त्रिककुब्धाम पवित्रं मङ्गलं परम् ॥

agrāhyaḥ śāśvataḥ kṛṣṇo lohitākṣaḥ pratardanaḥ ।
prabhūtas-trikakubdhāma pavitraṁ maṅgalaṁ paraṁ ॥

He is called *Agrāḥyaḥ* as it is difficult to grasp Him. He is impalpable, inaccessible and invincible. But it is a question of time and place which an aspirant has to wait patiently and cover gradually. Patience and perseverence with dedication and determination will bear fruit ultimately as the Lord is available at all time and in all places. He is *Śāśvataḥ* eternal, perennial and ever ready to give audience to His devotees in His private chamber, the heart that articulates and attracts one and all. That is why He is called *Kṛṣṇa*.

While explaining the etymology of the word *kṛṣṇa*, the author of the *Mahābhārata* says, 'the word *kṛṣ* means 'existence' and *ṇa* means 'bliss'. Hence, the Lord *Kṛṣṇa* is a pleasant blend of existence and bliss. This is what the sage says about the Lord. The Lord Himself explains the expression in a fascinating way by saying, 'I am called *Kṛṣṇa* because I am of dark-blue colour. The spirit behind this interpretation is typical of the sportive character of the Lord who combines wit and wisdom in all He does and says.

The name that follows *Lohitākṣaḥ* is also interestingly and perhaps significantly too speaks of colours. Here it is red, an exhilarating shift from the dark-blue. This reminds us of the epithet *Nīlalohita* used by *Kālidāsa* for *Śiva*. The poet prays to Lord *Śiva* to redeem him from re-birth.

The next name *Pratardanaḥ*, meaning the destroyer or diminisher of the entire creation during the dissolution of the world is rightly placed as it expands the significance of the name *Lohitākṣaḥ*, the Red-eyed.

The Lord is then named *Prabhūtaḥ* (well-endowed or fully equipped with all the qualities that go to shape what He is and should be). This is followed by the name *Trikakubdhāma* meaning one who dwells and sanctifies the three regions of the world--the lower, the middle and the upper. The word *dhāma* adds lustre to His three dimensional habitation.

The last two names- *Pavitram* and *Maṅgalaṁparam* are closely related in their purport and almost complementary. The Lord stands as a model for purity and therefore can purify anything and anyone by mere example and occasionally by showering His grace. It is this quality that makes Him, the Most Auspicious *maṅgalaṁ param*. He is *Maṅgalam* in its purest form. The presence of His Holiness is the most blissful blessing for all.

The Very Breath Of Life

How the Lord, very breath of life, breathes life into all living beings and makes life as dear as gold, as fragrant as earth and as sweet as grace that glitters is explained in the following verse:

ईशानः प्राणदः प्राणो ज्येष्ठः श्रेष्ठः प्रजापतिः ।
हिरण्यगर्भो भूगर्भो माधवो मधुसूदनः ॥

īśānaḥ prāṇadaḥ prāṇo jyeṣṭhaḥ śreṣṭhaḥ prajāpatiḥ I
hiraṇyagarbho bhūgarbho mādhavo madhu-sūdanaḥ II

The simple meaning of the first name *Īśānaḥ* is one who rules. But as it is followed by two attributes, *Prāṇadaḥ* and *Prāṇaḥ* connected with life-breath, the name *Īśānaḥ* has to be construed in the light of the two names that followed. Obviously, it has something to do with life-breath or the vital air. The word *īśānaḥ* is composed of two constituents--*īśa* (the ruler) and *aṇaḥ*, derived from the root '*an*' meaning 'to breath'. It is therefore clear that the word *īśāna* in this context not merely means the ruler or controller of the vital air in the cosmos but also the chief life-giving force which is usually termed *prāṇa*, the life-wind.

Taking the three names together, we can conclude that the Lord is depicted here as the main reservoir of life not merely supplying life-wind to all living beings but also regulating its flow in a phased and poised manner. *Īśāna* is therefore the main principle of life *mukhya prāṇa* stationed in the heart which controls the five life-winds--*prāṇa* in the lungs, *apāna* which goes downwords and out of the *aṇus*, *samāna*, seated in the cavity of the naval regulating *prāṇa* and *apāna* and helping digestion, *vyāna* diffused through the whole body and *udāna* the upward breath which rises up the throat and enters into the head. All these five life-winds are controlled by the primal and principal *prāṇa* which is termed here *Īśāna* as it is the main source for all life and life-breath. The Lord is therefore depicted by the term *Īśānaḥ*.

The next two names *Prāṇadaḥ* and *Prāṇaḥ* only elaborate this point. The Lord is called *Prāṇadaḥ* as He is the life-giver and the life-taker too when He withholds the same at the time of the withdrawal. He is the *prāṇa* of the *prāṇa (prāṇasya prāṇaḥ)* as the *Kenopaniṣad* puts it.

This point is further clarified by the two epithets that follow-*Jyeṣṭhaḥ* and *Śreṣṭhaḥ* which mean the eldest and the best or the seniormost and the most superior. *Nārada* while describing the unique personality of *Rāma* for the benefit of *Vālmīki* presents him as *Jyeṣṭha* and *Śreṣṭha* using the same words as are found here.

As He is the most ancient and the most magnificient deity, He is named *Prajāpatiḥ*, the Lord of all living beings. Immediately after uttering this name, *Prajāpatiḥ*, the *Ācārya* instantly remembers the Vedic expression *Hiraṇyagarbhaḥ* (the godhead shaping the universe in the form of a golden egg and dwelling in it). What a wonderful image of the world we live in and the whole universe that surrounds us! It is coated and decorated with pure gold, natural gold and the unadorned gold, hence the best adorned. The Vedic seers visualized this abode of the Lord which alone existed in the beginning and exclaimed with inexplicable joy--purely internal--that *Hiraṇyagarbhaḥ Samavartatāgre* (in the beginning there existed only 'One' inhabitant of a golden egg).

The next name *Bhūgarbhaḥ* presents the other side of the coin making the picture complete and comprehensive. That *Hiraṇyagarbhaḥ* has the whole universe in Himself. Not only that, He is present in every atom of the very universe. He is in the universe and the universe is in Him. Here the two words *hiraṇya* (gold) and *bhuḥ* (earth) are highly significant as they form the *garbha* (the inbuilt womb or campus for the Lord, the principal source of all creation), and also represent the two types of abodes for the Lord-one celestial and the other terrestrial. They may be termed in the mystic language, *Śrīdevī* and *Bhūdevī* who are believed to be the two consorts of the Cosmic figure.

There is yet another pair of epithets or attributes of the Lord which have vibrations sanctifying the three worlds--the Earth, the Heaven and the Eternal Abode of all existence, excellence and exuberance.

These two names are *Mādhavaḥ* and *Madhusūdanaḥ*. In a way, these two names summarize the glorification of the Lord *Īśānaḥ*. the main thrust of this verse. The monosyllable word *Mā* means *Lakṣmī*, the Goddess of wealth, prosperity and also learning *vidyā*. Therefore *Mādhava* would mean the Lord of *Lakṣmī* with all Her attributes. This is very simple and in fact the word *mādhava* is popular only in this sense. But *Chāndogya* speaks of *madhuvidyā*, a spiritual practice which enables the aspirant to obtain the grace of the Lord. The *Yoga* also speaks of *madhumatī bhūmikā*, a particular plane of consciousness where there is no distinction between happiness and sorrow, pleasure and pain and other dualities. So, the word *mādhava* can be interpreted as God head, the Lord of *Lakṣmī* or a deity propitiated through the spiritual practice called *Mādhuvidyā*. In any case, *Mādhava* is an enchanting name for the Lord, particularly for His incarnation as *Kṛṣṇa*. *Rādhā* and *Mādhava* go together. In *Mahābhārata*, the concept of *mādhava* is interpreted as a result of three spiritual practices--*Mauna* (silence), *Dhyāna* (meditation) and *Yoga* (psychic discipline).

The second name of the Lord in this duet is *Madhusūdana*. The Lord destroyed a demon called *Madhu* and so He is named *Madhusūdana*. The *Mahābhārata* says that this demon was killed by *Viṣṇu* at the instance of *Brahmā*. The demon may be a symbol of 'Sweet will' of evil-minded people which causes damage to peace and prosperity of the rightminded.

The Excellence Unexcelled

Having extolled the Lord as the primordial force of life, the *Ācārya* proceeds to present the excellence of His Excellency that cannot be excelled. The verse reads:

ईश्वरो विक्रमी धन्वी मेधावी विक्रमः क्रमः ।
अनुत्तमो दुराधर्षः कृतज्ञः कृतिरात्मवान् ॥

īśvaro vikramī dhanvī medhāvī vikramaḥ kramaḥ ।
anuttamo durādharṣaḥ kṛtajñaḥ kṛtir - ātmavān ॥

The trend-setting attribute of the Lord in the present verse is *Īśvaraḥ* meaning the omnipotent competent to control the entire universe. With His great strides, He can make His presence felt everywhere with or without any traversing process. He is therefore called *Vikramaḥ* as well as *Kramaḥ*. In His incarnation as *Vāmana*, He projected Himself as *Trivikrama* covering the three worlds with His three feet. As *Rāma*, He covered the vast area from *Ayodhyā* to *Laṅkā* on foot. He is the master of His movements. So, He is *Vikramaḥ*. He has a bow with miraculous powers and marvellous achievements. He could break the bow of Lord *Śiva* in a minute by just handling it casually. When His arrow killed *Rāvaṇa*, it pierced into the earth and came back to him as if to report to him that the Mother Earth has been kept informed of the pleasant news of her daughter's release from the cruel hands of *Rāvaṇa*. All these instances project the Lord as *Dhanvī*, the expert bowman. His extraordinary intellectual brilliance projects Him as *Medhāvī*.

The level of excellence manifest in the marvellous and mysterious acts of the Master cannot be surpassed by any other person, power or force. So, He is *Anuttamaḥ* . He is unsurpassable physically, intellectually and spiritually. He is an embodiment of excellence that excells all the norms.

He is also unassailable either by demons or by others. So, He is adored as *Durādharṣaḥ* . He identifies Himself with His action so deeply that He becomes the action itself. Because of this peculiar phenomenon, He does not have to exert Himself or make any special efforts in executing His will. He is both *Kṛtiḥ* and *Kṛtajñaḥ,* He is action personified,one who acts according to His will and also one who accords due recognition to the deeds of others. This is the real workmanship and work-culture which the Lord demonstrates through His own actions for the benefit of mankind.

The last name in the verse is *Ātmavān* which sums up the whole divinity. *Ātman* (the soul) is the source of all divinity as well as humanity. One who realizes the soul within can visualise the potential divinity latent in him. It is therefore this capacity to rise up the level of being *Ātmavān* (of one's own real and inner self) that elevates humanity to a level where it can excel even divinity as it happened in case of *Rāma*, the incarnation of the Lord .

Compassion All-compassing

The loving looks of the Lord reach each and every individual soul on earth and in heaven and provide practical solutions to all kinds of problems His children may be facing at any point of time and in any part of the globe. This universality in His outlook and compassion for the distressed is the central theme of the following verse containing ten names of the Lord:

सुरेशः शरणं शर्म विश्वरेताः प्रजाभवः ।
अहः संवत्सरो व्यालः प्रत्ययः सर्वदर्शनः ॥

sureśaḥ śaraṇaṁ śarma viśva-retāḥ prajā-bhavaḥ |
ahaḥ saṁvatsaro vyālaḥ pratyayaḥ sarva-darśanaḥ ||

He is called *Sureśaḥ* because even the celestial deities come under His purview for protection and partonage. Our mythology is full of episodes where the Lord had to come down to the terrestrial sphere to protect the celestials from the onslaughts by the dreadful demons. He uses all His devices both divine and human to set things right and ensure proper enforcement of Justice.

He is so considerate even to His rivals and opponents that He is prepared to entertain them and accommodate their needs if only they seek His shelter in right earnest and surrender themselves uncoditionally.

The instance of *Vibhīṣaṇa* seeking *Rāma's* intervention and protection is a glorious example. In fact Lord *Rāmacandra* was prepared to pardon even *Rāvaṇa* if he changes his mind and surrenders himself at his feet as *Vibhīṣaṇa* has done. He performs funeral rites for *Jaṭāyu* who sacrificed his life for protecting *Sītā*. This shows how open-minded the Lord keeps Himself to shower His mercy on each and every person on a sincere request made with a pious heart. This all-compassing compassion of the Lord explains His name *Śaraṇam* which means refuge. He never refuses any one seeking refuge under Him. The saint-singer *Tyāgarāja* appeals to his Lord to entertain him as he cannot be a burden to Him when He inhabits the whole universe.

The next name of the Lord *Śarma* meaning bliss, happiness, pleasure or delight indicates that whoever comes under His patronage will have all the bliss available for the blessed souls.

All the beings are His children. He is the cause and source of the entire creation. So, He is called *Viśvaretā* the universal cause. Not a single particle in the Universe can come into existence without His intervention. That is why He is called *Prajābhavaḥ,* the originator or the generator of all living beings.

Even the Time (the endless and systematic passage of time covering days, months, years and so on without rest and without haste) is His operational mechanism. That is why He is named *Ahaḥ* the day *Saṁvatsaraḥ,* the year and *Vyālaḥ* the serpentile movement of the time-reptile. These three names are primarily indicative of the passage of time over which none but the Lord has any control. In *Gītā,* the Lord identifies Himself with this Time Eternal whose job is to devour all that gets exhausted as ordained by Him.

It is understandable if the Lord is identified with the Time Eternal as He Himself declared so. But how the words *ahaḥ* meaning the day, *Saṁvatsaraḥ* the year and *Vyālaḥ* the vicious elephant or snake or a beast of prey can fit in as the names of the Lord needs some clarification. Taking these words by their derivation, one can easily find that they symbolise creativity, habituality and the inevitable termination of the limited span of life. Looking at these three names as symbolic, one wonders how these names are followed by a highly philosophical term *Pratyayaḥ,* which means confidence, conviction and well-settled mind. This assemblage of names indicates that the Lord is the sole source of solace and confidence in times of distress and uncertainty . The word, *pratyayaḥ* also means 'thorough knowledge of the self and spiritual experience' which we usually call *prajñā*. In the *Upaniṣads*, this advanced state of consciousness called *prajñānam* is identified with *Brahman*. *Prajñānaṁ Brahmā* is the most popular Vedic verdict.

One who is endowed with this knowledge and experience can see everything in any thing. The Lord identifies Himself with the realized souls of this Cosmic vision. So, He is named *Sarvadarśanaḥ* (one who sees everything).

The Lord Of All

The Lord of all is never born as He is the Supreme Soul seated in the hearts of all living beings. It is with this unique feature of the unborn that we start the next verse :

अजः सर्वेश्वरः सिद्धः सिद्धिः सर्वादिरच्युतः ।
वृषाकपिरमेयात्मा सर्वयोगविनिःसृतः ॥

ajaḥ sarveśvaraḥ siddhaḥ siddhiḥ sarvādir-acyutaḥ I
vṛṣākapir-ameyātmā sarva-yoga-viniḥsṛtaḥ II

The Vedic verdict declares that He was never born nor will He be born *na jāto na janiśyate.* The Lord Himself says in the *Śāntiparva,* 'I was never born, nor am I born, nor will I have any birth in future'. But He has a confirmed and permanent birth in the sacred hearts of all who are bound to be born. Hence He is called *Ajaḥ*. The word *ajaḥ* can also mean 'one who takes his origin from the sacred syllable- *a* - born of- *a*'. The unborn Lord declared that He is the syllable '*a*' (अ) among the various syllables *akṣarāṇām akāro'smi.* This first syllable in the alphabet (*varṇamālā* to be more authentic) is the initiating sound of *Praṇava* (*Omkāra*). This way too, He is *Ajaḥ*. The whole human vioce originates from this first vowel sound just as the whole universe takes its origin in the Supreme Soul - *Paramātmā.* He is the soul of souls.

The next attribute, *Sarveśvaraḥ* meaning the Lord of all is not a new concept. In the verse 4, the first name was *Sarva* and the last one was *Īśvaraḥ*. Both combined make *Sarveśvara*. There is nothing in the universe which does not come under the purview of His governance. So He is *Sarveśvara*. This expression figures very frequently in *Upaniṣads* and allied scriptures. But the names *Sarvaḥ* and *Iśvaraḥ* appear only once in the entire text of this *Sahasranāma*. *Sarveśvaraḥ* also comes only once. But in combination of other names and in different contexts, these words, *Sarva* and *Īśvara* are very frequently used even in this text e.g. *Sarvavāgīśvareśvaraḥ* (the Lord of all the presiding deities of all forms of articulation). Really a wonderful name which we shall discuss while dealing with the verse 86. However all the names belong to Him as He is the Lord of all.

The next two names *Siddhaḥ* and *Siddhiḥ* are so much inter-related that one speaks for the other. The first one *Siddhaḥ* means 'one who has attained' and the second one *Siddhiḥ* stands for the attainment itself. The 'means' and the 'end' merge into the process of taking the means to the desired end. The Lord of all is always with all means of attainment and also with the aspirant who has attained.

The Lord marks the beginning of all attainments. He inaugurates all attempts and aspirations because He is the First of all. There was nothing before Him.

The next name in the verse *Acyutaḥ* is highly sanctified and significant name. The vedic verdict proclaims,

स्वरूपसामर्थ्यात् न च्युतो, न च्यवते, न च्यविष्यत इति अच्युत:

[तैत्तिरीय आरण्यक]

svarūpasāmarthyāt na cyuto, na cyavate, na cyaviṣyata iti acyutaḥ

[Taittirīya Āraṇyaka]

He has not lapsed and is not lapsing and will not lapse from His Supreme Role as the Soul of all souls. Hence He is *Acyuta* (Incidentally we complete the first 100 names of *Śrī Viṣṇu Sahasranāma Stotram* with this sacred name.

The first name in the second hundred names is *Vṛṣākapiḥ*, a peculiar name from many angles. In the scriptural and spiritual parlance, The word *vṛṣa* stands for *dharma* (the right conduct) as it pours out fruits of all actions in the form of spiritual showers. *Kapi* which means the great Boar which protected the earth from waters and hence the most auspicious and the best. Thus *Vṛṣākapi* has come to mean the highest form of righteousness.

The next name *Ameyātmā* means immeasurable, undefinable and unimaginable. This resembles the name *Aprameya* which we already discussed [Verse-6].

The last name in this verse is quite lengthy - *Sarva yoga viniḥsṛtaḥ.* He is realized through *yoga* preached in several scriptural sciences. He is the essence of all the types of *yoga* practised and perfected. All the learning springs from Him and resides in Him.

The Soul Of Equanimity

Self-realisation, the ultimate goal of all yogic practices, can be achieved only by God's grace which is possible only when there is prefect harmony, equanimity and balance of emotions, passions and aspirations. A pure thought from a pure heart is the most effective means of communication with the Lord seated in our hearts. The following verse indicates the path of cultivating this faculty of direct communion with the deity through equanimity in body, mind and soul.

वसुर्वसुमनाः सत्यः समात्मा सम्मितः समः ।
अमोघः पुण्डरीकाक्षो वृषकर्मा वृषाकृतिः ॥

vasur-vasumanāḥ satyaḥ samātmā sammitaḥ samaḥ ।
amoghaḥ puṇḍarīkākṣo vṛṣa-karmā vṛṣākṛtiḥ ॥

The terrestrial and the celestial spheres spinning round and round without a stop or even a pause derive their propulsion from the dynamic Spirit, the Universal Soul inhabiting the entire universe. This Omnipresent and Omnipotent force is called *Vasuḥ* in this context. He provides an inbuilt mechanism to motivate, modulate and activate all the individual souls inhabited by Him. The human body with nine doors and several windows and chambers is designed and decorated by Him so that His children feel comfortable and lead a peaceful and pleasant life. He stays with them to ensure their safety and salvation. So He is our *Vasu,* (boss) granting bliss, bread and butter for our sustenance.

If we can live upto His expectations without disturbing ourselves and His set-up, we shall realize how tranquil and equanimous He Himself is and He expects us to be. This is the substance of the attribute *Vasumanāḥ* the mind moderated by blissful living. Be where you are and he happy - should be the motto.

The next name *Satyaḥ* though very close to *Stayam*, primarily meaning truth and in the scriptural parlance, the first among the three facets of *Brahman* (*Satyam, Jñānam* and *Anantam* - existence, knowledge and infinity) has a special connotation in this context. It is more relevant to interpret it here as the abode of *Brahman* and of truth, the uppermost of the seven worlds or *lokas* above the earth, the other six below it being *Bhūr-loka, Bhuvar-loka, Svar-loka, Mahar-loka, Janar-loka* and *Tapar-loka. Satya-loka*, the uppermost, is immediately above the *Tapar-loka*, the plane of penance. No penance is higher than truth, the basis of the *Satya-loka*. The Lord as existence personified is the source of all these worlds including *Satya* or *Brahma-loka*. But *Brahman* is free from all blemishes and differentiation and maintains perfect equanimity not only in all these seven *lokas* but also in the other set of seven *lokas* below the earth. Hence, the name *Satyaḥ* here stands for perfect and universal equanimity which forms the basis for all existence. This is the end of knowledge, but endless in its universality.

The same quality of euqanimity is emphasized in the next name, *Samātmā*, the soul of souls with inbuilt equality ingrained in the very nature of the soul-individual or universal.

This attribute of the Lord leads to the conclusion that there is no limit to this equanimity with the single exception of the very concept of equanimity. That is why the Lord is named *Sammitaḥ* well-modulated. This name is also read as *Asammitaḥ* but it hardly makes any difference in the purport of the nomenclature. He is both modulated and beyond all modulation.

The succeeding name and the concluding one in the *Sama* - series is *Samaḥ* the shortest and the sweetest attribute summarizing the significance of equanimity. It is enough if we say the Lord is simply *Samaḥ* (even, free from all aberrations, aversions and angularities). That is the Beauty of the Absolute Truth which is not affected by any worldly vagaries and variations. The word *sama* is also interpreted as one always associated with *Mā* or *Lakṣmī* who is believed to be always with the Lord or His ornament settled on His bosom *Vakṣasthalavāsinī.*

The second line of this verse starts with the name *Amoghaḥ* (never failing in granting His grace to His devotees). He is always fruitful in His actions in fulfilling the aspirations of His devotees. No worship offered to Him will go waste as the Lord assures His devotees saying, 'There is no such thing as defeat or disappointment for my true devotees' na me *bhaktaḥ praṇaśyati.*

His looks resemble the lotus. He looks as if there are two lotus flowers merged into one casting their compassion and concern for the welfare of the world He has created. As the *Taittirīya Āraṇyaka* says, this lotus *puṇḍarīka* of the Lord is always seated in the heart, the centre of the human body, purifying the whole space- outer and inner - and occasionally looking around to ensure that everything is going on well-as well as it should be. Hence, the name *Puṇḍarīkākṣaḥ.*

The last two names in the verse *Vṛṣakarmā* and *Vṛṣākṛtiḥ* help us in visualizing the actions and appearances of the Lord charged with a spirit of righteousness in sense and spirit. *Dharma,* the righteous conduct, is at the core of all that He does and all that He sees.

Holy Sound Dispels Fear

The next verse presents the Lord in the form of *Rudra* who is all compassion for His devotees and drives away all evils and fears from them. He is also fond of sacred hymns and their vibrations.

रुद्रो बहुशिरा बभ्रुर्विश्वयोनिः शुचिश्रवाः ।
अमृतः शाश्वतस्थाणुर्वरारोहो महातपाः ॥

rudro bahuśirā babhrur viśva-yoniḥ śuciśravāḥ |
amṛtaḥ śāśvata-sthāṇur-varāroho mahā-tapāḥ ||

The word *rudra* is derived from the root *rud* meaning to cry. This is a common and popular name for *Śiva* or *Śaṅkara* who is said to be the most prominent among 11 *Rudras*. He makes evil forces like *Rāvaṇa* cry though He grants boons to them on the basis of the penance they perform. He appreciates worship and chanting of sacred hymns like *Rudrādhyāyī* but does not make any compromise in matters of justice.

He is myriad-headed like most of the deities and is therefore called *Bahuśirāḥ*. As this hymn is dedicated to *Viṣṇu*, this word *rudra* too glorifies Lord *Viṣṇu* and His qualities. He is *Sahasraśīrṣa* as *Viṣṇu* and *Bahuśirā* as *Rudra*. Both are the same.

He is also named *Babhruḥ*, the supporter. He supports all the worlds and the living beings inhabiting them. He inhabits the whole universe and is the principal cause of the Universe. He is *Śuciśravāḥ* because He is fond of listening to sacred sounds invented and promoted by the great sages. The mere utterance of the hymns glorifying His universal excellence pleases Him. This is, in fact, the code language to invoke His blessings which He spontaneously grants the moment the holy sound reaches His ears.

He showers His blessings like nectar. So, He is called *Amṛtaḥ*. He grants immortality to pious souls who chant His hymns. The most popular *mantra* propitiating the deity referred to as *Mṛtyuñjaya mantra* is from the sacred hymn *Rudrādhyāyī*. In this *mantra*, *Rudra* is extolled as *Tryambaka*. The Lord is eternal and firm in His existence and efficacy. So, He is described as *Śāśvatasthāṇuḥ*.

Once His grace is granted, the devotee or the aspirant in the path of spiritual attainment goes on ascending the heights - one after another. His is a path of no return which has ascent and ascent alone. So, the Lord is glorified here as *Varārohaḥ*, the most covetable assent.

If the aspirant takes to asceticism, the Lord will take him to the highest plane of realization and spiritual attainment. That is why the Lord is called *Mahātapaḥ*. He is the ultimate goal of all penance. When *Rāma* goes to *daṇḍka,* he finds many saints and seers who have been eagerly waiting for him. They consider his *darśana* or at least a glimpse of his appearance more blissful and fruitful than all the penance they have been engaged in. *Śarabhaṅga* who was about to be escorted to the highest plane of realization by *Indra* stops for a whole on seeing *Rāma* approaching him and offers all his penance to *Rāma*. *Rāma* in His characteristic way smiles at the offer and tells the sage that his immediate need is a suitable place for stay during the period of his exile and He could manage the other things Himself. The Lord is the ultimate goal of all penance. So, He is called *Mahātapāḥ* because no penance can match His presence.

Blissful Blend Of Radiance And Wisdom

Wisdom is the basis of all radiance. But the real treat for the soul is a perfect blend of both radiance and wisdom which we find in the Lord and His devotees. This is the main theme of the verse that follows:

सर्वग: सर्वविद्भानुर्विष्वक्सेनो जनार्दन: ।
वेदो वेदविदव्यङ्गो वेदाङ्गो वेदवित्कवि: ॥

sarvagaḥ sarva-vid-bhānur-viṣvakseno janārdanaḥ ।
vedo vedavid-avyaṅgo vedāṅgo vedavit-kaviḥ ॥

He is everywhere-wherever you go. He knows everything whatever anybody knows and can know. He shines like the sunnay, the Central Sun of all suns. His access to all the areas of this vast universe makes Him *Sarvagaḥ* - a universal figure found anywhere and everywhere. His Omniscience as radiant as the Sun makes Him a *Sarvavid-bhānuḥ* the omniscient Sun. Whatever shines in the world shines after Him, says the *Muṇḍakopaniṣad* [2.2.10].

He excels not merely in radiance, but also in militancy with his army stationed in all strategic points to destroy evil and establish order. That is why He is called *Viṣvaksenaḥ* (The modern surname *Saksenā* seems to be very close to this name of the Almighty). The next name *Janārdanaḥ* explains the purpose of the Lord's militant attitude. The simple meaning of the word *janārdana* is the chastiser of wicked people. That is the purpose for which He organizes His forces. By destroying or distorting the evil forces, He is protecting the innocent and righteous people. So, the name *Janārdanaḥ* is often interpreted as the Lord who protects His devotees.

Now follow some names connected with Vedic scriptures. The first one is *Vedaḥ* itself. The Lord is identified with Vedic learning. He is Himself *Veda*, embodiment of all scriptures connected with Vedic learning. This is followed by the name *Vedavit*, one who is well - versed in Vedic learning. These two names describe the Lord as the embodiment of the *Vedas* and also as a scholar with profound knowledge of the *Vedas*. The next two names -*Avyaṅgaḥ* and *Vedāṅagḥ* have the emphasis on the parts or the branches of Vedic literature. The Lord is full-fledged and perfect in the Vedic learning. So He is *Avyaṅga* with no part or branch of the knowledge left untouched. The other name *Vedāṅgaḥ* means He is the same as any branch of Vedic learning. There are six branches of Vedic learning and they are all divine limbs of the Lord. In other words, the Lord is being described here as *Veda* personified.

The fifth name in the Vedic series is the same as the second one - *Vedavit*. This is not obviously a meaningless repetition. There are many repetitions of the same name in this hymn. But they convey different meaning in different contexts. Here the repetition is so close that it is not easy to make out the difference. The possible difference seems to be that the former one means - one who is thorough with *Vedas* and the latter should mean one by whose grace, the Vedic knowledge becomes revealed. Thus the knower and the means of knowing are both identified with the Lord. We try to know the Lord with the strength derived from His own grace. In other words, we can know Him only when He enables us to know. This is a wonderful series of five names connected with Vedic knowledge.

This chain of names of the Lord reminds us of a line in *Gītā* where the Lord Himself tells *Arjuna* that He is the subject worth knowing through Vedic studies, He alone is the composer of the essence of all *Vedas* and He again is the knower of this learning with perfection. This identification of the knowledge with the knower and the known is the special feature of these five names.

The last name in this verse *Kaviḥ* summarizes the content conveyed through the five names. The word *kavi*, though sounds secular to an average person, is essentially a Vedic term. *Īśāvāsya* (an integral part of the Vedic compilation) speaks of the Lord as *Kavi* equating Him with *Manīśī*, *Paribhūḥ*, and *Svayambhūḥ*. Obviously the word *kavi* in this context is not a mere poet in the secular sense of the term. He is Lord Himself.

It is very much in the fitness of things to describe the Lord as *Kavi* after identifying Him with the Vedic wisdom along with all its branches and also with the Vedic scholars. This is what makes the subject matter of this verse, 'a fine blend of radiance and wisdom'.

Presiding Over, While Residing In

It may be recalled that *Bhīśma* in his introductory verses referred to the presiding deity of the sacred hymn in seven significant epithets starting from *Jagatprabhu* (the Lord of the Universe) and ending with *Jagannātha* (the Master of this mysterious and mobile Universe). These two names - the first and the last start with the word *jagat* (the moving world) while the other five intermediate names start with the word *loka* (literally the visible world or worlds). There are 14 *lokas* in all - seven upper and seven lower with reference to the earth or our phenomenal world. The five names enumerated by *Bhīśma* in his prologue in terms of *Loka* are: *Śarvalokamaheśvaraḥ* (the Supreme Lord of all the worlds), *Lokādhyakṣaḥ* (the Presiding deity of the entire Universe), *Lokānāṁ kīrti vardhanaḥ* (the promoter of the prestige of all the worlds), *Lokanāthaḥ* (the Rector of the Universe) and *Lokapradhānaḥ* (the Principal Force behind the Universe).

It will help us in understanding the basic theme of the following verse in our sacred hymn in the light of the seven names mentioned above because this verse starts with homage paid to three presiding deities - *Lokādhyakṣa, Surādhyakṣa* and *Dharmādhyakṣa* specifying their areas of jurisdiction. It is not necessary that the three areas are controlled by three different deities. The same Supreme Lord of the Universe - the Omnipresent, the Omnipotent and the Omniscient - has His hand in this Supreme Command. How this is organized, we can see in the following verse:

लोकाध्यक्षः सुराध्यक्षो धर्माध्यक्षः कृताकृतः ।
चतुरात्मा चतुर्व्यूहश्चतुर्दंष्ट्रश्चतुर्भुजः ॥

lokādhyakṣaḥ surādhyakṣo dharmādhyakṣaḥ kṛtākṛtaḥ |
caturātmā catur-vyūhaś-catur-daṁṣṭraś-catur-bhujaḥ ||

The first three names glorify the Lord's complete hold on the visible world of worlds *loka*, the celestials *suras* and also *dharma*, the Eternal Law ensuring justice and righteous conduct. The irony and the beauty in this administration of universal justice, law and order is that the Lord manages all this without making His appearance. He is there in every atom of the universe but not visible to the mortals and even to most of the celestials. He resides in all living beings as an integral part of life and presides over all their movements, actions and thoughts. He administers justice on the basis of His personal observations in a systematic and self-designed manner. In *Gītā*, He reveals this secret to *Arjuna* and tells him that He takes His firm standing in the heart of hearts of all human (living) beings and makes them move like machines governed by unwritten but well-administered laws.

All this he does without any feeling that He is doing it. Even the persons affected by this machinery do not have any means to find out who is doing it and how. This mysterious process is explained in the next name *Kṛitākṛtaḥ*. He is the doer, but nobody including Himself feels that this is so. He is *Kṛta* (the doer) as well as *Akṛta* (non-doer). *Gītā* recommends this attitude to all the learned people as the ideal way of doing one's own duty without any feeling of involvement and attachment leading to the bondage of *karma*. Do you must, but do it with detachment or non-attachment so that what you do as your duty *karma* may assume the form of *yoga*, the gateway to the ultimate goal of life.

The name *Kṛtākṛtaḥ* is also read as *Kṛtākṛtiḥ* in which case it provides a clue to the next four names *Caturātmā* etc. There is a self designed form of the Lord devised in a fourfold structure - *Caturātmā* (fourfold forms of His nature), *Caturvyūhaḥ* (fourfold facets of His manifestation), *Caturdaṁṣṭraḥ* figuring through His four norms (or teeth) and *Caturbhujaḥ*, the four armed. He is quadruple in form, quadruplicated in essence, four-peaked and four armed.

Among these four designs of the Supreme Lord of four fold existence, excellence, enchantment and enlightenment, the *Caturbhuja* form is the most popular one. The Lord holding Conch *Śaṅkha*, the Sword warding off all evils *Nandaka*, the wheel of life-cycles (the *Sudarśana cakra*), the Club of Intelligence *Gadā* and the bow of interplay of the senses *Śārṅgadhanu* in His four arms is adored and worshipped by all His devotees. This is the figure which *Arjuna* wanted to see after he visualized the entire cosmos in the physical structure of *Kṛṣṇa*. This sums up the cosmic vision of the Lord. The sacred text of the thousand names of the Lord also concludes with the description of these weapons of the Lord which serve as offence for the evil forces and defence for the pious souls.

The name *Caturātmā* reminds us of the Upanishadic observation that this *Ātman* is *Brahman* and the same *Ātman* has four *pādas* (quadrants) - *vaiśvānara, taijasa, prājñā* and *turīya* representing the four states of awakening, dreaming, dreamless sleep and complete identification of the individual with the universal. These four states are also identified with the four components of the primordial sound *Om*.

Viṣṇupurāṇa too throws some light on the significance of this quadruple nature of these four names. *Śaṅkara* quotes this while commenting on the name *Caturātmā*. According to this interpretation, the Lord manifests Himself in four forms while performing the functions of creation, preservation and dissolution. *Brahmā, Viṣṇu* and *Rudra* are the key figures in these three sets of operative agencies. Of the other three, time and all creatures are common. *Dakṣa, Manu* and the god of death are the special personalities co-opted for the purpose.

The name *Caturvyūhaḥ*, the second in this quartet is also interpreted by *Vedavyāsa* himself as the four manifestations of *Viṣṇu* - *Vāsudeva, Saṅkarṣaṇa, Pradyumna* and *Aniruddha*.

The third name *Caturdaṁṣṭraḥ* can be related to the incarnation of the Lord as *Narasiṁha* and also to the mystic symbol *Vṛṣabha* having four horns, three feet, two heads, seven hands and tied up in three phases.

The last name *Caturbhujaḥ* has already been discussed. All these four names form a highly suggestive group of names of the Lord of the Universe and lend themselves to several modes of interpretation and assimilation. The saint poet Kabir also refers to the Lord with four arms and prefers to worship Him as a Cosmic figure with innumerable arms *jā ke bhujā anantā*.

The Radiance Resplendent

The resplendent radiance of the Lord that excells all, endures everything and promotes the continuity of the creative genius in His creation is explained in the following verse :

भ्राजिष्णुर्भोजनं भोक्ता सहिष्णुर्जगदादिजः ।
अनघो विजयो जेता विश्वयोनिः पुनर्वसुः ॥

bhrājiṣṇur-bhojanaṁ bhoktā sahiṣṇur-jagad-ādijaḥ ।
anagho vijayo jetā viśva-yoniḥ punar-vasuḥ ॥

Radiance is the inexhaustible essence of the Lord. So, He is called *Bhrājiṣṇuḥ*. He is the source of all radiance and radiance itself just as He is the source of all creation and creation itself. He is the source of all commodities that are consumed and also the consumption and the consumer Himself. This is brought out in the next two names : *Bhojanam* and *Bhoktā*. He is the food that grows out of His grace and He is also the delightful and sportive consumer of the food that is served. He is thus the consumption, the commodity and the consumer-all in one.

None can excel, endure or subdue Him as it is He who excels all, endures all and subdues all. That is why He is called *Sahiṣṇuḥ* the matchless.

He is the ABC of all creation. The whole creation starts with Him.

So, He is adored as *Jagadādijaḥ*, the first manifestation at the commencement of the Universe.

He is sinless as no sin can reach Him. Besides Him, none who is close to him or dear to Him can be effected by any sin. Where He is, there can be nothing but virtue - no vice, no sin, no defeat, no depression. This sinlessness is the key to all success - both secular and spiritual. That is why the Lord is identified with 'Victory' in general. Victory is bound to be there where His grace exists.

The beauty is that He is not only *Vijayaḥ*, victory incarnate but also *Jetā*, the 'Victorious'. He is both Victory and Victorious. In the concluding verse of *Gītā* [18-78], *Sañjaya* tells *Dhṛtarāṣṭra*:

यत्र योगेश्वरः कृष्णो यत्र पार्थो धनुर्धरः ।
तत्र श्रीर्विजयो भूतिः ध्रुवा नीतिर्मतिर्मम ॥

yatra yogeśvaraḥ kṛṣṇo yatra pārtho dhanurdharaḥ I
tatra śrīrvijayo bhūtiḥ dhruvā nītirmatirmama II

Where there is Lord *Kṛṣna*, the Mastermind of *yoga* and where there is *Arjuna* (the partner, representing all the mortals) with his *Gāṇḍīva* (bow) in his hands, there is bound to be virtue, victory and prosperity. This is my firm conviction.

The *Sahasranāma* which identifies the Lord as both victory and Victorious goes a step forward. This is *Bhīṣma* who asserts this and it was *Sañjaya* who predicted it. But that prediction could not effect the blind mind of the King *Dhṛtarāṣṭra* while the subtle suggestion of *Bhīṣma* could influence *Yudhiṣthira* here who is convinced that it was neither he nor the *Pāṇḍavas* who conquered, it was the back-drop of the dark complexioned *Kṛṣṇa* which brought them the Victory.

The next name *Viśvayoniḥ* which we discussed earlier (verse 13) meaning the root-cause of all success in life herein and hereafter sums up the essence of the ten names in this verse including the forthcoming name *Punarvasu.* The word *punarvasu* literally means 'one who dwells again and again to rehabilitate those who are displaced'. This is exactly what Lord *Kṛṣṇa* did in the *Mahābhārata* War and *Rāma* in His March in search of Righteousness.

The Gigantic Dwarf

Humility takes humanity closest to divinity because the heart that is humble is best suited to the blissful Lord to inhabit. This spiritual truth is conveyed in a compact package containing 12 names of the Lord in the following verse :

उपेन्द्रो वामनः प्रांशुरमोघः शुचिरूर्जितः ।
अतीन्द्रः संग्रहः सर्गो धृतात्मा नियमो यमः ॥

upendro vāmanaḥ prāṁśur-amoghaḥ śucir-ūrjitaḥ |
atīndraḥ saṅgrahaḥ sargo dhṛtātmā niyamo yamaḥ ||

The Lord in His magnanimity chose to be born as the younger brother of *Indra* to please the pious couple *Aditi* and *Kaśyapa*. He also chose to be a dwarf *Vāmana* though He later grew so gigantic that He occupied the three worlds to teach the arrogant king *Balī* a fitting lesson and make him realize the immense potentialities of being humble. As the younger brother of *Indra*, He was called *Upendra* and as a dwarf in physical form He was called *Vāmana*. But these two features did not lower the stature of His intrinsic divinity, rather enhanced His greatness and made Him an incarnation. This greatness acquired through unassuming simplicity made Him a *prāṁśu* (a stalwart figure). Thus the three names *Upendra, Vāmana* and *Prāṁśu* bring out the value of humility and simplicity the basic virtues of a respectable person.

The result of this cultivation is explained in the three names that follow: *Amoghaḥ, Śuciḥ* and *Ūrjitaḥ* meaning fruitful, pious and powerful respectively. The first name shows that any effort made in a humble way with sincerity never goes in vain and certainly bears fruit. The second name attributes this success to the pious heart with which the task is undertaken, executed and dedicated to the humankind without any personal interest. The third name *Ūrjitaḥ* attempts to assess the enormous power and energy generated by such noble and generous acts promoting general good in the world around us.

In the next line in this verse, the Lord is eulogized as *Atīndra* (Super *Indra*), the first name in the line. When we compare *Upendra*, the first name in the first line with this *Atīndra*, the starting name in the second line, we easily realize how the younger brother has grown in majesty and magnanimity by virtue of his soft and sophisticated temperament, tempo in work - culture and total dedication to the universal well-being.

All this has been possible because of collective feeling of community and composite outlook towards life in general. So, the Lord is named *Saṅgrahaḥ*, the Companion of all. This is the basis on which the Lord creates this wonderful, beautiful and purposeful universe. This is very well brought out in a simple word *sargaḥ*. He is the creator and He is the creation. This identification of the creator with His creation is what makes the creative process really creative and recreative.

It is worth recollecting, in this context, how the great epic poet *Kālidāsa* uses the two words *vāmana* and *prāṁśu* in his humble preamble to his epic poem, *Raghuvaṁśa*. He wonders how a dwarf like him can catch the fruit on the top of a tall tree. He says *prāṁśu labhye fale lobhāt udbāhu riva vāmanaḥ* (I am stretching my hands just in my craze craving for the fruit accessible only to a tall person). He sincerely feels that he is going to face humiliation. But his creative genius coupled with composed humility makes him not a dwarf but a gigantic poet with three monumental poems - *Raghuvaṁśa, Kumārasambhava* and *Meghadūtaṁ* and also three outstanding plays - *Abhijñāna Śākuntalaṁ, Vikramorvaśīyaṁ* and *Mālavikāgnimitraṁ*. His *Ṛtusaṁhāram* plays the role of his *Kratu saṁahāram* (summation of his poetic worship).

While poets like *Kālidāsa* derive inspiration from the names of the Lord in this sacred text, the exponent of this garland of names, reminds us of a significant observation made in *Kaṭhopaniṣad* about the *Vāmana* in a highly metaphysical context. This deity *Vāmana* located in between *prāṇa* and *apāna* (the upward and the downward life-winds) is worshipped by a group of ten deities called *Viśvedevas* [*Kaṭha* 2-2-3]. Thus the assemblage of sounds and their sense in these names is highly significant and deep in their implications.

The last three names - *Dhṛtāmā, Niyamaḥ* and *Yamaḥ* speak of the self discipline needed for a disciple aspiring for the realization of the Absolute Self. These names also refer to the Lord who controls the whole universe by exercising and enforcing perfect discipline. He holds full control over all the individual souls Himself being the Universal one. Hence the name *Dhṛtātmā*.

The next two names - *Niyamaḥ* and *Yamaḥ* have reference to *Aṣṭāṅga Yoga* described in *Yoga Śāstra* of *Patanjali. Yama* means restraint of the mind, the first of the eight steps *aṅgas* of Yogic practice. *Niyama* comes next in the list of the eight steps though in the present context the *Ācārya* chose to name *Niyama* first and then *Yama*. In either case, the emphasis is on the perfect control over self which ensures the realization of potential divinity in all the living beings.

The Supreme And The Superb

Whatever is supreme and superb in any branch of knowledge, its application is identified as divine. This Ever-manifest and Ever-lasting exuberance of the Absolute is glorified in the following verse:

वेद्यो वैद्यः सदायोगी वीरहा माधवो मधुः ।
अतीन्द्रियो महामायो महोत्साहो महाबलः ॥

vedyo vaidyaḥ sadā-yogī vīrahā mādhavo madhuḥ |
atīndriyo mahāmāyo mahotsāho mahābalaḥ ||

He is the source and the subject-matter of all that is to be known and can be known. So He is *Vedya*. He is the one Absolute glorified by all the *Vedas* and allied scriptural sciences. He is not only the knowledge that is knowable, but also the knower of all learning and skills that promote wisdom and provide path-way to salvation. So, He is adored as *Vaidya*. He is the ultimate source of all cures - physical and metaphysical. In this sense too, He is *Vaidya*.

He is an eternal *yogī*, not confined to a point of time or space or branch of yogic practice. In fact, He does not practise any *yoga* as He Himself is *Yoga* and a perfect example of *yoga* in action. He utilizes all His knowledge and wisdom for the destruction of evil forces and promotion of righteousness. He is, therefore, called *Vīrahā*. The word *vīra* also means excellence in expression or its antonym. He promotes word-culture by condemning misuse of holy scriptures.

The next two names *Mādhava* and *Madhuḥ* also relate to His perfect control over the right knowledge and its palatable promotion. The word *Mādhava* was already discussed in verse 8 where it was followed by the name *Madhusūdanaḥ*. Here it is followed by just *Madhuḥ*. The sweetest thoughts are those who come out of a pious heart. *Mādhava* means the Lord of knowledge and also the Lord of *Lakṣmī*, the grace that grants all grandeur to the Universe. In both the cases, the message has to be as sweet as honey so that it may instantly get into the innermost layers of consciousness.

Whatever be the mode and method of absorbing knowledge and wisdom with the blessings of the Lord, it should transcend the plane of all sensuous pleasure. The Lord is not within the reach of our senses or sense-objects. So, we have to cultivate the faculty of deriving the highest form of pleasure or bliss *ānanda* beyond the sensuous plane. That is why the Lord is depicted here as *Atīndriya* (transcending all senses). In *Gītā*, this is what was described and prescribed as *ātyantikasukha* (the highest form of happiness) which can only be accessible through *buddhi*, perception and intelligence. It is *buddhigrāhyam* (felt only by pure intelligence) and *atīndriyam* (beyond the senses).

There are three more names of the Lord in this verse - all starting with *mahā*. The names are *Mahāmāyaḥ*, *Mahotsāhaḥ* and *Mahābalaḥ*. In the first among these names, the Lord is presented and adored as the greatest of all illusionists as He subjects even the masters of illusion to utter illusion in no time. He Himself describes His *māyā* (illusion) as something which can not be overcome *mama māyā duratyayā [Gītā* 7.14].

The Lord is as dexterous in His diligence and energy as He is an expert in the technique of illusion. He is therefore called *Mahotsāhaḥ* . His strength is also equally supreme. So He is worshipped as *Mahābalaḥ*.

Whatever attribute we use to eulogize His glory, it cannot be anything less than Supreme and Superb. He excels all in excellence because He is the essence of all excellence.

His Majesty

The superlatives used to glorify the Lord in the previous verse continue to be multiplied in the coming verse as they can neither be concluded nor contained in secular language.

महाबुद्धिर्महावीर्यो महाशक्तिर्महाद्युतिः ।
अनिर्देश्यवपुः श्रीमानमेयात्मा महाद्रिधृक् ॥

mahābuddhir-mahāvīryo mahāśaktir-mahādyutiḥ /
anirdeśyavapuḥ śrīmān-ameyātmā mahādridhṛk //

Being greater than the greatest of intellectuals, the Lord is called *Mahābuddhiḥ*. *Gītācārya*, Lord *Kṛṣṇa* tells *Arjuna* in clear terms that it is He who grants intellect *buddhiyoga* to those who deserve and pray for it. He also says, 'When your intellect crosses the mire of delusion, then you realize that all the conditioned knowledge you have acquired through the word of mouth has wasted your ears all the time and once this realization takes place, you become wise, your intellect stays firm and steady and you will qualify for the *yoga*' the everlasting union with God. [*Gītā* 2.52, 53].

The might of the Almighty operates with equal vigour in generating energy that promotes peace and prosperity for one and all. In this sense, the Lord is hymned as *Mahāvīryaḥ*, possessed of energy that makes man great, The word *mahat* is a technical word which is the next stage to *buddhi* and springs up to attain the highest place of *puruṣa* as mentioned in the *Kaṭha Upaniṣad* [1.3.10,11].

As in intellect and energy, the Lord stands as a glorious goal in matters of power. Hence the name *Mahāśaktiḥ*. As the *Kaivalya Upaniṣad* says, His power is inconceivable, as He derives this from the Divine Mother. The *Saundarya Laharī* starts with the glorification of this transcendental power *Śakti* without which the Lord *Śiva* can not move even an inch in His march *śivaḥ śaktyā yukto yadi bhavati śaktaḥ prabhavituṁ*.

In respect of radiance or splendour too, the Lord is an all-surpassing specimen, *Mahādyutiḥ* - both internally and externally. He is acclaimed as *Svayaṁjyoti* (Self-radiant) and *Jyotiṣāṁjyotiḥ* (the Light of lights) by the sages of the Upanisadic vision.

Because of these supernatural and hence divine attributes, it is extremely difficult- almost impossible, to define and delineate the real form of the Lord. Hence, He is *Anirdeśyavapuḥ* (of indefinable form).

All these attributes contribute to His Majesty which becomes all the more magnificient with the august association of Her Excellency, *Lakṣmī*, the presiding deity of all prosperity. As long as He is with Her, He excels all and is worshipped as *Śrīmān*. The credit goes to *Śrīmatī*. The name *Śrīmān* figures in four contexts in this sacred hymn. This is the second time we are blessed with this auspicious name. These names are so popular among Indians, particularly the devotees of *Viṣṇu* and *Lakṣmī*, that the words *Śrīmān* and *Śrīmatī* are used in the sense of Mr. and Mrs. Sometimes the simple syllable *Śrī* serves both the purposes.

We now proceed to the next name *Ameyātmā*, meaning immeasurable, inconceivable and beyond all conjectures and imaginations. Such is His *prajñā* too as described in the *Māṇḍūkya Upaniṣad* [2-5]. We cannot visualize it, negotiate with it, grasp it, define it, think of it or compare it with something else. We can only experience it when the whole *prapañca* (world - consciousness) cools down, generates peace within and without. We see good and only good, one and only one. That is the nature of *ātman,* identical with *paramātman.*

The last name in this verse is *Mahādridhṛk* or *Mahādridhṛt* (according to another reading). There are two instances when the Lord had to lift a mountain. The first was when He supported the *Mandāra* assuming the form of a tortoise *Kūrmāvatāra* at the time of churning the milky ocean. The second one was in His incarnation as *Kṛṣṇa* when he had to hold the whole *Govardhana* mountain to protect the cows and cowherds under its shade.

The word *adri* also means clouds and thunderbolt. The Lord protects the people not merely from the physical and natural hazards but also from the supernatural and providential calamities when His intervention is needed. He is not only *Govardhanoddhārī,* (the supporter of mountains like *Govardhana*) but also *Āpaduddhāraka* (one who rescues people from their day to day disasters).

The Bow That Binds

The series of names that start with the prefix *mahā* conclude, for the time being, with the name *Maheṣvāsaḥ* the first name in the next verse which runs as follows :

महेष्वासो महीभर्ता श्रीनिवासः सतां गतिः ।
अनिरुद्धः सुरानन्दो गोविन्दो गोविदांपतिः ॥

maheṣvāso mahībhartā śrīnivāsaḥ satāṁ gatiḥ I
aniruddhaḥ surānando govindo govidāṁ-patiḥ II

The word *maheṣvāsa* literally means 'an archer with a mighty bow in his hands'. The Lord, in His incarnation as *Rāma*, is known for His astonishing skill in handling the bow. He could shoot thousands of arrows in one spell in such a way that those who are targets of this shots cannot see Him. This surprised even expert archer like *Rāvaṇa*. Another special feature in His shots is that the arrow will come back to Him after striking down the target. He could bend the bow of *Śiva* in a minute without any effort - not even sweating on His forehead. This won Him the hand of *Sītā*, the paragon par excellence.

Besides this simple meaning of the word *Maheṣvāsa*, the name also indicates a figurative meaning implying the bow of the primordial sound *Om* as mentioned in the *Kaṭhopaniṣad* where it is described that the sound *om* is the most effective and perhaps the sole means of reaching the ultimate goal, *Brahman*, the Supreme Being. The *Māṇḍūkya Upaniṣad* also sings the glory of *Om* as the essence of the Universe and identical with the Lord of the Universe.

The next name *Mahībhartā* continues this glorification of the Lord as the supporter of the earth and all its inhabitants. In His incarnation as the Divine Tortoise *Kūrma,* the Lord upheld the whole earth saving it from being sub-merged in the waters of deluge.

He is not only the protector and patron of the planet earth but He also patronizes *Lakṣmī*, the goddess of prosperity always dwelling on His chest. Therefore, He is called *Śrīnivāsaḥ*. The name has two shades of meaning. One who is the abode of *Lakṣmī* (uṣually referred to as *Śrī*) and also the one who always stays with Her. *Śrī* and *Śrīmān* are inseparable. Thus the two names - *Mahībhartā* and *Śrīnivāsaḥ* project the Lord as the consort of *Bhūdevī* and *Śrīdevī* - representing Earth and Heaven respectively.

He is the saviour of all those who are good at heart. So, He is called *Satāmgatiḥ*. He promotes good and patronizes all the followers of good.

In His mission of this promotion and patronage, nothing can obstruct His will. His will shall prevail. So, He is called *Aniruddhaḥ*.

Even gods and demigods depend upon His patronage. He is responsible for their happiness and pleasure. So, He is called *Surānandaḥ*.

The next two names *Govindaḥ* and *Govidāmpatiḥ* have several shades of meaning. The word '*go*' (गो) means earth, heaven, speech, cow, vedic vibrations, thunderbolt and the disc of the Sun. So, this name covers many areas of the Lord's governance. He unites earth and heaven with His skill in articulation. It is, after all, the sound or the speech that binds all living beings. Even inanimate objects like waves, stones, wind, flames and for that matter any friction can create sound and this is in His hands. He is the prime mover of the primordial sound *om*. Sound is the characteristic feature of the space which is the body for the Lord *ākāśa śarīraṁ brahma*.

The Splendour Of The Resplendent

All that is brilliant, refulgent and resplendent in the world derives its radiance from Him. The next verse starts with this observation :

मरीचिर्दमनो हंसः सुपर्णो भुजगोत्तमः ।
हिरण्यनाभः सुतपाः पद्मनाभः प्रजापतिः ।।

marīcir-damano haṁsaḥ suparṇo bhujagottamaḥ ।
hiraṇya-nābhaḥ sutapāḥ padmanābhaḥ prajāpatiḥ ।।

Marīci means splendid. Whatever is splendid derives its splendour from the most resplendent, the source of all that shines.

It is this resplendent splendour that drives away all darkness in the hearts of the devotees of the ford. So, He is called *Damanaḥ*. He watches carefully those who do not perform their duties and sets them right. He also inculcates the habit of self-restraint in His devotees. The very thought of the Lord residing in the innermost layers of our heart makes us pious and god-fearing. This self-discipline leads to self-realization in course of time.

The next name *Haṁsaḥ* reveals the pleasant and placid movement of the pious soul who realizes the presence of the Lord within the mortal frame at all moments. He is an integral part of the very breath of life. The respiration - system produces this sound which carries the sense of this incessant and inherent motion. *Kaṭhopaniṣad* [5-2] sings the glory of this vibrant radiance that inhabits the hearts of the pious souls. Like the Sun enlightening and illuminating the inner and the outer regions of this phenomenal world, the Lord, who is the central figure of all the centres of this radiance, is everpresent in all the places dissiminating His divine splendour. This, the *Upaniṣad* asserts, is the basic truth *ṛtaṁ bṛihat* the essence of all thc rhythm that supports the existence and excellence of the Universe He has created.

This radiance can be found in the reverberating wings of the Celestial Bird *Garuḍa* who serves the Lord as His vehicle. That is why He is identified with the wings of the bird as He Himself is the source of their energy. In fact, He provides locomotion to all the moving creatures, birds and animals. Therefore He is *Suparṇaḥ* one with automobile and fascinating wings.

The next name *Bhujagottamaḥ* takes us to the realm of reptiles. The Lord, again, identifies Himself with the most magnificient specimen of the reptiles. *Bhujaga* means one who moves on the strength of his shoulders and is usually used in the sense of serpents. *Bhujagottama* means the most celebrated of this species. He is the best of the divine serpents like *Vāsukī and Ādi śeṣa.*

One interesting thing in the two names above is that the Lord is as much endeared to *Garuḍa*, the destroyer of serpents as to the best of the serpents. The two opposites can co-exist in the heart of the Lord. He is fascinated by the excellence achieved by the species in His creation. All forms are equally dear to Him.

The last three names of this verse deal with the nucleus of the 'atmic' splendour - more powerful than the atomic energy. This starts with the name *Hiraṇyanābhaḥ* which means one with gold in his navel. It is the gold that is hidden in His navel that imparts radiance to all precious and fascinating objects in the world. *Śaṅkara* uses a highly significant epithet to this golden navel. He calls it *Kalyāṇī Nābhī* meaning a navel that provides a centre to all the activities going on anywhere and at any point of time. Whatever be the point from which we see, the Lord is at the centre of all points. It was this *Hiraṇyagarbha* who was at the centre of creation right from the beginning.

Seated in this central point from all sides and controlling the gravitational force from the navel rich in faculties of creation, the Lord becomes accessible to all engaged in penance and other austerities. The *Upaniṣads* say that the ultimate goal of all penance and austerities is the realization of the potential divinity hidden in the mortal frame of all living beings. That is why the Lord is called *Sutapā.* The prefix *su* indicates that the penance performed should be for the betterment of all living beings in general. It should be done with a good heart. Then only it merits the grace ot the Lord.

If this is done, *Hiraṇyanābha* will shower His blessings as *Padmanābha,* having a navel like the lotus flower. The human heart is often compared to a lotus because that is the source of all beauty, benevolence and beatitude that one aspires for in life and expects from the Lord.

The concluding name of the verse is *Prajāpatiḥ* the protector of all living beings. All are His children and He is the patron, guardian and the great grand father of all.

No Birth - No Death

Birth and death are mere sensational scenes projected by the Almighty on the screen of the eternal entertainment for those who are born to enjoy the film of existence, excellence and engrossment. But the Omniscient is absolutely free from this phenomenon. His detachment from birth and death and their cause does not, however, keep Him away from His concern for creation, preservation and disposal of life in general. He keeps a watch through His universal vision and innate awareness of all that happens to each and every soul subjected to these transitory events. This is explained in the eleven names enumerated below :

अमृत्युः सर्वदृक् सिंहः सन्धाता सन्धिमान् स्थिरः।
अजो दुर्मर्षणः शास्ता विश्रुतात्मा सुरारिहा॥

amṛtyuḥ sarva-dṛk siṁhaḥ sandhātā sandhimān sthiraḥ |
ajo durmarṣaṇaḥ śāstā viśrutātmā surārihā ||

A realized soul is untouched by death because he knows that it is just a transition from one stage to the other, mere change of body like change of outer garments. Lord *Kṛṣṇa* explains this to *Arjuna* in so many words. The same truth is enunciated here by glorifying the divine nature of the Lord as *Amṛtyuḥ* free from death. Birth or death has no meaning for Him. His concept of birth is entirely different. He is never born. If at all He makes us feel that He is born, He is ever born. But what He is concerned with is a watch and ward over the self-operated cycle of birth and nescience.

This He does with a universal vision. So He is eulogized as *Sarvadṛk* He sees all, observes everything and exercises an effective control over proper practice of the Eternal law of nature.

He is impartial and meticulous in the implementation of the basic norms in this respect. Like a lion, He keeps all living beings on their toes while, at the same time, treating them with love, affection and compassion. He is depicated as *Siṁhaḥ* in this respect. He assumed the form of *Narasiṁha* to teach *Hiraṇyakaśipu*, a lesson and save his son *Prahlāda* from the inhuman treatment meted out to him. It is His compassion for the victims of the occasional vicious circle in the world that compels Him to take such drastic action.

The next three names which inaugurate the 'third hundred' of the 'thousand names' of the Lord enlighten us on how meticulous He is in His just and balanced decrees so that there is no room for any grievance from any quarter. This makes Him a perfect *Sandhātā* one who grants to all people the fruits of their actions in a well organized manner.

The system is so self-sustained that the Lord is also not exempt from the outcome of this machinery. He also enjoys the fruits of his actions without any attachment. Therefore, He is called *Sandhimān*.

While all living beings keep on changing in this system, the Lord who is the chief remains constant so that the continuity is maintained. In this sense, He is termed *Sthiraḥ*, constant.

The next name is *Ajaḥ* which was discussed earlier [verse 11]. Here this is with reference to the divine dispensation of justice and is closely associated with the name *Amṛtyuḥ*. The subject taken up here is the cycle of birth and death. Therefore, the name *Ajaḥ* has to be understood in the same context. In *Gītā*, the Lord depicts Himself as *Aja* (unborn) but declares in the next moment that He takes birth on His own *māyā*. He takes birth on His own *māyā* (*sambhavamyātmamāyayā*). The Lord subjects Himself to the Law enforced by Him with a slight modification.

When the Lord comes down to set things right, He spares none. He cracks down with a heavy hand. So, He is called *Durmarṣaṇaḥ*, hard to put up with.

All this He does with a tender heart to improve the situation by teaching a lesson to those on the wrong side. So, He is *Śāstā* , the Mentor who tries to mend to the extent possible.

All the scriptures glorify the unique role played by the Lord in this respect. Hence, the name *Viśrutātmā* the renowed self.

The last name in the verse, *Surārihā* tells us that the Lord does not spare anybody who creates trouble in the dispensation of justice assigned to the celestial bodies and deities. He destroys them and restores order without any hesitation.

The Light-house That Preaches

The very presence of the Lord, the universal preceptor, promotes wisdom, truth, valour, voice and generosity. He shapes and moulds His devotees into master - minds in no time. This miraculous power of the Lord is brought out inthe following verse:

गुरुर्गुरुतमो धाम सत्यः सत्यपराक्रमः ।
निमिषोऽनिमिषः स्रग्वी वाचस्पतिरुदारधीः ॥

gurur-gurutamo dhāma satyaḥ satya-parākramaḥ ।
nimiṣo'nimiṣaḥ sragvī vācaspatir-udāradhīḥ ॥

He is not only the Master *Guru* of this mysterious universe, but also the Master of several masters who put the common man in the right path. He is the most illustrious of all masters, preceptors and spiritual guides. He is therefore, worshipped as *Gurutamaguru* (the most outstanding of all *gurus*) as He is always seated in the hearts of His devotees and guide them on the right lines correcting them at every stage through the inner voice, His Master's voice.

He is the abode of all learning, the celebrated store-house of all wisdom and the power-house of all intellectual and spiritual brilliance. He is the Light of Life and hence hymned as *Dhāma,* the lustre that nurtures the whole universe, His own creation.

He is the absolute truth personified. There is no distinction between truth *satyam* and Him who stands for it. His entire strength lies in truth. Hence, He is glorified as *Satyaparākrama. Vālmīki* is very fond of this epithet which he uses frequently for *Rāma*, the man of his vision. *Rāma* himself says in *Citrakūt* that truth and truth alone is God. There is no divine virtue which is more sacred than truth according to him. *Bharata* considers *Rāma* as his *Guru* and *Viśvāmitra* discovers *Rāma* for the first time as *Satyaparākrama.* Thus the two twin-names *Guru* and *Gurutama* and *Satyaḥ* and *Satyaparākrama* remind us of the dual qualities of the hero of *Vālmīki.*

The next two names *Nimiṣaḥ* and *Animiṣaḥ* meaning 'deep meditation' and 'unwinking vigilance' also apply equally to the watchful eyes of *Rāma* who protected the *yāga* of *Viśvāmitra* by spending six sleepless nights in the *Siddhāśrama.* Whenever some intricate problem used to confront him, he used to retreat into deep meditation mounting to meditative slumber. He is godly because of his *animeṣa* (unwinking) character and above gods because of his meticulous vigilance.

He is hymned in the next name as *Sragvī,* the Garlanded. He is always adorned by a mystic garland made of the five rudiments- sound, touch, form, taste and fragrance - collectively called *Tanmātrās.* When *Ahalyā* lost these five due to the curse cast by her husband *Gautama*, it was *Rāma* who restored her to the normal sensation of these rudiments. This is the garland which every individual gets as a gift from the Lord of all senses and sensation.

The last name in the verse speaks of two qualities connected with voice and wisdom or speech and nobility. It is a combination of two names - *Vācaspati*, the Lord of speech and *Udāradhīḥ* generous in granting the intellectual brilliance to His devotees. Lord *Kṛṣṇa* assures His devotees that once they are on the right path, they can rest assured of *Buddhi* the intellect that follows them automatically. They can take it for granted that speech and generosity go hand in hand. It is the voice that promotes wisdom. This basic truth about 'word-culture' is glorified and illustrated by *Vālmīki* through almost all his characters. *Rāma* notices this word-culture in its most refined form in *Hanumān* even at the first sight. He misses the mellifluous voice of *Sītā* when she was abducted by *Rāvaṇa*. He recollects that soul-elevating sweetness of her expression again and again when he looks at the placid and pleasant flow of the water in *Pampā*. The epithets like *Vākyajñaḥ* (an expert in expression) *Vāgvidāmvaraḥ* (the most celebrated among the scholars of expression and *Vadatāṁvaraḥ* (the best in articulation) are abundant in the *Rāmāyaṇa* of *Vālmīki*.

The present verse in the sacred hymn, *Śrī Viṣṇu Sahasranāma* is a glorious tribute to the speech-culture coupled with intellectual generosity fostered and formulated by the Lord of the Universe.

Direction From All Directions

The leadership of the Lord directing proper administration of justice and formulation of the basic norms through His Myriad-faced, Myriad-eyed and Myriad-stepped personality is the mainthrust of the next verse which runs as follows:

अग्रणीर्ग्रामणीः श्रीमान् न्यायो नेता समीरणः ।
सहस्रमूर्धा विश्वात्मा सहस्राक्षः सहस्रपात् ॥

agraṇīr-grāmaṇīḥ śrīmān nyāyo netā samīraṇaḥ |
sahasra-mūrdhā viśvātmā sahasrākṣaḥ sahasrapāt ||

He is the leader of those desirous of attaining the Supreme State of Consciousness. He is ahead of all *Agraṇī* directing His devotees towards the right path which takes them to the august assembly of the liberated souls. He is the head of all living beings and carries the team with Him. All this shows the magnanimity of the Lord. He is at the forefront of His followers as *Agraṇī* and leads the team with a high morale. Hence, He is called *Grāmaṇī*. He is also *Śrīmān.* This is His standing attribute because of his majesty and magnanimity.

All that He does and says in the form of a direction stands to reason. He makes no compromise with the requirements of Justice. He is justice *Nyāya* personified. All His decrees are just and balanced. He has the full control over the machinery He handles and never allows any deviation from His directions. He is an ideal leader of the entire Cosmos. Hence, He is eulogized as *Netā*, the Leader of all leaders regulating, directing, rectifying and promoting the wonderful order He laid down for the universal peace, prosperity and welfare.

The name *Samīraṇaḥ* speaks of His indispensable leadership for the vast mass of living creatures. He is the very breath of life. He is a part and parcel of the pleasant breeze that we breath in. Like the everflowing air which makes us live, He breathes life into us.

He combines in Him all the individual souls. So He is glorified as the Universal Soul or the Universal Self, *Viśvātmā*. The whole universe is His manifestation. There is no particle that can exist without Him as He is the permanent and constant resident of the Universe, His own creation.

He inhabits the universe in thousands and millions of forms, visualises, overseas and supervises the various acts and events of this multidimensional world with thousands of eyes, contemplates on each and every aspect of His creation with thousands of heads and hearts and moves in the Cosmos with thousands of His cosmic feet. That is why He is hymned in this verse as *Sahasramūrdhā* (thousand headed), *Sahasrākṣaḥ* (thousand eyed) and *Sahasrapāt* (thousand footed). In fact all heads are His, all eyes are His and all feet are His. As an integral part of each and every particle in the universe, He controls, directs, leads and protects all that happens here. He is one with the Cosmos.

The second line in the verse reminds one of a similar line in the *Puruṣa Sūkta* where the Supreme Being is presented, praised and eulogized as

sahasra śīrṣā puruṣaḥ sahasrākṣaḥ sahasrapāt.

In fact, He is not confined to the Universe alone. His expansion is much wider. The Universe we know is only one fourth of His Cosmic existence.

The Synthesis Of Day And Night

As the spirit behind the eternal cycle of brith and death, day and night, fire and wind, the Lord is instrumental in all the vicissitudes of life but maintains a balance between the extremes with a synthetic approach. This synthesis is illustrated in the nine names of the following verse:

आवर्तनो निवृत्तात्मा संवृत: सम्प्रमर्दन: ।
अह: संवर्तको वह्निरनिलो धरणीधर: ॥

āvartano nivṛttāmā saṁvṛtaḥ sampramardanaḥ I
ahaḥ saṁvartako vahnir-anilo dharaṇī-dharaḥ II

Āvartana means the cycle of birth and death or the wheel of worldly life. This is generated and operated by the Lord. But He Himself is not bound by this. He is beyond but behind this as a sponsoring spectator. He is completely unattached but not unconcerned. This quality is brought out in the second name - *Nivṛttātmā* (unbound). He is covered by the veil of nescience *avidya*. He is aware of it but not involved in it. He is beyond darkness but creates darkness to make the radiance look relatively much brighter. This makes Him *Saṁvṛtaḥ* (enshrouded).

It is this synthetic approach that enables Him to destroy the evil with a remote control. Hence He is hymned as *Sampramardanaḥ*. He does not do this destruction with malicious intention. Far from it, all his destructive operations are constructive in spirit and purpose. It is not just *mardana* (crushing) but *sam* (sophisticated) and *pra* (recreating) form of reformation.

As the day dawns at His command, He is glorified as the regulator of day, night and seasons. The entire system of the diurnal and annual motion of planets is controlled by Him as He is the time-maker. He is therefore depicted here as *Ahaḥsaṁvartakaḥ* (the regulator of day or time in general).

He is always the moving spirit behind fire(*vahni* and wind *anila*. The fire is called *vahni* because it is the god of fire who carries the oblations offered in the religious rituals to the gods concerned. As the wind *anila*, He is all-pervading without a point of origin or absorption. He carries the fragrance to the farthest points of space. The Fire *vahni* and the Wind *anila* are vedic terms as these are worshipped as deities. Eulogizing the wind, the *Upaniṣad* (*Īśa*) says, *Vāyuranilaṁ amṛtam* (the air as wind is deathless as it does not dissolve). What dissolves is the body and not the wind within, says the *Upaniṣad*. Similarly, the same *Upaniṣad* concludes with the prayer, Oh, *Agni*, lead us through the right path to the highest state of Supreme Consciousness *agne naya supathā rāye*. The last name in the verse, namely, *Dharaṇī-dharaḥ* presents the Lord as the supporter of the earth. Like a huge mountain, the Lord supports the earth and if need be, He can lift the mountain itself to save the earth. He is the ultimate support to all objects which support something else.

The Man, The Divine

The divine grace is so universal, liberal and spontaneous that it becomes accessible even to the lowest and does not recognize any distinction. Very often the divinity manifests itself through humanity. The Lord speaks to the devotees in their own language, the language of the soul. His grace is so unlimited that the whole universe can come under its purview. He is so sweet and soft in His temperament that nothing can disturb Him. This state of equanimity and tranquility makes Him more human than the mankind and more divine than all the celestial deities. He is both *Nārāyaṇa* and *Nara* combined in one. These are the attributes of the Lord eleborated in the 11 names in the following verse:

सुप्रसादः प्रसन्नात्मा विश्वधृग्विश्वभुग्विभुः ।
सत्कर्ता सत्कृतः साधुर्जह्नुर्नारायणो नरः ॥

suprasādaḥ prasannātmā viśva-dhṛg-viśva-bhug-vibhuḥ I
sat-kartā sat-kṛtaḥ sādhur-jahnur-nārāyaṇo naraḥ II

He is so gracious in his looks, words and movements that the grace of being gracious finds an inspiring specimen in Him. He is always cheerful and merciful to the core of His heart, calm and quiet in His facial complexion and ever ready to shower His grace whenever a devoted and deserving soul approaches Him.

So, He is *Suprasāda*, admirable in His august and auspicious personality. The next name *Prasannātmā* also explains the same quality of equanimity and divine grace. It is His crystal-clear consciousness that elevates His devotees to higher and higher planes of spiritual excellence at the mere sight, thought and admiration. It is this characteristic feature of *prasāda* which *Gītā* glorifies as the universal remedy for all sorrows *prasāde sarva duḥkhānām hānirasyopajāyate -[Gītā* 2.65].

Vālmīki visualizes this *prasannatā* (transparent tranquility) in the crystal-clear waters of the river *Tamasā* transmitting waves of radiance beyond all darkness-both internal and external *tamasaḥ parastāt.* It is this radiance that the epic poet tries to depict in the movements of *Rāma*, the Man of his vision and it is the same Man *nara* who is being elevated to the level of *Nārāyaṇa* purely and solely by the transparency of his thoughts, words and deeds.

Before the present verse is concluded with the key attributes *Nārāyaṇa* and *Nara*, the exponent of the sacred hymn tries to explain the universality of the human dignity worth equating with divine grace in seven more names that follow the first two and precede the last two.

He is the potential supporter and sustainer of the entire universe *Viśvadhṛk*. He is also the most delighted spectator and also the dictator of the Cosmos which is His own creation. So, He is also hymned as *Viśvabhuk*. Virtually it is the creator who consumes the essence of his creation as he alone is competent to assess the potentialities of his creation. In this respect, the Lord who is both the sustainer and the dispenser of His creation is very appropriately described in a two syllable word *Vibhuḥ*, the Supreme, the master of all masters, the ruler of all rulers, the Sovereign Power - all pervading.

The Lord is as docile as He is divine because His Supremacy lies in

His simplicity. He is respected by all because He respects every one. He is *Satkartā* (one who respects, honours and appreciates the good in each and every one) and hence *Satkṛtaḥ* (respected, admired and adored by all). The two episodes of *Ahalyā* and *Śabarī* provide ample illustration to these two qualities. *Rāma* never felt that he had done a great favour to *Ahalyā*. He was all admiration for the spectacular penance she had performed for years and she deserved the redemption by virtue of her patience and penance. As per *Vālmīki, Rāma* and *Lakṣmaṇa* touch her feet with immense pleasure *pādau jagṛhaturmudā* and this honour done to her is immediately reciprocated by *Ahalyā* with deep gratitude remembering the words of the sage *Gautama -pratijagraha sā hi tau.* This shows how the Lord has more admiration for the reverence of his devotees than for the grace He showers on them. Same is the case with *Śabarī.* So is his attitude towards *Vibhīṣaṇa* He was in fact prepared to pradon even *Rāvaṇa* if he surrenders himself. These are the qualities extolled in the two names *Satkartā* and *Satkṛtaḥ*. That is why He is called *Sādhu*, a prefect being, a pious soul whose divinity lies in His humility. One who is straight forward is also called *Sādhu.*

The Lord is so straight forward, direct and perfect in His execution of justice that he can set right anything that is not straight. Anything that is crooked, perverted and palatable automatically takes the right course with the divine touch of the Lord. It is in this sense that He is named *Jahnu. Jahnu* is also the name of a King who drank up the waters of the river Ganges when the water inundated his sacrificial ground. But soon at the request of the gods, he released the whole water through his ears. That is why the Ganges is called *Jāhnavī* whom the king adopted as his daughter. This is how the Lord keeps His devotees always alert and ensures that they never go wrong. If they do, they will have a fitting lesson which will change them in a minute.

The Lord is so intimate with His devotees that He never makes them feel that they are too small for Him. He equates Himself with them. The way *Kṛṣṇa* played the role of charioteer for *Arjuna* and set him right when he was overpowered by false notions of duty and commitment to the basic norms of human justice. The sincere *Pārtha* (*Arjuna*) never felt that his intimate friend, guide and mentor *Pārthasārathī* was away from him. Both are as intimate as *Ātman* and *Paramātman*, *Nara* and *Nārāyaṇa*, the individual and the universal. This is what has been brought out in the last two names - *Nārāyaṇa* and *Nara* in this verse.

The Bestower Of Distinction

It is very difficult to measure the magnanimity of the Lord. He grants what we deserve and desire in our heart of hearts even before such aspirations are spelt out. He has distinguished Himself in the art of granting distinction to His devotees according to their status and stature in the spiritual scale without any external assessment. This is what the following nine names tell us:

असंख्येयोऽप्रमेयात्मा विशिष्टः शिष्टकृच्छुचिः ।
सिद्धार्थः सिद्धसंकल्पः सिद्धिदः सिद्धिसाधनः ॥

asaṅkhyeyo'-prameyātmā viśiṣṭaḥ śiṣṭakṛc-chuciḥ I
siddhārthaḥ siddha-saṅkalpaḥ siddhidaḥ siddhisādhanaḥ II

The Lord's grace cannot be assessed in terms of number, quantity, commodity or validity. Numbers cannot count it. Units cannot measure it. So, He is adored as *Asaṅkhyeyaḥ* (un-countable) and *Aprameyaḥ* (immeasurable). He is also invisible like *ātman.* We can only feel, experience and invoke His gracious presence and the presence of His grace though it is beyond expression.

That is why He is called *Viśiṣṭaḥ* the Transcendental. He is beyond the phenomenal world. He is the transcendent Eternal *paraṁ brahma*, the supreme Abode *paraṁ dhāma*, the purest of the pure *pavitraṁ paramaṁ* as *Arjuna* glorifies the Supreme Soul [*Gīta* 10-12]. But the speciality about the distinguished personality of the Lord is that the moment some pious soul comes into contact with Him, he gets transformed into an embodiment of divinity. That is the miracle behind the touch of the Absolute. This is what is conveyed through the name *Śiṣṭakṛt*. He is not only *Viśiṣṭa* (distinguished) but also bestower of the distinction within Him *śiṣṭakṛt*.

He is purity personified *śuciḥ*. So anyone who comes close to Him gets purified. He is stainless untainted by any illusion or *māyā*. All *māyā* vanishes when His mercy dawns.

The second line in the verse consisting of four names is all admiration for the concept of *Siddhi*, which is so natural for the Lord to impart and for His devotees to imbibe. He is *Siddhārthaḥ*, one whose very thought of achieving something is the same thing as achievement. 'Think of it and you have it' is the maxim of His methodology. In case of His devotees, it may be true to say that they get what they desire. But as far as the Lord is concerned, His proposition to have something done is done then and there. Such is the sanctity behind His thought or *Saṅkalpa*. There is absolutely no distinction between His *Saṅkalpa* and *Siddhi*. That is why He is adored as *Siddhasaṅkalpa*. He grants *Siddhi* to those who deserve it and not to all who just desire for it. So He is called *Siddhidaḥ*. He prepares His devotees for the accomplishment of the achievements and grants them at the appropriate time in a fitting manner. One has to wait patiently and impassionately for the mercy of the Lord. It comes in a moment, when the Lord feels inclined. It is like a shower of mercy which pours down, often unexpectedly and that is the distinguished merit of the divine grace which knocks at your door and pats on your back and make you feel that you are 'caught' unawares.

The Showers That Sustain

Dharma, the eternal law of universal existence is the main theme of the following verse. But the word *dharma* is not directly mentioned in any of the nine names incorporated in the verse. The word *vṛṣa* has been used instead. In common parlance, *vṛṣa* means a bull and the root *vṛṣ* from which the word is derived means to rain, shower or pour down. As *dharma* is supposed to shower the fruits of all virtuous deeds and righteous conduct the word *vṛṣa* is symbolically used in the sense of *dharma*. The word *vṛṣabha* meaning bull also stands for *dharma* in the religious and the spiritual sense. The verse glorifying the rewarding nature of *dharma* reads as follows:

वृषाही वृषभो विष्णुर्वृषपर्वा वृषोदरः ।
वर्धनो वर्धमानश्च विविक्तः श्रुतिसागरः ॥

vṛṣāhī vṛṣabho viṣṇur-vṛṣaparvā vṛṣodaraḥ I
vardhano vardhamānaś-ca viviktaḥ śruti-sāgaraḥ II

Lord as the embodiment, supporter and revealer of *dharma*, the righteous conduct showers its radiance like the solar rays emerging with the day-break. The word *vṛṣa* stands for *dharma* and *ahaḥ* for the radiance it emits for the benefit of those who are aware of it and also those who are not aware. The rays of *dharma* pierce into the hearts of all souls-pious or otherwise. It is for the receiving end to benefit by the merciful showers it pours down.

The next name *Vṛṣabhaḥ* further clarifies the grace of these showers which brighten the hearts and enlighten the minds of the followers of *dharma*. Those who protect *dharma* are, in turn, protected by it.

Then comes the name *Viṣṇu* the presiding deity of this sacred hymn, *Śrī Viṣṇu Sahasranāma*. *Viṣṇu* is also one of the twelve *ādityas*. *Bhagavān* says in *Gītā*, 'I am *Viṣṇu* among the *ādityas* [*Gītā* 10-21]. It is significant to note that the name *Viṣṇu* is placed at the centre of the four names starting with *vṛṣ*. It appears as if these four names on either side of the Lord stand for His four arms.

The two names that precede throw light on the brilliance and radiance of *dharma* with which the Lord identifies Himself. The next two names *Vṛṣapravā* and *Vṛṣodaraḥ* tell us that the strict observance of the basic norms of *dharma* lead the aspirant to the highest state of bliss and this *dharma* is universally applicable to all living beings. *Viṣṇu*, the Lord of the Universe, is the abode of all forms of *dharma*. He contains them within and transmits their radiance to the entire creation.

These showers of radiance emerging from the Lord sustain the entire creation promoting growth - physical, intellectual and spiritual. These are the showres that nourish and protect those who adore and absorb them. That is why the Lord is hymned here as *Vardhanaḥ* the sustainer and *Vardhamānaḥ* ever growing with the universe. But at the same time, the Lord is all alone - keeping Himself apart. He is a part and patron of the Universe, yet apart from it. He is like the ocean of all learning which imparts learning, but He does not store it for Himself. In short, He is not a part, but the whole of it.

The nine names of this verse, thus, present a blissful imagery of *dharma*, transmitting brilliance and radiance to the whole world like the rays of the sun and the ocean of learning helping the process by responding to the call of the solar radiance resulting in the sweet showers of pious feelings when it rains at the command of the Lord. These are the showers that sustain the existence of the Universe.

Valiant Vibrant And Radiant

The Lord of lords stands as an outstanding specimen for valour, voice and splendour that sustain the universe. This multidimensional personality is brought out in the following verse:

सुभुजो दुर्धरो वाग्मी महेन्द्रो वसुदो वसुः ।
नैकरूपो बृहद्रूपः शिपिविष्टः प्रकाशनः ॥

subhujo durdharo vāgmī mahendro vasudo vasuḥ I
naikarūpo bṛhad-rūpaḥ śipiviṣṭaḥ prakāśanaḥ II

The handsome figure with mighty arms protecting the Universe with grace and grandeur spontaneously gets installed in the hearts of the devotees. So, the Lord is called *Subhujaḥ*. But it is difficult to grasp Him and more so to catch Him. He is not easily accessible though He is seated in the heart. But He lends all support and imparts all strength from within. He enables us to pass through unsurmountable problems and unbearable pains if only we cultivate ourselves to feel His presence within us. This makes Him *durdharaḥ*, the relieving support in the intricate circumstances in life.

He is *Vāgmī*, the Eloquent. It is not only His speech that is eloquent, but His silence is often more eloquent than His speech. In fact all that happens in the world is nothing but His verbal expression. He manifests

Himself in various forms - in pleasures and pains, in wealth and health, in knowledge and ignorance and, in short, in good and bad. He tells us what is right and what is wrong. But unfortunately we do not listen to Him, though we are able to hear Him. His vibrations reach our ears, but we do not pass them on to our hearts and minds. Hence the troubles and the whole tragedy of life. But He continues to transmit His internal vibrations to us and also try to install them at the door - steps of our consiousness - carefully watching the moments when we can catch them. Such is His voice - ever vibrating within and without, day in and day out. The realization will dawn when the day comes bidding farewell to the dense darkness of the night.

He is *Mahendra*, the Lord of all lords. As the Lord of splendour, strength and prosperity, in this particular context, He bestows all that is required to make life cheerful, secured and graceful. He provides all the equipment - material, intellectual and spiritual - that shapes life into a comprehensive, composite and coordinated whole.

This wholesome nature of His concern for all His children is glorified in the next two names - *Vasudaḥ* and *Vasuḥ*. He is the bestower of wealth and also the wealth itself. Wealth is where He is. *Lakṣmī*, the goddess of wealth is an integral part of His personality. She stays always with Him keeping His breast (bosom) abreast of all that is auspicious.

The word *vasu* also means a cover or a veil. The Lord who is called *Vasu* here veils Himself in granting the material prosperity to His devotees. As *Vasu*, He inhabits the outer space as *Kaṭhopaniṣad* puts it - *Vasurantarikṣasad* [2.2.3]. Thus He is an outer cover for the entire universe and is pervaded by the outer rays. *Iśopaniṣad*, therefore, appeals to the Lord to withdraw His outer rays so that we can have a glimpse of the most auspicious light within *tejo yatte rūpaṁ kalyāṇatamaṁ tatte paśyāmi.*

Just as all the names are the attributes of the Lord, all forms also belong to Him. He can assume any form and therefore any name can depict His form. The fact is that He is nameless and formless. They are the attributes conjured up by His devotees according to their conceptual vision. So, He is hymned in this verse as *Naikarūpaḥ* (not confined to one particular form) and also *Bṛhadrūpaḥ* (one with all-compassive form). *Kaṭhopaniṣad* presents the multiplicity of the forms assumed by the Lord in a highly enchanting and enlightening language where the Lord, representing the eternal truth and the Cosmic rhythm *ṛtam-bṛhat* appears as *Haṁsa* (the Sun) purifying and sanctifying the space he traverses, as *Vasu* inhabiting the outer space, as the *Hotā* in the Vedic rituals, as the honoured guest occupying the most meritorious place and so on. All these observations lead to one conclusion that the fromless has many forms because all forms are His.

The next name *Śipiviṣṭaḥ* has a myriad shades of meaning. It is difficult for an average student of *Saṁskṛt* language to comprehend the real sense behind this name. The word *śipi* means 'a ray of light'. It also means water. So, the name *Śipiviṣṭa* can be interpreted as one who inhabits the rays of light. The real significance of the name can be understood only when we connect the rays to the water. Sun's rays pierce into the water in the rivers and in the Sea and the water evaporated in the process forms the clouds and comes back to the source in the form of rain-water. This is the *Yajña* (ritualistic process of natural resource development) that goes on forever in nature. The Lord is the cosmic force behind this. In a sacred hymn eulogizing the significant role played by the Sun, the visible God, the sage *Agastya* says, 'The Sun is both the creator as well as the destroyer. He scorches the surface of the earth and also protects and preserves the prosperity of the inhabitants by showering rays that generate light and life, radiance and rain.' *pāyatyeṣa tapatyeṣa varṣa tyeṣa gabhastibhiḥ* [*Āditya Hṛdayam*-22].

The next and the last name in the verse *Prakāśanaḥ* substantiates this interpretation of the preceding name *Śipiviṣṭaḥ*. Both the names present the Lord of myriad forms and millions of names as the Cosmic Controller of the rays that shine and the clouds that shower. This is how the Light and Life are coordinated by the Supreme Spirit working behind this Cosmic existence.

The Light Of Life

Life is delightful because it is enlivened, energized and enlightened by the Lord. He breathes life into the mortal frame as *ojas* (the sap of life), imparts strength to the body as *tejas* (sharpness) and makes it resplendent as *dyuti* (the light of knowledge). The following verse is a glorification of these three components which contribute to the stability, splendour and radiance that the Lord combines in Him:

ओजस्तेजोद्युतिधरः प्रकाशात्मा प्रतापनः ।
ऋद्धः स्पष्टाक्षरो मन्त्रश्चन्द्रांशुर्भास्करद्युतिः ॥

ojas-tejo-dyuti-dharaḥ prakāśātmā pratāpanaḥ ।
ṛddhaḥ spaṣṭākṣaro mantraś-candrāṁśur-bhāskara-dyutiḥ ॥

The very first name of this verse enlightens us on the three ingredients of both humanity and divinity. *Ojas*, *Tejas* and *Dyuti* are the three gifts granted by the Lord. These qualities promote tranquility and equanimity within and lead the aspirant to the highest state of bliss. Like the Sun, the Lord gives us light, heat and energy. So, He is adored here as *Prakāśātmā* (the radiant self) and also *Pratāpanaḥ* (promoter of energy).

This key-note explaining the significance of cultivating these basic principles of life is followed and amplified by indicating the process through which this can be achieved. The five names that follow present the outline. The first of these names *Ṛddhaḥ* means right conduct, right vision and right knowledge. This is the first step (and perhaps the final one as well in a way) in the direction. This ensures the proper assimilation of the intrinsic rhythm ever present in the universe. The next name stresses the need to cultivate clear articulation of our thoughts and verbal expression deriving inspiration from the Vedic vibrations discovered by sages. This is what is conveyed by the attribute *Spaṣṭākṣaraḥ*. If the vision is right and the voice is clear, all expression becomes enlightening, elevating and enchanting making our prayers *mantras* (sacred spells). This is articulated in the next name *Mantraḥ*.

Once this stage is attained, the aspirant can visualize the Lord within him as *Candrāṁśuḥ* (as pleasant and blissful as the moonlight) and also as *Bhāskaradyutiḥ* (as radiant as the rays of the Sun). It is worth remembering in this context that the source for the sunshine and the moonlight is the same, though the effect is apparently different.

The Lord clarifies this point in His message in *Gītā* by proclaiming that the radiance present in the Sun, in the Moon and in the fire is mine *tattejo viddhi māmakam*. There is only one light, the Light House of all light that makes life delightful and that is the presence of the Lord which projects various forms and norms of existence, excellence and enlightenment.

The Truth Thy Strength

Truth is the mightiest asset of the Almighty who Controls the whole universe with the strength derived from His inbuilt and inherent truth. This is the subject matter of the seven names that follow:

अमृतांशूद्भवो भानुः शशबिन्दुः सुरेश्वरः ।
औषधं जगतः सेतुः सत्यधर्मपराक्रमः ॥

amṛtaṁśūdbhavo bhānuḥ śaśabinduḥ sureśvaraḥ ।
auṣadhaṁ jagataḥ setuḥ satya-dharma-parākramaḥ ।

The Lord is the source behind the emergence of the Moon with ambrosial rays from out of the milky ocean when it is churned. That is why He is called *Amṛtāṁśūdbhavaḥ*. The word *amṛta* means nectar or ambrosia, *aṁśu* means rays. The source or origin for the Moon with ambrosial rays is the same as the source of solar rays as well. So He is called *Bhānuḥ*. These two names reaffirm the concept explained in the last two names of the previous verse where the Lord was hymned as *Candrāṁśuḥ* and *Bhāskaradyutiḥ*. The Lord effects these two forms of radiance with the strength derived from truth *satyam* and righteousness *dharma*. It is because of these two basic and eternal forces that the Sun and the Moon enlighten the hearts and souls of all living beings.

The next name *Śaśabinduḥ* elaborates the same theme by

describing the hare-mark we find in the moon as the trade-mark of the Lord of the Universe. The Moon is therefore called *Śaśāṅkaḥ*.The word *śaśa* means hare. The word *bindu* means a drop or a dot. This dot denotes the nectar that rains from the moon.

Besides the Sun, the Moon and also the Fire, all the celestial bodies and deities derive their radiance from the Lord. That is why He is called *Sureśvaraḥ*, the Lord of the celestials.

This nectar or ambrosia which emerged from the milky ocean with the Divine will provide a cure for all the evils and ailments of life. These rays are able to cure the diseases because of the presence of the Lord in them. He is the medicine. Hence, He is adored here as *Auṣadham*. He also enables the disabled to cross over all unsurmountable problems and obstructions in life. So, He is named *Jagataḥ setuḥ*, the bridge across the Universe. He connects the physical with the metaphysical, the terrestrial with the celestial and also the life herein *iham* and hereafter *param*. *Kaṭhopaniṣad* substantiates this concept of bridging the mortal plane of consiousness with the immortal *yaḥ seturījānānām- akṣaraṁ brahma yatparaṁ*. The absolute *Brahman* with whom the Lord is identified here serves as a link between the two worlds (the world of reality and the world of relativity).

The last name in the verse summarizes the essence of the Eternal Existence which the Lord promotes with His two innate attributes: truth *satyam* and righteousness *dharma*. He strides in the three worlds and even more at His command with the strength of these two attributes which almost form His foot-steps. He thus maintains balance between the two. *Satyam* (*truth*) takes *dharma* (righteous conduct) in the proper direction and *dharma* demonstrates the inbuilt strength behind *satyam*. That is why the Lord is eulogized here as *Satya-dharma-parākramaḥ* . He covered the three worlds with His three steps in His incarnation as

Vāmana. Àgain in His manifestation as *Rāma*, He showed by His own example that humanity can transcend the powers of divinity if a perfect balance is maintained between *Satyam* (*truth*) and *Dharma* (righteousness). *Vālmīki* was very fond of this expression *Satya dharma parākrama* to depict the personality of *Rāma*. Very often, the sage poet used the epithet *Satyaparākrama* for the man of his vision and described him as *dharma* personified *vigrahavān dharma*. When *Kaikeyī* sticked to her stand on the basis of truth and *Daśaratha* appealed to her to have basic consideration for *dharma, Rāma* could solve the crisis created by the conflict between the two in a minute by saying that he is prepared to satisfy both by voluntarily proceeding to the forests as desired by his stepmother. So, ultimately, it is the spirit of sacrifice that solves the most complicated crisis in the world. That is what is meant by *Satya dharmaparākrama,* a glorious attribute of the Lord.

The Dispenser Of All Desires

Desires are the root- cause of all evils, ailments and aberrations of human existence. The Lord is the generator, curator and controller of all such disorders. The way He dispenses with these passing phases of life is explained in the ten names that follow :

भूतभव्यभवन्नाथः पवनः पावनोऽनलः ।
कामहा कामकृत्कान्तः कामः कामप्रदः प्रभुः ॥

bhūta-bhavya-bhavan-nāthaḥ pavanaḥ pāvano'nalaḥ ।
kāmahā kāmakṛt-kāntaḥ kāmaḥ kāmapradaḥ prabhuḥ ॥

The Lord has full control over all the living beings that had been in existence so far, that are yet to come into existence and that are already in existence at present as He resides in them and presides over all their movements, thoughts and aspirations. He is not confined to a particular point of time or space as He is present everywhere and at all times. He is Time itself and Time exists because of Him. So, He is glorified and adored as *Bhūta-bhavya-bhavan-nāthaḥ* (the Lord of all beings that have been, are and will be in existence). This first name in the present verse strikes the key-note for the ideas that follow in the nine names that succeed.

The next three names - *Pavanaḥ, Pāvanaḥ and Analaḥ* - are so closely interrelated that they need a coordinated and comprehensive study and assimilation. At a glance, they look almost synonymous. But a deep insight into the various shades in which they are presented as indicative of the inexplicable movements of the Alimighty, these names form the three angles of a triangle whose sides are endless and angles are always variable making the whole virtually wholesome.

The word *pavanaḥ* usually means air or wind. *Bhagavān* identifies Himself with *pavana* (the wind) among those who purify *pavanaḥ pavatāmasmi* - [*Gītā* 10.31]. In general anything that purifies can be called *pavanaḥ*. So, by implication, the word is used in the sense of a householder's sacred fire and water too. The quality of purifying things is what is significant in this context.

Similarly, the word *pāvanaḥ* also meaning 'purifying' or 'freeing from sin' is used in the sense of holy, pure and sacred objects like fire, incense, water, penance and so on. In short, any means of purification can be called *pāvanaḥ*. The only subtle difference between the two words *pavanaḥ* and *pāvanaḥ* is that *pavanaḥ* is what purifies directly and *pāvanaḥ* is what causes or becomes instrumental in the process of purification. In the common parlance, however, the word *pavanaḥ* is used in the sense of life-giving air, breeze or mild wind. The word *pāvanaḥ* is broader in its sense and essence. It causes air, water and fire. The common trait in all the three is purity, sanctity and sagacity.

The third name in the 'trinity' which we are discussing as a whole is *Analaḥ*. Literally, the word means 'that for which there is nothing like 'enough' *alam*. The sense of satisfaction or saturation is totally missing and it can consume anything in any quantity. That is why the word *analaḥ* has come to mean 'fire' *agni*. It is the highest and the most powerful consumer of all consumable objects.But this consumption is basically intended for purification and not for annihilation. That is why it is very sacred and worshipped as the prime deity. The Vedic seers called it *purohitam*, the first and the foremost among the well-wishers of the well being of all living beings *agnimile purohitaṁ*. Of all the words which convey the meaning of *agni* (fire), the word *analaḥ* is the finest and the richest in sound and sense. There is no such thing as *alam* (enough) in its operational field. So, it is *analaḥ*. With slight modification in the sound, the word can be changed into *anilam* or *anilaḥ* which means wind. As the fire can consume all, the wind can cover all the places without any restriction. By starting with *pavanaḥ* and concluding with *analaḥ*, the author of the sacred hymn has placed the two cosmic forces, wind and fire, in such a fine juxtaposition that the central name *pāvanaḥ* fits into the pattern and presents the Lord, the embodiment of purity, with the wind on one side and the Fire on the other.

Then the verse proceeds to the world of desires, designs, hopes and aspirations of the living world. We get a series of names containing *kāma* (desire) as the common factor concluding with a presiding name *prabhuḥ* (the Lord). It is an exhilarating experience to recite the names of the Lord of all desires-passionate and dispassionate- and discover in the final name *Prabhu* how the Lord controls, sustains, absorbs, absolves and bestows the best of these desires to His blessed devotees and dedicated souls.

The first name is *Kāmahā* the destoryer of evil desires. By doing so, He enables His devotees to divert their attention to higher values of life. In fact, the Lord tries to keep His devotees away from the passionate way of living to start with. The next name *Kāmakṛt* has two meanings - generating desires and also putting an end to them. The Lord is so diplomatic in this respect that He sees to it that the aspirants themselves change their mind looking at the dreadful consequences of evil desires. At the same time, He fulfils the sacred desires of the saintly persons whose intention is to work for the betterment of all living beings in general. Such selfless desires are promoted and sometimes even sponsored by the Lord. That is why He is called *Kāntaḥ* the enchanting.

The next name *Kāmaḥ* presents the Lord as the desire itself. He is the most desired person in the world. So, the concept of *Kāma* (pious intentions) starts from Him. He is the originator, supporter and sustainer of *kāma* as long as it is in conformity with the basic norms of *dharma*, the righteousness. The Lord proclaims in *Gītā* that He is of the form of *kāma* which is not opposed to *dharma* - *dharmāviruddho bhūteṣu kāmo' smi.* Where *kāma* is cultivated to promote *dharma*, He grants such pure *kāma* (love without lust) to His devotees.

As a sort of summing up these attributes of the Lord pertaining to pure love and pious desires, He is eulogized in the end as *Prabhuḥ*. As the Lord of all desires, ambitions, hopes and aspirations, He exercises full control over the maintenance of the Law of Emotions in His realm of righteousness.

Invisible, But Innumerable

Just as the formless and the nameless assumes millions and millions of forms and accepts myriad names, the ageless alone has the power to generate ages that are endless. He inaugurates all ages though He does not belong to any particular age or aeon. All ages *yugas* are His just as all names and forms belong to Him. This originator and coordinator of all ages, forms and names in this phenomenal world is surprisingly invisible to the naked eye though He is present in each and every being in innumerable forms. This is the theme of the following verse:

युगादिकृद्युगावर्तो नैकमायो महाशनः ।
अदृश्यो व्यक्तरूपश्च सहस्रजिदनन्तजित् ॥

yugādikṛd-yugāvarto naikamāyo mahāśanaḥ |
adṛśyo vyakta-rūpaś-ca sahasrajid-anantajit ||

He is the innovator of the *yugas* (ages) as the cycle of the *yugas* right from the dawn of existence of the universe started with Him. Therefore He is the *Yugadikṛt* the generator of aeons. He is the genius behind all this genetic code and sequence of generations and also the well-designed units of time rolled into ages that are set in motion with His Master-mind.

As the prime-mover of this cyclic movement of aeons and endless ages, He moves with the times. He creates time though He Himself is timeless. He is the *Yugāvartaḥ* the time- mover though neither these aeons nor their cycle can bind Him. He is boundless with no binding, but binds every one and everything with the bondage of time and space. This is the illusion He creates, promotes and patronizes with a well conceived purpose. This illusion which we call *māyā* is of multiple forms. There are innumerable ways in which He manifests His *māyā* (illusion). That is why He is eulogized here as *Naikamāyaḥ* His *māyā* is mainfest in many ways. The ways are many, but the purpose is one. So His *māyā* can not be measured or counted. All that we can say is that it is not just a set single pattern. The pattern changes with the passage of time and the purpose of projection. The calculus of time and space (*deśa-kāla-kalanā* as *Śaṅkara* puts it) is designed by His ingenuity or illusion *māyā-kalpita.*

Creation and consumption always go hand in hand. This is true in case of Creator of this world as well. The Lord who creates the universe also consumes the whole of His creation at the time of dissolution *pralaya.* Even in the material world, all consumers are consumed in the process of consumption as proclaimed by the scriptures *annamannādo bhavati.* But the consumption as the dissolution by the Lord of creation is of a very high magnitude as it effects the whole universe. That is why the Lord is hymned here as *Mahāśanaḥ* (the great devourer).

But the beauty is that none can witness this process as the whole thing is consumed. That is why the Lord is called *Adṛśyaḥ* the invisible. But the seers and *yogīs* can visualize Him in their hearts. He manifests Himself in His universal and eternal form to those who have acquired that special vision through the inner eye. So, the Lord is called *Vyakta-rūpaḥ* manifest in His own way. He is self-radiant to those who have realized the self within themselves.

This is His divine sport *līlā* through which He conquers all in His myriad forms and mysterious ways. That is why He is worshipped as *Sahasrajit* conqueror of thousands and *Anantajit* also of infinite variety of beings.

The Beloved Of The Blessed

Universal love is the basic attribute of the Lord of the Universe. Those who love Him and those whom He loves are both blessed as love is His best and the choicest blessing. The celestial sage *Nārada* defines devotion *bhakti* as the highest and the purest from of love [*Bhakti-Sūtra*]. It is this bond of 'love eternal' that binds the individual with the Universal. This is the subject matter of the verse that follows.

इष्टोऽविशिष्टः शिष्टेष्टः शिखण्डी नहुषो वृषः ।
क्रोधहा क्रोधकृत्कर्ता विश्वबाहुर्महीधरः ॥

iṣṭo'viśiṣṭaḥ śiṣṭeṣṭaḥ śikhaṇḍī nahuṣo vṛṣaḥ ।
krodhahā krodhakṛt-kartā viśva-bāhur-mahīdharaḥ ॥

The first name in this sequence is *Iṣṭaḥ*. This word is derived from the root *yaj* which means 'to worship, to propitiate'. The Lord is worshipped, adored and eulogized by His devotees either for material benefits or for the attainment of the highest state of absolute bliss. That is why He is called *Iṣṭaḥ*. In common parlance, the word *iṣṭa* means one who is dear to the heart, the beloved. In this sense also, the Lord is the most beloved of almost all living beings. Even those who do not like to express their love or admiration for Him always think of Him out of curiosity or fear.

The next name which can be read either as *Viśiṣṭaḥ* or *Aviśiṣṭaḥ* clarifies this bond of love or admiration between God and man in clearer terms. The Lord is called *Viśiṣṭa*, the distinguished as He has some unique qualities or attributes which a normal human or living being does not usually possess. Though He dewells in the heart of hearts of all living beings, it takes time for the individual souls to feel, visualize and realize the universal soul within them.

Whether we worship him or not, feel His presence or not, it makes absolutely no difference for Him. He is all love and affection for all living beings whom He treats as His own children. In this sense, He is one with us - *aviśiṣṭa* - though He is virtually *viśiṣṭa* - distinguished in all respects. He is both the nearest and the farthest friend of ours. The distance depends upon our degree of devotion, dedication and identification with Him, the Great Grand Father of His Great Grand Children. He is equally dear because of His proximity to the innermost layers of human consciousness. It is in this sense, He is hymned in this context as *Śiṣṭeṣṭaḥ*. He is *iṣṭaḥ* dear because He is *śiṣṭa* (Refined, good-humoured and benevolent). He is both *śiṣṭa* (polished) and *iṣṭa* (endeared) and hence *Śiṣṭeṣṭa* (the blissful beloved of the blessed souls).

The next three names - *Śikhaṇḍī* , *Nahuṣaḥ* and *Vṛṣaḥ* are all symbolic of the universality of the Lord. *Śikhaṇḍī* means a peacock, *Nahuṣaḥ* means a serpent and *Vṛṣaḥ* means a bull. But in mythological sense, *Śikhaṇḍī* is a character in *Mahābhārata* who is neither a male nor a female and on that account helped *Arjuna* in keeping *Bhīṣma* neutral in his attack. This name can surprisingly apply even to *Kṛṣṇa* as he wears peacock-feathers on his forehead. In all these shades, the name fits in to hymn the Lord of the Universe, *Viṣṇu* who can take any form and justify any name to serve the cause of upholding righteousness.

Similarly the name *Nahuṣaḥ* meaning a serpent stands for an arrogant king of heaven who ordered the sages to drive his palanquin to the chamber of *Śaci*, the queen of the heaven. He was fittingly cursed by the sages to become a serpent. He was after all a king designated temporarily for a specific purpose and he misused it to the extreme limit of insulting the sages who taught him a leasson. Thus this name, when attributed to the Lord, indicates that He can be as humble as harmful as time demands.

Another beauty about these two names is that the former stands for a peacock and the latter for a serpent and the two are utterly opposed to one another. This shows that the two opposites can coexist in the realm of the Lord as long as His blessings are there to protect them. He is the beloved of the blessed and His blessings are so blissful that all differences disappear the moment He touches them with His divine hand.

The third name in the series is *Vṛṣaḥ* which literally means a bull, but in the metaphysical symbolism, it stands for righteous conduct or righteousness itself. It showers all benevolence of the Lord and in that sense too, the name is a proper attribute for the Lord.

The next line in the verse takes up anger or temper for its theme to start with. The first two names-*Krodhahā* and *Krodhakṛt-kartā*-depict the Lord as one whom anger dreads to approach. It is not that He never shows anger, but He never loses His temper on that account. He keeps it completely under His control and expects the same from His devotees. He is *Jitakrodhaḥ* conquerer of temper, being *Krodhahā* keeping Himself away from it.

However, when He is forced by circumstances to resort to the expression of His anger, He does it with a purpose and for a specified time. This moderate and well-modulated manifestation of anger makes Him *Krodhakṛtkartā* (one who resorts to anger as a temporary measure in order to achieve something higher and more benevolent for the betterment of the Universe in general.

The next name *Viśvabāhuḥ* explains the wide range of the shoulders which the Lord wields to cover the entire universe. The Universe is the limit in determining the jurisdiction of His mercy. Protection is normally assured by extending the hands and fore-arms. While extending his whole-hearted support to *Rāma, Sugrīvā* extends his hands saying, 'Here is my hand extended to you expecting you to respond and reciprocate *bāhureśaprasāritaḥ*. Then *Rāma* takes his hands into his and embraces him. This is the magnanimity of the Lord. Hence the name, *Viśvabāhu.*

The last name in the verse is *Mahīdharaḥ* the supporter of the World or the Earth in particular. Earth is often spoken as *Bhūmātā.* She is Mother Earth for us and *Devī* for the Lord. She is as dear to Him as *Śrīdevī* (the Goddess of Wealth-*Lakṣmī*). *Śrīdevī* and *Bhūdevī* are equally dear to Him. *Ramā* and *Dharā* - *Lakṣmī* and *Prithivī* - are His two sides.

That is why Saint *Nārāyaṇa Tīrtha* in his *Kṛṣṇalīlā-taraṅgiṇī* sang the glory of the Lord depicting Him as both *Dharānātha* and *Ramānātha* (the Lord of both the Earth and the Heaven). Heaven shines when earth thrives.

The word *Mahīdharaḥ,* in common usage, means mountain. In this sense also, the Lord is the most magnificient mountain supporting the entire Universe.

The Main-stay

The eternal and the everlasting establishment of the Almighty with resources never failing and attention never distracted is the main thrust of the next verse in the sacred hymn :

अच्युतः प्रथितः प्राणः प्राणदो वासवानुजः ।
अपां निधिरधिष्ठानमप्रमत्तः प्रतिष्ठितः ॥

acyutaḥ prathitaḥ prāṇaḥ prāṇado vāsavānujaḥ ।
apāṁ nidhir-adhiṣṭhānaṁ-apramattaḥ pratiṣṭhitaḥ ॥

The unswerving Lord never deviates from His line of action and order of priorities in administering justice to the truthful citizens of this universe and hence He is *Acyutaḥ*. As the *Mahānārāyaṇa Upaniṣad* says, He is eternal *Śāśvatam*, auspicious *Śivam* and unswerving *Acyutam*. Incidentally, the name *Acyuta* is the first among the three names considered to be most auspicious for chanting, the other two being *Ananta* and *Govinda*.

It is because of this unfailling and unswerving nature, the Lord is celebrated as the Supreme Power controlling the whole creation. So, He is called *Prathitaḥ* the renowned, well-established and first and foremost.

He is the life-energy *prāṇaḥ* and also the supplier of this energy to the material world consisting of men and material. He energizes the matter and makes it operative. He is both *prāṇaḥ* the life energy and *prāṇadaḥ* the energizer.

Though He breathes life into all celestial beings as well, He assumed the role of the younger brother of *Indra*. *Indra* provides shelter to gods and all other living beings in the world- the lower and the upper. *Indra* is called *Vāsava* because he houses the heaven and the earth. The Lord provides shelter to *Indra*. But as a gesture of divine humility, He chose to be born as his younger brother and son of *Aditi* and *Kaśyapa*.

It is the Lord who provides water to all including the oceans which are supposed to be the perennial reservoirs of water. All the river water flows into the seas. But the sea-water comes back to rivers through the radiation designed by nature in collaboration with the rays of the Sun. This is organized and controlled by the Lord through the systematic functioning of the forces of nature - evaporation, cloud - formation, rains and proportionate distribution of rain-water. Thus the Lord is the Chief Controller of water resources in the world. He is therefore called *Apāṁnidhiḥ* in this name. The *Mantrapuṣpam* glorifies this role the Lord plays in channeling the water resources and says that those who can identify and appreciate the eternal boat sailing in the waters is the one who has the mainstay in this management of matter and energy.

योऽप्सुनावं प्रतिष्ठितां वेद प्रत्येवतिष्ठति

yo'psunāvaṁ pratiṣṭhitāṁ veda pratyevatiṣṭhati

It is this attribute of the Lord that is glorified in the next name, *Adhiṣṭhānam* the main-stay as it literally means. That is also the eternal establishment instituted by the Lord for establishing eternal flow of matter and energy and also maintaining proper balance in them.

This is what is conveyed in the next name *Apramattaḥ* never unaware. That is why the machinery has become well-established *Pratiṣṭhitaḥ* as the final name indicates.

It is worth noting the harmony between the first and the last of the nine names in this verse. The Lord is called *Acyutaḥ* in the first name and *Pratiṣṭhitaḥ* in the last one. He is established because He is unswerving. Where there is no *cyuti* (lapse), there will be proper order, *pratiṣṭhā*.

The Grace That Condescends

The Divine Grace drops down like a shower of mercy the moment a desperate call from a dedicated soul reaches the Lord with its own momentum and in a well-knit wave-length. He comes down with tender steps audible only to the ears within and attends to the call within the split of a second and returns to His abode as if nothing happened at all.

This imperceptible flow of divine grace is picturesquely presented in the nine names of the following verse:

स्कन्दः स्कन्दधरो धुर्यो वरदो वायुवाहनः ।
वासुदेवो बृहद्भानुरादिदेवः पुरन्दर ॥

skandaḥ skanda-dharo dhuryo varado vāyuvāhanaḥ /
vāsudevo bṛhad-bhānur-ādidevaḥ purandaraḥ //

The Lord comes down to the lowest level in order to grant a graceful lift to the lowliest and the down-trodden. The episodes of *Gajendra, Prahlāda, Dhruva, Draupadī, Ahalyā* and several others illustrate this condescending divine grace of the Lord. That is why He is called *Skandaḥ* one who comes down and also *Skandadharaḥ*, one who holds the down-trodden and the grief-striken in His arms. He bears the burden of His devotees and relieves them from all worldly worries. He is therefore called *Dhuryaḥ*. In fact He is the bearer of the yoke of the entire creation consisting of all living beings.

He grants boons to the blessed souls who worship Him with a spirit of self-surrender. He is, therefore, called *Varadaḥ* He grants what is good for His devotees at His own discretion. One does not have to ask for anything. He knows how to keep His devotees in good cheer depending upon their standing. This is what is implied in the word *vara* (the best and the choicest).

The next name *Vāyuvāhanaḥ* is highly significant and conveys several ways the Lord chooses to bless His devotees. He makes *vāyu* (the all - pervading wind) His vehicle and reaches any point of space in no time. There are seven types of *vayus* starting from *āvahaḥ* and spreading upto *parivahaḥ*. All routes are open to Him as He is the prime-mover of all these seven winds. He makes us feel His touch through these winds wherever we are stationed - ranging from the surface of the earth to the pole-star.

As the indwelling and enveloping light of the Universe, the Lord provides shelter to all the living beings and also lives with them and within them. He is, therefore, worshipped as *Vāsudevaḥ*. One who realizes the presence of the Lord in each and every atom of the universe is the real seer and the realized soul. *Gītā* says that such a great soul or *Mahātmā* is very rare *sa mahātmā sudurlabhaḥ* In the daily prayers, the devotees of *Vāsudeva* sing His glory saying, that all the three worlds are inhabited by the essence of His existence and He dwells in all the souls:

vasanād vāsudevasya vāsitaṁ te jagat-trayaṁ
sarvabhūtanivāso'si vāsudeva namo'stu te

The Lord is also called *Bṛhadbhānuḥ,* the greatest source of illumination. He is the biggest sun of all the suns in the celestial sphere. All sources of light draw from Him the power of illumination.

As the first and the foremost of all the celestial deities, He is worshipped as *Ādidevaḥ.* Everything shines when He shines. It is His brilliance that imparts light to all that is bright. As the scriptures say: It is His radiation that is reflected in all that radiates- *tasya bhāsā sarvamidaṁ vibhāti.*

He is the destroyer of all demons and their holdings. No devilish activity can thrive under His governance. So, He is called *Purandaraḥ.*

The Lotus That Looks After

There is nothing to worry when the Lord is there looking like a lotus that transforms the pond into cosmos, *brahmāṇḍa.* This paternal care of the Lord looking after the whole universe with love, affection, compassion and consideration is glorified in the ten names that follow:

अशोकस्तारणस्तारः शूरः शौरिर्जनेश्वरः ।
अनुकूलः शतावर्तः पद्मी पद्मनिभेक्षणः ।।

aśokas-tāraṇas-tāraḥ śūraḥ śaurir-janeśvaraḥ ।
anukūlaḥ śatāvartaḥ padmī padma-nibhekṣaṇaḥ ।।

There can be no affliction where there is the affection of the all-compassionate Lord. He is Himself *Aśoka* (uninflicted) and therefore does not allow any trace of trouble, turmoil or terror to step into His realm. He is therefore *Aśokaḥ* .

He enables all souls to cross over the ocean of the worldly bondage of birth and rebirth (*saṁsāra*). He is, therefore, hymned as *Tāraṇaḥ*. He is the Savior who frees the devotees from all pains of birth and death. So, He is called *Tāraḥ*.

By virtue of His intrinsic and inbuilt valour, the Lord is eulogized here as *Śūraḥ* the valiant. In another sense, He is *Śauraḥ* being the grand son of *Śūraḥ,* the father of *Vasudeva.* In His incarnation as *Kṛṣṇa,* He was called *Vāsudeva*, son of *Vasudeva* and *Śauriḥ* as the grand son of *Śūraḥ*, the father of *Vasudeva*. This can also be interpreted in terms of valour that the Lord commands. No valour in the world can compete with Him. He is the most valiant in combating all wickedness, crookedness and devilish activities. Hence, He is *Śūraḥ* as well as *Śauriḥ*.

As the Lord of all beings, He is also called *Janeśvaraḥ*. In this capacity, He adapts Himself to all circumstances, deals with all types of people and handles all situations. He is therefore described as *Anukūlaḥ*, accommodative, adaptable. Even in the most unfavourable conditions, He makes every turn favourable for Him and flows like the pleasant and placid water of a river. Nothing can go against His current. He makes everything concurrent with Him.

Like the gigantic river that crosses innumerable hurdles, surmounts ups and downs on the way and takes the well-designed course to irrigate the land around and make the people happy with its perennial flow, the Lord too keeps His march in the right direction so as to promote general good and the ultimate salvation of all pious souls. For this purpose, He comes down to the earth in several forms which we call incarnations. It is in this sense that the Lord is glorified here as *Śatāvartaḥ*.

But whatever He does, He does it with grace. It is a pleasure to follow the path shown by the Lord who always holds a loving lotus in His hand and looks like a lotus whenever He intends to convey something which no human language can express. The looks of the lotus in His hand coupled with His own looks which resemble the lotus convey world of message. The last two names in this verse - *Padmī* and *Padmanibhekṣaṇaḥ* convey this in a language that blossoms like a lotus.

As the most cherished and enchanting beauty of this grand universe, the Lord of the Universe is very fittingly depicted here as *padmī* (one who has a lotus) and also *Padmanibhekṣaṇaḥ* (one who looks like a lotus).

The Ever-growing And The Ever-lasting

The song of the Lotus that the Lord represents continues in the next verse also with new dimensions touching higher and higher planes:

पद्मनाभोऽरविन्दाक्षः पद्मगर्भः शरीरभृत् ।
महर्द्धिर्ऋद्धो वृद्धात्मा महाक्षो गरुडध्वजः ॥

padmanābho'ravindākṣaḥ padmagarbhaḥ śarīrabhṛt ।
maharddhir-ṛddho vṛddhātmā mahākṣo garuḍa-dhvajaḥ ॥

The first name *Padmanābhaḥ* is one of the most popular names of the Lord. This is the third time, the name occurs in the text. The simple meaning of the name is the one having a navel looking like a lotus. The Lotus actually is symbolic. It means the source of the universe. The whole universe emerges from Him. The word lotus also stands for the heart. The Lord is supposed to be located in the centre of the heart which looks like a lotus. The word *padma* also means the most cherished achievement of life, namely, visualizing the Lord in the lotus of the heart. In this sense also the name *Padmanābhaḥ* fits in. Both words *padma* and *nābha* are highly suggestive. Hence, the name *Padmanābha* lends itself for several shades of meaning.

The second name *Aravindākṣaḥ* literally means one whose eyes look like lotus. Here the word *aravinda* is used in place of *padma* in the same sense. But the word *aravinda* presents a special picture of the lotus where the emphasis is on the petals of the lotus. The full figure of the lotus is formed with number of petals which constitute it. This picture indicates that the Lord who is compared to the lotus with various petals represents the Universal Soul which is a collective form of all individual souls. The emphasis is also on the word *akṣa* which is the second part of the compound word *aravindākṣaḥ*. This gives us a picturesque image of the Lord where He is at the centre of all living beings on whom He always keeps an eye - an affectionate eye.

The next name *Padmagarbhaḥ* also has the lotus - imagery in it. Here the word *padma* stands for the heart where the Lord is seated. He is, therefore, meditated upon as the centre of the heart that looks like a lotus.

The Lord seated in the heart looks after the needs of the body and supports it with food, water and energy. He not only provides nourishment to the body but also helps in the process of proper digestion.

In *Gītā*, the Lord identifies Himself with the all-consuming fire *vaiśvānara* within the body and assures the living beings that He is there to consume all the four forms of food by controlling the outgoing and the incoming life breath [*Gītā* 15.14]. That is how the body is looked after by the Lord from within. Obviously He is located in the heart of the mortal frame like a lasting lotus. That is why He is called *Śarīrabhṛt.*

This Lotus-Lord seated in the hearts of all living beings is not only everlasting but also evergrowing. The body may go; but the spirit behind it never dies, never fades away, but on the other hand grows and grows forever. This evergrowing nature of the soul within the soul is brought out in the next three names *Maharddhiḥ, Ṛddhaḥ* and *Vṛddhātmā.*

There is no limit to the growth of an individual soul. The closer He is to the universal soul, the greater he grows in his spiritual splendour. This growth can be as great and matured as the universal soul itself. One who realizes *Brahman* becomes one with *Brahman,* as the scriptures say. This is the limit to which the individual can elevate himself with the grace of the great grand guardian, the Lord of the Lotus-Heart. This is the purport of the name *Maharddhiḥ* (the splendid).

One who has achieved this highest elevation in the spiritual growth is called *Ṛddhaḥ.* He is grown to the optimum point and is one with the Lord.

At this stage, he merges into the oldest and the most ancient self, the *Paramātman.* He becomes indentical with *Vṛddhātmā.* The Lord blesses these elevated souls with a magnanimous look. He is *Mahākṣaḥ.* His axis of coordination becomes so vast that His gracious look is enough to grant redemption from all bonds of worldly life.

In the form of *Mahākṣaḥ* as explained above, the Lord having *Garuḍa* as His emblem can grant immortality to the mortals. *Garuḍa* who carries the Lord on his wings is famous for hoarding nectar for the betterment of humanity and divinity as well. The Lord having such a celestial bird as His vehicle and emblem is appropriately eulogized in the last name of this verse - *Garuḍadhvajaḥ.* The word *Garuḍa* also means antidote for poison. There can be no poison where *Garuḍa,* the vehicle of *Viṣṇu* is. Such is the magnificience of the Lord who chose to have *Garuḍa* as His emblem.

The Incomparable

There can be no comparison or counterpart for the Lord as He excels in all the attributes that one can imagine. He is an embodiment of all virtues and a model for modesty, majesty and magnanimity. This unique supremacy of the Lord is brought out in the following verse :

अतुलः शरभो भीमः समयज्ञो हविर्हरिः ।
सर्वलक्षणलक्षण्यो लक्ष्मीवान्समितिञ्जयः ।।

atulaḥ śarabho bhīmaḥ samayajño havirhariḥ I
sarvalakṣaṇa-lakṣaṇyo lakṣmīvān-samitiñjayaḥ II

By virtue of His unique position in the Cosmos, the Lord of the Universe is without an equal. He is, therefore, adored as *Atulaḥ* the incomparable. All brilliance, splendour and radiance that men and material exhibit in the world is the manifestation of the majestic munificence of the Lord. Hence, He is called *Śarabhaḥ*. The word *śara* is used in this context in the sense of the mortal frame and *bha* means splendour. The presence of the Lord in the mortal frame generates brilliance and grandeur to it. The word *śara* is also used in the sense of *ātman* (the self). The primordial sound *om* is said to be the bow *dhanu* and the individual soul within the mortal frame is compared to the arrow *śara* and *Brahman* is the object to be achieved by the aspirant. In this sense, the name *Śarabhaḥ* can be taken to mean, the radiance inherent in the individual which enables him to realize the 'Absolute' within him. The Lord is, therefore the Soul of all souls, the Supreme Self latent in the individual self.

The Lord is tender at heart, but terrific in power and energy. He can cause terror to any body however mighty he may be. No might or strength can stand the stupendous force behind the Divine Power. He is Almighty, the mightiest of all. Hence, the epithet *Bhīmaḥ* for Him. Some read this name as *Abhīma* (not so terrible). This is also justified because of the nature of the Lord who is as kind to His devotees or gods as dreadful to the demons.

At times He is *Bhīma* (terrific) and at some other times He is *Abhīma* (tender). He knows when to exercise His power to destroy the evil and when to shower His mercy on the pious souls. Hence, the name *Samayajñaḥ*. He makes a tryst with time and sticks to His resolve.

One can split the word *samayajña* as *sama + yajña* and interpret as the one who promotes equanimity *samatā* and accepts it as the most refined form of *yajña*. There can be no better form of worship than maintaining equanimity in the day to day affairs overcoming all weaknesses, passions and excitements. The best way to realize the divinity within is to dive deep into the tranquility present in the deepest layers of consiousness.

If this is accepted as a form of worship *Yajña*, then all offerings and oblations used in this ritual go to the Lord and He grants all that the aspirant has in mind. He destroys all the sins the moment the devotee thinks of Him with a wholesome heart. Hence, the name *Havirhariḥ*. He is both *havi* (the offerings or oblations) and also *hari* (one who absorbs and absolves all).

The illustrious Lord stands as an example for all the excellences that one can imagine and try to imbibe. Whatever ideal we think of, we find it amply illustrated in the sports of the illustrious Lord. Hence, the attribute, ***Sarvalakṣaṇa-lakṣaṇyaḥ.*** The sportive deeds of the Lord form the treasure-house of knowledge-both theoretical and practical.

As *Lakṣmī*, the goddess of prosperity always resides on His bossom, He is always blissful and graceful. He is therefore adored by all as *Lakṣmīvān*. When *Rāma* leaves for the forests, *Sumitrā* consoles his mother *Kausalyā* saying that there is nothing to worry about him as *Sītā* has accompanied him like *Lakṣmī* or *Lakṣmī* hereself has accompanied him in the form of *Sītā*. *sītevānugatā lakṣmī, tasya kiṁnāma durlabham.*

Victory is where *Lakṣmī* is. So, the Lord is assured of His victory wherever He goes and whatever He does. He is therefore adored as *Samitiñjayaḥ*. Similarly, the blessed souls who have always in their heart the vision of the victorious Lord are also assured of their success in all their efforts to make their life meaningful.

All-enduring And Never-decaying

Like matter, the material world too can neither be created nor destroyed. If it is created at all, it is only for its absorption in the essential existence of the Universe. That is why the Lord never identified Himself either with the perishable or with the imperishable. He says, He is beyond these two and that is why He is adored as *Puruṣottama* who is beyond *kṣara* (perishable) and *akṣara* (imperishable). Then what is He? The author of this sacred hymn finds a nice word to express this mysterious form of the Lord. He is called *Vikṣaraḥ* He is neither *kṣaraḥ* nor *akṣaraḥ*, He is *Vikṣaraḥ.*

This concept is explained in all its implications in the following ten attributes of the Almighty :

विक्षरो रोहितो मार्गो हेतुर्दामोदरः सहः ।
महीधरो महाभागो वेगवानमिताशनः ॥

vikṣaro rohito mārgo hetur-dāmodaraḥ sahaḥ ।
mahīdharo mahābhāgo vegavān-amitāśanaḥ ॥

The first name *Vikṣaraḥ*, as stated above,conveys something beyond what is perishable or decadent and what is not so.Whatever is divine is eternal and everything else appears to be temporal until it merges into the eternal flow of universal existence. This process of creation, cremation and transcreation is sponsored and executed by the Lord in collaboration with Nature. Whatever dissolves will be regenerated in some form or other.As the *Kaṭhopaniṣad* says, all mortals are born and reborn after changing their mortal frame like the crop in the field. *sasyamiva martyaḥ pacyate, sasyamivājāyate punaḥ*.

This is conveyed in the next name *Rohitaḥ* derived from the root *ruḥ* meaning to grow,spring up,emerge or rise. The word *rohitaḥ* also means a fish.The great fish *mahāmatsya* re-generates the entire creation after the deluge. The so-called death is therefore but a change of form. There is nothing like destruction in the absolute sense.

The path through which the mortal passes to realize his basic immortality is in the hands of the Lord.Hence,the attribute, *Mārgaḥ*. One has to discover this path or route to find out the root-cause of this creation ,preservation and dissolution of the life herein well-connected with the life hereafter. This is what is implied in the name *Mārgaḥ* -- a simple word with a world of substance.

The Lord is the central force behind this transformation of energy from one form to the other. He is the root-cause. So, He is described as *Hetuḥ*.

The Lord contains the whole universe in Him. Hence, He is called *Dāmodaraḥ*. In His incarnation as *Kṛṣṇa*, the Lord demonstrated this supernatural character of His body for the benefit of mankind and to the amusement of His foster mother *Yaśodā*. She could not bind Him with a cord. But He chose to be bound only to grant redemption to the poor and pious souls transformed into trees by a curse. The word *dāma* means a rope or a cord and also a garland. The rope which the mother used to bind her mystic child turned out to be a garland for Him.

This episode illustrates the endurance or forebearance of the Lord who patiently underwent the trial of His innocent mother and ultimately made her realize how patient and compassionate the Lord can be just to please and favour those who are near and dear to Him by virtue of their devotion and penance. These are the qualities of the Lord which are glorified in the name *Sahaḥ* a name so short, yet so significant. The word *sahaḥ* means 'surpassing'.It also means 'with'. The Lord is always with us wateching us and guiding us. No force in the world can test Him or protest against Him. In this sense also, He is *Sahaḥ* the surpassing.

As the Bearer of the earth and also as a consort of the Mother Earth *Bhūdevī*, the Lord is adored as *Mahīdharaḥ.* He is also called *Śrīdharḥ* being the consort of *Lakṣmī*, the goddess of prosperity. The next name *Mahābhāgaḥ* meaning the most fortunate perhaps refers to this grandeur of the Lord. He has *Śhrīdevī* on one side and *Bhūdevī* on the other both contributing to the harmonious nature of the Lord.

He is eulogized as *Vegavān* in the next name which means ' the most dynamic or the swiftest'. The *Īśopaniṣad* glorifies the Supreme as faster than the mind *manaso javīyo.* He does not appear to be moving at all, but yet He is swifter than the swiftest.

Similarly, He does not consume anything to sustain Himself, but He is praised here as *Amitāśanaḥ,* one who has the maximum and unlimited appetite. It is true because the Lord Himself said in *Gītā,* that He sits in the body of all beings and helps them in digesting all the food they consume. Indirectly, it is He who consumes all that is consumed in the world of His creation.

The Spirit Behind Creation

One who creates is normally different from what is created. But in case of the Supreme Lord of all creations, there is no potential difference between creation and the creator. How this happens is explained in the following lines:

उद्भव: क्षोभणो देव: श्रीगर्भ: परमेश्वर: ।
करणं कारणं कर्ता विकर्ता गहनो गुह: ।।

udbhavaḥ kṣobhaṇo devaḥ śrīgarbhaḥ parameśvaraḥ I
karaṇaṁ kāraṇaṁ kartā vikartā gahano guhaḥ II

The first name, *Udbhavaḥ* presents the Lord as the presiding deity of the whole creation.The word *udbhava* or even the latter part of word *bhava* means creation, advent, emergence or just coming into being. In fact the word *bhava* has been used here to denote creation and the Lord is called *Udbhava* as He is above the creation causing and effecting it both materially and instrumentally. This is further illustrated in the names that follow.

The next name *Kṣobhaṇaḥ* explains how the Lord materializes the process of creation by energizing the primordial matter *prakṛti* and motivating the imperishable *puruṣa* and the perishable *prakṛti* through His power of *māyā*.This was stated by the Lord Himself in *Gītā* [ch.9-

10]. The Lord uses the word *adhyakṣa* (the overseeing or the presiding deity) of the entire creation and Nature *prakṛti* brings forth the creation consisting of sentient *cara* and insentient *acara* beings. This is how the wheel of *Saṁsāra* goes on and on, the Lord says.

This is sustantiated by the next three names, *Devaḥ* (the presiding deity), *Śrīgarbhaḥ* containing *Śrī* or glory or the grandeur of the whole universe within Him and hence *Parameśvaraḥ* (the Lord of lords, the supreme Lord). *Bhagavān* uses the word *bhūtamaheśvaraḥ* for Himself in this context [*Gītā* 9-11]. Thus the five names in the first line of this verse illustrate the role of the overlord of creation in setting the wheel of creation in motion in the universe.

The next line clarifies the role played by the Lord in this process. He is the Instrument, *Karaṇam* , the cause *Kāraṇam* and also the Doer *Kartā*. As instrument, He is the most effective *Sādhakatamam* - to use the grammatical terminology devised by *Pāṇini*. As the material and effective cause of creation, He is the *Kāraṇam* and as an independent executive *Svatantraḥ kartā* , He is the most powerful doer and so powerful that He can mould His operation in any form as *Vikartā* . He can do and undo or overdo at His discretion. He is all in all.

His ways are mysterious - so mysterious that no one can imagine the logic behind them nor can challenge Him or atleast understand His line of thinking or course of action. That is why He is acclaimed and admired as *Gahanaḥ,* immensely deep in His thinking and doing. Human mind cannot comprehend Him nor can human voice describe Him. He is mysterious, concealed in Himself and not accessible for any deliberation. Hence the name *Guhaḥ*. He is believed to be resting in the innermost layers of the hearts of all beings--unnoticed, but watching everything at the same time.

It is refreshing and rewarding to recollect the words of the Lord spoken to *Arjuna* on this subject using almost the same terminology. The actual utterance of the Lord is:

कर्मणो ह्यपि बोद्धव्यं बोद्धव्यं च विकर्मणः ।
अकर्मणश्च बोद्धव्यं गहना कर्मणो गतिः ॥

karmaṇo hyapi boddhavyaṁ boddhavyaṁ ca vikarmaṇaḥ I
akarmaṇaś-ca boddhavyaṁ gahanā karmaṇo gatiḥ II

[*Gītā*: 4-17]

The truth of action and action needs a deep understanding as also the truth about what is peculiar. Mysterious are the ways of the Master and His actions.

The Grace That Grants

In matters of spiritual diplomacy, administration and organization, the Lord as the Supreme Commander of the entire Universe has an established pattern with decency, decorum, grace and grandeur. This is brought out in the following ten names:

व्यवसायो व्यवस्थानः संस्थानः स्थानदो ध्रुवः ।
परर्द्धिः परमस्पष्टस्तुष्टः पुष्टः शुभेक्षणः ॥

vyavasāyo vayavasthānaḥ saṁsthānaḥ sthānado dhruvaḥ |
pararddhiḥ parama-spaṣṭas-tuṣṭaḥ puṣṭaḥ śubhekṣaṇaḥ ||

Strong and positive determination is the foundation of the mass-administration the Master-mind runs with a universal code of conduct. This is what the architect of this sacred hymn chose to call *Vyavasāyaḥ*. This word occurs in *Gītā* in a similar context where *Bhagavān* says, 'An intellect determined to proceed in proper direction never deviates from the designed path while the one wavering in different directions cannot follow the right path' [*Gītā* 2-41]. This is the real sense of the word *vyavasāya* which is the key-note of any pursuit or proposition which pleases the Lord.

This also forms the basis *vyavasthānaḥ* for all progress and achievement in all fields of life, branches of knowledge and spheres of spiritual advancement and self-realization. That is why the Lord is adored here as *Vyavasthānaḥ*. Thus the *Vyavasāyaḥ* contemplated in the previous name assumes the form of an establishment, with a coordinated system of functioning for the betterment of global welfare, peace and prosperity.

The next name *Saṁsthānaḥ* is the standing and the ultimate goal of life, the abode of the Lord which not only directs, guides, controls and commissions various establishments, institutions and organizations working for this highest and the supreme cause of truth, righteousness and fellow-feeling in the world but also ensures stability in their status. Hence, the two names, *Sthānadaḥ* that which grants proper placement and organizational set up for the other bodies engaged in this global task and *Dhruvaḥ* the stable. Like the pole-star *dhruvatārā*, this central point provides guidance to all other points of enlightenment.

Among the five names in the second line of this verse, the last name *Śubhekṣaṇaḥ* is the most significant name qualified by the four attributes preceding it. The first one *Pararddhiḥ* means the most prosperous, affluent, exalted, gracious and magnificient. That is the limit for all excellence where the Lord is located looking after the welfare of all living beings stationed in various locations. Anyone can notice that excellence because it can be felt both within and without. Hence, the name *Paramaspaṣṭaḥ* clearly manifest in each and every atom of the Universe. That abode of the Lord is an illustration for the utmost satisfaction that one can imagine. He is satisfaction or contentment *tuṣṭi* personified. Besides this contentment, the Lord also presents an example for the highest form of plentitude. It grants the highest bliss in the fullest form. Hence, the Lord of this abode is adored as *Tuṣṭaḥ* and *Puṣṭaḥ*. He is both content and plentiful.

It is worth recollecting, in this context, *Vālmīki's* description of *Rāma Rājya* (the kingdom of *Rāma*) where the whole kingdom was immensely happy, pleasant, content and rich in all respects. The actual wording of the sage-poet resounds with these names--*prahṛṣṭa mudito lokaḥ - tuṣṭaḥ puṣṭaḥ sudhārmikaḥ*. This plentitude is mainly because of the righteousness practised by all the subjects with zeal.

The last and thc most significant name in the verse is *Śubhekṣaṇaḥ*, one with auspicious looks. The mere sight of the Lord and the feeling of His auspicious looks should suffice to run the world with peace and prosperity.

This reminds us of a memorable incident in the *Rāmāyaṇa* where *Vālmīki* describes how millions and millions of eyes were focussed on *Rāma* when He was walking towards the palace of His father, King *Daśaratha* in the early hours of the day of the proposed coronation. Every eye was on *Rāma* and *Rāma* too was trying to peep into all the eyes. The poet says, 'Blessed are those whose eyes were cast on *Rāma* and more blessed are those whom *Rām's* eyes could catch and those who are deprived of this blissful experience have really lost the taste of life'.

This is the beauty of the looks of the Lord who is rightly called *Śubhekṣaṇaḥ*. Those looks contain all that is good in the entire globe. They are global eyes containing good and good alone because they are 'godly looks'.

The Right And Might Of The Lord

Though the name of *Rāma* does not find a specific mention in the previous verse depicting the divine looks of the Lord, one can easily feel the presence of the prince of *Ayodhyā* in each and every name that was incorporated there as it reminds us of His March *ayanam* in search of 'good' *sat* and truth *satyam*. The name proper, however, figures in the following verse:

रामो विरामो विरजो मार्गो नेयो नयोऽनयः ।
वीरः शक्तिमतां श्रेष्ठो धर्मो धर्मविदुत्तमः ॥

rāmo virāmo virajo mārgo neyo nayo'nayaḥ I
vīraḥ śaktimatāṁ śreṣṭho dharmo dharma-vid-uttamaḥ II

Once the divine grace glances at the blessed souls deeply engrossed in spiritual practices, the eternal bliss dawns and enlightens the absolute conciousness hidden in the hearts of the *Yogīs*. According to *Padmapurāṇa*, it is this bliss that is adored as *Rāma* (the embodiment of eternal bliss). As son of *Daśaratha* too, *Rāma* granted this bliss to several saints, seers and seekers of divine grace. *Rāma* is where this bliss *Ānanda* is or *Ānanda* is where *Rāma* is.

If *Rāma* is the embodiment of the eternal bliss of life *virāmaḥ* is the ultimate goal of life, the net result of all that one achieves in life.

When *Rāma* asks *Śabarī* whether her penance was progressing well, she replies that the fruit of all penance is at hand the moment she is blessed with His presence. The sight of *Rāma* is the ultimate goal of life. The same feeling was expressed also by the sages like *Śarabhaṅga* and *Sutīkṣṇa* and also demons like *Virādha* and *Kabandha*. *Rāma* continues to be a blissful blessing even if He assumes the role of *Virāma*. The very thought of *Rāma* even in the last moment of life when life comes to a stand-still *virāma*, the soul is blessed with the eternal bliss. Even the antonym of *Rāma* has the power to save His devotees and grant salvation to them.

Rāma is the most dispassionate character in the *Rāmāyaṇa* as it hardly mattered for Him whether He was king of *Ayodhyā* or an ascetic prince in the forests. He tells *Lakṣmaṇa* in clear terms that kingdom *rājyam* or forest *vanavāsa* does not make any difference and perhaps the forest-life may open up new potentialities and possibilities to serve humanity *rājyam vā vanavāso vā, vanavāso mahodayaḥ [Rāmāyaṇa* 2.22.29].

In this sense, *Rāma* is not only *Virāma* but *Virataḥ* passionless too. Hence, the name *Virataḥ* attributed to the Lord. This name is also read as *Virajaḥ* by some. That also fits in as He is completely free from lust and dust of passionate mind. He is Bliss personified untouched by the vagaries and vanities of life.

The Lord is named *Mārgaḥ*, the path of salvation. Follow the path of *Rāma* (*Rāmāyaṇa*), you will be free from passions, bondage and blemishes of indisciplined life. Seek Him for proper guidance, He will guard you against all evils and evil effects. The path of equanimity and tranquility both within and without is the only way to realize the potential divinity present in all living beings. There is no other way as the Vedic verdict ad ises: *nānyaḥ pantha vidyate'yanāya*.

Then follow three names all based on the root verb *nī* meaning to conduct, lead, carry. These three names *Neyaḥ, Nayaḥ* and *Anayaḥ* convey the three dimensional implications of the code of conduct contemplated in their coinage. The first name *Neyaḥ* means the conduct that is to be cultivated. The second name *Nayaḥ* means righteous conduct, political wisdom, statesmanship and in simple terms, just virtue and good conduct. The third and the final one in the series *Anayaḥ* appears, at the outset, to be just the opposite of the preceding name *Nayaḥ*. But a careful understanding of the etymology of the word reveals that it is the antonym of the word *ayaḥ* and not necessarily of the word *nayaḥ*. From this point of view, the attribute means adaptable even in adverse circumstances. Even when justice *nayaḥ* is openly violated, the Lord tries with all His might and right to set right what goes wrong by the irony of fate and ensure that ultimately the established code of conduct *nayaḥ* is resorted. This is a highly significant quality of the Lord which every human being should cultivate. Thus the three names-- *Neyaḥ, Nayaḥ* and *Anayaḥ* clarify the right course of conduct which leads to allround peace and harmony in the world of ups and downs, pleasures and pains, hospitality and hostility, virtue and vice and, in short, good and bad. The good should be promoted to the extent possible so that the bad will automatically gradually diminish and ultimately vanish. This is the essence of practical philosophy preached by *Rāma* in His march of life *ayanam*- not by precept, but by his own example.

The next line in the verse contains four names-- *Vīraḥ, Śaktimatāṁ śreṣṭhaḥ, Dharmaḥ* and *Dharmaviduttamaḥ.*

The first two glorify the might of the Almighty and the next two reveal how right He is in sticking to the norms of the Eternal Law of Existence *dharma.*

The quartet starts with a short epithet, *Vīraḥ* which simply means the valiant. As far as *Rāma* is concerned, He is both *Dharma-vīra* and *Karma-vīra* as He manifested Himself as the unique personality of His times in upholding right conduct and right policy. He excelled in His dedication to truth *satyam* and righteousness *dharma* and maintained commendable balance between both facing all consequences, very often threatening His own comfort and composure. That is why He is eulogized in the next name as *Śaktimān-śreṣṭhaḥ* (one who excels in his strength--both mortals and immortals).

In matters of *Dharma* (the eternal law of existence and the basis for all beauty, stability and validity of life), He is glorified as *Dharma* itself. He is *Dharma*, personified--(*Vigrahavān dharmaḥ*). It is significant to note that this tribute was paid to *Rāma* not by any saint or seer; but by his own opponent *Mārīca* who later became His admirer and devotee. It was His dispassionate compassion towards this helpless soul that brought about this remarkable change in a devilish character like *Mārīca*. To invoke *Rāma*, it is enough to think of *Dharma*. *Rāma* and *Dharma* are almost synonymous.

The last name in the verse *Dharmaviduttamaḥ* meaning the most authoritative exponent of *dharma* presents a full-fledged picture of *Rāma's* wholesome personality. He not only knows the implications of *dharma* but also puts them into practice unmindful of the disasters that He may have to face in the process.

Thus the whole verse containing eleven names of the Lord looks like the picturesque and graphic description of the Great Grand March (*ayanam*)of *Rāma*, the Man who excelled divinity through His unassuming human dignity. Thus these eleven names relate the story of *Rāmāyaṇa* in short and significant words.

The Puruṣa Who Nourishes

Puruṣa, the Supreme Being presides over the entire creation while residing within it. How this is done is explained in the following verse :

वैकुण्ठः पुरुषः प्राणः प्राणदः प्रणवः पृथुः ।
हिरण्यगर्भः शत्रुघ्नो व्याप्तो वायुरधोक्षजः ॥

vaikuṇṭhaḥ puruṣaḥ prāṇaḥ prāṇadaḥ praṇavaḥ pṛthuḥ ।
hiraṇya-garbhaḥ śatrughno vyāpto vāyur-adhokṣajaḥ ॥

The cosmological concept of *Puruṣa*,the Supreme Being starts with the coordinating force behind it which is named *Vaikunṭha* here.The etymology of the word *Vaikunṭha* is that which saves the universe from disintegration or in other words the coordinating force which promotes integration of various elements *tattvas* to make it an organic whole where life can originate,expand and enrich itself. This is done by the Supreme Being *Puruṣa* by effecting an integrated assemblage of the five elements: the earth, the water, the fire,the wind and the ether with due regard to the order of precedence.The Lord brought the universe into existence by uniting the ether with air, air with fire, fire with water and water with earth.This process of integration created the Universe. This is exactly what the word *Vaikuṇtha* means. Hence, this place where this integration took place and continues to take place to provide placement to life and living beings is the abode of the Lord, who is called *Puruṣaḥ* in this context.

Once the process of integration and synthesis is over, the life-breath, *prāṇaḥ* had to be invented and this was done promptly and properly. Then the Lord breathed life into the living beings and kept the movement of this life-breath completely under His control. Hence, the name *Prāṇadaḥ*. The word *prāṇadaḥ* means both life-giver and life-taker. He controls both so that a perfect and programmed balance is maintained between the inward and outward flow of life. This flow is perennial, eternal and uninterrupted. It is ever fresh and ever-flowing. Hence, the name *Praṇavaḥ*. Like the primordial sound, *Om* which is an integral part of the life-breath-incoming and outgoing, this process is as old as the universe and as novel as the navel of the body from which life springs up every moment. As long as there is movement in the Universe, these movements record there output and disposal according to a systematic turnover. This process is as wide as the vast mass of earth and perhaps the other planets too where life exists in some form or other.

Thus the six names in the first line of this verse present a dialogue between the Cosmos and Cosmic figure. In a way, this is something like *Puruṣasūktaṁ* where the creation is described in symbolic language so as to enable us to understand what *puruṣa* and *prapañca* mean and how this *prapañca* is related to *Brahman,* the Cosmic Consciousness.

The next line starts with the name *Hiraṇyagarbhaḥ,* the primordial form of life. Vedic seers visualized this golden egg which the Supreme Being brought forth to set the Universe in motion. They sang the glory of this *Hiraṇyagarbha* saying that He and He alone existed before the Universe came into existence and He was the Lord of this vast mass of configuration of the five basic elements - ether, air, fire, water and earth.

In the next name, this cosmic figure is described as *Śatrughnaḥ* as He succeeded in surmounting all the obstructions and destroying all evil forces standing in His way.

He spread Himself and the net work He sponsored like the air carrying life and fragrance to all corners of this globe. Hence, the name *Vāyuḥ* given to Him.

The last name *Adhokṣajaḥ* is highly substantial and suggestive in its meaning. One interpretation is that the word *adhaḥ* means the earth, *akṣa* means heaven and *ja* means born. According to another interpretation, He was born as *Vairaja* (the illustrious splendour) in the intermediate region between the earth and heaven. As this lustre or radiance never diminishes, it is called *Adhokṣajaḥ*. But what appears to be sound and sensible is that one becomes aware of this Cosmic Consciousness seated in the heart of all living beings when the senses take a downward course towards the inner self.

The subject matter of this verse consisting of eleven names of the Lord of the universe is however highly enlightening about the origin, growth and purpose of the Cosmos and needs a discerning eye to dive into it.

The Prime-mover Of Time

The Lord is as abstract as Time Eternal and as blissfully pleasant as the colourful and sportive manifestation of the seasons. He is as gracious as fearful and as stable as dynamic. This multifaceted mysterious disc the Lord keeps in His hand which is usually referred to as *Sudarśana* is the main theme of the next verse in the text:

ऋतु: सुदर्शन: काल: परमेष्ठी परिग्रह: ।
उग्र: संवत्सरो दक्षो विश्रामो विश्वदक्षिण: ।।

ṛtuḥ sudarśanaḥ kālaḥ parameṣṭhī parigrahaḥ ।
ugraḥ saṁvatsaro dakṣo viśrāmo viśva-dakṣiṇaḥ ।।

Time is abstract though accurate and accountable. But the seasons like spring, autumn, winter and monsoon are as visible and vivid as the spokes of the divine disc *Sudarśana* that the Lord handles as the prime mover of time. So, the first three names, *Ṛtuḥ, Sudarśanaḥ, Kālaḥ* present the Lord as the motivating and controlling force behind the passage of time, change of seasons, light and darkness and the colourful display of nature dancing to the tune of the sweet melodies of the Master.

In *Gītā*, the Lord identifies Himself with the spring season *Vasanta* or *Kusumākara* of all the seasons as it blossoms in colourful petals of fragrant flowers. He also says that He favours the month of *Mārgaśīrṣa* normally December to provide warmth to the worthy citizens of the Kingdom He commands. He also expresses His identity with time *kālaḥ* as the most effective and accurate measuring agency. *Kālaḥ kalayatāmaham* [*Gītā* 10.30].

The next name *Parameṣṭhī* is chosen to glorify the Lord as He chooses to stay in the most auspicious and awe-inspiring place in the heart of hearts of all beings. He stations Himself in the uppermost layers of the outer space and also manifests Himself in the individual souls as a tiny figure of the size of a thumb *aṅguṣṭha mātraḥ puruṣaḥ* shining like a smokeless radiance *Jyotirivādhūmakaḥ*.

Wherever He is, He is accessible to all and listens to all with concern and compassion.Where He feels that His intervention is intended,He attends to each and every one with equal attention and affection. This unaccountable and unlimited affection and mercy the Lord showeres on His devotees makes Him *Parigrahaḥ* ready to receive all and accept anything that they offer as a token of love and dedication.

But the fascinating beauty of nature nurtured by everchanging seasons sometimes becomes ferocious, frightful and at times even fatal. This is the formidable phase of the same *Sudarśana-cakra*, the wheel of overwhelming power controlling the globe. This is what is termed *Ugraḥ* and the Lord is named after it. He is *ugra* because He has to run the show in a well-disciplined manner. The *Upaniṣads* say that the wind blows, the sun rises, the rain falls, the fire burns and even death crashes down just out of fear the Lord creates in the minds of all elements and components of nature. The intention in maintaining this discipline is, however, to make the life livable.This is what the next name of the Lord *Saṁvatsaraḥ* clarifies.

The word *saṁvatsara* literally means an abode where the inmates can live happily. This is the abode of the Lord that provides shelter for all living beings. Life exists, flourishes and merges into its eternal abode making use of the amenities provided in this material abode, called *Saṁvatsara.* This word is popularly used in the sense of year, a unit of time covering 12 months, 6 seasons and 2 *ayanas -- uttarāyaṇa* and *dakṣiṇāyana* indicating the march of the Sun northwards and southwards according to specified schedule. The sacred hymn *Yopāṁpuśpaṁ* describes this cycle of days and nights, full moon and new moon and the planetary motion keeping the year as a primary unit in a highly significant and symbolic language. The hymn concludes with an observation that he who knows the significance of this cycle and the abode of the basic unit of time, (the year or *Saṁvatsara*) will be blessed with a gift of sailing in a boat across the perennial flow of the time eternel and ultimately attain immortality crossing the barriers of time and space *yopsu nāvaṁ pratiṣṭhitāṁ veda pratyeva tiṣṭhati.*

The whole thing is managed so effectively and efficiently that nothing goes wrong despite the daring challenges and vicissitudes of time and tides.Hence, the name *Dakṣaḥ,* the competent controller of the entire Cosmos.

As the ultimate solace for all living beings, the Lord is adored as the embodiment of *Viśrāmaḥ* the tranquility of the soul.The famous prayer glorifying the Lord as peace personified,resting on the serpent making it his comfortable couch, having lotus springing from His navel, the Lord of all celestials, the sustainer of the Universe, as vast as the sky, charming like the laden cloud, auspicious in every inch of His body, the Consort of *Lakṣmī,* eyes shining like the lotus, accessible to the seers in the innermost layers of their hearts during meditation, the remedy for all fears of the world and the Lord of all the worlds occurs to us while contemplating on this name *Viśrāmaḥ*. The Lord was earlier glorified as

Rāmaḥ and *Virāmaḥ*. This name *Viśrāmaḥ* supplements the concept of blissful tranquility that the Lord displays for the benefit of His devotees.

The last name in this verse *Viśvadakṣiṇaḥ* glorifies the universal character of the Lord who is always keen in protecting the rights of all righteous people and pleasing all His subjects with His love, affection, compassion and consideration. As the Lord Himself says, 'I am equally amicable to all, I hate none, favour none, whoever seeks my grace with a devoted heart, they are within me and I am in them' [*Gītā* 9-29].

The Source Of All Resources

As long as the divine will stands behind the mobilization of all resources in the world, there will be no dearth or scarcity for the basic necessaries of life - physical, intellectual and spritual. As the eternal and everlasting source of all resources, the Lord maintains a perfect balance between the mobilization and utilization of all material and power components for peaceful and harmonious living. This principle is brought out in simple and scintillating words in the following verse:

विस्तारः स्थावरस्थाणुः प्रमाणं बीजमव्ययम् ।
अर्थोऽनर्थो महाकोशो महाभोगो महाधनः ॥

vistāraḥ sthāvara-sthāṇuḥ pramāṇaṁ bījam-avyayaṁ |
artho'nartho mahākośo mahābhogo mahādhanaḥ ||

The Lord has under His control a very wide expanse as vast as the universe. There is no space in the universe which does not come under this huge expanse. Hence, the Lord is adored as *Vistāraḥ*. He is spread over the entire space - the outer as well as the inner.

Despite His wide canvas covering each and every corner of the Cosmos, He is surprisingly stable and stationary. Hence, the name *Sthāvaraḥ*. He does not move, but makes everything mobile. The immobile controls the mobile. This is what the *Upaniṣad* (*Īśa*) confirms by saying, 'That moves but yet is stationed' *tadejati, tannaijati.* As the prime-mover of all that moves, the Lord is not only stable and stationed but also steady and firm - *sthāṇuḥ.* No force on earth or heaven can displace or disturb Him. He is therefore both *Sthāvaraḥ* (stable) and *Sthāṇuḥ* (steady). He is like the Huge Mountain deepply rooted in the fathomless layers of the earth and at the same time reaching into the highest orbits of the celestial splendour. Thus the two attributes *Sthāvara* (stable) and *Sthāṇu* (steady) combine to glorify the Lord as *Sthāvarasthāṇuḥ.* He is stable *Sthāvaraḥ* like the *Himālayas* and steady *Sthāṇuḥ* like *Śiva*, the presiding deity of the *Himālayas,* the Lord of *Kailāśa.*

One may just wonder at this paradoxical phenomenon and ask himself, 'Where is the proof for all this ?' The answer comes from within. He Himself is the proof - *pramāṇam* - for this as the Seed of Creation once sown by Him never decays but multiplies itself without causing any damage to the original seed, generating infinite variety of forms that make the Universe colourful and delightful. He is the seed that knows no decay. Hence, He is glorified as *Bījamavyayam.*

The next two names *Arthaḥ* and *Anarthaḥ* create yet another paradoxical situation which needs careful understanding . The word *artha* in the popular usage means 'wealth', material possession or the meaning of a word. Taking the context into account, one can interpret this word used as an attribute to the Lord of the Universe as 'the meaning of life in general or the most cherished goal of life'. Self-realization or achievement of the Absolute Bliss with the Grace of the Almighty may be accepted as the real meaning of life *Puruśārtha* or *Paramārtha* and the name *Artha* can be interpreted accordingly.

But the real problem comes with the name *Anarthaḥ* which follows immediately. If *arthaḥ* is the ultimate goal of life and the highest achievement in life, what should be the implication or connotation of the term *Anarthaḥ.* Obviously it cannot be the antonym of *Arthaḥ.* The only possibility that sounds feasible, in the context, is the possibility of a situation where nothing remains to be achieved when the highest has been achieved. Just as *Hanumān* feels on seeing *Jānakī* in *Laṅkā* that there is nothing else worth seeing after seeing her,the paragon of beauty and beatitude.Similarly, the Lord is the highest entity to be prayed for. There is no room for other material means - *artha* - when the most meaningful *paramartha* has been achieved.

In this sense, the Lord is both *arthaḥ* 'what is to be sought' and also *anarthaḥ* who leaves no room for any other aspiration or expectation in life.

That is why He is glorified as *Mahākośaḥ* (the most precious treasure of all pleasures), *Mahābhogaḥ* (the most blissful experience in life) and *Mahādhanaḥ* (the richest wealth that one can imagine in the material sense as well).

These three names - all in superlative attributes - adore the Lord as The Great - *Mahā* - in the real sense of the term. He is the greatest treasure-house of all the five sheaths of life - *anna, prāṇa, manas, vijñāna* and *ānanda.* He takes us step by step from matter to energy, from energy to intellect, from intellect to awareness and finally from awareness to the absolute bliss *ānanda.* Hence he is *Mahākośaḥ.*

Similarly, the joy that one feels in the presence of the Lord is of the highest form. Hence, He is *Mahābhogaḥ.* He is *Mahādhanaḥ* because no material wealth can equal the immesurable sense of perfection that comes through divine grace.

The Nave Of All Constellations

Divinity and depression never go together.Where there is divinity,there can be no depression -- either mental or spiritual. The very feeling of the presence of the Lord - within or without - drives away all depression. The Lord is undepressed *Anirviṇṇaḥ* because He is greater than the greatest and stronger than the strongest. He is therefore worshipped as *Sthaviṣṭhaḥ.* This greatness and godliness extends to all corners of both the celestial and the terrestrial spheres. Therefore He is glorified as *Bhūḥ* (the Existence itself). He is praised as *Abhūḥ* also as He is beyond the cognizable existence transcending the terrestrial sphere. He is the Nave of all celestial bodies like stars and constellations. He is therefore rightly named as *Nakṣatranemiḥ.*

This majestic form of the Almighty is the main theme of the next verse in the text:

अनिर्विण्णः स्थविष्ठोऽभूर्धर्मयूपो महामखः ।
नक्षत्रनेमिर्नक्षत्री क्षमः क्षामः समीहनः ॥

anirviṇṇaḥ sthaviṣṭho'bhūr-dharma-yūpo mahā-makhaḥ |
nakṣatra-nemir-nakṣatrī kṣamaḥ kṣāmaḥ samīhanaḥ ||

The first three names, as already explained, stand for the undepressed *Anirviṇṇa*, migtiest *Sthaviṣṭha* and ever- existing essence of all existence *Bhuḥ* and also what can be conceived beyond all existence within our reach *Abhuḥ*.

The next name *Dharmayūpaḥ* explains the Lord's commitment to *dharma* the eternal law of existence and all the ethical principles connected with it. He binds all living beings to the strict adherence of the tenets of *dharma* as if they are tied up to a sacrificial post. The implication is that there is no compromise in respect of *dharma*, as it is the foundation of all existence,you have to follow it if you mean to survive.This is the Law of Nature enforced by the Lord through a self-operated machinery. The results of following or violating *dharma* are automatic and cannot be modified or condoned. This strict attitude of the Almighty who is *dharma* personified leads to the next name *Mahāmakhaḥ*, a great *yajña* prescribed as an integral part of life. Any activity of a living organism under-taken and executed by him just to serve and survive is a kind of *yajña* (ritualilstic offering at the altar of life) and so it becomes a universal phenomenon which the sacred hymn calls *Mahāmakhaḥ*.

Even the celestial bodies like stars, sun, moon, pole-star and other planets come under this obligatory adherence to the Almighty's orders. Stars twinkle, planets shine, sun rises,wind blows and so many other activities go on in the celestial sphere every moment without rest and without haste in obedience to the schedule laid down by the Lord who is the Nave of all stars and constellations. Even the path of the moon is laid down and the asterisms scheduled to come into cantact with the Moon is pre-destined and determined according to the Calculus of time and space. Hence, the name *Nakṣatranemiḥ*.

The pole-star which controls the movement of all other stars with the help of the winds of its command is also under the overall supervision of the Lord of the entire universe.He is called *Nakṣatrī*. He Himself is a

Nakṣatra functioning as the prime-mover of all the celestial bodies causing time. Fascinated, perhaps, by the beautiful moonlight which keeps the creation in good humour and also sustains it by showering nectar of mercy on the vegetation, the Lord declared in *Gītā* that He is the Moon *Śaśī* among the stars *Nakṣatrānām-ahaṁ Śaśiḥ.*

At the time of deluge or dissolution of the entire creation the Lord maintains utmost calm and compassion. Ultimately He and He alone survives only to revive the whole scene. His intentions are wholesome, positive and constructive. Hence, the final name *Samīhanaḥ,* the well-meaning Lord who never allows His sportive process of creation to come to a stop. He operates the wheel of creation with a dexterous and determined will. His *īhā* is always well-designed and executed with elegance and excellence.Therefore, He is hymned as *Samīhanaḥ* towards the end of this verse which unites the terrestrial life with the celestial splendour.This reminds one of a highly significant observation made in the *Kaṭhopaniṣad* which concludes that 'whatever is here is there in the other sphere too (*yadeveha tadamutra*)' and reinstates the theory by spelling out its converse version 'whatever is there is here too (*yadamutra tadanviha*)'.

The Object Of All Worship

The verse that follows is in continuation of the well -formulated concept equally well-articulated in the utterance of the name *Mahāmakhaḥ* which elevates every action to the level of a great grand worship or *yajña*. The following verse carries this thought further depicting *yajña* in various forms :

यज्ञ इज्यो महेज्यश्च क्रतुः सत्रं सतां गतिः ।
सर्वदर्शी विमुक्तात्मा सर्वज्ञो ज्ञानमुत्तमम् ॥

yajña ijyo mahejyaś-ca kratuḥ satraṁ satāṁ gatiḥ I
sarvadarśī vimuktātmā sarvajño jñānam-uttamaṁ II

The first name *Yajñaḥ* used as a qualifying name for the Lord of our hearts and of the universe equates the act of worship with the deity worshipped . He is worship itself and He Himself is worshipped. The *Taittīriya Saṁhitā* says, 'sacrifice or worship is indeed identical with *Viṣṇuḥ*'. This is true, in a way, because the very idea of worship originates when one thinks of the deity in mind. Thought of doing something is more powerful and effective than the actual deed itself. So, He is the source of inspiration and the object of the worship both. This is what is re-affirmed in the name that follows : *Ijyaḥ*, the object of worship.

The object of worship, in the ultimate analysis,is to identify the source of all inspiration latent in the heart of our hearts, but unmanifest because we have not tried to realize or visualize it. Even though the object of worship is within us, we wander around to identify it. As the saint poet Kabir puts it, 'Your Lord is seated within you just as the fragrance is an integral part of the flower.' The flower, ironically, does not realize how fragrant it is or where that fragrance is coming from. It is this search for the reality dwelling within and driving us into action that is actually termed *yajña*. The word *yajña* can be split into two parts *yat* and *jña* which will mean 'to know' or 'find out' whence all this is originated ? It is that absolute source of all existence, excellence and exhilaration that is to be worshipped *ijyaḥ* and it is the form of that worship that is named *yajñaḥ*. Thus *yajṇaḥ* and *ijyaḥ* are one and the same. We worship Him who is worship and also the object of worship.

The next name, *Mahejyaḥ* takes us a step further to tell us that He is the greatest object of worship. Other deities are capable of granting only temporal pleasures while the Lord, the embodiment of worship, grants the highest gift-the eternal bliss-leading to salvation through self-realization.

Having said that the highest form of worship is to worship the Supreme Self seated in one's own self, the sacred hymn takes us to various forms of worship classifying them into two broad categories-the individual or isolated form of worship and the collective or cosmopolitan form of worship. The former is termed *Kratuḥ* and the latter *Satram*. The mythology depicts *Indra* as the distinguished and accomplished performer of ritualistic worship called *Kratu* hundred times. That is why He is called *Śatakratuḥ* (or *Śakra* in the form of initials). Though the word *kratu* by convention, means a religious sacrifice or *yajña*, it implies any manifestation of innate talent, deliberation, offereing or worship. Mostly it is individual - orientated while *satram* aims at massive appeal and collective activity intended for the betterment of the worshippers and seekers of knowledge in general. *Satram* also means a spiritual session leading to well-thought out ideals and ideologies transmitted to posterity for further processing and promotion. In both the forms -*Kratu* and *Satram*, it is the spirit of worship that is glorified making *yajña* as the basis.

The main idea of discussing the significance of the real form of worship *yajña* is to emphasize the need to chalk out a line of enlightenment and a purposeful enterprise for the elite in larger interests of promoting the common cause of 'general good'. It is this aspect of worship that is hinted at in the last name in the first line of this verse *Satāmgatiḥ*. In fact the word *Satram* also points out to this aspect as it literally means that which protects the rightminded from the onslaughts by the evil forces. This is the sole asnd the highest objective of all forms of worship.

The highest form of worship, naturally, aims at and leads to the right type of vision, all-compassing which is designated as *Sarvadarśī* in the name that follows. The right vision - all round in its canvas leaves no area of awareness untouched. So it definitely leads to ultimate liberation of the immortal soul from the mortal constraints. It is in this sense that the Lord is adored as *Vimuktātmā* in the next name.

He who sees all - *Sarvadarśī* - knows all that too. That is how the next name *Sarvajñaḥ* continues the thought of vision leading it to the next higher region - the realm of knowledge or awareness. The Omniscient *Sarvajña* leaves nothing unknown to the seekers of knowledge. They become aware of all that needs to be known. The best and the highest form of knowledge becomes accessible to them and this becomes possible with the grace of the omniscient Lord who is identified here with the best form of knowledge - *Jñānaṁ-uttamam.*

The Loving God

The onmiscient is also an expert in winning the hearts of all.He is an embodiment of love, peaceful promoter of all that is good, pleasant in speech and good at heart.These qualities which project the Lord as a 'loving god' are brought out in a sweet language in the following verse:

सुव्रतः सुमुखः सूक्ष्मः सुघोषः सुखदः सुहृत् ।
मनोहरो जितक्रोधो वीरबाहुर्विदारणः ॥

suvrataḥ sumukhaḥ sūkṣmaḥ sughoṣaḥ sukhadaḥ suhṛt ।
manoharo jita-krodho vīrabāhur-vidāraṇaḥ ॥

The genuine love of the Lord for all living beings and His strong determination to protect them from all evil forces make Him *Suvrataḥ*. He makes no compromise in matters of upholding the righteousness and never hesitates to accept any challenge to achieve this end. When *Vibhīṣaṇa* seeks shelter from his cruel brother, *Rāvaṇa*, the Lord in His incarnation as *Rāma* accepts him inspite of the counsel from his well-wishers. He declares in open that whoever comes to him seeking his support and shelter, he makes it a point not to disappoint him whatever may be the consequence and whoever he may be. This, he says, is my *vratam* (conviction or sacred vow). Hence, the Lord is glorified here as *Suvrataḥ*.

He is always cheerful, pleasant and sweet in His countenance. He is, therefore, named *Sumukhaḥ*. Lord *Gaṇeśa,* the destroyer of all obstacles, is also called *Sumukhaḥ*. In common usage, the word *sumukha* means favourable and also good-looking. In every sense of the term, the Lord is *Sumukhaḥ*.

The next name *Sūkṣmaḥ* shows how shrewd, subtle and meticulous the Lord is in His judgements. He takes the most minute things into account while passing His final decrees. He is present in all living beings and in every atom of the Universe and in this sense also He is adored as *Sūkṣmaḥ*.

The way the Lord speaks gives out His heart along with the noble thoughts He expresses. Hence, the name *Sughoṣaḥ*, pleasant in speaking.

Whatever the Lord contemplates, communicates and actually does leads to the welfare and happiness of the people whom He looks after like His own children and they are so indeed. This consideration for the promotion of general good in His thoughts, words and deeds projects Him as *Sukhadaḥ*. His main intention is to make people happy because He is good at heart. Hence the name *Suhṛit*.

These six names all starting with the syllable *su,* are applicable to anybody involved in service to humanity without any cosideration, whatsoever, of any benefit in return. The last word *suhṛt* summarizes the basic principle underlined in all public service. How nice it will be if these names of the Lord are kept in mind while serving the cause of humanity. In a way, these can be adopted as basic principles of public administration.

The starting syllable '*su*' common to all the six names indicates that a person dedicated to these values is not only respected but admired, adored and even worshipped with reverence like the Lord. He becomes the loving god for the common people. In *Saṁskṛit* language, the particle *su* is used in the sense of handsome, excellent and respectable. The grammarians add *pūjanīyata* (adorability) also to this particle *Suḥpūjāyām*. By glorifying the grace and grandeur of the Lord with these six names starting with *su*, the hymn has enhanced the sanctity of the vibrations it has produced.

The next line in the verse presents four names projecting the prominent features of the Lord which promote the well-being of all living beings in the world. He is glorified as *Manoharaḥ* as He easily wins the hearts and minds of His devotees by His pleasant countenance and benevolent behaviour towards them. He never loses temper and maintains a perfect balance in his facial complexions even in critical conditions. For instance, when *Rāma* came out of the private chamber of *Kaikeyī* with the orders for his exile, nobody standing outside, bubling with enthusiasm to see his coronation, could notice any change in his complexion. Even when he is furious while fighting in the battle, he maintains this calm. He never allows his temper to overcome him. He is therefore called *Jitakrodhaḥ*.

But he does not spare his enemies. He is *Vīrabāhuḥ* armed by valiant arms and shoulders. He is also described as *Vidāraṇaḥ* who tears away his opponents when they transgress the limits of proper conduct and violate the basic norms of propriety and decorum.

Normally, He showers His love and affection on all; but does not hesitate to teach a lesson to anyone who is treacherous and proves a traitor to the cause of human values and dignity.

The Abode Of Affection

The multi-faceted and multi-dimensional personality of the Lord is basically affectionate and compassionate for those who are gentle though at times He becomes rash and rude in order to restore order in times of crisis. The following verse presents this phase:

स्वापनः स्ववशो व्यापी नैकात्मा नैककर्मकृत् ।
वत्सरो वत्सलो वत्सी रत्नगर्भो धनेश्वरः ॥

svāpanaḥ svavaśo vyāpī naikātmā naika-karma-kṛt ।
vatsaro vatsalo vatsī ratna-garbho dhaneśvaraḥ ॥

At times, the way the Lord conducts Himself makes us stupefied, spell-bound and aghasted as if we are witnessing a dream. This is what makes us feel that He is lulling us to sleep. So we call Him *Svāpanaḥ*.In fact the whole world or the worldly life is a dream which is caused by the Lord. When we wake up, only then we realize that we have been sleeping all the time.

This is how He keeps us under control. He puts us to sleep and again it is He who wakes us up. He does not like us to feel that we are independent. Rather He reminds us again and again that we are entirely in His hands. Hence, the name *Svavaśaḥ*, keeping everything under His control.

He is Omnipresent. So, everything is under His purview. Nothing can escape His attention. Similarly, nobody can exist without His affectionate care, the parental touch. He is, therefore, worshipped as *Vyāpī*, all-pervading.

He has many forms. He can assume any form at any time entirely at His will. He is therefore named *Naikātmā*, not of one form. He assumed the form of a fish, tortoise, boar, lion-like man and so on. He may hide Himself in a mountain, flow with a river, fly with the wind, shine with the stars and smile like a flower. All forms and names suit Him. He can fit into any.

Similar is the case with His deeds, sportive activities. He was just a charioteer for *Arjuna* in the great battle of *Mahābhārata*. But still He was the person who brought victory to *dharma* practised by the right-minded *Pāṇḍavas*. Hence, He is glorified as *Naikakarmakṛt* -- not confined to a single field of action.

The next three names-- *Vatsaraḥ, Vatsalaḥ* and *Vatsī*-- are all full of affection the Lord showers on those who like Him and whom He likes. He is the abode of affection. He gave shelter to the whole *Gokula* by holding the *Govardhana* on the tip of His finger. His main objective is to uphold *dharma* righteousness and turn down what is not *dharma* so that the world can live in peace and take the full advantage of the rich treasures of nature created by Him for them.

The name *Ratnagarbhaḥ* reveals the inexhaustible treasure hidden in our oceans, mountains, soil and innumerable forms of energy. These resources are meant for proper utilization. The Lord is keen to ensure this by using His powers. But this is not possible without a bond of mutual love and affection among the inhabitants of this vast universe and also between them and Him.

The last name *Dhaneśvaraḥ* presents the Lord as the presiding deity of all the wealth the world has under its standing reserve. There is a continuous flow of this wealth. The Lord tries to ensure that there is enough goodwill prevailing in the world to promote full benefit of this wealth--a gift of nature. Lord is the proprietor of this enormous wealth and all living beings are trustees.

The Guardian Of Dharma

The basis of all existence, enrichment and enlightenment is the proper observance of *dharma*, the righteous conduct. If *dharma* is sound, everything else is safe. The Lord, therefore, gives top priority to the protection and promotion of dharma so that the creation proceeds on right lines. The next verse in the text concentrates on this significant role the Lord plyas as the guardian of *dharma*.

धर्मगुब्धर्मकृद्धर्मी सदसत्क्षरमक्षरम् ।
अविज्ञाता सहस्रांशुर्विधाता कृतलक्षणः ॥

dharmagub-dharmakṛd-dharmī sad-asat-kṣaram-akṣaraṁ I
avijñātā sahasrāṁśur-vidhātā kṛta-lakṣaṇaḥ II

The main purpose of the incarnation of God from time to time is the establishment of *dharma* whenever there is a crisis. The chief oncern of the Lord is, therefore, the proper protection of *dharma*. He is accordingly acclaimed here as *Dharmagup*, the guardian of *dharma*.

In order to ensure that the whole world follows the principles of *dharma* with care and caution, the Lord Himself sets an example during His incarnation as to how the ethical code of conduct should be followed. Besides His personal demonstration, He tries to preach the importance of *dharma* in the proper setting and in an appropriate manner as the

Lord *Kṛṣṇa* did in the battle-field. This is what is implied in the next name *Dharmakṛt,* the Lord as the practitioner of *dharma* Himself.

This is followed by a very short and simple name *Dharmī* which means the supporter of *dharma.* It was in this capacity that He supported *Pāṇḍavas* in the greate battle of *Mahābhārata.* In His incarnation as *Narasiṁha* (Man-Lion), He supported the boy *Prahlāda.* As narrated in the *Rāmāyaṇa,* the Lord supported several victims of *adharma* (non-righteous conduct) like *Sugrīva* and *Vibhīśaṇa* and taught a fitting lesson to *Vāli* and *Rāvaṇa.*

Dharma in its basic form supports whatever is real *sat* and condemn whatever is not real *asat.* What is right has to be re-established when what is not right tries to dominate over the right. The Lord has therefore to study both and then proceed to strengthen the right of what is right and destroy what is contrary to it. The two names--*Sat* and *Asat* explain this position of the relative values of the two. The Lord maintains balance between the two.

These two names can also be interpreted in terms of Reality--in absolute as well as conditioned forms. The Supreme *Brahma* is the absolute reality and He also plays another role as a conditioned reality. From this point of view, both *Sat* and *Asat* stand for the Lord in different forms.

Similarly, the next two names *Kṣaram* and *Akṣaram* also need to be understood with special reference to their usage in the scriptures. The Lord is there even in the beings which perish though he is potentially imperishable. What is perishable is *Kṣaram* and what is imperishable is *Akṣaram. Gītā* clearly states that all beings are perishable, but the key-person *Kūtastha* seated in the key-position is imperishable. Hence, He is called *Puruṣottam- atosmi loke veda ca prathitaḥ puruṣottamaḥ.* He is the soul of all souls.

So is the area of knowledge professed and promoted by the Lord. His is the absolute knowledge free from the misconceptions fostered by the *jīva* who thinks that he is the knower. It is true that he knows a few things and that too in a confused manner. He thinks that he is doing everything while the reality is that it is *Ātman*, the real doer at the instance of the *Paramātman*. The Lord is the real knowledge and the knower both. He is therefore called *Avijñātā* which literally means non-knower. What He does not know is the perverted knowledge of the *jīva*. Once the grace of the Lord dawns on the *jīva*, he becomes aware of the absolute state of affairs as different and distinct from the confused knowledge.

The real radiance also comes from the Lord and not from the sun or the moon or the stars. He is the original source of all illumination from which all the celestial bodies derive light. *Bhagavān* says in clear terms [*Gītā* 15.12] that the light which is in the sun, the moon and the fire is mine.

He is also the supporter, sponsorer and coordinator of all luminaries. So, He is called *Vidhātā*.

The last name, *Kṛtalakṣaṇaḥ* projects the Lord as the Eternal Consciousness which postulates the characteristics of all scriptures. He is the author of all authentic texts. The whole knowledge is authored and authorized by Him. He is the *Lakṣya* (the source). Everything else is *Lakṣaṇa* (substance) authenticated by Him.

The Prime And The Supreme

As the prime and the supreme deity among all celestial deities, the Lord is at the centre of all existence - terrestrial and celestial. This unique status of the Lord controlling the whole universe is explained in the following verse :

गभस्तिनेमिः सत्त्वस्थः सिंहो भूतमहेश्वरः ।
आदिदेवो महादेवो देवेशो देवभृद्गुरुः ॥

gabhasti-nemiḥ sattvasthaḥ siṁho bhūta-maheśvaraḥ ।
ādidevo mahādevo deveśo devabhṛd-guruḥ ॥

Being the original source and the controlling force for all the rays of the planetary systems, He is worshipped as *Gabhasti-nemiḥ*. The word *gabhasti* means a ray of light in general. The sun and the moon draw this light from the Lord, the nave of all light and heat. It is through this system that the clouds are formed and the crops grow. In this way, the system of transmitting rays from one central point ensures not only proper living for all beings but also lays foundation for the existence itself. It is this radiation that provides and promotes natural strength inborn to all living beings. It is the basic strength and inherent power of which a person is made. This is called *sattva* also known as the quality of goodness or purity and regarded as the highest of the three *guṇas*. This is supposed to be present predominantly in the celestial bodies and deities. The Lord is supposed to be the resident promoter of this virtue among His devotees. Hence, the name *Sattvasthaḥ*. He resides in the heart of those who cultivate this virtue. This virtue is also responsible for the spiritual radiation that a few blessed ones are endowd with. The realized souls are, however, beyond these three categories--*sattva, rajas* and *tamas*. The Lord expects His blessed devotees to trascend these and attain the stage of *nistraiguṇya* so that they get firmly established in the Eternal Existence *Nitya Sattvasthaḥ* of the Lord. It is this highest state of divinity that is glorified in the name *Sattvasthaḥ*.

These two significant names as have been discussed so far are immediately followed by a two-syllable name *Siṁhaḥ* which simply means a lion or a Valiant lion at the most. But the lion is supposed to be the king or head of all animals and beasts. The lion has a majestic stature inherent in its looks and movements. The backward glance of a lion (often referred to as *siṁhāvalokanam*) has a significance as through this peculiar movement, the head of the animal kingdom connects the events that precede and follow. This is what the Lord also does. Lord *Kṛṣṇa* traces the knowledge of *yoga* to *Vivasvān* (the sun) and transmits the same to *Arjuna*. So, the lion has a tendency to connect the past with the present and make the future an improvement over the two. That is how the name *Siṁhaḥ* attributed to the Lord here has a world of significance. That is, perhaps, why the Lord chose to assume the form of *Narasiṁha* (half man and half lion) to destroy the evil deeds of the demon *Hiraṇyakaśipu*.

The next name *Bhūtamaheśvaraḥ* literally means the overlord of all beings. He is the great lord of all other lords. Being the Eternal Existence Himself, He breathes life into all beings and exercises full control over them. That is why He is worshipped as the Great Grand Master *Maheśvara* of all living beings *bhūtas*.

Besides all living beings, He has perfect control over all celestial bodies as well including deities. He is therefore glorified as *Ādideva*, the Prime and the Supreme deity among all heavenly deities.

The *Ādideva* (the first deity) is then glorified as *Mahādeva* (the great deity) as well. His greatness lies in His intimate involvement in the process of Self-realization practised by the *Yogis*. Realizing Him and His presence in the Self is the highest form of *yoga--mahāyoga*. One attains this highest state of consciousness with His grace. Hence, the name *Mahādevaḥ*.

He is *Deveśaḥ* too. He is the Lord of all *Devas* (deities). Anything offered to any deity ultimately goes to Him as per the scriptures which say that all salutations finally reach *Keśava*, the Lord of all deities *sarvadeva namaskaraḥ keśavaṁ prati gacchati*.

The last name in the verse *Devabhṛdguruḥ* indicates that all knowledge is imparted by Him not only to the practitioners of *yoga* but also to the number of deities worshipped through yogic exerceises and practices. He is the highest authority in the science of *yoga - Yoga Śāstra*. He is the teacher of teachers *Gurūṇām Guruḥ*, *Jagadguru* (the universal guide) in the real sense.

The Tranquil Joy Of Bliss

As revealed in the previous verse, the Lord transcends all limits of the real and the unreal, the perishable and the imperishable, the terrestrial and the celestial and all pleasures and pains of the material and the spiritual world. Placed on the highest pedestal, higher than the highest, He finds Himself deeply absorbed in the highest form of Supreme Bliss; but takes pleasure in sharing it with the material world consisting of common consumers who are blissfully ignorant of the fact that what they think they are consuming is already consumed and converted into a blissful essence for the mutual benefit of the mortal frame and the immortal soul. This is what is explained in the following verse:

उत्तरो गोपतिर्गोप्ता ज्ञानगम्यः पुरातनः ।
शरीरभूतभृद्भोक्ता कपीन्द्रो भूरिदक्षिणः ॥

uttaro gopatir-goptā jñānagamyaḥ purātanaḥ I
śarīra-bhūta-bhṛd-bhoktā kapīndro bhūridakṣiṇaḥ II

The deliberation starts with a simple name *Uttaraḥ* which means higher, superior or transcendental. It can also be interpreted as the Saviour who saves His devotees from the bondage of birth and death and also trivial troubles and turmoils of worldly life.

How He does this is explained in the next name *Gopatiḥ* with an illustration. Just as a cowherd looks after his cattle sitting and moving with them, the Lord stays with all His beings as a part of their mortal frame - detached superficially but virtually attached. He is invisible to the naked eye, but vibrant to the inner heart-beats. That is why He is described as *Goptā*, the hidden one. The word *goptā* also means one who protects. He protects the individual body and soul without being detected. The word *go* in the name *Gopatiḥ* and the root *gup* in the next name are both very vast in their meaning. In *Saṁskṛt*, the word *go* means not merely a cow, but several other things like the sky, the earth, the human voice, the ray of light, a diamond, heaven and arrow. Therefore, the Lord named here *Gopati* stands for all these things. So vast is His jurisdiction that almost all that finds a place between earth and heaven comes under His area of protection. The whole universe is His body. He is the Master of the entire creation and dwells in all He creates to share the Bliss of Life with them.

But the way He works this out can be grasped only through true knowledge *jñāna*. Action *karman* alone cannot help us in understanding His machinery. A blend of action *karman* and knowledge *jñāna* too does not help much. True knowledge and pure consciousness will pave the way for realizing His real shape, what He does and why and how He does it. That is why the Lord is hymned as *Jñānagamyaḥ*, who can be conceived and comprehended only through concentrated knowledge--undiluted and unpolluted.

It is not possible to find out His background as He is the most ancient *purātanaḥ*. He is older than the oldest. He existed when nothing else was in existence and He will continue to exist as long as the concept of being remains in the world of comprehension and contemplation. The name *Purātanaḥ* traces His existence to the timeless antiquity because He Himself is Time.

The first name in the next line *Śarīrabhūtabhṛt* is slightly longish. In the first nine names (*nāmanavamī* as we called it) of this *Sahasranāma*, the name *Bhūtabhṛt* occurs as the sixth one preceded by another similar name *Bhūtakṛt*. It will facilitate right comprehension if we study the present name *Śarīra-bhūta-bhṛt* in relation to these earlier names. The name *Bhūtakṛt* means the creator of beings and *Bhūtabhṛt* means the sustainer of beings. If we apply this cannotation to the present name, it will mean one who sustains the beings created by Him giving them a mortal frame to cover the various elements of the body. The Lord takes the responsibility of sustaining the body created by Him by Himself dwelling in it in the form of *prāṇa,* the vital breath. This is what is conveyed through the name *Śarīra-bhūta-bhṛt*. But the meaning becomes complete when we connect it with the next name *Bhoktā* meaning the enjoyer, one who experiences the joy of sustaining and supporting the wonderful boby created for the purpose. While reading the two names rapidly, one feels that they make one single name, *Śarīra-bhūta-bhṛt-bhoktā*. This will mean that the Lord who has created the body nourishes it with all consumable material and also shares the pleasure of the supreme bliss that results from the process of consumption. The fascinating part of it is that the consumer gets only nourishment coupled wiht some satisfaction. But the thrill of the Supreme Bliss is entirely the monopoly of the Lord. The individual has to qualify himself to share this bliss with the Lord by realizing the presence of the Supreme within him. Otherwise, the Lord is the main *bhoktā* and the *jīva* remains a mere *upabhoktā* (sub-consumer).

This name *Bhoktā* , therefore, is a very significant name which, if properly understood, tells us how the individual soul can elevate himself to the level of a real enjoyer of the thrill behind experiencing this Supreme Bliss *Pramānanda*.

Incidentlly, we complete the first half (500 names) of the sacred text *Śrī Viṣṇu Sahasranāma* with this name *Bhoktā*. This makes the name all the more significant. In fact it conveys the essence of all spiritual experiences whose ultimate goal is to experience the Supreme Bliss with the blessings of the Lord.

The name that follows is *Kapīndraḥ* which means the Lord of the monkeys. In His seventh incarnation as *Rāma* , the Lord mobilised the monkey army to fight and win the battle with *Rāvaṇa*. *Hanumān* is also *Kapīndra*, the mightiest of all the monkeys and very close to *Rāma* and *Sītā*. He was the key person in bringing about the re-union of *Sītā* and *Rāma*. He was *Bhakti* (devotion) personified. It is a pleasant coincidence that the previous name of the Lord *Bhoktā* (The last among the first 500 names) glorifies the thrilling experience of the Supreme Bliss as a form of *bhukti* (consumption) while the next name *Kapīndra*, the first among the second half of the text presents a person who can serve as a specimen for *bhakti* (devotion). This is a soul-elevationg juxtaposition of *bhukti* (Consumption) and *bhakti* (devotion).

The verse concludes with the name *Bhūridakṣiṇaḥ*, the height of magnanimity. The grace the Lord showers on *Hanumān* and several other devotees and the realized souls of the world speaks volumes about the magnanimity of the Lord.

The central theme of the text - the soulful singing of the glory of the Lord in myriad names - is blissfully presented in this verse.

Victor, Rector And Protector

The Lord is as charming as the moon, as delicious as the ambrosia, as firm as truth, as victorious as *ātman* (the soul) and as Cosmic as the Cosmos. These are the rare attributes of the Lord which find a masterly treatment in the scintillating stanza that follows:

सोमपोऽमृतपः सोमः पुरुजित्पुरुसत्तमः ।
विनयो जयः सत्यसंधो दाशार्हः सात्वतां पतिः ॥

somapo'mṛtapaḥ somaḥ purujit-purusattamaḥ ।
vinayo jayaḥ satyasandho dāśārhaḥ sātvatāṁ patiḥ ॥

The first three names *Somapaḥ, Amṛtapaḥ* and *Somaḥ* are inter-related and discuss about the Moon and the mythology connected with nector and *Soma-rasa*, a beverage of the gods and those who perform *Soma-yāgas.*

In the first name, the word *soma* is used in the sense of the sacred beverage prepared with the juice of a plant called *soma.* The Lord is very fond of this as it is symbolic of the succesful performance of the *yāgas* named after *soma.* Hence, the name *Somapaḥ*, one who enjoys this beverage. The priests also take it and the Lord joins them as He is not only pleased with the *yāgas* but Himself is *yajña* or *yāga* performed by His devotees.

The second name *Amṛtapaḥ* is attributed to the Lord as He helped the celestial deities in protecting the nector *amṛta* which emerged from the ocean of milk when it was churned. Lord *Viṣṇu* protected the vessel containing this ambrosia *amṛta* from the demons and handed it over to the gods so that their immortality is safe-guarded. The name *Amṛtapaḥ* may mean either one who protected the *amṛta* or the one who shared it with the inhabitants of the heaven. It is worth noting in this connection that the moon is also called *Amṛtāṁśuḥ* as he transmits rays saturated with nectar *amṛta* and promotes the proper growth of the plants.

The third name *Somaḥ* relates mainly to moon. Etymologically people relate it to Lord *Śiva* also as the word can be split as *Umayā saha* (the one who is always associated with *Umā*). This interpretation places *Viṣṇu* at par with *Śiva*. It may be recalled that in the course of the churning of the ocean of milk, poison came first and *Śiva* swallowed it at the instance of *Viṣṇu* and *Viṣṇu,* in turn, took charge of the pot of nectar and protected it from the demons for the sake of gods. Thus the name *Somaḥ* applies to both *Viṣṇu* and *Śiva.* The scriptures hold that there is no potential difference between them.

The next name *Purujit* opens up a new chapter in the discourse on the sacred hymn. This deals with the victorious nature of the Lord. *Puru* means many. *Purujit*, therefore, stands for the conqueror of many. *Puru* was also the sixth monarch of the lunar race and was also the ancestor of the *Kauravas* and *Pāṇḍavas.* Lord in the form of a Victor subdued several *Purus*. Hence, the name *Purujit.*

The next name, closely connected with this, is *Purusattamaḥ*. Here, the word *puru* stands for heaven, the world of immortals. Thus the word *purusattamaḥ* will mean the most celebrated among the heavenly personalities and celestial deities.

In both these names, the expression *puru* can be interpreted as 'One who is ahead of all'. In that case, the name *Purusattamaḥ* can be taken to mean 'the most advanced' or 'the most victorious' whose victory is taken for granted even before the actual battle starts. This is exactly what happened in the great war of *Mahābhārata.* Lord *Kṛṣṇa* tells *Arjuna* in clear terms that most of the warriors on the side of the *Kauravas* are already slain in his records. Apart from this divine prediction, *Bhīśma, Droṇa* and even *Karṇa* were quite sure about their defeat. This is what is exactly meant by naming the Lord as *Purujit* and *Purusattamaḥ*. Where the Lord is, victory is already there. Those who know what *Kṛṣṇa* means by *dharma*, can easily visualize victory where He is because His *dharma* stands by Him.

The first name in the next line is *Vinayaḥ* immediately followed by *Jayaḥ* and *Satyasandhaḥ*. These three names together present a picturesque description of the methodology which the Lord adopts to win over His opponents. He starts with humility *Vinaya* and when He finds that it does not work, He smiles which ensures a definite and positive victory by virtue of the intrinsic potentialities of truth *satyam*. Thus *dharma* and *satyam* put together make sure that victory is on His side.

The last two names *Dāśārhaḥ* and *Sātvataṁpatiḥ* project the Lord's concern, consideration and compassion for those who are near and dear to Him. *Dāśārhaḥ* is the name of a tribe of cowherds in which *Kṛṣṇa* was born. The tribe is so named because they are authorised or privileged to receive gifts from others. This tribe was patronized and protected by Lord *Kṛṣṇa*. Even now this tribe is seen in some parts of our country. In Andhra Pradesh, they are called *Dāsaris* who sing devotional songs in the early hours of the sacred month called *Dhanurmāsa* when the Sun is in the constellation of Sagittarius. Gifts are offered abundantly to them.

Similar is the tribe of *Sātvatas* who are mentioned in the next name. The Lord is glorified in this name as *Sātvatāṁ-patiḥ,* the patron and protector of the *Sātvatas* who are *sāttvik* (gentle) in nature and practise some rituals--mostly *tāntrik*--for the welfare of society. Lord likes them.

The Heart Of Heaven And Earth

The Lord is the heart-beat of all living beings - both in heaven and on earth. Starting from *Jīva*, the living organism right upto *Anantātmā*, the unending Absolute in Time, Space and matter.He is the be - all and end-all of all that we witness wilingly or unwilingly. This is the central theme of the stanza that follows:

जीवो विनयितासाक्षी मुकुन्दोऽमितविक्रमः ।
अम्भोनिधिरनन्तात्मा महोदधिशयोऽन्तकः ॥

jīvo vinayitā-sākṣī mukundo'mitavikramaḥ ।
ambhonidhir-anant-ātmā mahodadhi-śayo'ntakaḥ ॥

The first name *Jivaḥ* used as an attribute to the Almighty implies that there is no difference between *Jīva* and *Brahman* (the living being and the Supreme Being). This is the basic concept in *advaita*- *jīvo brahmaiva nāparaḥ.*

Inspite of His supremacy, the Lord comes down to the level of the individual soul and as a gesture of His modesty, witnesses all the movements of His children with love and affection.This humility on the part of the Almighty imparts courage and conviction to the individual souls to rise to level of universal consciousness.This aspect of divinity manifest in the modesty of the Lord is brought out in the name,

Vinayitāsākṣī. Some people read the expression *sākṣī* in this name as *asākṣī* (non-witnessing) and interpret that the Lord being Omnipresent does not go beyond what He is, but yet knows everything being Omniscient. But basically this wonderful name of the Lord brings out His most unassuming attitude towards all living beings inspired by parental affection and meticulous care about their welfare .

The next name *Mukundaḥ* explains the intention of the Lord to confer salvation to His devotees as and when they qualify themselves for the same.

Amitavikramaḥ ,the name that follows, glorifies the immeasurable prowess of the Lord. In His incarnation as *Vāmana*,He covered all the three worlds with His feet to the great surprise of the King *Balī* who never imagined that such a thing would happen.The prowess *vikrama* of the Omnipotent is therefore immeasurable *amita* and unimaginable. Hence, He is adored as *Amitavikramaḥ.*

Ambhonidhiḥ is a multidimensional name for the Lord. At the first sight, the name appears to be glorifying the oceanic nature of the Omnipresent Lord.But the word *ambhas* has a wide canvas of meaning. The scriptures say that there are four fold *ambhas* - the gods, men, manes and *asuras* -- all under the protection of the Lord. He provides abode to all the four.The word *ambhas* also means *tuṣṭi* in philosophical terms, meaning thereby that the Lord who is glorified as *Ambhonidhiḥ* is acquiescence of the soul.The term *ambhas* also stands for power, splendour and fruitfulness.This covers both earth and heaven.Thus the name *Ambhonidhiḥ* covers an ocean of meaning and hence a fitting tribute to the Lord who is an ocean Himself - ocean of all treasures and pleasures that bring plenty and prosperity to the whole universe.

The excellences of the Lord are endless, infinite, and undefinable.

He is therefore praised in the next name as *Anantātmā* . He is unlimited in His powers and potentialities.He is everywhere, everything and everlasting.

Even an ocean cannot contain Him. The entire universe has to become an ocean to accomodate Him. He needs not an ordinary ocean,but a vast ocean, *Mahodadhi* as vast as the space.During *pralaya*, He reduces the whole creation into an ocean of universal dimensions and happily relaxes in that peaceful (pacific) ocean.He is therefore called *Mahodadhiśayaḥ* .He enjoys a sound sleep in the deep waters with roaring waves. He maintains calm even in calamity.

In fact the End is as pleasant and palatable for Him as the Beginning.When He says 'Start', it starts and when He says 'Stop' it stops. It is so simple and routine matter for Him because He knows how to merge and emerge again and again. He is therefore glorified in the last name of this verse as *Antakaḥ* , the Master Merger of the mysterious world, His own creation.

The Bliss And The Blissful

The Endless does not have a beginning either.So, the Lord is unborn or self-born.Being the very breath of life for all-living beings,He need not be born like others. *Bhagavān* says in *Gītā* that those who know in essence how I am born and how I act merges in me and is never born again [Ch. 4-9]. In the same breath, *Bhagavān* also says, 'I am birthless *ajaḥ* and deathless *avyaḥ* but being the Lord of all beings, I manifest myself through my own *yogamāyā* (divine potency) keeping my nature *prakṛti* undere my control'.This is the secret behind the advent (not birth) of the Lord. The next verse in the text starts with this explanation of the divine manifestation of the Lord :

अजो महार्हः स्वाभाव्यो जितामित्रः प्रमोदनः ।
आनन्दो नन्दनो नन्दः सत्यधर्मा त्रिविक्रमः ॥

ajo mahārhaḥ svābhāvyo jitāmitraḥ pramodanaḥ |
ānando nandano nandaḥ satya-dharmā trivikramaḥ ||

The first name *Ajaḥ*, at the first sight, looks like a deliberation on the birthlessness of the Lord. Of course, that is also one of the significant interpretations of the name - viewed particularly from the statement of *Bhagavān* Himself in *Gītā*. If we go deeper into its inner meaning, we get more and more enlightened as is the case with most of the names in this remarkable hymn. For instance,the word *ajaḥ*, can be interpreted as *kāma* (passionate love) as it is believed that *kāma* is born of *Viṣṇu.*The syllable *a* stands for *Viṣṇu* and on this basis the word *ajaḥ* has been interpreted as the *kāma* (Cupid) the son of Lord *Viṣṇu.* But what sounds more sensible is to understand it as 'the unborn Lord' as He Himself explained in His *Gītā*

In the light of this,when we proceed to the next name *Mahḁrhaḥ* which means, 'highly precious', we realize how precious the manifestation of the Lord is for the material world caught in the mesh of birth and death, pleasures and pains and worthless positions and possessions that only strengthen the bondage. It is therefore wise to have a relook at our values and try to spend our valuable time to attain the most precious status which the Lord *Mahārhaḥ* alone can grant us. It is His grace that is most precious. The sooner it is realized, the better.

Then follows the name *Svābhāvyaḥ* the most natural name for the Lord. When *Arjuna* wanted to know from *Kṛṣṇa* as to what, indeed, is meant by spirit or spirituality *adhyātma,* the Lord readily replied, in a word, saying that *adhyātma* is nothing but *svabhāva.* To become one's own real self and realize the supremacy of that self is the ultimate goal of all spirituality. This is what *Bhīṣma* is trying to impress upon *Yudhiṣṭhira* here by naming the Lord as *Svābhāvyaḥ.* If at all the Lord is born of or emerges from something, it is this *Svabhāva* (self manifestation). We feel the presence of the Lord the moment we are blessed with this realization.

The next name *Jitāmitraḥ* tells us that the Lord has no enemies and whoever is not friendly is won over in no time. All are equal in the eyes of the Lord.

He is ever joyful, full of delight. So He is called *Pramodanaḥ.* He shares His joy with others because whoever approaches Him and seeks

His grace will instantly be freed from all sorrows and sufferings of the physical world.

The next three names - *Ānandaḥ, Nandanaḥ* and *Nandaḥ* are all torch-bearers of the Suprem Bliss fostered by the Lord who is not only blissful, but also Bliss personified. Bliss or *ānanda* is His nature. Of the five sheaths of the human body, *ānanda* is the most refined and the Lord resides in it. One has to pass through the gross layers like *anna* (matter), *prāṇa* (vital air), *manas* (intellect) and *vijñāna* (knowledge) to reach the highest state, *ānanda* (bliss). The *Taittīriya Upaniṣad* concludes after several deliberations that *ānanda* is *Brahman*, the Supreme Being as the whole creation emerges from it, flourishes with its nourishment and ultimately merges into it.

Being the embodiment of bliss, the Lord makes His devotees blissful. So He is *Nandanaḥ* who makes others blissful--free from worldly troubles. He is *Nandaḥ*, the delight of being blissful.

Thus the three names project the Lord as Bliss personified. The source of this bliss is indicated in the next name *Satyadharma*. A blissful blend of truth *satyam* and righteousness *dharma* ensures the attainment of the Supreme Bliss.

The last name in this verse is *Trivikramaḥ* which refers to the incarnation of the Lord as *Vāmana* who covered the three worlds with three steps. This name finds frequent reference in this hymn in several forms.

He Knows What He Does

The very first name in the next stanza containing seven names of the Lord springs a little surprise as it names the great *Kapila* as synonymous with *Viṣṇu*, the presiding deity of this hymn. The other names are also slightly abstract. These names,therefore, need a special attention. The verse reads as follows :

महर्षि: कपिलाचार्य: कृतज्ञो मेदिनीपति: ।
त्रिपदस्त्रिदशाध्यक्षो महाशृङ्ग: कृतान्तकृत् ।।

maharṣiḥ kapilācāryaḥ kṛtajño medinī-patiḥ |
tripadas-tridaśādhyakṣo mahāśṛṅgaḥ kṛtāntakṛt ||

The sage *Kapila* is known as the fifth incarnation of *Viṣṇu* according to *Śrīmad-Bhāgavata.*There are different versions of the origin of this great sage in authentic works like *Mahābhārata*. He is depicted as the incarnation of *Agnidevatā* (the god of fire) and also as the son of *Brahmā*, the Creator. He figures in the *Rāmāyaṇa* as a great sage who reduced 60,000 sons of *Sagara* into ashes when they misbehaved with him. In Indian philosophy, however, the name of *Kapilācārya* is well-established as the founder of the *Sāṅkhya* system according to which *jñāna* (knowledge) finds a superior place in relation to *karma* (action). *Ācārya Śaṅkara* in his commentary on *Brahma Sūtra* mentions *Kapilācārya* as the founder of *Sāṅkhya* system and clarifies that he is not the same sage who destroyed the sons of *Sagara*. In his commentary on the present text *Śrī Viṣṇu Sahashranāma* (which is being discussed here), *Śaṅkarācārya* says : 'He was a great sage, *Maharṣi* as he visioned the entire *Veda* whereas others visioned only a part of it. *Kapila* taught the knowledge of pure self and called it *Sāṅkhya*'. This observation made by *Ādi Śaṅkara*, the great commentator, seems to be convincing.

What is relevant to us in this context is the significance of the special mention of this sage, the founder of *Sāṅkhya* system of philosophy as the starting name in this verse. Lord *Kṛṣṇa* also says in *Gītā*, ' I am the sage *Kapila* among the realized souls - *siddhas' (Siddhānām kapilo muniḥ)*. It is worth noting that *Gītācārya* calls him a *muni* and not *maharṣi*.

Whatever it is, the contribution of *Kapila's Sāṅkhya* system to Indian philosophy is no doubt very substantial. It is in this respect that this name should be studied here. *Gītā* does not consider *Sāṅkhya* as totally different from *yoga*. In fact *Gītācārya* repeatedly tries to emphasize the equal importance of both. The essence of *yoga* preached by Lord *Kṛṣṇa* is that you have to do your duty but you should do it with awareness, knowing fully well what you are doing, why you are doing and how you should do it. This is the maxim which the *Saharsanāma* wants to highlight here by bringing the great sage *Kapila* to the forefront. As *Śaṅkara* said in his lyrical composition *Bhaja Govindam, Gītā* and *Saharsanāma* are one and the same in their purport *Geyam Gītānāma Saharsam*.

This point is verey lucidly brought out in the next name *Kṛtajñaḥ* - one who knows what he does. This conclusion is again confirmed in the third name *Medinīpatiḥ* that follows immediately. This is to say that action supported by awareness or knowledge of the pure self as *Śaṅkara* puts it is bound to lead the aspirant to the highest peak of spiritual awareness. He becomes the master of the metaphysical world

Medinī-patiḥ.

The second line in the verse changes the topic for diversion. It starts with the name *Tripadaḥ.*This has direct reference to the Upanishadic expression, *trayo asya pādāḥ.* There are three steps to take to reach the ultimate goal. These are interpreted as *om, tat* and *sat* - In secular language these three fold appelations of the Absolute are explained in terms of Truth- *sat,* Consciousness - *cit* and Bliss- *ānanda* [*Gītā.* 17-23].

The next name *Tridaśādhyakṣaḥ* is explained in terms of the three states - woken, dreaming and sound sleep - referred to in the *Māṇḍūkya Upaniṣad.*They correspond to the three phases of the primordial sound *Om.*

Mahāśṛṅgaḥ is the next name which clearly refers to the Great-horned fish, the *Matsya* incarnation of the Lord who is presented here as the protector at the time of delude *Pralaya.*

The last name *Kṛtāntakṛt* also refers to the withdrawal of the universe at the time of *Pralaya* (dissolution).

The Infinite Variety

Having mentioned *Mahāśṛṅga,* the great - horned fish as the *Matsyāvatāra* (the fish incarnation) of the Lord,the *Ācārya* proceeds to mention the other incarnations also. The next stanza presents a glimpse of the infinite variety of forms assumed by the Lord from time to time. This exposition starts with *Varāhāvatāra* (the incarnation as the great Boar).

महावराहो गोविन्दः सुषेणः कनकाङ्गदी ।
गुह्यो गभीरो गहनो गुप्तश्चक्रगदाधरः ॥

mahāvarāho govindaḥ suṣeṇaḥ kanakāṅgadī ।
guhyo gabhīro gahano guptaś-cakra-gadādharaḥ ॥

The Lord in His incarnation (the third one) as the Great Boar, *Mahāvarāha* holds the whole earth on His large teeth.Thus He saved the earth from sinking.

The word *varāha* can also mean an auspicious day and *mahāvarāha* would mean the most auspicious day.The day on which we remember the Lord,worship Him and adore Him is the most auspicious and fruitful day, well-spent for the betterment of the whole race of humanity and other living beings. In this sense also, the name is highly significant, suggestive and enlightening.

The next name *Govindaḥ* is the most popular name of the Lord. As *Kṛṣṇa*, the Lord played the role of a cowherd - mixing with cows, cowherds and the village folk. The name *Govinda* is also an auspicious start for any prayer. The single syllable-word *go* as we discussed earlier in some other context ,is a multi-dimensional name. It means sky, earth, voice, senses and so on. By worshipping, promoting or cultivating these faculties, we will be closer and closer to divinity. *Govinda* leads us from darkness to light, ignorance to knowledge and despair to aspiration.

The Lord is then depicted as *Suṣeṇaḥ*, having a well organized army behind Him. In His incarnations as *Rāma* and *Kṛṣṇa*, one can see how the Lord mobilized His forces with resourceful mind and strategic skill. *Kṛṣṇa* entered into the battle with a promise that He would not use any weapons. But still *Arjuna* preferred Him to the vast army offered to him as an alternative. Poor *Duryodhana* exercised his choice in quite reverse way and had to pay heavily for it. The real army was the Lord Himself. This *Duryodhana* could not realize.

The next name *Kanakāṅgadī* presents the charming personality of the Lord with golden armlets. It is a feast for the eyes - both inner and outer and also for the soul - to see the Lord in this form. He turns iron into gold with His majestic touch.

How He does it is very mysterious. The next name *Guhyaḥ* explains this.The Lord has many secrets with Him, but does not reveal them to all. He tells *Arjuna* in confidence that He was revealing several aspects of His divine *māyā* and *ātmayoga* to him as He has immense confidence in him. It requires a noble mind and a pious heart to win the confidence of the Cosmic figure like *Kṛṣṇa* or *Rāma*. *Hanumān* enjoyed this. *Prahlāda* was favoured with this. Even *Gajendra* was qualified for this rare privilege.

The next two names - *Gabhīraḥ* meaning deep and *Gahanaḥ* meaning impenetrable - also elaborate the same point with different illustrations in appropriate terms. The ways of the Lord are too deep for common understanding. One can fathom into the intentions of the Lord only when they bear fruit and come out to the pleasant surprise or otherwise of average people.

They are kept strictly confidential, top-secret and concealed even from the closest of friends. The intention is not to keep others away, but to promote general good and materialize what is actually good for the universe as a whole and not favourable for a chosen few for the time being. The accent is on *śreya* (the ultimate good) and not on *preya* (the immediate benefit).

The Lord indicates this motive hidden in His deeds through two ornaments He puts on. These are the *Sudarśana Cakra* (the discus symbolizing the intellect - *manas*) and the *Gadā* (the mace symbolizing perception - *buddhi*). Hence the name *Cakragadādharaḥ* the last name in this verse.

The sum and substance of His philosophy of movement and motivation is that He knows what He does, how He does and why He does. But we can not guess until He does it. This is the difference between divinity and humanity.

The Unconquered

As the self-ordained ordainer of the Cosmic order, the Lord stands as firm, steady and majestic as the Divine tree stationed at the centre of His Creation as *Vedhā* the ordainer , *Kṛṣṇa,* the centre of attraction , *Ajitaḥ*, the unconquered and *Mahāmanaḥ*, the Supreme in thought. These are the main attributes brought out in the following verse :

वेधाः स्वाङ्गोऽजितः कृष्णो दृढः संकर्षणोऽच्युतः ।
वरुणो वारुणो वृक्षः पुष्कराक्षो महामनाः ॥

vedhāḥ svāṅgo'jitaḥ kṛṣṇo dṛḍhaḥ saṅkarṣaṇo'cyutaḥ ।
varuṇo vāruṇo vṛkṣaḥ puṣkarākṣo mahā-manāḥ ॥

It is the Lord who originates the existence, excellence and also the extinction of the Universe. He is the Creator, the preserver and the disposer of this mysterious world. He is therefore worshipped as *Vedhāḥ*, the ordainer of this Cosmic order.

All this is self-ordained as the Lord who has done all this is neither subordinated to nor cordinated with any other agency. He has His own mechanism - organic and inorganic - to effect this marvellous creation. He operates this with His own apparatus, organizational equipment and technical skill. Hence He is called *Svāṅgaḥ,* having His own instruments, limbs or tools for this job.

He is also hymned as *Ajitaḥ,* one who has never been conquered, excelled or surpassed in this line. In all His incarnations, the Lord never experienced any difficulty, faced any problem or failed to achieve what He proposed. He never witnessed any defeat in His mission of re-establishing *dharma,* the eternal law of justice and righteous conduct by undoing all that was done to destroy the Cosmic order and the natural rhythm of the Creation.

In short, this invincible, yet invisible Supreme Spirit standing by what is sane has been expressed in a single, simple, short and scintillating name *Kṛṣṇaḥ.* the captivating force behind all that we see, do and think in the day to day life. There is some 'divine drive' behind all our activities.This is not visible. But the invisible hand draws us into its tender touch and puts us in motion

The word *Kṛṣṇaḥ,* here, need not necessarily be confined to the incarnation of the Lord as *Kṛṣṇa,*the son of *Devakī* and *Vasudeva.* It stands for the captivating divine force in general appealing to and appeasing the entire globe. The three names that follow confirm this assumption. He is very firm in His determination and deliverance. Hence He is *Dṛḍhaḥ.* He does not compromise with His policy of supporting the righteous and condemning the evil minded. In matters of *dharma,* He is very firm. The next two names, *Saṅkarṣaṇaḥ,* attracting, withdrawing and cultivating and *Acyutaḥ,* the unswerving are taken together by many commentators including *Śaṅkara Bhagavatpāda.* In the combined form, they may even refer to *Balarāma* and *Kṛṣṇa.* Even otherwise the qualities attributed and glorified in these three expressions - *Dṛḍhaḥ, Saṅkarṣaṇaḥ* and *Acyutaḥ* - apply to any form of the Lord whose sole purpose of descending on earth is to promote commitment to the basic values of healthy and happy living in the larger interests of universal peace and prosperity.

The next name, *Varuṇaḥ* stands for the evening sun who witholds his rays for the time being. *Varuṇa* is also the presiding deity of the direction west. He is also depicted as the king of the ocean. When he is mentioned in his association with the morning sun *mitra*, he stands for the particular phase of the sun who represents the withdrawal of the rays while *Mitra* breathes life into all beings through his radiance in the morning time. *Mitra* and *Varuṇa* thus stand for the rising sun and the setting sun. In the daily prayers invoking the blessings of the rising and the setting suns,we appeal to *Varuṇa*, the setting sun not to deprive us of the life and energy granted to us *mā na āyuḥ pramoṣīḥ*. In other words, we pray to Him for protection from untimely demise or unhealthy conditions interfering with the preservation of our lives granted by divine decree.

The next name *Varuṇaḥ* may refer to the son of *Varuṇa* (either *Vaśiṣṭha* or *Agastya*) or it may simply mean the functioning of the *Varuṇa*, the presiding deity of the western quarter. The ocean is also referred to as *Varuṇālaya*, the residential place of *Varuṇa*. Both the names *Varuṇaḥ* and *Vāruṇaḥ*, are in any case, interrelated and stand for the withdrawal or summing up of life.

Whether it is granting or withdrawing life, the Lord maintains an order and balance and acts as an ordainer *Vedhāḥ* in both the functions. He stands firm as a majestic and magnanimous tree with divine stature and stability - all alone, unsupported, but yet supporting all - ever growing, ever green and ever graceful. Hence, the name *Vṛkṣaḥ* for the Lord who provides shelter to all the living beings who can always bank upon Him like the free flying birds on a widespread tree with innumerable branches, pleasant leaves, delicious fruits and refreshing shade. It is this tree that is glorified in the *Upaniṣads* and compared to the Lord who stands firm providing shelter for all on earth and in heaven. *Vṛkṣa iva stabdho divi tiṣṭhatyekaḥ* .

The Lord has always a place in our hearts if only we keep it neat like a lake full of lotus-flowers. Where there is bliss,there is Lord.He is *Puṣkarākṣaḥ*. He has a magnanimous mind which can create a univerese of its own at His mere will. He is, therefore, glorified here as *Mahāmanāḥ*, of mind with immeasurable potentialities.

Bhagavān

Bhagavān (the Blessed) is the most popular name of the Lord. What exactly is meant by this celebrated name is explained in all its implications in the following verse:

भगवान् भगहानन्दी वनमाली हलायुधः ।
आदित्यो ज्योतिरादित्यः सहिष्णुर्गतिसत्तमः ॥

bhagavān bhagahā-nandī vanamālī halāyudhaḥ ।
ādityo jyotir-ādityaḥ sahiṣṇur-gati-sattamaḥ ॥

The word *bhagavān* in the common parlance, is used in the sense of God, any God in general and of any religion like *Viṣṇu, Śiva, Mahāvīr, Buddha* or any other deity worshipped with reverence as the final refuge of all living beings. As an epithet, the word *bhagavat* means glorious, illustrious, celebrated, blessed, divine, venerable and is used to glorify even demi-gods, holy and respectable personalities, celebrated works like *Śrīmad Bhagavad Gītā, Śrīmad Bhāgavatam* and so on. This word *bhagavān* is used as a glorious attribute of Lord *Viṣṇu* in the present text *Śrī Viṣṇu Sahasranāma Stotra* only once while the name *Viṣṇuḥ* occurs thrice, *Kṛṣṇaḥ* twice and *Rāmaḥ* once.The speciality about the name *Bhagavān* is that it refers to the god-head in general and not to any incarnation of God like *Rāma* and *Kṛṣṇa*.

The *Viṣṇupurāṇa* defines the word *bhagavān* as one who is endowed with six attributes technically called *Bhagas,*namely, *Samagra Aiśvarya* (Supreme Lordship), *Dharma* (the ethical authority), *Yaśas* (glory and fame), *Śrī* (the grace and grandeur), *Jñāna* (the absolute knowledge) and *Vairāgya* (detachment from the world of relative values). This explanation is further elaborated in the same *Purāṇa* defining the word *bhagavān* as one who knows the origin and the end, the arrival and the exit of all living beings as well as the distinction between *vidya* and *avidya* [V.P. 6-5-74,78].

The word *bhaga* also means fortune, happiness, excellence, loveliness and beauty. *Bhaga* is also one of the 12 forms of the sun and in this sense stands for brilliance and radiance. Thus the name *Bhagavān* is not merely the most popular but also the most significant with multidimensional meaning.

In short, the word *bhaga* stands for all that is splendid, blissfull and blessed and God is endowed with all this and showers this on the universe created by Him. He presides over His creation and resides in it to keep His children hale and healthy, wise and vibrant and pleasant and perfect. The two syllables *bha* and *ga* in the celebrated word *bhaga* stand for radiance *bhāti* and dynamism *gacchati. Bhagavān* is the most radiant and the most dynamic spirit behind His Cosmic manifestation. Hence, He is *Bhagavān.*

The next name *Bhagahā* speaks of the role that the Lord of the Universe plays at the end of an aeon when He destroys all that He has created to establish a new system. The Lord derives pleasure in this because the whole process of creation has to undergo a total and radical change giving place to the new order. This is the bliss *ānanda* which, according to *Taittirīya Upaniṣad,* is the source of all creation, the supporting force behind all preservation and the ultimate goal or the final deluge of all existence. Hence, the Lord is named *Ānandī,* the Blissful or the Bliss itself. The *Upaniṣad* concludes the deliberation saying that this *ānanda* itself is *Brahman*, the Supreme - *ānando brahmeti vyajānāt.*

The next two names *Vanamālī* and *Halāyudhaḥ* present two concrete examples to illustrate this point. The first is that of *Kṛṣṇa* and the other one is His elder brother *Balarāma* - the former adorned by a long garland of gracious flowers upto his knees and the latter holding ploughshare as a weapon. The garland of *Kṛṣṇa* symbolizes the five subtle elements - *tanmātrās*, namely, the sound, the touch, the form, the essence and the fragrance while the plough on the shoulders of *Balarāma* serves two purposes simultaneously, namely, ploughing the land and producing food to sustain the Universe and destroying dust and dirt at the time of deluge giving place to new vegetation and habitation.

Then folows two names of the Lord - almost twins - as both are based on the concept of *āditya.* The first of these two names is just *Ādityaḥ* which can mean sun without any explanation. By implication, it can also mean the son of *Aditi* and *Kaśyapa,* namely the *Vāmana* incarnation of the Lord. In either case, this name stands for the enlightenment, radiation and illumination drawn from the deity of worship. The second name *Jyotirādityaḥ* is more specific focussing on the illumination or radiance part of the term *āditya*. It can also be taken for the deity of divine radiance residing in the disc of the Sun, *Āditya hṛdayam* (the heart of the sun).

Thus the two names jointly glorify the Lord's divine radiance which leads the living beings from darkness to light, from ignorance to awareness and finally from despair to hope. The Lord is not a mere *āditya* but an *āditya* endowed with *jyoti*. He is, indeed, not a mere *joyti* (illumination) either, but *Paraṁ Joyti* (the Eternal Light) that leads the inhabitants of the mortal frame from the temporal to the eternal.

That is why, the Lord is adored in the next name as *Sahiṣṇuḥ* who promotes endurance, forbearance and also excellence. He transmits these powers to His devotees as well. Divine grace usually starts with a series of sufferances, then introspection, contemplation, meditation and finally leads to the Supreme Bliss. The Divine Radiance has a blazing nature with it in the beginning but ultimately results in the highest form of bliss. The Lord is both blazing and blissful at the same time.

The last name *Gatisattamaḥ* shows that He and only He is the ultimate goal of life and He is also the safest and the best resort for all whatever be their walk of life. All ways lead to Him as He walks for us and with us whatever way we follow.

He Gives What You Want

The Lord is well-equipped and well-armd to bestow the best of wealth to His devotees and punish the evil-minded. How this is done is explained in the following verse :

सुधन्वा खण्डपरशुर्दारुणो द्रविणप्रदः ।
दिविस्पृक्सर्वदृग्व्यासो वाचस्पतिरयोनिजः ॥

sudhanvā khaṇḍa-paraśur-dāruṇo draviṇa-pradaḥ ।
divi-spṛk-sarva-dṛg-vyāso vācaspatir-ayonijaḥ ॥

The Lord has an auspicious bow in His hand. Hence, the name *Sudhanvā*. Lord *Viṣṇu* is known for His expert handling of the bow called *Śārṅga* which symbolizes the five senses and egotism *ahaṅkāra*. This auspicious and characteristic form of *Viṣṇu* figures almost towards the end of this sacred text *Śārṅgadhanvā* (996). In this context, however, the auspicious bow referred to seem to be the bow handled by *Rāma* the son of *Daśaratha* who handled not one, but many bows to establish peace and harmony in the world. This is supported by the name that immediately follows, namely *Khaṇḍaparaśuḥ* or *Akhaṇḍaparaṣuḥ* which obviously refers to *Paraṣurāma*. Both the personalities had an encounter on the question of handling the bows of different origin and dimensions. *Dāśarathī Rāma* married *Sītā* having performed the wonderful feat of bending the bow of Lord *Śiva*. Later when he was challenged by

Bhārgava Rāma i.e. *Paraśurāma*, he handled the bow of Lord *Viṣṇu* with equal ease and subdued the challenger by making him almost impotent and ineffective. Thus *Rāma,* the son of *Daśaratha* could handle the divine bows of both *Viṣṇu* and *Śiva* and thus combined the powers of both within him. Later the great sage *Agastya* also gave him another bow when he was in exile. All these weapons came very handy to him in his spectacular battle with *Rāvaṇa.* Thus *Rāma* used his bow or bows or for that matter all the missiles that *Viśvāmitra* bestowed on him as a reward for his valour with the noble intentions for the betterment of the world. When *Sītā* questioned whether it was right on the part of a noble prince like *Rāma* to destroy the demons without adequate provocation, *Rāma* clarified that it was his sacred duty as a prince to destroy all evil forces and establish peace in the world. The Lord, in His incarnation as *Rāma*, is therefore aptly admired and adored as *Sudhanvā*, one who uses his weapons (bows in particular) for noble and peaceful purposes.

The next name *Khaṇḍaparaśuḥ* or *Akhaṇḍaparaśuḥ* stands for *Bhārgava Rāma* or *Paraśurāma* as He punished (rather finished) the whole group of His enemies with His sharp edged axe which knew no defeat. This unfailing axe is the most powerful weapon that *Paraśurāma* uesd to terminate the *Kṣatriya* race as revenge.

In both the incarnations-*Rāma*, the son of *Daśaratha* and *Rāma*, the son of the sage *Jamadagni*, the Lord wielded the most powerful weapons terrorising His foes. Hence, the name *Dāruṇaḥ,* a terror for the evil forces.

But the ultimate aim of the Lord in wielding these invincible weapons was to grant peace and prosperity to those who were on the path of righteousness. It was to protect and support them that He had to do all this. Even the evil doers were ultimately granted salvation and made to repent for their devilish activities. It was *Mārīca* who praised *Rāma* as the embodiment of *dharma* - *Vigrahavān dharmaḥ*. Even

Rāvaṇa admired *Rāma* in the end as *Nārāyaṇa,* the non-ailing - *Nārāyaṇa-manāmayam. Vāli* too realized in the end after hearing *Rāma* with patience that the treatment he received in the hands of *Rāma* was in the larger interests of the establishment of the right values which ensure justice to those who are not unjust.

This spirit behind the acts of the Lord testifies His positive attitude to the establishment of truth and justice granting what people deserve and desire. He gives what you want provided you exercise your wisdom in presenting your wants. This is what is implied in the name *Draviṇapradaḥ,* the bestower of wealth--real wealth to the really deserving people.

The next two names *Divispṛk*, as high as the Heaven and *Sarvadṛgvyāsaḥ*, the Omniscient and All-compassing extol the encircling and ennobling vision which the Lord of the Universe manifests in His acts. He has the entire Universe in His mind's eye while executing His plans. He is analytical like the sage *Vyāsa*, who classified the entire Vedic literature into various heads and synthetic in His outlook like the sky with a heavenly touch.

The last name in the verse *Vācaspatirayonijaḥ* glorifies the Lord's excellence in His expression which no other being born in the usual process of procreation can cultivate. His is a voice of vision, the language of the Soul, the articulation of the heart and the essence of all sense that the Sound unheard alone can spell out. That is the reason why He is worshipped as *Vācaspatirayonijaḥ*, the Eloquent Master of Speech that needs no source. His expression is the source of all expressions and this is the source of all resources of Sound and Sense that create speech. He is the original sound *a-kāra* which is the beginning as well as the end of all *vāk*.

The Song, The Supreme

The whole life is a song sung in the glory of the Supreme Singer who breathes life into the inbuilt music and the inherent rhythm of this universe. That is what *Bhagavān* meant when He said in His Song celestial *Śrīmad-Bhagavadgītā* that He is the *Sāma Veda* among the *Vedas* and the *Bṛhatsāma* among all the Samavedic utterances. This aspect of divinity finds expression in the following verse :

त्रिसामा सामगः साम निर्वाणं भेषजं भिषक् ।
सन्यासकृच्छमः शान्तो निष्ठा शान्तिः परायणम् ॥

trisāmā sāmagaḥ sāma nirvāṇaṁ bheṣajaṁ bhiṣak |
sanyāsa-kṛcchamaḥ śānto niṣṭhā śāntiḥ parāyaṇaṁ ||

The identification of the Lord with the *Sāma Veda* and the scared hymns called *Trisāmas* or *Devavrata* is brought out in the first three names. The Vedic scholars sing His glory in the three scared hymns as the Lord is believed to be present in these hymns. Hence, the name *Trisāma*, the Lord manifest in the form of the three *Sāma*-hymns.

The next name *Sāmagaḥ* means one who chants the *Sāmaveda*. Here this is used as an attributive term to the Lord Himself who, of course, joins the scholar while chanting the scared hyms. It can also mean that the best way to reach the Lord is through chanting the scared hymns of *Sāmaveda* like *Bṛhatsāma*.

Sāmaveda is acclaimed as the most enchanting, pleasing, appeasing and awarding of all the *Vedas.* There is an interesting story prevalent among the Vedic scholars that a scholar solely engrossed in chanting the *Sāma*-hymns never allowed his wife to kiss him lest his lips sanctified by the chanting of the *Sāma* should be polluted by the kiss.

सामगायन-पूतं मे नोच्छिष्टमधरं कुरु।
उत्कण्ठितासि चेद् भद्रे वामकर्णं दशस्व मे ॥

sāmagāyana-pūtaṁ me nocchiṣṭamadharaṁ kuru |
utkaṇṭhitāsi ced-bhadre vāmakarṇaṁ daśasva me ||

So high was the esteem the Vedic scholars had for the *Sāmaveda.* Hence, the Lord identified Himself with this sacred scripture. The third name *Sāma* stands as a synonym for the Lord. Name Him, the Song is sung. There is absolutely no difference between the Vedic vibrations and the Lord. This is what the name *Sāma* speaks for itself. In these three names, *Trisāmā, Sāmagaḥ* and *Sāma*, the Lord is identified with the celebrated hymns of the *Sāmaveda*, the cheif objective of chanting these hymns and the entire text of *Sāmaveda.* In short He is *Sāma* (equanimity) personified as the word *sāma* stands for equanimity.

The next name *Nirvāṇam*, meaning final liberation tells us that the chanting of the Vedic hymns with total dedication, perfect harmony within and absorbing articulation of each sound is the surest and the safest way to merge in the Almighty. This is what is referred to here as *Nirvāṇam* which means the complete emancipation from matter and reunion with the Supreme Spirit. This *Brahmanirvāṇam* extolled in the *Sāṅkhya-yoga* of *Gītā* is possible through singing the glory of the Lord deriving inspiration from the enchanting vibrrations of *Sāmaveda.* Hence, the Lord is depicted here as *Nirvāṇam* itself.

The next name *Bheśajam* means medicine, remedy or cure. The chanting of the Vedic hymns is the best medicine to get liberated from the worldly bondage and this becomes possible only with the grace of God. So, God is not only liberation *Nirvāṇam* but also the means and medication for it *Bheśajam*. Not only that, He is the *Bhiśak* the physician too. He is the medicine, the cure and also the object of the whole treatment. One word or name standing for the Lord is enough to attain the eternal bliss.

The next line in the verse starts with the attribute *Sannyāsakṛt*. *Sannyāsa* is the final state- *āśrama* - in life leading to the ultimate goal of life, namely attaining oneness with the Lord. But it is not given to each and every person to take up this venture of becoming a real *Sannyāsin*. This, again, requires His grace, One can attain this stage only under the pleasure of His Majesty. It depends entirely on His Supreme Will. Hence, the name *Sannyāsakṛt*.

The only requisite for adopting this final (the fourth) stage in one's life is perfect calmness, quiescence, stability to withstand and overcome all temptations of the material world. This state of mind is what is known as *Sāmaḥ* and one who is endowed with this quality is called *Śāntaḥ*. *Sannyāsī* is one who has this tranquility in him and it is this tranquility *sāmaḥ* which takes him closer and closer to divinity. Both the attributes, *Sāmaḥ* (the state of tranquility) and *Śāntaḥ* (one who has cultivated this state) are, therefore, deified and used as synonymous with the Supreme Spirit in these two names.

The next name *Niṣṭhā* means strict and steadfast adherence to the desired objective in mind. This is a pre-requisite to attain tranquility. This is also a divine virtue as it promotes divinity in humanity by stages in degrees. This is, therefore, glorified as an attribute of the Lord.

Śāntiḥ follows automatically when all these stages are passed through. *Śāntiḥ* or peace takes the individual nearest to the universal one. He rises above the petty differences and considerations and trains himself to think in terms of the whole, and not to confine himself to his pleasures, achievements and aspirations. The *Upaniṣads* emphasize the need to cultivate and promote this concept of peace - universal and multidimensional peace. Each *Upaniṣad* starts and ends with the prayer for peace repeated thrice to cover the material, intellectual and spiritual areas of peace.

The last name *Parāyaṇaṁ* sums up that this is the ultimate goal of life.

The Bestower Of Peace

Peace, Peace and Peace alone is the foundation for the welfare of all beings. This is the central theme of the verse that follows :

शुभाङ्गः शान्तिदः स्रष्टा कुमुदः कुवलेशयः ।
गोहितो गोपतिर्गोप्ता वृषभाक्षो वृषप्रियः ॥

śubhāṅgaḥ śāntidaḥ sraṣṭā kumudaḥ kuvaleśayaḥ ।
gohito gopatir-goptā vṛṣabhākṣo vṛṣapriyaḥ ॥

The deep blue sky spread over the entire canvas of the whole cosmos constitutes the most auspicious body of the Lord. The scriptures accordingly adore Him as *Ākāśa Śarīram* (whose body is the sky). His limbs are spread over everywhere and are visible where good prevails. Where there is good, there is God. He manifests Himself only to promote good. That is why He is glorified as *Śubhāṅagaḥ* in the starting name of this stanza.

Because there is nothing but Good wherever He maifests Himself He promotes peace. Peace is the result of all the good thoughts, words and deeds cultivated by the inhabitants of this universe. He is therefore worshipped as *Śāntidaḥ,* the bestower of peace. The Lord is worshipped by His devotees as of peaceful countenance - *Śāntākāram.* As His image itself is peaceful, it goes without saying that peace percolates to all layers and corners of His cosmic manifestation.

He is the *Sraṣṭā*, the creator of the universe. So it is His duty to see that there is happiness, prosperity, peace and bliss wherever He spreads His auspicious limbs. That is why He is glorified in the next name as *Kumudaḥ*, one who imparts bliss to the earth. As the presiding deity of the whole universe, He stays on earth in the hearts of all inhabitants and relaxes in the deep waters of the sea. Hence, He is glorified as *Kuvaleśayaḥ,* one who reclines on *kuvala* (Ocean, that surrounds the earth). The word *kuvala* also means a powerful serpent named *Takṣaka* who bit the King *Parīkṣit* hiding himself in a fruit called *Badarī.* This may also refer to the divine serpent *Śeṣa* or *Ādiśeṣa* who offers himself as the bed for the Lord. The whole earth is supported by this gigantic serpent. This serpent is also said to be the divine source of all human expression. Thus the name *Kuvaleśayaḥ* has multiple meanings and implications. Whatever be the connotation, the purport is that this is the resting place of the Lord *Kuvaleśayaḥ*. It may be the *kuṇḍalinī,* the serpent-power coiling round the *mūlādhāra*, the base of the human body.

The next three names- *Gohitaḥ, Gopatiḥ* and *Goptā* are also deep in their meaning. As the present theme is the universe, the immediate purport is that the Lord is always favourable and friendly towards the world He has created. Whatever He does is in the larger interests of the general good of the people whom He created. Hence, the name *Gohitaḥ* favourably inclined to the inhabitants of the earth.

The next name *Gopatiḥ* simply means the Lord of the earth, though it reminds us of Lord *Kṛṣṇa* who acted as the leader of the inhabitants of *Gokul.* He was friendly to the cows and cowherds and protected them from the anger of *Indra.*

The name *Goptā* presents the Lord as the protector of those who approach Him for help, shelter and salvation.

The last two names *Vṛṣabhākṣaḥ* and *Vṛṣapriyaḥ* project the Lord's patronage for *dharma*, the righteous conduct. The word *vṛṣa* means *dharma* (righteousness) too in addition to its primary meaning, bull. The bull is a symbol of righteousness and serves as vehicle *vahana* for Lord *Śiva*. The word *vṛṣabhaḥ* too has the same connotation, but has an additional factor of radiance because of the last syllable *bha*. *Dharma* or righteousness has two qualities one is showering the fruits of action on the right-minded people and the other, imparting radiance or brilliance. The name *Vṛṣabhākṣaḥ* which is being discussed here speaks of these two qualities of the Lord. He grants what we want with love and delight. His looks are full of spontaneity of His delightful love. Hence, the name *Vṛṣabhākṣaḥ*. In fact Truth and Righteousness *satyam* and *dharma* are His two eyes.

He is fond of these two virtues and likes people who cultivate them. Hence, He is worshipped as *Vṛṣapriyaḥ*. He likes those who like *dharma*, the fountain- head of all that is good.

Nothing But Good

The path of righteousness which alone can lead to peace is the path of no return or retreat. 'Arise and Awake and Achieve the Absolute' is the motto which the followers of this path should have in their mind. The march goes on and on under the leadership of the Lord who accepts nothing but good - *Śivam*. This is what the names that follow tell us in blissful vibrations :

अनिवर्ती निवृत्तात्मा संक्षेप्ता क्षेमकृच्छिव: ।
श्रीवत्सवक्षा: श्रीवास: श्रीपति: श्रीमतांवर: ॥

anivartī nivṛttātmā saṅkṣeptā kṣema-kṛcchivaḥ ।
śrīvatsa-vakṣāḥ śrīvāsaḥ śrīpatiḥ śrīmatāṁ-varaḥ ॥

The Lord leading the aspirants of the absolute bliss does not allow any retreat in the march. There is no place for return or withdrawal *nivartan*. Hence, He is glorified as *Anivartī*. If at all there is any question of going back or giving up, it will be in respect of worldly pleasures, wants and temptations. When *Ātman* is the goal, anything other than that is just ignored. It is to drive this point into the minds of the aspirants and readers of this sacred text that the *Ācārya* re-affirms the strong determination of the followers of this path by glorifying the Lord by the name *Nivṛttātmā*, turned away from tempting pleasures of life. Thus the way to salvation or the absolute bliss is the way that accepts no defeat and yields to no temptation.

The Lord is then adored as *Sṅkṣeptā,* the condenser. He can reduce the whole universe into an atom and create it again. He does not destroy but compress the expanded existence into a subtle form at the time of *pralaya* or disintegration. But He does this for the safety and security of the Universe as a whole. Hence, He is adored as *Kṣemakṛt,* the well-wisher or the harbinger of good. He does everything for the good of all. There can be nothing that is not good in the Kingdom of god as He is Good solidified.

This Good-ness of God is expressed in a single word *Śivaḥ*, the Auspicious. He is the concrete illustration of the Vedic expression *Śāntaṁ Śivaṁ Advaitam.* He is the purest of the pure and can therefore purify anything and anyone with the mere touch or thought of the Good that He symbolizes.

Having completed 600 names of Lord *Viṣṇu* with this highly significant name *Śivaḥ, Bhīṣmācārya* presents a series of fourteen soul-elevating names starting with *Śrī* of which the first four appear in this verse itself.

The first among this series is *Śrīvatsavkṣāḥ* which describes the auspicious mark called *Śrivatsa*, symbolizing *Śrī, Lakṣmī,* the consort of the Lord, permanently impressed on the majestic chest of the Lord. It is just a curl of hair and nothing else. But it presents the most gracious image of the Goddess of wealth, prosperity and beauty that can *Śrī*-face the whole universe.

No wonder, if the Goddess has chosen to make this mark Her home, the inbuilt habitat made for Her by Her Lord, the Lord of the Universe. This is beautifully brought out in the next name *Śrīvāsaḥ.* This name lends itself to two facets of the same idea. It means that the Lord is the resting place for the Lady and also that the Lady is the abode of the

Lord. He resides in Her and She resides in Him. It will be worth comparing this relation with that of the deity and the devotee as well.Deity is the ultimate resort for the devotee and devotee for the deity in the same way. The Lord Himself makes this statement in *Gītā* saying ' They (the devotees) are in me and I in them' - *mayi te teṣucāpyahaṁ*.

The next name *Śrīpatiḥ* clarifies this position further. The name simply means that He is the Lord of *Śrī*. Here *Śrī* refers to *Lakṣmī*, the Goddess of wealth in its multidimensional and universal sense. *Lakṣmī*, who emerged from the ocean of milk when it was churned out by the gods and the demons. As *Parāśakti* (the Supreme Power), She chose Him as Her husband. This is, therefore, a Cosmic union of matter and energy giving rise to the multifaceted manifestation of the universe in its colourful and resourceful form.

The last name in the verse is *Śrīmatāṁvaraḥ*, the Most distinguished personality adored and honoured by *Śrī*, the Supreme Power governing the material, intellectual and spiritual wealth of the whole universe.

Śrī The Treasure-house

Śrī-mālā, the series of names glorifying the grace and grandeur of *Śrī-devī* continues in the following names :

श्रीदः श्रीशः श्रीनिवासः श्रीनिधिः श्रीविभावनः ।
श्रीधरः श्रीकरः श्रेयः श्रीमाँल्लोकत्रयाश्रयः ॥

śrīdaḥ śrīśaḥ śrīnivāsaḥ śrīnidhiḥ śrīvibhāvanaḥ I
śrīdharaḥ śrīkaraḥ śreyaḥ śrimānlloka-trayāśrayaḥ II

Being the most benevolent bestower of wealth as the well-wisher of all His devotees, the Lord is adored as *Śrīdaḥ*. The wealth He bestows is not merely the material one, but mostly the wealth of wisdom and spiritual awareness.

He has all the wealth with Him. He keeps it under His control and distributes it among the deserving at the appropriate time and in a judicious manner. Hence, He is *Śrīśaḥ*. He is the Lord of wealth. According to *Iśopaniṣad,* there is no wealth-worldly or otherwise, which is not controlled by him. It is with His grace and absolutely under His pleasure that people enjoy the wealth. He is the Comptroller of wealth in general.

He is where *Śrī* (Excellence) is. He stays with gifted people endowed with this spiritual excellence and adds radiance to their personality. *Śrī*, the Mother *Lakṣmī*, is of cource, the permanent resort for the Lord. She is never without Him and He is never withour Her. Hence He is *Śrīnivāsaḥ*.

He is *Śrīnidhiḥ* the treasure-house of all the treasure that one can cherish and aspire for. The area of richness or plenitude covered by *Śrī* is not confined to any one class or category of riches. Anything that enriches the wholesome and harmonious personality of an individual comes under the purview of this treasure for which the Lord and the Lady of the Universe are the soul trustees. This is a treasure *nidhi* which is accessible and available for all living beings who enjoy the grace of its master.

Śrī has been defined in the Scriptures as the treasure house of learning contained in the three *Vedas* - *Ṛk*, *Sāma* and *Yayur* which the sages admire and adore as *amṛtā* as it makes them immortal. *Ṛk sāmāni yajū ̐ṣi sā hi śrīramṛtā satām.*

The next name *Śrīvibhāvanaḥ* can be interpreted by common understanding as distributor of wealth. The Lord distributes this common-wealth among His children according to their standing, needs and deserving qualities. But a deeper insight into the word *vibhāvana* reveals a treasure of meaning hidden under the name. In Indian poetics, the word *vibhāva* has special connotation. A person, object or event which gives rise to a sentiment *rasa* is called *vibhava*. If the sentiment is based on divine love or devotion, the *Vibhava* is the deity and His deeds, sports and events connected with His incarnations. From this point of view, the name *Śrīvibhāvanaḥ* used as attribute to the Lord clearly means the source of inspiration for cultivating total dedication to the deity of worship. This inspiration also comes from the Lord. As *Gosvāmī Tulasīdās* puts it, wisdom does not dawn without the divine grace and it is this wisdom, the gift of God, which takes the devotee closer and closer to His deity. Sometimes, a silent repetition of a prayer is an adequate *Vibhāvana* (source of inspiration) for identity with the deity. It is in this sense that the name *Śrīvibhāvana* gains special significance in this *Śrī-mālā* garland of names glorifying the grandeur of Mother *Śrī* -*Śrīmātā*.

The Lord of the Universe constantly keeps *Śrīdevī*, the Mother of the Universe on His chest. Hence, He is worshipped as *Śrīdharaḥ* the Bearer of *Śrī*.

As He is both the instrumental and the material cause of all wealth and prosperity in the world of His own creation, He is adored as Śrī-*karaḥ*, the Creator of Fortune and Prosperity.

Fortune is again of two kinds- the one which we like and the other which elevates us. The former is called *preyas* (lovable, appeasing) and the latter is known as *śreyas* that is ultimately good for us. As the *Kaṭhopaniṣad* says, normally most of the people are content with *preyas*, the immediate pleasure while the wise and the realized souls prefer the latter, *śreyas*, the ultimate good. The Lord grants the latter one and hence projected here as *Śreyaḥ*, one who grants and promotes the absolute good which remains good for all time to come and for all classes of people whether they like it immediately or not. Thus this name *Śreyaḥ* instructs us, by implication, not to be led away by the momentary pleasures and seek the grace of God for acheiving the highest good, the unfailing fortune.

The last name starting with *Śrī* in this series *Śrīmālā* is very simple and popular even in common usage. In this name, the Lord is simply designated as *Śrīmān*, the Celebrated. He is the most celebrated among all as all other *Śrīmāns* get originated from Him. In common parlance almost all the male members are called *Śrīmān* and the female counterparts (usually the wedded ones) are treated as *Śrīmatī*. This is a very good social practice as it enables almost all individuals to remember the name of the Lord and also the Mother of the Universe, though, in a casual way. Remembering the Lord in some form or other is, in itself , a great blessing.

The concluding name in this series *Lokatrayāśrayaḥ* meaning the Refuge of the three worlds, focusses our attention on the universal significance of these names with *Śrī* as their centre.

The Bliss Unsurpassed

The next verse in the text starts with glorifying the blissful beauty of the Lord manifest in His eyes and each and every limb. The Supreme Bliss and the Radiant Splendour of the Lord finds expression in this verse:

स्वक्षः स्वङ्गः शतानन्दो नन्दिर्ज्योतिर्गणेश्वरः ।
विजितात्माविधेयात्मा सत्कीर्तिश्छिन्नसंशयः ॥

svakṣaḥ svaṅgaḥ śatānando nandir-jyotir-gaṇeśvaraḥ I
vijitātmā-vidheyātmā satkīrtiś-chinnasaṁśayaḥ II

The first two names - *Svakṣaḥ* and *Svaṅgaḥ* describe the good-looking eyes and fascinating limbs of the Lord. The lovely eyes and the charming limbs are so beautiful that each and every aspect of this beauty gets multiplied and looks delightful to those who can see the Lord even by imaginary eyes in the innermost layers of one's own consciousness. He is, therefore, glorified as *Śatānandaḥ,* hundredfold in the blissful beauty. The beauty transformed into bliss produces immense delight in the spectators' mind, heart and soul and their blissful feelings become immeasurable. This Supreme Bliss is appropriately termed *Nandiḥ*. It looks as if the Lord is an embodiment of the Supreme Bliss.

As for the radiance in His face, it appears as if all the luminaries-both celestial and terrestrial are grouped in the blissful form of the Lord and He outshines them all. No single celestial beauty or bliss can match

Him as all these heavenly bodies have emerged from Him and will ultimately merge in Him. He is therefore adored as *Jyotirgaṇeśvaraḥ*, the Lord of the luminaries. The scriptures sing the glory of His radiance in superlative terms saying that all luminaries derive their light and delight from the Lord. It is His radiance that shines in all liminaries. Everything shines by His effulgence.

This is because the beauty, the bliss and the effulgence we find in the Lord has its origin in the *ātman* and not in the matter, It is not material splendour. It is the inner and the inbuilt radiance. Hence, He is *Vijitātmā*, the one who excels in all *ātmic* radiance. He is never surpassed and hence worshipped as *Avidheyātmā* not subjected to any external order or ordinance. He shines by His own splendour and transmits the same to others who come nearer to Him.

In name and fame too, He is unsurpassed. But He is most unassuming. He never feels that He excels others. In fact, He likes His devotees to imbibe these qualities and shine by themselves. He wants them to rise upto His expectations by their own efforts. He never boasts of His fame but shares it with His beloved devotees. That is why He is adored as *Satkīrtiḥ* - of unique fame that is neither isolated nor adopted. He spreads by His own radiance.

If one does not believe all this, the loss is entirely his and not His. Those who have faith in Him and realize His supremacy flourish. One who is free from doubts alone can visualize the potential divinity within. So the Lord wants us to have trust in Him and do our best. The rest is in His hands, handsome limbs and lovely eyes. This is very well expressed in the last name of the present verse - *Chinnasaṁśayaḥ.*

Bhagavān Himself says in His song Celestial *Gītā* that he who is devoid of faith and is always possessed by doubt is lost to the spiritual path and for him there is neither this world nor the world beyond, nor even happiness [*Gītā* 4.40].

The Dispeller Of Grief

The Lord of the Universe is the sole, eternal and unchanging power leading every soul of this vast universe with none beyond Him. His is the transcendental glory that encircles the globe and has an eye on each and every atom of this universe looking after global welfare and dispelling all grief. This point is brought out in the following verse :

उदीर्णः सर्वतश्चक्षुरनीशः शाश्वतस्थिरः ।
भूशयो भूषणो भूतिर्विशोक : शोकनाशनः ।।

udīrṇaḥ sarvataś-cakṣur anīśaḥ śāśvata-sthiraḥ I
bhūśayo bhūṣaṇo bhūtir-viśokaḥ śoka-nāśanaḥ II

The Lord rises on His own, ascends and soars high to the highest level so that He can have a telescopic vision of the whole universe which is under His charge. He is therefore called *Udīrṇaḥ*, one who grows and moves upwards with nothing to bar Him.

He can have a full vision of the land and the sky at a single, sharp and penetrating glance from all sides. He can see from distance anything above, below, beside and behind Him. Similarly, the seeker of His vision can also see Him likewise either within or without, far or near, right or left, over His head or below His feet, sitting or standing, awake or asleep, alert or abrupt. This all-round vision of the Lord makes Him adorable as *Sarvataścakṣuḥ* having His eyes on all sides.

There is no authority on earth or in heaven to question the lordship of the Lord. He is lorded over by none. He is the Lord of Himself and the Lord of the Universe. Hence, the name *Anīśaḥ*. He is the only *Īśvara* with none above Him.

The next name which further clarifies the lordship of the Lord of the Universe is *Śāśvatasthiraḥ*. This combines two qualities of the governance of the Lord-permanence *Śāśvataḥ* and stability *Sthiraḥ*. A durable and stable government is the basic requirement for a welfare state safe and secured. This is fully ensured by the Lord ruling not one world, but all the worlds created so far and yet to be created.

Inspite of this heavy responsibility, the Lord relaxes on the green grass of His land or in the deep waters of the ocean or on the soft bed of the primordial serpent *Ādiśeṣa* supporting the whole earth from time immemorial. The Lord is calm and quiet cooly observing the ups and downs of the roaring waves around and passifying them with the radiant rays of the celestial luminaries coming from above-eager to greet them and treat their ailments - physical, mental and spiritual. This is what makes the Lord adorable as *Bhūśayaḥ*, recumbent on the earth.

He is not just a recumbent, but a radiant, jubilant and ornamental source of inspiration for the inhabitants of this Universe - an admirable admixture of pleasure and pain, union and separation, hopes and despairs and delight and depression. The Lord with His playful sprit adds new life and new colour to the mundane way of living. He is, therefore, admired and worshipped as *Bhūṣaṇaḥ*.

By virtue of this transformation of life herein from the most mechanical and morose pattern to the transcendental way of looking at things, the Lord is glorified in the next name as *Bhūtiḥ*. The feeling of existence which elevates the human to the divine level is the most precious gift of God. If we feel that we are, we are. Otherwise we are nowhere. This basic belief in the real existence of all that we see, hear, understand, absorb and identify ourselves with is the divine grace, the transcendental glory of this temporal world making it eternal, enduring and elevating.

There is no such thing as grief in the great grand diction of the Lord. He is free from all grief *Viśokaḥ* and makes others also free from it. He is, therefore, glorified as *Viśokaḥ,* free from all griefs and hence *Śokanāśanaḥ*, dispeller of grief. No grief can exist in His transcendental vision and mission. There can be only Bliss, Bliss and Bliss alone.

Arch Light

The next verse in the text starts with a name glorifying the lord as the arch-light, the light of lights, the light that is worshipped by all luminaries- both terrestrial and celestial and the light that purifies the whole universe. The word used for this type of light *arciḥ* is also highly significant. The word *arciḥ* or *arciṣ* means a ray of light. As a verb *ac* means to adore, worship, salute, welcome with respect. It is the light that is worshipped in this sense because the word *arca* means worship or the idol to be worshipped. Of the nine forms of devotion *Navadhā Bhakti* enumerated in *Śrīmad -Bhāgavataṁ*, *arcanam* is the fifth (incidentally the central). Daily worship performed by devout householders is also called *Arcanā* which has a system of its own. In general, any form of worship or reverence paid to deities is called *Arcanā*. The whole concept of *Arcanā* therefore seems to be centred round the term *arciṣ* meaning a ray of light. In this context, it means 'the original ray of light' from which the whole radiance of this universe emerges. The glorification of this arch-light runs as follows :

अर्चिष्मानर्चितः कुम्भो विशुद्धात्मा विशोधनः ।
अनिरुद्धोऽप्रतिरथः प्रद्युम्नोऽमितविक्रमः ॥

arciṣmān-arcitaḥ kumbho viśuddhātmā viśodhanaḥ ।
aniruddho'prati-rathaḥ pradyumno'mita-vikramaḥ ॥

The Lord is glorified, adored and worshipped as *Arciṣmān* as He is the centre and source of all radiance, brilliance and illumination in the Universe. He is called *Arcitaḥ* in the next name as He is worshipped not only by the devotees, but also by the celestial deities like *Indra, Varuṇa, Brahmā* and *Śaṅkara.*

He is, then, adored as *Kumbhaḥ* which superficially means only a pot, a vessel or a container. As a container, the Lord contains the whole creation. Everything is contained in Him and derives existence, excellence and enlightenment from Him. He provides light *bhā* to the earth *kum.* Hence, He is worshipped as *Kumbha.* There is a popular festival called *Kumbha* celebrated on the basis of the movement of three planets--Jupiter, Sun and Moon. This is also a festival of faith celebrating the perennial flow of the essence of life (the ambrosia of animate existence despite the temporal nature of the life-span). The concept of *kumbha* (a pot full of elixir of life) indicates that the life is always full-fledged *pūrṇam* in its own way. *Pūrṇamadaḥ Pūrṇamidam* is the prophetic assertion of this eternal existence symbolized in the image of this adorable and adored pot of water. The Lord is therefore worshipped as *Kumbha* the eternal container of the everlasting existence.

A pure soul can purify all other souls. As the purest of all souls, the Lord purifies anybody or anything the moment he or she or it comes into contact with Him. That is why the Lord is glorified as *Viśuddhātmā* and *Viśodhanaḥ* in the next two names. The scriptures are all admiration for the marvellous effect of *Brahma-Saṁsparśaḥ* the touch of the Absolute.

Nothing can obstruct the divine course of purification. *Gītā* assures that even the worst of all the sinners can get salvation once he becomes aware of the Supreme Spirit within him. He will cross all barriers with the help of the boat of this absolute knowledge. The Lord is therefore glorified as *Aniruddhaḥ* unimpeded and *Apratirathaḥ* unrivalled. No force on earth can drive against the chariot of the Master and nobody can stop Him when He starts driving and goes ahead.

He is the most radiant and brilliant in His movements. Hence, the name *Pradyumnaḥ*. His is divine radiance which excels even the celestial one. His valour *vikramaḥ* is also unlimited *amita*. Hence, He is adored as *Amitavikramaḥ*, unequalled in power and unaffected in prowess.

Lord Of The Three Worlds

How the Lord exercises control over the three worlds - *svarga* (heaven), *martya* (the world of mortals) and *pātāla* (the nether world)- by destroying the devilish element and patronizing the peaceful and pious souls is brought out in the following verse:

कालनेमिनिहा वीरः शौरिः शूरजनेश्वरः ।
त्रिलोकात्मा त्रिलोकेशः केशवः केशिहा हरिः ॥

kāla-nemi-nihā vīraḥ śauriḥ śūra-janeśvaraḥ |
trilokātmā trilokeśaḥ keśavaḥ keśihā hariḥ ||

Kālanemi literally means the 'wheel of time' which is controlled by the Lord of the universe. He moves with the time, identifying Himself with it and make the whole world move with it as if by force. This is His illusive power *māyā* which causes all the beings rotate and revolve round this wheel according to the *karma* they have to their credit (or discredit).

There was a demon called *Kālanemi,* the grandson of *Hiraṇyakaśipu.* The Lord destroyed both these demons when they transgressed the limits of righteous conduct. But the same Lord protected *Prahlāda*, the son of *Hiraṇyakaśipu* as He sticked to his stand of devotional attachment to the Lord inspite of threats by his cruel father. This is how the Lord maintains the standards of truth and justice in the time-bound temporal life. The name *Kālanemi-nihā*, therefore, justifies its inclusion in the thousand names of the Lord as it projects the Lord as 'the destroyer of the wheel of time' and also as the slayer of the demon *Kālanemi*.

The second name *Vīraḥ* meaning the valiant glorifies the valour the Lord has at His command just to destroy the 'evil' and support the 'good'.

The Lord, in His incarnation as *Kṛṣṇa* was born in the *Śūra*-clan of the *Yādavas*. Hence, He is glorified in the next name as *Śauriḥ*.

He is not only one of the *Śauris*, but the Head of this clan of valiant people. He is, therefore, adored as *Śūrajaneśvaraḥ*, the Lord of the valiant. Indeed He is admired, adored and worshipped by the whole community of warriors because of His Supreme and supernatural martial powers.

The next two names *Trilokātmā* and *Trilokeśaḥ* glorify the Lord as both the insider and outsider of the three worlds. He is an integral and indivisible part of the three worlds as no world or creation can exist apart from Him. Hence He is *Trilokātmā*. He is also the Lord of the three worlds which are entirely and exclusively under His control.He is, therefore, *Trilokeśaḥ*. He is the Creator and also the Master of His creation--*Loka* and *Lokeśaḥ* both.

The next name *Keśavaḥ* sounds as if it is in continuation of the sense conveyed by the previous name *Trilokeśaḥ*. The word *keśaḥ* normally means 'hair' in general. But it also means 'a ray of light'.Thus this attribute used for the Lord can be interpreted as 'one with beautiful hair' and also as 'one who shines with His inbuilt radiance transmitted through His lock of hair covering His head like a crown'. The Lord with the vast outer space as His body transmits radiance to all the lumineries through His hair which shine like rays of light.

The word *Keśava* can also be interpreted as the Lord *Īśa* or *Brahmā*, the creator *Ka*. The word can be split up into three parts -- *ka* + *īśa* + *va* -- which combined come to mean the Lord who excells in His power as the Supreme authority in Creation.

Keśava is also one of the most sacred names of the Lord.This is the first of the 24 names (*Keśava, Nārāyaṇa, Mādhava, Govinda* etc. ending with *Śrī Kṛṣṇa*) which are chanted at the beginningof the daily prayer *Sandhyā vandanam* or any other ritual propitiating any deity. The three basic energies of creation, preservation and assimilation operated by the Trinity *Brahmā, Viṣṇu* and *Śiva* are also called *Keśas* in the Vedic parlance *trayaḥ keśinaḥ*. The fact that the name *Keśavaḥ* starts with the sound *keśa* with which its preceding name *Trilokeśaḥ* ends has its own significance. The three worlds which the Lord holds under His control need not necessarily be confined to the global demarcations but several other dimensions -- ethical, spiritual and cosmological. Wherever there is the divine radiance, there is *Keśava* as *Trilokeśa*.

Keśi is the name of a demon whom the Lord killed. Hence, the name *Keśihā*. Beauty without radiance has no divinity in it and is therefore not patronized by the Lord. In this sense also He is *Keśihā*. *Keśī* had fascinating hair but they had no radiant brilliance in them. That is why He did not enjoy the blessings of the Lord.

The last name *Hari* is one of the most popular names of the Lord. He absolves all the sins of His devotees, puts an end to all the sinners and bestows all bliss to the great souls who visualize *Paramātman* in every atom of the Universe. Incidentally *hari* means many things besides *Viśṇu*. *Hari* means a ray of light , fire, wind, lion, horse, monkey, frog, parrot and so on. The root-meaning of the word *hara* or *hari* is one who takes away or brings back. Taking an object from one place to the other is *haraṇa*. With slight modification, *Hari* (*Viśṇu*) becomes *Hara* (*Śiva*). Thus the name *Hariḥ*, the last name in the verse, has the widest canvas of meaning and the most enchanting effect on the devotees who chant this name for the attainment of the Supreme Bliss *Paramānandam*.

The Deity Of Desires

Desires are the motivating forces in life as long as they are moderated by what the desirer really deserves.God is always prepared to fulfil our desires to the extent they are designed to promote the universal good. Otherwise He curbs them and directs them to purification by sublimation in due course. The way the Lord presides over all our desires, passions and sentiments is explained in the following verse:

कामदेवः कामपालः कामी कान्तः कृतागमः ।
अनिर्देश्यवपुर्विष्णुर्वीरोऽनन्तो धनञ्जयः ॥

kāmadevaḥ kāmapālaḥ kāmī kāntaḥ kṛtāgamaḥ ।
anirdeśya-vapur-viṣṇur-vīro'nanto dhanañjayaḥ ॥

The word *kāmaḥ*, though generally means desire, has different connotations depending upon the degree and nature of the object of the desires and the way they are aspired for or cultivated. *Bhagavān* acts as the presiding deity of all these desires. Hence the name *Kāmadevaḥ*. In *Gītā* while enumerating His divine glories, the Lord identifies Himself with *kāmaḥ* the love or desire of sensual enjoyments as long as they are not against *dharma* the natural law of righteousness. In this respect, *kāmaḥ* is one of the *puruṣārthas* (the objectives of life) and is placed at par with *dharma* (righteousness), *artha* (wealth) and *mokṣa* (liberation). Even the desire of carnal gratification is supposed to be pious when its main objective is to promote procreation as a contributory measure for creation in general. It is in this sense that *kāma* is deified and *Kāmadevaḥ,* the God of love is viewed with respect and reverence. The Lord is the presiding deity of such pious desires. Hence, He is adored as *Kāmadevaḥ.*

The next name *Kāmapālaḥ* enlightens us on the desirability of exercising control and restraint over this basic passion so that it does not assume the proportions of violence, giving rise to devastating fire of passion or inflaming fire of love. It is to ensure this that the Lord is eulogized as *Kāmapālaḥ.* He fulfils the legitimate and peace-promoting desires of all well-meaning beings and also ensures that such desires do not violate the basic norms of general welfare.

As the well-wisher of His devotees who never transgress the limits of righteous conduct in matters of their aspirations, the Lord Himself asssumes the role of a lover *Kāmī* whose universal love demonstrates to the loving world how pure the form of love can be so that there is no room for the mad rush of lust in the realm of love. The two major incarnations of the Lord - *Rāma* and *Kṛṣṇa* - have ample illustrations to clarify this point. The very sight of *Rāma* could liberate *Ahalyā* from her husband's curse.She became one of the five sacred women *pañca-mahākanyās.* The entire canvas of *Kṛṣṇa* was full of love-- love elevated to the highest form of devotion where the pious hearts forget the whole world in their pure thoughts. This is the role the Lord plays as *Kāmī,* the promoter of pious desires.

This *Kāmavallī,* the quartet advocating and singing the glory of pure love concludes with a wholesome name *Kāntaḥ* which means 'handsome'. In all His incarnations, whatever form He assumed, He excelled all the species in that form. As an archer, He displayed His skill in handling all types of bows and shooting the arrows with remarkable skill when He was *Rāma.* As an ardent admirer, practitioner and promoter of fine arts like music, dance and communication, He left an indelible mark on the lovers of these fine arts as *Vaṁśīdhar* (flute-master), *Rāsa-līlā* expert, a charioteer and several other areas when He was *Kṛṣṇa*. He brought splendour to all the aesthetic fields He entered in. Thus He is, in the real sense of the term, a *Kāntaḥ*, the most fascinating and captivating figure in the field of all fine arts and finer means of mass mobilazation.

He is not only an expert in the execution of His thoughts, but also an accomplished articulator and formulator of Cosmic Vision.His reverberating voice stays in the hearts of all living beings who have respect for the art of living. Hence, He is glorified as *Kṛtāgamaḥ*, the author of all sacred scriptures including the *āgamas*. The word *āgamaḥ* literally means arrival, approach, acquisition and, by implication, knowledge of scriptures or the voice of Vision.All scriptures and other sources of knowledge in their absolute form derive their inspiration from the thoughts,words and deeds of the Lord in His incarnations. They emanate from Him. So, He is the invisible articulator of all the Vedic vibrations. Hence the name *Kṛtāgamaḥ*

It is difficult and almost impossible to define the form and nature of the Lord. He is, therefore, adored as *Anirdeśyavapuḥ*, of undefinable form. This name already figured once along with *Śrīmān* - *Anirdeśyavapuḥ Śrīmān*. Here the name is followed by *Viṣṇuḥ*, the presiding deity of the sacred hymn. He is all-pervading, and hence hymned as *Viṣṇuḥ*. Eventhough he is all pervading, His effulgence can only be felt, experienced and enjoyed but cannot be defined or described.

In the next three names *Vīraḥ, Anantaḥ* and *Dhanañjayaḥ*, three characteristics of this divine form are explained. The word *vīraḥ* literally means a hero, warrior or champion. The Lord is all this in His various manifestations. In addition, *Vīraḥ*, in this context, can mean one who has a distinguished form of expression through which He manifests His divinity. The root *vī*, according to *Śaṅkara*, denotes swift movement. That way, He moves fast and with majestic gait. He covered all the three worlds with His three steps when He assumed the form of *Vāmana*, the gigantic dwarf.

Anantaḥ is a very common name for the Lord. He is of the form of truth- *satyam*,knowledge-*jñānam* and the infinite *anantam*. The word *ananta* also denotes the name of a divine serpent.The Lord in His divine glories identifies Himself with this peculiar *nāga*. He says, I am *Ananta* among all the *nāgas* - *anantaścāsmi nāgānāṁ* [*Gītā* 10.29]. This *ananta-nāga* is a semi-divine being, having the face of a man and the tail of a serpent. This is supposed to be in *pātāla* and is worshipped as a serpent-god.

The third and the last name in this verse, *Dhanañjayaḥ* is also the name of *Arjuna*, the central figure of the five *Pāṇḍavas.* Lord *Kṛṣṇa* tells *Arjuna*, while narrating His divine glories that He is *Dhanañjaya* among the *Pāṇḍavas.* This is one of the best illustrations of the divine wit the Lord indulges in, in sportive moods. One can imagine the feeling of *Arjuna* when the Lord said this to him.That shows how intimate,affectionate and unassuming the Lord was to His closest friend who turned out to be His dearest devotee in the end. The word dhanañjaya *dhanañjayaḥ* —as confessed by *Arjuna* himself means one who gathers immense wealth in his victories and this is a tribute paid to *Arjuna* by his votaries and admirers. The 'wealth' *dhana* spoken of here may be spiritual wealth as well.

The Learning Of The Learned

Brahman, the Supreme Being, the soul and spirit of the Universe and the essence from which all created things are produced and into which they are absorbed is the central theme of the following verse conisting of ten names all starting with the word *brahman, (Brahmā).*

ब्रह्मण्यो ब्रह्मकृद्ब्रह्मा ब्रह्म ब्रह्मविवर्धनः ।
ब्रह्मविद्ब्राह्मणो ब्रह्मी ब्रह्मज्ञो ब्राह्मणप्रियः ॥

brahmaṇyo brahmakṛd-brahmā brahma brahma-vivardhanaḥ ।
brahmavid-brāhmaṇo brahmī brahmajño brāhmaṇa-priyaḥ ॥

The first among the series of these ten names which we may term *Brahmavallī* is *Brahmannṇyaḥ* which simply means relating to *Brahman.* It includes anything that promotes the concept of *Brahman* and its contributory factors. It is therefore necessary to understand the meaning and significance of *Brahman* before we proceed to make out what exactly is meant by *Brahmaṇyaḥ*. What is dear to *Brahman* is *Brahmaṇya. Brahman* is identified with truth, knowledge and the infinite in *Taittirīya Upaniṣad.* The single syllable and the primordial sound *Om* is also equated with *Brahman* in several *Upaniṣads* and also in *Gītā*. Thus the term *Brahma* means the Supreme Spirit and *Brahmaṇyaḥ* is anything that relates to the acquisition of sacred knowledge, holy and pious contemplation, meditation, study and recitation of Vedic and other sacred texts. The Lord has a warm affection and soft corner for those who are committed to this pursuit of absolute and unconditioned learning or wisdom which leads to salvation though self-realization.

The next name *Brahmakṛit* projects the Lord as the promoter of this learning by creating advanced forms of learning like *yoga, tapasyā* (penance) and *svādhyāya* (systematic and regular study of the scriptures). Any sacred word, sanctified statement *mahāvākya* or spiritual practice comes under this divine enterprise of the Lord who commissions realized souls to disseminate this wisdom among the common people.

As creator of the whole Universe, the Lord is extolled in the next name as *Brahmā* who is the first among the trinity-*Brahmā*, the creator, *Viṣṇu*, the preserver and *Maheśvara*, the destroyer. Here, *Viṣṇu*, the presiding deity of this sacred hymn, is glorified as *Brahmā*, the creator as *Viṣṇu* is the creator of the Creator, *Brahmā* who is said to have emerged from His lotus-like navel.

Brahma, as distinguished form *Brahmā* the Creator, is the next name in the verse. We have already discussed about this name and found that it stands for the Supreme Spirit, the subject matter of all scriptures including *Vedas Upaniṣads* and *Brahma Sūtras. Brahma* is the holiest of all that is holy, the most pious of all that is pious and the most auspicious of all that is auspicious. He is the landmark of all sacred learning. In the real sense, He is the Learning personified.

As promoter of this highest form of learning, He is extolled as *Brahmavivardhanaḥ*. He promotes learning while being the most learned of all the learners and the learned.

This knowledge of the highest order is what is usually acclaimed as *Brahmavidyā*, the awareness of the *Brahman*, all-pervading. Those who are endowed with this kbowledge are referred to as *Brahmavettā* or *Brahmavid*. As the Lord is the first among them and in fact the subject matter of all such knowledge, He is worshipped as *Brahmavid.*

One who is learned and well-versed in the science of spiritual awareness and the knowledge of *Brahman* is called a *Brāhmaṇaḥ*. The Lord is also eulogized here as *Brāhmaṇaḥ*.

Brahmī, the name that follows, tells us that the Lord is the prime possessor of all forms of *Brahman*. Whatever is meant by the term *Brahman*, that is present in the Lord,in His form and nature and in all that He thinks,utters and acts. Hence the name *Brahmī.*

As He knows all about *Brahman*, He is glorified as *Brahmajñaḥ* in the next name.

He is also fond of scholars who are masters in this branch of learning called *Brahmavidyā*. As these scholars are designated as Brahmins or *Brāhmaṇas*, the Lord as lover of these learned persons is called *Brāhmaṇapriyaḥ*. It should be noted that the Lord is fond of *Brāhmaṇas* because of their learning, not because of their birth in a caste called *Brāhmaṇa*. It is the learning that counts, not the birth.

The Greatness Of The Great

God is great because He appreciates whatever is great and promotes the greatness of His grand creation. He is the spirit behind the greatness of all great things and great personalities and the grandeur they have brought to the Universe He inhabits. He is great *mahān* because His universe is great. He is not different from the great grand universe He has created. The following verse glorifies this great grandeur in scintillating words :

महाक्रमो महाकर्मा महातेजा महोरगः ।
महाक्रतुर्महायज्वा महायज्ञो महाहविः ॥

mahākramo mahākarmā mahātejā mahoragaḥ ।
mahākratur-mahāyajvā mahā-yajño mahā-haviḥ ॥

The steps of the Lord are glorified in the first name *Mahākramaḥ*. He is gigantic in His strides as can be seen in His incarnation as *Vāmana*. The *Upaniṣads* also extol Him as *Urukramaḥ*, taking wide strides.

He is as wide in His strides as He is great in His actions and accomplishments. Hence, the name *Mahākarmā*, Great in deeds.

In radiance and transmission of light to the luminaries, He is again great-greater than all other sources of light. He is the Great Light that imparts radiance to the sun, the moon and other celestial bodies. As the

Lord Himself says, He is the radiance present in all radiant bodies *tejastejasvināmaham*. Hence, the name *Mahātejā*.

He is the most outstanding personality in all species of living beings. He is glorified as *Mahoragaḥ* as He is the greatest serpent in the Universe. He identified Himself with *Vāsuki* -*sarpānāmasmi Vāsukiḥ*.

He makes His presence felt in all religious rituals and sanctifies them. Hence, He is *Mahākratuḥ*. He identifies Himself not only with *kratu* (the ritual) but also with the person who performs the ritual. He Himself performs *yajñas*. Hence, He is *Mahāyajvā*.

Of all *yajñas*, *japa* (chanting the name of the Lord or any sacred syllable) is considered to be the most effective and the Lord says, 'I am the *japa-yajña* of all forms of *yajña*'. He is, therefore, worshipped as *yajña-puruṣa* or *yajña* itself. Any ritual becomes effective or great when there is the participation of the Lord in it. That is why He is eulogized as *Mahāyajānaḥ*.

Even the offering that is made in such ritualistic acts is identical with the Lord. He not only accepts these offerings but also identifies Himself with them. Hence, the name *Mahāhaviḥ* a great offering.

All the eight names in this verse which can be termed *mahāmālā* glorify the greatness of the Lord from all angles, in all objects and in all actions that the devotees perform. The devotion makes the deity closest to the devotee. This identification of the deity with the devotee makes any devotional act great. This is the greatness of the Lord.

Hymn The Lord And Have His Grace

The Lord is fond of hymns-particularly the Vedic hymns whose vibrations have a special appeal to Him. According to *Patanjali, Om* is the name of the Lord *tasya vācakaḥ praṇavaḥ*. The best way to invoke the grace and blessings of the Lord is, therefore, to sing His glory in the hymns invented by the sages and seers whose voice is the voice of vision. The following verse extols the glory of the Lord as a hymnist, hemn-lover and also as the hymn itself :

स्तव्यः स्तवप्रियः स्तोत्रं स्तुतिः स्तोता रणप्रियः ।
पूर्णः पूरयिता पुण्यः पुण्यकीर्तिरनामयः ॥

stavyaḥ stavapriyaḥ stotraṁ stutiḥ stotā raṇapriyaḥ /
pūrṇaḥ pūrayitā puṇyaḥ puṇya-kīrtir-anāmayaḥ //

The Lord is the most praiseworthy *stavya* celebrity in the Universe as the whole Universe belongs to Him and all praises, prayers, offerings and oblations ultimately reach Him. All the *Vedas*, as the *Kaṭha Upaniṣad* says, hymn the glory of His gracious position *sarve vedā yat padamāmananti.* He is the celebrity extolled, adored and worshipped in several forms and from several quarters. Hence, He is glorified as *Stavyaḥ*, the commendable celebrity deserving all hymnical invocations.

He is fond of such utterances as these are the code-words to establish a dialogue with the divinity latent in all beings and also in the be-ness *sattā* of the Supreme Being. He does not gain anything by our singing His glory. We are the beneficiaries and He is only keen to pass on that benefit to us in our own interest. Hence, He is *Stavapriyaḥ*, the lover of hymnical prayer and praise.

He is so absorbed in the hymnical process that He becomes one with the text of the hymn itself. When we offer any *stotram* (hymnical expression) to Him, He resides in every syllable of the hymn and sanctifies it. It is our feeling of His gracious presence within us in our thought and word that sanctifies the process. He is, therefore, adored as *stotram*, the hymn itself.

He is also a part of the actual act of offering this prayer to Him. He becomes *Stutiḥ*, the act of praising or praying for His mercy, grace and blessings.

The last name in this *stuti-mālā* (the garland of hymnical worship) is *Stotā,* the hymnist. He is the one who sings for us when we offer our hymnical salutations. The voice is ours, but the spirit behind the voice is He, His grace, His compassion and His divine touch.

These five names dealing with the hymnical offering to the Lord project Him as the celebrity to receive these offerings, the lover of such practices, the text itself of the hymns and finally the real one who does all this for us.

Then follows a very strange name *Raṇapriyaḥ*, a lover of battles. What a change from the love for music to the love for a battle. This is again a battle fought by Him for us. This is the battle of life fighting against the odds and adversities of day to day life which keep our body and mind away from the soul within. The Lord joins us in this battle as well with the same spirit of love, affection, compassion and consideration with which He sings for us in our prayers to Him. This means that He is always with us promoting our good thoughts, expressions and actions and also in granting the fruits of our good deeds. He is both *Stavapriyaḥ* and *Raṇapriyaḥ*. He sings for us and also fights for us.

Thus He makes us fully accomplished giving the entire credit to us. He is a perfect whole *Pūrṇaḥ* and hence imparts that wholeness to us as well *Pūrayitā*. Only the one who has perfection, complete-ness in Him can grant these qualities to others. It is this magnanimity of the Almighty that is glorified in the two names-- *Pūrṇaḥ* and *Pụrayitā*. He is the one who personifies all plentitude in Him and also the one who grants and imparts all this to His devotees who approach Him with wholesome and holy fellings.

Similarly, His Holiness makes His devotees too equally holy if not more. He shares all pious thoughts and deeds with His dearest devotees. He confers holiness on them and drives away all sins making them as wholesome as He is. This is explained in the two names *Puṇyaḥ* and *Puṇyakīrtiḥ*. He is holy, He makes His devotees holy and He spreads holiness throughout the whole universe making it holy and wholesome in all respects.

There can be no ailment-physical, mental, intellectual or spiritual in the world when such holy atmosphere pervades the whole environment. Holiness leads to healthy thinking, healthy living and healthy practices - secular and spiritual. All this is brought out in the concluding name of this verse *Anāmayaḥ,* free from all aliments, worries, obsessions and aggressions. His Holiness ensures a clean, clear, clam and composite human culture with no aberration if only we sing for Him for a minute.

Livable Is Lovable

God lives in all living beings in the form of love as Love is God and God is love. The *Bhakti-sūtras* of *Nārada* extol devotion or *Bhakti* as *parama-prema-rūpā* (the highest form of love). In order to cultivate love for God, we have to understand how lovable is the life gifted by God. This love for life is explained in the following verse:

मनोजवस्तीर्थकरो वसुरेता वसुप्रदः ।
वसुप्रदो वासुदेवो वसुर्वसुमना हविः ॥

manojavas-tīrthakaro vasuretā vasupradaḥ ।
vasuprado vāsudevo vasur-vasumanā haviḥ ॥

The Lord moves from one corner of the Universe to the other sometimes with the speed of the wind and usually with the speed of the mind. Even wind and mind cannot match His fleet as He is not only swift in His movement but He also makes His presence felt everywhere at the same time. Even mind can not,possibly, do this unless it comes close to the soul. That is why the Lord is extolled here as *Manojavaḥ* (as swift as the mind). This is only an approximation.

Wherever He is, that point of space gets purified and becomes a holy place-- a pilgrim centre which enables the pious souls to cross the ocean of *Saṁsāra*, the cycle of birth and death. He is therefore worshipped as *Tīrthakraḥ*. He converts any place into a sacred centre of spiritual learning, the moment the devotees think of Him in their heart of hearts. Once the mind is set to receive Him, the heart makes room for His stay and He is there with life full of love. All the spritual wisdom dawns in a second, the moment His looks start glancing at the four corners of the place He inhabits.

The whole universe came into existence because of His Power of spreading the Golden Germ of creation in all waters, the elixir of life. He is thus the originator of life in the globe which He converted into a golden egg, the prime source for *Brahmā*, the Creator. Being the seed of Creation, He is extolled as *Vasuretā*, the essence of existence.

Having created the universe, He made it livable and lovable too. He filled the whole habitation with all the means--material, emotional, and spiritual so that there is real meaning in life. He is, hence, eulogized as *Vasupradaḥ*, the bestower of wealth. He showers His choicest blessings on His devotees so that their life may become meaningful, fruitful, purposeful and beneficial for themselves and their fellow beings. One does not live and cannot or should not live all alone for himself. He lives for others too. This reciprocacity in life makes it lovable in the real sense. It is to project this aspect of the wealth of life that the *Sahasranāma* repeats the name *Vasupradaḥ* immediately. The repetition of names is a common phenomenon in this sacred hymn. But this is the only instance where a name is repeated without any gap. This is to hint at the special significance of the wealth of life *vasu* which the *Vasuretā* (the Golden Germ) grants to His children. He makes their life fruitful herein and also hereafter by granting perfect union with the universal soul in the end. The name repeated without any intervention also shows that what is here is there hereafter, as the *Kaṭha* says, *yadeveha tadamutra yadamutra tadanviha.* It is worth noting that there is a repetition in this Upanishadic saying too. What is here in this world is there in the other world too and what is there in the other world is there here as well.This makes the statement complete and confirmed.

Now comes the name *Vāsudevaḥ*, the Lord Himself, the son of *Vasudeva.* This needs no special explanation as the implication is so explicit that the Lord descends to the level of the devotees the moment they utter this name.

Then the deity is adored simply as *Vasuḥ* who dwells in all beings in the form of the basic 'Be-ness' *sattā*. He is there in you,with you and around you.You have only to make yourself fit to feel Him, sing His glory, grace and grandeur in instant ecsatasy. As *Mīrā* asks her Lord to stay on in her eyes forever so that the beauty of life and love becomes a standing asset for her. This is the type of feeling that makes the Lord your real wealth *vasuḥ*. All other wealth is momentary; but the wealth of life sanctified and saturated with pure love for God is immortal and immemorable.

The author of this hymn wants to remind us that the Lord has an omnipresent mind. Hence, the name *Vasumanāḥ*. His mind is everywhere. Where there is a mind, He is already there.

The last name in this verse *Haviḥ* summarizes the essence of not only this verse but the whole 'Universe' that is God. The name reveals to us the highest truth that God is not different from us. He is not only a recipient of our offerings, but He Himself is an offering, *Haviḥ*. He is not only the Ultimate, but also the means to reach the Ultimate.

The One Existent

The main thrust of the next verse in the sacred hymn, *Sahasranāma* is to define and deliberate upon *sat* which broadly means what really exists as different from what appears to exist but does not really exist which is called *asat*.The stress, however, is on the positive side. *Sat* is presented in various contexts in relation to the Supreme Spirit *Brahman*.

What really exists and is good, virtuous, noble, venerable and sagacious is normally said to be *sat* which figures in all the five names of the first line of the following verse:

सद्गतिः सत्कृतिः सत्ता सद्भूतिः सत्परायणः ।
शूरसेनो यदुश्रेष्ठः सन्निवासः सुयामुनः ॥

sad-gatiḥ sat-kṛtiḥ sattā sad-bhūtiḥ sat-parāyaṇaḥ ।
śūraseno yaduśreṣṭhaḥ san-nivāsaḥ suyāmunaḥ ॥

The real wisdom lies in identifying the difference between good and bad, right and wrong, real and unreal, temporal and eternal and then follow the path of what is good in general. This is what the first name *Sadgatiḥ*, the right path tells us. The word *sat* also stands for the Supreme Spirit in which case the name *Sadgatiḥ* will mean the path which leads the aspirant to the absolute reality, real existence or the Supreme Spirit. It is again the Lord who has to show us this path. Real wisdom never dawns without the divine grace. Hence, the Lord is adored as *Sadgatiḥ* in this name.He is the path, He is the guide and He is the goal. All these aspects are further illustrated in the names that follow.

The next name *Satkṛtiḥ* means right action. If you do what is right, you reach the right place. God will help you in reaching your right destination if you do what is right and avoid all that is wrong. What we do and what we learn in course of our life will decide our status and placement towards the end of our life. God keeps a watch over all this and tries to induce good coduct in us. But even God helps those who help themselves.

The third name is wholly based on the concept of *sat* (the existent). What really exists for all time to come without any limitations or modifications is what is named here *Sattā*, the One that is Existent. It knows no extinction. As *Bhagavān* says in *Gītā*, What is not real does not exist and what really exists never ceases to be. *nā sato vidyate bhāvo, nābhāvo vidyate sataḥ*. *Sat* is ever-existing and *a-sat* can not exist forever. Hence the name *Sattā* has been attributed to the Lord. He is the One ever-existent in the Universe because the Universe has no existence apart from Him.

Sad-bhūtiḥ, the next name, means 'the glory of the One Existent'. His glory is all-pervading. He exists in all living beings and also in the inanimate objects. *Bhagavān* Himself narrates His endless glories or forms of existence and concludes with a generalized statement that any being endowed with extraordinary glory, grace and grandeur is a part-manifestation of His own glory. Any manifestation of remarkable and superhuman power is therefore to be taken for the manifestation of the Lord Himself. The ultimate goal of all godly men charged with divine power by the grace of the Lord is the Lord Himself. Hence, the name *Satparāyaṇaḥ*, the abode of all true knowledge, excellence and eternal existence.

The next four names glorified in the second line of the stanza present illustrations to clarify the excellence of His Excellency. The first among these names *Śūrasenaḥ* refers to almost all incarnations of the Lord and particularly to *Rāma* and *Kṛṣṇa* who had to fight against the evil command. *Hanumān, Vibhīṣaṇā, Arjuna, Bhīma, Yudhiṣṭhira* and several others were commissioned by the Lord for these battles.

The second name *Yaduśreṣṭhaḥ* confirms the name of *Kṛṣṇa*, the Chief of the *Yadus*. As a spiritual statesman and martial chief, Lord *Kṛṣṇa* mobilized all resources and brought victory for *Paṇḍavas* who were entirely dependent on *dharma* (righteousness).

The next name *Sannivāsaḥ* literally means 'One who stays with the virtuous and meritorious'. All the well-meaning people devoted to the Lord and dedicated to the establishment and revival of the basic human values have the full support of the Lord who provides shelter to them. He is their abode, the eternal one for that matter.

The last name *Suyāmunaḥ* too refers to Lord *Kṛṣṇa* who was the most respected, distinguished and deified personality on the banks of the river *Yamunā*. He brought new life in the area distressed and disturbed by several evil forces. But the Lord converted it into a spiritual, devotional and celestial habitat for healthy and holy activities. Hence, He is glorified as *Suyāmunaḥ*. Really the river *Yamunā* was blessed by the Lord as almost all the celestial deities were present there to assist the Lord in some form or other. They became cowherds to share the bliss of the Lord's presence in the beautiful land chosen by Him for *Dharmasaṁsthāpana*, establishment of righteousness.

The Be-ness Of All Beings

God appears to be nowhere for a casual spectator with normal or blurred vision. But for a seer who can perceive the Supreme Spirit in all beings with an inner eye, He is everywhere. He is the real being in all beings seated in the innermost layers of consciousness. This fact is brought out in the ten names of the following verse :

भूतावासो वासुदेवः सर्वासुनिलयोऽनलः ।
दर्पहा दर्पदो दृप्तो दुर्धरोऽथापराजितः ॥

bhūtāvāso vāsudevaḥ sarvāsu-nilayo'nalaḥ |
darpahā darpado dṛpto durdharo'thāparājitaḥ ||

The abode of the Lord is the dwelling place for all beings and the Lord, in turn, resides in the heart of hearts of all beings. Hence, He is adored, in the first name of this verse, as *Bhūtāvāsaḥ*, the habitat of all beings.

But the Lord envelopes the whole universe with His divine *māyā* (illusion). Therefore, He is not visible for the common man with the normal vision. But He is the Resident Deity of the whole universe who accommodates all beings in His Eternal Abode and makes His presence felt by them within if only they try to energize their inner eye. Hence, the name *Vāsudevaḥ* about whom Lord *Kṛṣṇa* Himself says in *Gītā* [ch.

7-19], that it is only a great soul *mahātmā* who can realize and visualize the Omnipresent *Vāsudeva* in all beings in all places and at all times. *Vāsudeva* is all that you can see wherever you are and in whatever form you are.

The Lord, in the next name *Sarvāsunilayaḥ* is projected as the power-house of all life-energies which keep the beings alive. He controls the *prāṇa* of all living beings. He is the indestructible life-force behind all living beings the life-breath of the whole universe.

Another speciality about His control over the life-breath of all the living beings is that these energies stored in Him have no limit. They never get exhausted. The treasure-house of all these energies is always full. Addition or subtraction has absolutely no effect on the balance-sheet of this data processing. He is, therefore, worshipped as *Analaḥ*, the unlimited. Fire is also called *Analaḥ* as it is inexhaustible and unquenchable in thrust and thirst.

Ignorant people who are unaware of this process of life-giving feel proud of their own achievements like longevity, sound health, physical strength and handsome personality little knowing that these are all assets entrusted to the individual for safe custody and proper utilization. Hence, the Lord as *Analaḥ*, 'the living flame that never dying burns the ages through' takes care of the *Anilaḥ*, the wind or the life-breath of the body. He also helps the digestion of food that the body takes by assuming the role of *Vaiśvānara*, the fire of digestion.

God also knows how to keep the ignorant and the arrogant people who claim all the credit for this under constant control. He knows how to subdue them. Hence, the name *Darpahā*, the Repressor of Pride. He also knows how to give credit to those who attribute all this to the Almighty and entirely depend upom Him for this excellent and endearing treatment they receive in the hands of their Master. He gives them all credit and grants them the highest form of bliss as a reward for their awareness of the real self - the self within the self. Hence, He is glorified as *Darpadaḥ* -one who grants the due credit and a legitimate sense of pride to those who are sensible.

The Lord is personally happy about all this and He feels that He has done what He is supposed to do. He is, therefore, glorified as *Dṛptaḥ*, He feels exalted for the excellence His devotees have attained.

But one should always remember that it is not easy to visualize the Lord and realize His Might and Magnificience. Any amount of contemplation or meditation will not help in the proper and perfect comprehension of the Cosmic nature of the Lord. He alone should help us in understanding Him. Hence He is eulogized as *Durdharaḥ* difficult to grasp through contemplation or meditation without His grace.

Finally, He remains unconquered even By His devotees. He is therefore adored as *Aparājitaḥ*, never conquered by any. He is the conquerer in all His encounters. There is no counter where one can bargain with Him. He grants His grace as a gift unasked for. It comes from above like a shower of mercy.

The Unmanifest In Myriad Forms

The Lord has no form of His own and there is no single name by which He can be known. All names emanate from Him and all forms emerge from Him. The following verse presents the infinite forms of the formless in a fascinating series of names ending with the word *mūrtiḥ*, meaning form.

विश्वमूर्तिर्महामूर्तिर्दीप्तमूर्तिरमूर्तिमान् ।
अनेकमूर्तिरव्यक्तः शतमूर्तिः शताननः ॥

viśvamūrtir-mahāmūrtir-dīptamūrtir-amūrtimān /
aneka-mūrtir-avyaktaḥ śata-mūrtiḥ śatānanaḥ //

The first name *Viśvamūrtiḥ* projects the Lord as universal in form. He is, indeed, the Universe itself. As *Iśopaniṣad* states at the very beginning, the whole Universe is inhabited by the Lord.

He is then glorified as *Mahāmūrtiḥ*, great in His form. Any thing that is great has the blessings of the Lord. So He manifests Himself in various forms of greatness. He is adored as the greatest of all endowed with greatness. The word *mahat* itself means great. Wherever there is greatness, it is the manifestation of the Lord in some degree. Similarly intellectual brilliance and spiritual radiance are also partial manifestations of the glory of the Lord. Hence the name, *Dīptamūrtiḥ*. Even otherwise

He shines with a radiance that can brighten the whole universe. He imparts radiance to all.

But He does not have a form of His own. Hence, He is glorified as *Amūrtimān,* the formless. The formless has many forms. He can choose any form to suit His convenience depending upon His design and mission and incarnate Himself in that form. He can transform Himself into a fish, a tortoise, a boar, a dwarf, a prince, a charioteer and then come back to His original form - *Viśvamūrti* the Universe as His basic form. As the Universe does not have a uniform shape, He too is formless, *Amūrtimān.*

One advantage in not confining to a particular form is that He can assume several forms. Hence, He is glorified as *Anekamūrtiḥ.* Sometimes He manifests Himself in some form and at times He recedes to His original formless complexion that is the universe in general. This unmanifest form of the Lord is worshipped as *Avyaktaḥ.* The myriad forms of the Lord merge into one single form.

When He finds it necessary, He can assume hundred or hundreds of forms at the same time. Hence, He is called *Śatamūrtiḥ* having hundreds of forms and *Śatānanaḥ,* having hundreds of faces.

Rāma appeared to the army of *Rāvaṇa* in thousand forms. Wherever they saw, they found *Rāma* and *Rāma* alone with his bow and arms. After some time they were not able to see *Rāma,* but they saw only his arrows piercing into the force. This demonstrates the glory of the Lord who can multiply Himself in a moment and then withdraw all the forms in a second.

This is what makes us feel that the Lord is as pervading as the Universe because He is Universe itself.

The One, But Not One

The Supreme spirit that is really existent is one and only one. But it is realized, visualized and adored in various forms depending upon the status of the devotee or the aspirant. The various stages of this spiritual quest to identify the Supreme Spirit are presented in the following verse in short and significant names of the Lord :

एको नैकः सवः कः किं यत्तत्पदमनुत्तमम् ।
लोकबन्धुर्लोकनाथो माधवो भक्तवत्सलः ॥

eko naikaḥ savaḥ kaḥ kiṁ yat-tat-padam-anuttamam ।
loka-bandhur-loka-nātho mādhavo bhakta-vatsalaḥ ॥

The first two names *Ekaḥ* and *Naikaḥ,* at the outset, appear to be contradicting. The first name depicts the Lord as 'One' and the second name immediately presents Him as 'Not One'. The conclusion is that He is One, but not one, but this is the real truth. There is no contradiction in it if properly understood. The fact is that *Paramātman,* the Supreme Self or the Universal Self is One who is beyond cause and effect and is eternal, pure, absolute consciousness. He is Omnipresent, Omnipotent and Omniscient. The first name refers to this One and the only one existent. The second name *Naikaḥ* (not one) refers to the individual souls, all the living beings in the universe who are potentially divine and derive their radiance and life-energy from the Supreme Self. The scriptures confirm this position by declaring that the eternal existent *sat* is one *ekaṁ sat*. But this is qualified by the divine will about which the same scriptures state that the Supreme Self was one, but He willed to multiply Himself *ekohaṁ bahuśyāma*. This answers the query about the contradiction in the two terms glorifying the same entity. In simple language, this means that *Paramātman* is one but His manifestation in the form of *Jīvātmās* is manifold. It is not one. It can be many or any form He chooses to assume for the fullness of the Universe and a wholesome living in His Cosmic order.

The next name *Savaḥ*, meaning extraction of *soma* juice for offering in a religious sacrifice *yajña* stands for the whole creation as a *yajña*. Besides sacrificial offering, the word *savaḥ* has several other meanings derived from its root *sū* to bring forth, produce, yield. If the eternal existence that excels all other forms of existence in the world is *Brahman*, the Supreme Spirit, the process through which this One existent multiplies is called *yajña* (religious sacrifice). *Gītā* presents this cyclic system of sacrifice that is going on in the Universe automatically starting from *brahman* and leading to the production of food *annam* and concludes by saying that the all-pervading, indestructible Supreme Spirit *Brahman* is always present in *yajña--nityaṁ yajñe pratiṣṭhitaṁ*. Thus the name *Savaḥ* explains how the 'one' becomes 'many' and identifies Himself with 'all' in general, and 'any' in particular.

Now arise many questions 'who', 'what', 'which', and 'wherefrom' followed by a positive reply that 'That which' is the source of all this is the One ultimate goal of all the process and the processors or sponsorers involved in the process. These queries and conclusions are expressed in five codified words *kaḥ*-who, *kiṁ*-what, *yat*-wherefrom, *tat* - that and *Padam-anuttamam*, the Absolute goal of all. These grammatical and somewhat mystic expressions, when decodified into common mode of communication will mean : who is the root-cause of all this *yājñik* process of multiplication; what is the purpose and mission; 'Where from' all this current of continuous cycle of emergence, evolution and dissolution is flowing incessantly and what is That One all-pervading and everlasting Superhuman and Supreme Spirit, the Absolute goal of life.

The preceptor of the sacred hymn *Śrī Viṣṇu Sahasranāma* has thus compressed the entire philosophy of life into a single line consisting of sixteen syllables and eight names of the Lord glorifying His divine hand in the dynamic cosmology we witness. These eight names *Ekaḥ, Naikaḥ, Savaḥ, Kaḥ, Kiṁ, Yat, Tat* and *Padam-anuttamam* form the *aṣṭādhyāyī* of the Absolute, if we may say so. Every name in this compendium is a chapter by itself opening up new vistas of wisdom for those who have a mind to think, heart to feel and eyes to have an insight into the 'abstract' of the 'absolute' knowledge.

The next line presents four names of the Lord in a refreshing tone. The first among them is *Lokabandhuḥ*. The Lord is the friend, well-wisher, patron and protector of all beings who look for Him in times of need. All the needs will be looked after by him if we pay heed to His unaccountable attachment and involvement in the universal peace, harmony and material prosperity.

He is also glorified as *Lokanāthaḥ*, the Lord of the Universe. He rules over the land He created to provide shelter and solace for all beings. He leads us on the right path to the right goal unless we mismanage and misguide ourselves. He is the friend in need *bandhu* and also the guide *nātha* in matters of good conduct and peaceful and harmonious co-existence.

He is very sweet in temperament, attitude and affection that touches the heart of all His subjects *prajā*. Hence, He is named *Mādhavaḥ*, sweet in all respects. He incarned Himself in the scan of *yādavas* led by a person called *Madhu*. That also accounts for His acclamation as *Mādhava*.

Finally, He is worshipped as *Bhaktavatsalaḥ*. He treats His devotees as His own children and looks after them with parental affection. There is no need for His devotees to ask Him for something. The mere thought will do. He will rush to the spot and takes care of them as He did in case of *Prahlāda, Dhruva, Gajendra, Draupadī* and *Kuntī*. Mother *Kuntī*, in fact, welcomes all troubles and turmoils in life so that she can have an opportunity to see the sweet-smiling face of the fascinating figure *Kṛṣṇa*.

Saint *Tyāgarāja* also tells his deity *Rāma* that it is for him to come and see his children from time to time and look after them just like a dutiful mother with an innate bond of maternal love and care for her children.

This is the affection which the Lord *Bhaktavatsala* has in His heart for all living beings in the world and particularly for His devotees. Devotion is an integrating force which unites the deity with His devotees.

All Gold For The Golden God

In the beginning, there was water and water alone which was partially converted into a golden Egg to habilitate *Brahmā*, the Creator. *Viṣṇu* being the Self of this *Hiraṇyagarbha* is also adored as the *Hiraṇmayaḥ puruṣaḥ*, the Golden Self. What exactly is this 'gold' attributed to the Lord is explained in the following names :

सुवर्णवर्णो हेमाङ्गो वराङ्गश्चन्दनाङ्गदी।
वीरहा विषमः शून्यो घृताशीरचलश्चलः ॥

suvarṇa-varṇo hemāṅgo varāṅgaś-candanāṅgadī ।
vīrahā viṣamaḥ śūnyo ghṛtāśīr-acalaś-calaḥ ॥

The first name *Suvarṇavarṇaḥ* extols the beauty of the Lord's complexion which shines like gold *suvarṇa*. Strictly speaking, the word *suvarṇa* need not necessarily mean gold. It generally means beautiful, brilliant, glorious, celebrated, but is often used in the sense of 'golden'. Here the Lord is called *Suvarṇavarṇaḥ* as His complexion is the most auspicious and it transmits radiation of blissful blessings to the devotees. In His incarnations as *Rāma* and *Kṛṣṇa*, He is not depicted as of 'golden' colour in particular. He was, nevertheless, admired of a complexion which enchants not only women, but also men *puṁsāṁ mohana rūpāya, puṇyaślokāya maṅgalaṁ*.

The word *varṇa* also means any letter of the alphabet *varṇamālā*. The Lord is worshipped with sacred hymns containing the choicest syllables, words and phrases. In this sense also, the name *Suvarṇa varṇaḥ* is a fitting attribute to the Lord. The root meaning of the word *varṇa* also suggests 'excellence' of a person. The best way to adore, please and worship the Lord is through the chiocest words and best actions.

Having projected the complexion of the Lord as golden or the most auspicious, the preceptor *Bhīṣma* says that He is *Hemāṅgaḥ*. Here the reference is direct. The word *heman* definitely means gold. The Lord is called *Hemāṅgaḥ* as His limbs shine like gold. All is gold in the body of the golden God as it was He who created the Golden Egg for the Creator.

The third name also speaks of the excellent and resplendent complexion of the golden deity and projects Him as *Varāṅgaḥ* shining with pleasing limbs.

The next name *Candanāṅgadī* admires the artistic armlets of the Lord transmitting fascinating fragrance like the sandal paste. In fact, the fragrance that is radiated is not due to the sandal but the divine radiance of the Lord. Wherever He is with His consort Goddess *Lakṣmī*, there is all-pervading fragrance that supports and sustains the whole creation *sugandhiṁ puṣṭivardhanam*.

He is as kind and considerate to the devotees as harsh and harmful to the evil forces who are violent and valiant. The Lord knows how to deal with these valiant foes. He finishes them in a minute without causing any damage to the other sections of population. That is why He is extolled as *Vīrahā* who just eliminates them from the path of righteousness to clear the way for the well-meaning and peace-loving pious souls. This is what He did in all His incarnations. Indian mythology is full of such stories which sing the glory of the Lord as the savior of the saints and devotees.

In this respect there is no match for the Lord. He is far above the level of others in destroying the evil and supporting the good. Even in other aspects like love, compassion, nobility and magnanimity, He transcends all norms and hence hymned as *Viṣamaḥ* unequalled.

The preceptor *Bhīṣma* suddenly springs a surprise on the *Pāṇḍavas* who were listening to the holy names of the Lord with rapt attention by glorifying the lord as *Śunyaḥ* which means nil, nothing or void. It was only a little while age that the *Ācārya* adored Him as *Pūrṇaḥ* full-fledged and now he says He is a virtuous void. What the *Ācārya* means is that it hardly makes any difference for the Lord whether He is all in all or none at all, whether He is showered with all flowering attributes or condemnd with a casual remark saying 'null and void'. He remains the same unmindful of and untouched by praise or blame. Hence He is both *Pūrṇa* and *Śūnya*. Both the points interact in Him and He treats them both with equal respect and reverence.

The Lord has all His blessings for His beloved and devoted and has nothing to expect from anyone. All His aspirations are for the betterment and welfare of the good. He is non-aspirant, but fulfils the aspirations of His aspirants to their utmost satisfaction. Hence, He is hymned as *Ghṛtāśīḥ*. He bestows His blessings like the fresh *ghī* from the sacred vessel. *Ghī* is the last stage of extraction of the milk passing curd, butter-milk and butter - the essence of the most cherished and nourishing liquid-food for all living beings. If other deties grant their boons like milk, the Supreme Deity hands over healthy and tasty *ghī* as His gift.

The last two names *Acalaḥ* and *Calaḥ* are antonyms - one contradicting the other. The meaning of the two names respectively is 'immutable' *acalaḥ* and 'mutable' *calaḥ*. The Lord is both. in *Īśopaniṣad*, the Supreme Soul is said to be 'movable' and also 'immovable' *tadejati, tannaijati.* He moves and also does not move because He need not move to move matters. The wind is there to carry out His orders. The light is there to illumine the space at His command. The Sun is there to shower the rain. The Moon is there to delight the nights and nourish the crops. Therefore it hardly matters whether He is variable or constant, mutable or immutable, dynamic or static. He transcends all these stages and acts as the prime-mover of all movements and moments that motivate the fast moving objects.

Adored By All But Himself

One who never thinks high of himself, but accords due recognition and credit to those who have done any good work at any time is always held in great esteem by all. Such people are very rare. It is this unique feature of the Lord which is glorified in the following verse :

अमानी मानदो मान्यो लोकस्वामी त्रिलोकधृक् ॥
सुमेधा मेधजो धन्यः सत्यमेधा धराधरः ॥

amānī mānado mānyo loka-svāmī triloka-dhṛk ।
sumedhā medhajo dhanyaḥ satya-medhā dharādharaḥ ॥

The most ideal and unassuming nature mentioned above is attributed to the Lord Himself who is adored by all but Himself. He never thinks that He is great and transmits His own greatness to others. He is therefore eulogized as *Amānī* who is never conscious of His greatness but is *Mānadaḥ* who gives due respect and credit to others. Hence, He is adored by all as *Mānyaḥ* revered, respected, honoured and admired for this rare quality.

This is the secret behind His success as the Lord of the Universe. He is therefore worshipped as *lokasvāmī*. He is the Lord of the fourteen worlds - the seven above and the seven below. He controls all this with His simple, unassuming and hence appealing and awe-inspiring temperament.

He is the Lord, not of one *loka* but three different *lokas* all supported and sustained by Him. Hence, He is hymned as *Trilokadhṛk*.

Naturally He has the sweet temperament and bright intellect to manage this vast area under His control. He is, therefore, adored as *Sumedhā* sharp, sweet and sophisticated mental make up to organize all this and ensure global welfare, peace and prosperity.

The word *medhaḥ* actually means a religious sacrifice like *aśvamedhaḥ* from which the word *medhas* or *medhā* is derived. This is the word we have in the current name *Sumedhā*. The word *medha* stands for retentive faculty, sharp memory. The Lord has this faculty automatically built up in His universal form. This is the result of the continuous *yajña* (religious sacrifice) that goes on every day and every moment in every part of the globe. The Lord derives this strength and power to conduct the affairs of all the worlds through this sacrificial ritual performed by His devotees and learned ritualists. He is, therefore, hymned as *Medhajaḥ*, the outcome of the religious sacrifice. He is often presented as a product of *yajña*, born in the sacrifice. *Rāma* and His three brothers were born as a result of the *putrakāmeṣṭi* (a sacrifice performed for getting children). *Draupadī* is called *Yājñasenī*, her patronymic name. *Sītā* was the offspring of the mother earth. *Hanumān* is supposed to be *Pavana sambhava*, the offspring of the Wind god.

Blessed are these great personalities who received the blessings from the Lord of the Universe who is adored as *Dhanyaḥ*, a celebrity who blesses all who have the required merit in them. The word *dhanyaḥ* which is used as the name of the Lord here has multiple meanings. Blessed, celebrated, auspicious, accomplished, fortunate, wealthy and many more epithets are associated with this word and they all fit into this word as the distinguished name of the Lord. In fact the Lord alone is *Dhanya* in the real sense while all others are just *dhanyaṁ-mānya* supposed to be '*dhanya*'. They consider themselves to be blessed and accomplished while the Lord does not even feel that He is blessed and takes pleasure in blessing others.

The next name *Satyamedhā* takes us back to the intellectual plane once again. The Lord was already praised as *Sumedhā*. Here He is projected as *Satyamedhā* -one with real, eternal and unfailing intelligence.

The last name *Dharādharaḥ* projects the Lord as the supporter of the entire land the never ending and ever enduring base for all beings - a model for endurance, forbearance and stability.

The Bearer Of Radiance

Physical strength or vigour *ojas*, intellectual brilliance *tejas* and spiritual radiance *dyutiḥ* are the gifts of God who grants these assets to the aspirants according to their background. He is the custodian of these assets. This point was explained in His glorious name *Ojastejo dyutidharaḥ* earlier (name.275). Here these qualities are discussed with special reference to the intellectual brilliance *tejas* and spiritual radiance *dyutiḥ* in the following verse:

तेजोवृषो द्युतिधरः सर्वशस्त्रभृतां वरः ।
प्रग्रहो निग्रहो व्यग्रो नैकशृङ्गो गदाग्रजः ॥

tejo-vṛṣo dyuti-dharaḥ sarva-śastra-bhṛtāṁ varaḥ ।
pragraho nigraho vyagro naikaśṛṅgo gadāgrajaḥ ॥

Being the reservoir of all intellectual brilliance *tejas,* the Lord showers it on the deserving like showers of rain. The rain comes on its own. Similarly the Lord's grace also showers such gifts unasked as pleasant surprise. Hence, He is hymned as *Tejovṛṣaḥ*. Lord *Kṛṣṇa* showered all His wisdom on *Arjuna* to make him fit for the battle right in front so that the righteousness *dharma* may get well-established uprooting the abuse of gentleness.

In physical plane also, the Lord directs the celestial luminaries to shower such grace of intellectual brilliance on the aspirants of global welfare. The Sun shines and provides light and heat for the benefit of one and all. He makes no distinction between the poor and the rich. Perhaps the poor enjoy His grace and mercy more than the rich.

The next name *Dyutidharaḥ* focusses our attention on the spiritual radiance which is the highest form of worldly splendour which the Lord keeps in reserve so that it may be made available to those who attain the proper stage to receive it. He is the treasure-house of such radiance. All the celestial deities draw this radiance from the Lord. Hence the name, *Dyutidharaḥ*.

The pole-star, also known as *Dhruva* is also the reservoir of such radiance through which the main luminary controls all other luminaries.

Having explained the intellectual and spiritual aspects of the Cosmic energy, the preceptor of the hymn touches upon its physical aspect also. In the third name, he quotes *Rāma* as the expert unexcelled in the art of handling all the mystic missiles. He names the Lord in this context as *Sarvaśastra-bhṛtāmvaraḥ*, the best of those who wield weapons. *Bhagavān* Himself says in His *Gītā*, 'I am *Rāma* among those who wield weapons'. But this valour of *Rāma* is not merely physical. It is supported and substantiated by the intellectual skill and spititual background. The mystic missiles *Rāma* received from the sage *Viśvāmitra* came handy in the battle which the prince of *Ayodhyā* had to fight in *Laṅkā*.

He had three qualities which stood by Him while using these missiles. He had a thorough grasp and shrewd handling which is described here as *Pragrahaḥ* as an attribute of the Lord.The second asset He had was *Nigrahaḥ* full restraint or control in the application of these skills. He had both theoretical and practical expertise in the field. He had all round vision which projects Him as *Vyagraḥ* or *Avyagraḥ*. His concern for the composite outlook and ensured outcome makes Him *Vyagraḥ* deeply concerned and His all-compassing vision presents Him as *Avyagraḥ*, unperturbed.

Coming back to the intellectual brilliance, the hymn chooses to adore the Lord as *Naikaśṛṅgaḥ* endowed with more than one horn. The Vedic seers visualised a symbolic bull with four horns - *catvāri śṛṇgaḥ*, three feet - *trayo asya pādāḥ*, two heads - *dve śirṣe*, seven hands - *sapta hastāsou* and bound by three ropes in three directions - *tridhā baddhaḥ*. This is the spiritual wisdom symbolized in the form of a bull which, again, stands for *dharma*, the eternal law of nature.

The last name in the verse *Gadāgrajaḥ* also deals with the efficacy of Vedic vibrations and the word power which promote the three basic faculties of physical strength, intellectual brilliance and spiritual radiance *ojas, tejas and dyuti*. The word *gadā* though literally means a weapon, here it refers to the Vedic hymn or a sacred utterance of a seer gifted with the voice of vision which leads the soul chanting such *mantras* or sacred syllables to the highest state of spiritual awareness. It is in this sense that the Lord is hymned here as *Gadāgrajaḥ*. In *Saṁskṛt* the word *nigadati* is used in the sense of (He or She) 'says'. Here, the prefix *ni* is dropped leaving the word *gada* to convey the sense of word-power which is perhaps more powerful than sword-power if properly cultivated and handled.

Four In One

The following verse presents the fourfold manifestation of the divinity of the Lord and concludes with a synthetic note that all the manifestations ultimately merge into one Supreme Spirit from which these forms have emerged. The verse sounds very musical and the melody appeals not only to the ears, but also to the heart, mind and soul.

चतुर्मूर्तिश्चतुर्बाहुश्चतुर्व्यूहश्चतुर्गतिः ।
चतुरात्मा चतुर्भावश्चतुर्वेदविदेकपात् ।।

catur-mūrtiś-catur-bāhuś-catur-vyūhaś-catur-gatiḥ I
catur-ātmā catur-bhāvaś-catur-vedavid-ekapāt II

The Lord manifests Himself in four forms - *mūrtis* - *Virāṭ* (the first progency of *Brahman*), *Sūtrātman* (the Soul with the nature of a string or thread), *Avyākṛta* (an elementary substance from which all things were created, considered identical with *Brahma*-prime germ of nature *pradhānaḥ* in *Sāṁkhya* philosophy) and finally *Turīya* (the fourth stage of the soul in which it becomes one with *Brahman* or Supreme Spirit). He also assumes four colours in the four forms: white - *sita*, red - *rakta*, yellow - *pīta* and dark blue - *kṛṣṇa*. Hence, the Lord is worshipped as *Caturmūrtiḥ*, having four forms of manifestation in four different shades.

The most popular form of the Lord (particularly as *Vāsudeva*) is of four arms. He is, therefore, hymned as *Caturbāhuḥ*, of four arms with the conch *Śaṅkha*, the wheel *Sudarśana-cakra*, the club *Gadā* and the lotus *Padma* in His hands. Saint Kabir, not satisfied with these four arms, imagines the Lord with infinite arms *jāke bhujā anantā*. *Arjuna*, puzzled with the Cosmic form of the Lord, requests Him to appear before him with four arms. The four-armed form of the Lord *Caturbhuja* is, therefore, the most popular one among the devotees who worship Him as *Viṣṇu* or *Vāsudeva*.

There are three more forms or manifestations of the Lord besides this *Vāsudeva* form. The othere three are *Saṅkarṣaṇa, Pradyumna* and *Aniruddha*. These four forms are also known as *Vyūhas* (manifestations) of the Lord. There is yet another set of four manifestations of the Lord which are also called *Vyūhas*. These are *Śarīra-puruṣaḥ*, the *puruṣa* in the body, *Chandaḥ-puruṣaḥ*, the *puruṣa* in the *Chandas* (the sacred text of the Vedic hymns or free will), *Veda-puruṣaḥ* the *puruṣa* in the *Vedas* and *Mahā-puruṣaḥ*, the *puruṣa* the Great. This is based on *Aitereya Āraṇyaka*. There can be many more ways of analysing the manifestations of the Lord. The figure four seems to be common in all these modes of presenting the manifestations. That is why the Lord is hymned as *Caturvyūhaḥ*, having four types of manifestations.

In the next name *Caturgatiḥ*, the four paths to reach the Lord are indicated. According to *Śaṅkara Bhagavatpāda*, these are the four *Āśramas - Brahmacarya, Gārhasthya, Vānaprastha* and *Sannyāsa*. These are the four stages (not exactly paths) of reaching the ultimate goal of life. The four paths indicated here can be the four principal objects of human life called *puruṣārthas*.These are *dharma* (righteousness), *artha* (wealth), *kāma* (desire) and *mokṣa* (salvation).

Caturātmā, the next name in the series of fourfold manifestations of the Lord, clearly refers to the *Māṇḍūkya Upaniṣad* where four phases of *ātman* are explained in detail. The first is *Vaiśvānaraḥ* the state of awakening, the next is *Taijas,* the state of sleeping and dreaming, the third is *Prājña* the state of sound sleep and finally the *Turīya* the fourth one where the *ātman* is in a state of absolute bliss. The *Upaniṣad* while describing this fourfold (four-footed, to be more accurate) *ātman* says that this *ātman* is *Brahman- ayaṁ ātmā brahma* and the self same *ātman* is of four foot-steps *soyamātmā catuṣpāt.* All the four states or stages through which the soul passes are the manifestations of the Lord. Hence the name *Caturātmā.*

The next name is *Caturbhāvaḥ*, the source of the four. As the consciousness in this final state is crystal clear, free from all desires and is one with the Supreme Soul for the time being, all the inner organs *antaḥkaraṇas*, the mind *manas*, the intellect *buddhi*, ego *ahaṅkāra*, and the mindstuff *citta* form the four phases or manifestations of the soul.

The last name in the series is *Caturvedavit*, the knower of the four *Vedas* or the one knowable through the perfect knowledge of all the four *Vedaa.* The Lord Himself is *Veda* (Vedic text), *Vedavit* (the scholar of Vedic wisdom), and *Vedavedya* (the one who can be comprehended by reading and chanting the Vedic hymns).

Having extolled the glories of the Lord and His fourfold manifestation in various forms, the verse concludes with a highly significant name *Ekapāt*, One-footed. Here all the four phases, modes, forms or manifestations merge into One, the One who manifests Himself in these forms. The *Puruṣa Sūkta* tells us that this whole universe is but one-fourth of the infinite glory of the Lord *pādosya viśvā bhūtāni.* The three-fourth is beyond our comprehension . In *Gītā*, *Bhagavān* also says, I stand holding the entire universe by a fraction of my yogic power [*Gītā* Ch. 10-42].Time and Space too are superficially four-fold but virtually are only single unit controlled by the Lord.

Get The Best And Forget The Rest

When the blissful presence of the Supreme spirit *paramātman* is felt, the rest of it seems to be insignificant. When the *ātman* realizes the *paramātmā* within, everything seems to have been achieved because there is nothing else to be achieved. This is explained in the following verse which almost strikes a valedictory note to the sacred hymn, *Sahasranāma*.

समावर्तोऽनिवृत्तात्मा दुर्जयो दुरतिक्रमः ।
दुर्लभो दुर्गमो दुर्गो दुरावासो दुरारिहा ॥

samāvarto'nivṛttātmā durjayo duratikramaḥ ।
durlabho durgamo durgo durāvāso durāriha ॥

The word *Samāvartaḥ*, the first name of the Lord in the present verse, means the return of a pupil to his home after completing a course of religious studies and holy scriptures under a Vedic scholar. The pupil returns home with the blessings of his *Guru* coupled with some specific instructions to him which will serve as guidelines for the future conduct and continuation of the learning process. This ceremony is called *Samavartana* (Valedictory function) which also marks the successful completion of *brahmacarya*, the first *āśrama* (stage) in life, the foundation for material prosperity and spiritual realization. *Satyaṁvada* (speak truth), *Dharmaṁcara* (do the right thing and be righteous) and

Svādhyāyān mā pramada (do not neglect furtherance of your studies and daily routine to keep abreast of advancement in Vedic texts) are some of the guidelines the pupil receives from his preceptor on such occasion.

Here the Lord is hymned as *Samāvartaḥ* meaning thereby that perfection in the field of spiritual knowledge enables the scholar to attain the highest status of *Brahmavid* (one who knows *Brahman*). Once this is acheived, the aspirant receives the blessings of the Lord and there is a summing up of scholarship acquired by him.

The word *samāvartaḥ* also means 'the turner of the wheel of worldly life'. This interpretation also supports the stand explained above. Formal and successful completion of programmed learning in the spiritual field is a significant stage in life which is very appropriately termed as *Samāvartaḥ*. As such an event can happen in life only with the grace of God. He too is remembered by the same term.

The next name *Nivṛttātmā* tells us that once the stage of spiritual awareness is reached, the scholar withdraws himself from the material, temporal and relatively less significant positions and possessions in life. This attitude also develops by divine grace. Hence, the name *Nivṛttātmā* who turns away from the worldly attractions and temptations. Some people read this name as *Anivṛttātmā* which means 'who never turns away'. In this sense the meaning will be that the scholar who has cultivated a taste for spiritual attainments will never turn away from the field. In both ways, the substance of both the names *Samāvartaḥ* and *A-nivṛttātmā* is that once a wise person gets into the most auspicious and the best line of living and thinking, he forgets and ignores the rest.

The next name *Durjayaḥ* glorifies the Lord as the unconquerable. He is the Supreme and Matchless. This is followed by another attribute *Duratikramaḥ* which means 'untransgressable'. It is extremely defficult to approach and reach anywhere near this Supreme Spirit. He is, therefore, adored as *Durlabhaḥ*, not easily accessible. Devotion or *Bhakti* is the only means to achieve His grace. The Lord Himself says in *Gītā* that He can not be realized, visualized or acquainted with by any other means except undivided devotion [*Gītā* Ch. 11-48].

He is *Durgamaḥ* difficult to reach, realize and retain in contemplation and deep meditation. He is as inaccessible and unapproachable as a strong fort. He is, therefore, adored as *Durgaḥ*, a fort.

Even after reaching Him and realizing Him, it is difficult to retain Him in our hearts during meditation. The wavering mind wanders here and there and the object of meditation gets lost-slipping from the grip every second. It needs a strong determination - stronger than the fort in which He is stationed - to retain Him in our hearts. We should be able to have His singular form in our minds, His feelings in our heart, His vision in our eyes, His voice in our ears, His gestures in our hands, His movements in our feet and His blissful beats in our nerves to retain His image and grace constantly with us, in us and around us without a break. This is what is conveyed in the name *Durāvāsaḥ* difficult to retain Him even for the great saints, seers and scholars. Perhaps, it may be easier for the single-minded devotees to reach Him, catch Him and retain Him with love, regard and respect - all compressed into a composite consciousness called devotion.

Once we have cultivated this near-ness and dear-ness to Him, He will keep all evil forces, temptations and distractions away from us. Hence, He is extolled as *Durāriha*, one who destroys the wicked and looks after our safety, security, and of course the ultimate goal of life, the one-ness with Him.

Beauty And Duty Combined

The concept of beauty as the manifestation of divinity is what makes the Lord most beautiful in the Universe. He presents a model for beauty that is auspicious, awe-inspiring and duty-oriented. This is what is explained in the following names of the Lord :

शुभाङ्गो लोकसारङ्गः सुतन्तुस्तन्तुवर्धनः ।
इन्द्रकर्मा महाकर्मा कृतकर्मा कृतागमः ॥

śubhāṅgo loka-sāraṅgaḥ sutantus-tantu-vardhanaḥ |
indra-karmā mahā-karmā kṛta-karmā kṛtāgamaḥ ||

The Lord is the most auspicious, august and gracious even in His physical formation and assemblage of limbs. The real beauty promotes pious feelings in the hearts of the spectators. It pleases the eyes, delights the heart and enlightens the soul. Hence, the Lord having this purest form of beauty radiant in all His limbs is eulogized as *Śubhāṅgaḥ* with auspicious limbs. Whatever is good, shining, asupicious, handsome and wholesome comes under the category *śubha* and resultant effect of this three dimensional (physical, intellectual and spiritual) beauty is *Śobhanam* transmitting this inspiring radiance to one and all in the universe. The smile in the face of a fragrant flower, the seven colurs in the rain-bow that conveys the message of the Master of all celestial deities *devendra*, the pleasant, placid and perennial flow of the running rivers, the jubilant waves of the meditative ocean, the golden rays of the rising sun and the silver shining of the saintly moon are all illustrious monuments of the eternal beauty that the Lord presents every moment for the delight of the dynamic life. This is the universal beauty which the Lord of the Universe manifests in His majestic figure as *Śubhāṅgaḥ*.

The fact behind the universality of this beauty is brought out in the next name *Lokasāraṅgaḥ,* One who collects the essence of the Universe like a bee and makes this essence His instrument in promoting decency, dignity and devotion to duty among all living beings. Even the physical beauty of the Lord is not exclusively His own. It is the essence of the beauty of the whole universe that collects itself in His complexion as He belongs to the universe and the universe belongs to Him.

He has nothing exclusive for Himself. The whole Universe is an expanded form of His personality. He is *Virāṭa* (the universal figure), a consummation of all the best the Universe has acquired or achieved with His blessings and grace. He is therefore glorified in the next name as *Sutantuḥ* having beautiful well-knit and auspicious expansion of His own Self in the whole of His creation. He has no existence or excellence apart from His universe. The whole beauty, grandeur and workmanship of the whole mass of humanity belongs to Him and He is proud of it. He is the key to this string of happiness. The word *tantu* actually means 'thread'. The thread-cermomy of Lord *Kṛṣṇa* celebrated on the full-moon day of the month of *Śrāvaṇa which* is called *tantuparva* (the festival of the sacred thread - *yajñopavītam*) and the tradition is still continued. There is a connecting link between the Supreme Spirit *Brahman* and His whole creation. This is what is implied in the sacred name *Sutantuḥ*. The prefix *su* indicates that this is a very auspicious link which promotes universality in all living beings.

There is no limit or terminal point for this link. It goes on expanding under the sponsorship of the Lord. Hence, He is adored as *Tantuvardhanaḥ*, the promoter and enhancer of the life-link existing in and sustaining the Universe.

Having established a beautiful link between all living beings, the Lord acts as a driving and dynamic force behind all activities of the inhabitants. In order to present an example, He Himself is always engaged in constructive work and makes others also work with a sense of duty, dedication and pride. This is what projects the Lord as *Indrakarmā*. He works like *Indra*, the chief of all celestial beings promoting general good, welfare and prosperity of the universe He has created.

What the Lord does in promoting work-culture in the world is not just mechanical or manual, but monumental. He created the Universe, then the five elements - earth, water, fire, air and ether and all the equipment - material, mental and metaphysical - to maintain peace and harmony leading to the attainment of the Absolute Bliss, the ultimate goal of life. He is, therefore, hymned as *Mahākarmā*, the Master-mind behind all major and monumental works and achievements in the world.

Having done the needful to make His universe a blissful abode for all blessed souls, the Lord feels a sigh of relief and delight that what had to be done has been well-done *sukṛtam*. Hence, He is glorified as *Kṛtakarmā*, one with a sense of fulfilment of the action He has contemplated. *Bhagavān* says in *Gītā* [Ch. 3-22] 'There is nothing for me to do in all the three worlds nor is there anything worth attaining unattained by Me; yet I engage myself in work'. This is the work - culture which the Lord promotes as *Kṛtakarmā* preaching the merit of action *karma* by example and not by precept.

The last name *Kṛtāgamaḥ* projects the Lord as a practical philosopher who has demonstrated the significance of all scriptural science including Vedic hymns and allied texts through His own conduct and the way He handles intricate problems in life with a smile of spritual vision and the heart of a human being. All *Vedas* sing the glory of His actions only for this reason.

The Living Looks Of The Lord

The birth and behaviour of the Lord as also His beauty should not be taken to be worldly. Those who realize the divinity in His actions, the Lord says, [*Gītā*. Ch. 4-9] will not be reborn in the world after leaving the body, but merge in Him. This divinity in the birth, beauty and behaviour of the Lord is extolled in the following verse :

उद्भवः सुन्दरः सुन्दो रत्ननाभः सुलोचनः ।
अर्को वाजसनः शृङ्गी जयन्तः सर्वविज्जयी ॥

udbhavaḥ sundaraḥ sundo ratna-nābhaḥ sulocanaḥ |
arko vājasanaḥ śṛṅgī jayantaḥ sarva-vijjayī ||

The first name *Udbhavaḥ* places the Lord on a higher plane in matters of birth *bhavaḥ*. He rises above the level of average human beings as He is born with a purpose and on His own. In all His incarnations, He had a mission and a divine will while taking birth at a particular point of time and space at His free will. This is what makes Him *Udbhavaḥ* of superior birth *ut+bhavaḥ*.

Like His birth, His physical complexion and the well-designed structure of His body are all mysterious. Nobody knows the background. But everybody is enchanted by His beauty which pierces into the hearts of all who see Him or those whom He sees. His movements are captivating, His words have a world of significance in thier sense and essence and His looks are full of life and love. Hence, He is adored in the second name as *Sundaraḥ* handsome and wholesome in all respects. In the very next name, He is glorified as *Sundaḥ*. The word *sundaḥ* speaks of the melting nature of the Lord. There is compassion in His looks. His heart melts when He looks at the miseries of His devotees. He has warmth in His heart but His eyes are 'moist' by compassion. His heart melts and spells out His feeling through His eyes. They have the living looks that breathe life into the suffering masses. Hence the *attribute Sundaḥ*.

His navel has precious feelings, ideas and intentions hidden under it. It looks like a jewel *ratna*. Hence, He is hymned as *Ratnanābhaḥ* of beautiful navel shining like a precsious jewel.

In the next name *Sulocanaḥ,* the charming eyes of the Lord are extolled. Their enchanting beauty speaks volumes about His love, affection and compassion.

He is, therefore, adored by all and worshipped even by those who are worshipped like *Brahmā*, the Creator. He is therefore, extolled as *Arkaḥ*, the adored. The word *arkaḥ* also means Sun, the visible God.

The Lord bestows food to all the beings. Therefore, He is worshipped as *Vājasanaḥ*. The word *vāja* means food.

The next name is *Śṛṅgī*, the Horned. In His incarnation as the great fish *Matsyāvatāra*, the Lord saved *Manu* and the seven sages from extinction when the whole earth was swept away by a flood. This name may refer to the Lord's incarnation as the Boar *Varāha* as well.

Being the well-wisher of His divotees and celestial gods like *Indra*, the Lord is eulogized as *Jayantaḥ*, ever Victorious.

The last name *Sarvavijjayī* has two components *sarva vid* (the omniscient) and *jayī* the victorious. These two components are together treated as a single name. This is to attribute His victory to His omniscient nature. It is His wisdom - particularly the spiritual wisdom - which brings Him victory. He helps His devotees in overcoming both the internal foes like passionate desire - *kāma*, anger - *krodha*, greed - *lobha* and the like and also the external enemies in fierce battles.

The Lord Of Lords Of The World Of Words

The Lord of the Universe is not only the Lord of worlds but also of the words. The secret behind His lordship lies in His heart full of love for the choicest sacred syllables, words, verbal expressions charged with a divine touch shining like the golden spot in the heart of all celestial bodies like the stars, planets and the polar points--the prime movers of the universe.It is this lordship which places the Lord as the real Lord of the Universe--the world of words.

The following verse presents a galaxy of such glittering golden spots in the empire of the Eternal Existence *sat*, complaisant and composed consciousness *cit* and the blissful exuberance *ānanda*.

सुवर्णबिन्दुरक्षोभ्यः सर्ववागीश्वरेश्वरः ।
महाह्रदो महागर्तो महाभूतो महानिधिः ।।

suvarṇa-bindur-akṣobhyaḥ sarva-vāgīśvareśvaraḥ |
mahāhrado mahā-garto mahā-bhūto mahā-nidhiḥ ||

The Lord of the Universe resides, according to His own confession, not in *Vaikunṭha*, His celestial palace, not even in the meditative minds of the sages and seers but in the devotional song sung by His dedicated devotees and their reverberating tones, tunes and melodies. This is the spot--the golden spot-- cited in the first name of this celebrated verse. He is glorified as *Suvarṇa-binduḥ*, the sacred syllables articulated by heart and concluded by an auspicious *anusvāra* (the nasal sound marked by a dot above the line) which always blongs to a preceding vowel *anunāsikāt-paronusvāraḥ [Pāṇini* VII. 3-4]. This is the deified dot which the Lord chooses as His resting place - the spritual resort to spend some time with His selected and blessed celebraties and devotees of sound *dhvani*, syllable *varṇa*, word *padaṁ* and sentence or sensible and sentimental statement *vākyaṁ*. These four are the bases of the blissful deity of word-culture which the Lord of the world of words presides over.

Once the Lord gives audience to His devotees in this 'golden dot' *suvarṇa bindu*, nothing can disturb or distract them. Hence, this golden spot or dot is glorified as *Akṣobhyaḥ* (unshaken)-- unshaken because it is a marvellous 'milk-shake' produced by the magnificient ocean of milk *Kṣīra-sāgara*, the private chamber of the presiding deity of all word-culture in the world. Hence, He is hymned as *Akṣobhyaḥ* in the second name of this verse- immediately preceded by the golden name *Suvarṇa binduḥ*.

The name that follows *Sarvavāgīśvareśvaraḥ* clarifies the implication of the two earlier names. The scriptures proclaim that the syllable *a* sums up the whole world of words and the substance of word-power *akāro vai sarvā vāk*. *Pāṇini* also concludes his *Aṣṭādhyāyī* with a short and significant aphorism *a a iti*. Say *a* in both the heard and the unheard forms, you have said everything. This is all that is meant by the word *vāk*. This is *sarvā vāk* (the sum and substance of all human expression) and this is headed by the Lord of the Universe at the highest level. Hence, the attribute *Sarvavāgīśvareśvaraḥ*.

This exposition on word-culture and speech-therapy is followed by four fascinating names - *Mahāhradaḥ, Mahāgartaḥ, Mahābhūtaḥ* and

Mahānidhiḥ. All the four names have the epithet *mahā*, 'the great grand truth' governing this world of words and word-culture.

In the first of these four names, the Lord is adored as *Mahāhradaḥ,* the great pond or lake in which these sacred syllables and words are whispered or chanted by the vibrant waves. In sharp contrast to this prestigious pond there is the *Mahāgarta* the Great Eddy of illusion from which the Lord saves all His devotees. This is the great gulf which stands in the way of the devotees of word-culture and practioners of the sacred words.The Lord helps them out of this hurdle.

Then the Lord is hymned as *Mahābhūtaḥ*, the Great Being. He is greater than the Supreme Being, *Brahman*. He has the five elements--earth to ether-- under His control and conducts the five subtle and primary elements -- sound, touch, form, taste and smell--associated with the five elements. The word *Mahābhūta* also stands for the Supreme Being. The deep meditation is often described as *Mahābhūta-samādhi.*

Finally, the speech -therapy discussed in depth in this sacred verse concludes with a glorifying name *Mahānidhiḥ,* The Great Treasure-house that can cater to any need or needs of the devotees dedicated to the sacred syllables, words and vibrations which are governed by the Lord of lords of the world of words.

The Heaven On Earth

The Lord descends on earth to make it heaven. He is equally fond of holding them both on his two shoulders. This patronage of the Lord to the Earth bringing Heaven down to it is extolled in the following verse:

कुमुदः कुन्दरः कुन्दः पर्जन्यः पावनोऽनिलः ।
अमृताशोऽमृतवपुः सर्वज्ञः सर्वतोमुखः ॥

kumudaḥ kundaraḥ kundaḥ parjanyaḥ pāvano'nilaḥ I
amṛtāśo'mṛta-vapuḥ sarvajñaḥ sarvato-mukhaḥ II

The single syllabled word *ku*,in *Sanskṛit*, means 'the Earth'. Whatever pleases the Earth is *kumudaḥ*. The Lord, being equally endeared to both Earth and Heaven, He decorates the Earth with vegetation, minerals, mountains, rivers, seas, oceans, clouds, birds, animals, and cultured men and women. He is glorified here as *Kumudaḥ* as He keeps the Earth in good humour by all these gifts and *Kumudaḥ* is also the name of a flower known as water-lily white in colour and said to open at moon-rise. The lotus, on the other hand, is patronized by the sun as it blossoms with sun-rise.Thus the Lord presents the white lily to the Earth and entrusts its care to the moon while He sends lotus also to the Earth under the patronage of the sun. Thus He maintains a balance in His affection to both Earth and Heaven through the moon and the sun.

The next name *Kundaraḥ* means a kind of grass which grows from within the soil as an off-spring of the Mother Earth.The Lord sits on this grass and plays with it along with others who have a heart for the greenery around.

The next name *Kundaḥ* also refers to the smiling face of the Earth. This word stands for a kind of Jasmine white and delicate. This shows how fertile and fragrant the Mother Earth is- excelling even Heaven in some respects.Lord *Veṅkateśvara (Bālājī)* of the templetown *Tirupati-tirumālā* is said to have come down to the Earth getting disgusted with his palacial residence *Vaikuṇṭha* not for a change but for permanent settlement (*Śrī Vaikuṇṭha viraktāya ...Ramayā Ramamāṇāya Veṅkateśāya maṅgalaṁ*). *Ramā Lakṣmī* also comes along with Him to see and enjoy the beauty of the Earth.

The next three names *Parjanyaḥ, Pāvanaḥ* and *Anilaḥ* respectively refer to the clouds showering from above, the purifying air and the ever-active winds controlled by the god of wind, a subordinate deity working under the Supreme Spirit. Thus the three names present the dynamic forces working under the overall supervision, direction and control of the Lord of the Universe who showers His love, affection and compassion for the benefit of the inhabitants of the Earth, purifies the atmosphere and environment and keeps the whole creation active, alert and accommodative.

The next line in the verse starts with the name *Amṛtāśaḥ* which means the enjoyer of the nectar that came out from the ocean of milk. It was the Lord who managed to pass it on to the gods and saw to it that the blessing of immortality goes to the right side. He too took a part of it just to give company to the gods.He,being the source of nectar, is adored in this name as *Amṛtāśaḥ*.

He is not only the participant in the enjoyment of nectar but He Himself is nectar being the Lord of immortality. Hence, the attribute *Amṛtavapuḥ*. He is Himself immortal and grants immortality to those who deserve it by virtue of their penance.

The last two names *Sarvajñaḥ* and *Sarvatomukhaḥ* respectively refer to the Omniscient and Omnifaced personality of the Lord. He knows everyone and everything and He is everywhere casting His eyes on each and every aspect of the Universe.

One With Trees

The Divine Grace covers a wide range of greatness from the Supreme Spirit to the common trees and plants. All are equal in the eyes of the Lord and each has a share of His perfection, power and prestige. Here are a few examples:

सुलभः सुव्रतः सिद्धः शत्रुजिच्छत्रुतापनः ।
न्यग्रोधोदुम्बरोऽश्वत्थश्चाणूरान्ध्रनिषूदनः ॥

sulabhaḥ suvrataḥ siddhaḥ śatru-jic-chatru-tāpanaḥ ।
nyagrodho-dumbaro'śvatthaś-cāṇūrāndhra-niṣūdanaḥ ॥

The first name *Sulabhaḥ* projects the Lord as easily accesible -but only for the real devotees. The very thought of the Lord originating from a pious soul makes His persence felt in the inner consciousness. He pleases His devotees as easily and readily as He Himself feels pleased and delighted by their devotion. This is what makes Him *Sulabhaḥ* - instant grace as great and grand as His simple smile.

He is *Suvrataḥ* - One with a pure consciousness and a strong determination. He never goes back from His words. He sticks to His promises and expects His devotees to maintain the same commitment to integrity in thought, word and deed.

He is perfect in all respects having attained the highest position in the spiritual field. He Has nothing more to achieve as everthing is available with Him. There is nothing worth attainable which He has not attained. Hence, the epithet *Siddhaḥ* the most accomplished with nothing more to aspire for. This He grants to His devotees too when they rise to that level.

As far as His enemies are concerned, He, for one, has no enemies. He treats all alike. But those who stand in the way of righteousness are not spared by Him. He teaches them a lesson by subjecting them to the most painful experiences. He ensures that they change by themselves. Otherwise He defeats and destroys them. Hence, He is glorified by two attributes -- *Śatrujit* victorious over His foes, and *Śatrutāpanaḥ* One who torments them till the end.

Now the preceptor of the sacred hymn names three trees which have imbibed the divine qualities of the Lord. The first among these three is a Banyan Tree for which the name chosen is *Nyagrodhaḥ*. The word *nyagrodhaḥ* means a tree which is very tall and covers a wide area with its branches coming back to the earth for rebirth. It provides shade to the casual hawkers and travellers and shelter to birds and animals. But no other tree can flourish under its shade.

The second tree mentioned and compared with the attributes of the Lord is *Udumbaraḥ*, a fig tree which grows upwards and the fruits are full of seeds and small insects. As it transcends the ether and provides health and nourishment to the people, it fits into the transcendental nature of the Lord.

The third one is the well-known *Pīpala* tree *Aśvatthaḥ*.The derivation of the word is very peculiar. It means, literally, that which does not last for the day that follows. But in fact this tree has the longest life and springs up without much external patronage. The leaves are very active in their motion and make melodious sound. The religious minded people worship this tree as the botanical form of Lord *Nārāyaṇa*. They call it *Aśvattha Nārāyaṇa*. It is believed that felling this tree is a sin. Normally it does not grow in residential houses. It is often found in temples.

In *Gītā* [ch. 15-1], *Bhagavān* glorifies the qualities of this tree from a spiritual angle. He says , 'He who knows the eternal nature of this tree *Aśvattha* with its roots upwards and the branches growing downwards and the scriptures as its leaves knows the essence of all learnng contained in the *Vedas*. Obviously the holy book *Gītā*, the Voice of the Lord, is referring to the cosmic form of the mystic tree *Aśvattha*, the glimpses of which we find in our familiar tree *Aśvattha*. What is 'impermanent' in the worldly sense is the Eternal one in the spiritual sense. One represents *Saṁsāra* while the other one stands for *Sanātana*. *Kaṭhopaniṣad* also refers to this tree as the holy tree with world of spiritual significance. One wonders why this divine tree is called *Aśvattha* (that which may not last till tomorrow). The proper name could have been *Śaśvatthaḥ* not *Aśvatthaḥ*.

The sacred hymn *Śrī Viṣṇu Sahasranāma* has rightly chosen this tree in the end with the Banyan and the Fig preceding it.The attachment of the banyan tree to the earth with branches turned into roots, the skyward fig unmindful of what is going on all around and the Eternal Tree *aśvattha or śaśvattha* addressing the world on theory of relativity in the language of the leaves that sound like Vedic hymns chanting the glory of the Absolute speak for themselves on the philosophy of life.

The last name *Cāṇūrāndhra-niṣūdanaḥ* refers to an episode in *Śrīmad Bhāgavatam* where the cruel king *Kaṁsa* sends a wrestler named *Cāṇūra* to kill *Kṛṣṇa*. This wrestler whose profession is to kill people at the royal command perhaps hailed from Andhra. Hence, He is referred to as *Cāṇūrāndhra* whom Lord *Kṛṣṇa* with His divine power despatched to the other world in no time.

The verse, on the whole, highlights the universal love of the Lord who cares more for the silent services rendered by stationary plants and trees than for the soul-less demons like *Cāṇūra* who lives upon the lives of others causing irreparable damage to life in general.

Fire And Fear Of God

Fire and fear are the most marvellous creations of God -as sacred and scaring as He Himself. Fire is distinct and visible when it is enkindled till it is extinct while fear is comparatively less visible except in external facial changes.One has a flexible form while the other is formless.But both are very predominant in the day to day life of people.Fire is worshipped as God and no form of religious ritual can be organized without lighting the lamp and offering oblation to the god of fire in *havan*. Fear, on the other hand, is something which every one tries to avoid except fear of God. God-fearing is considered to be a virtue which drives away all the fears. This relationship between fire, fear and God is brought out in the following nine names of the Lord.

सहस्रार्चिः सप्तजिह्वः सप्तैधाः सप्तवाहनः ।
अमूर्तिरनघोऽचिन्त्यो भयकृद्भयनाशनः ॥

sahasrārciḥ sapta-jihvaḥ saptaidhāḥ sapta-vāhanaḥ ।
amūrtir-anagho'cintyo bhayakṛd-bhaya-nāśanaḥ ॥

All the four names in the first line glorify the Lord in His manifestation as the sacred fire, the first to be worshipped by the Vedic seers *agnimīde purohitam*. There is no life without light and heat which are the main contributions of fire and power in some form or other. *Bhagavān* tells us in *Gītā* that the radiance existent in sun, moon and fire is His own. This radiance manifested in the form of sacred fire is glorified in these four names --*Sahasrārciḥ, Saptajihvaḥ, Saptaidhāḥ* and *Saptavāhanaḥ.*

The first among these four names, *Sahasrārciḥ* means 'One who radiates thousands and thousands of rays'. This need not necessarily refer to fire though the word *arciḥ* basically means 'a ray of light' and also fire or flame. The immediate sense conveyed through this name is, therefore, the Sun with innumerable rays which he radiates to the entire globe. The word *sahasra* also is not limited to thousand. It means myriad or innumerable. Thus the first name *Sahasrārciḥ* covers both light and heat in several forms.

The second name *Saptajihvaḥ* means 'one with seven tongues of flame'. *Śaṅkara* quotes *Muṇḍaka Upaniṣad* [1-2-4] to name the seven tongues of the flame with which the Lord is identified here. The seven tongues are *Kālī* - the black one, *Karālī* - the terrific one, *Manojavā* - swift as the mind, *Sulohitā* - the red one, *Sudhūmravarṇā* - purple coloured, *Sphuliṅginī* - emitting sparks, and *Viśvarucī* - supremely splendid. These are the seven quivering tongues of the goddess worshipped in all religious sacrifices. These goddesses lead the person who offers these oblations direct to the eternal abode of the Supreme Soul with the help of the radiant rays of the sun, says the *Upaniṣad.*

The next name *Saptaidhāḥ* indicates the seven flames that form themselves when the fuel is added and which grant prosperity, happiness and enlightenment to those who worship the 'god of fire' in the Vedic tradition.

The fourth name *Saptavāhanaḥ* like the first one *Sahsrārciḥ*, glorifies the sun again who is said to have seven horses for his riding. His horses are also named *Sapta* - the seven. In *Āditya hṛdayam*, a sacred hymn dedicated to the Sun-god, the Sun is glorified as *Haridaśva* (one with green horses). He is also glorified as *Sahasrārciḥ*, the name with which this verse starts.

Light and heat have no form as such but manifest themselves through the sun and the fire. So is the Lord who is formless, but assumes any form He likes when occasion arises. This is what is conveyed in the next name *Amūrtiḥ,* the Formless. He is also glorified as *Anaghaḥ*, the Sinless. Obviously, there can be no sin when there is no form. All sins are associated with the psycho-physical organism that the mortals are entrusted with. The immortals and the celestials are free from form and hence free from sins as well. The same thing applies to the Lord who maintains the same status even when He incarnates. He assumes a chosen form only to free the individual souls from all sins. But how He does it, ordinary living beings cannot even imagine. He is therefore adored as *Acintyaḥ,* the Inconceivable.

He causes fear and also despels it. He causes fear to those who are not afraid of committing sin and misuse or abuse the physical frame and material prosperity given to them. He does it to set them right by creating fear for God in their hearts. He is therefore adored as *Bhayakṛt*.

He dispels fear in the minds of His devotees as a reward for their virtue and righteous conduct. He is, therefore, glorified as *Bhayanāśanaḥ*. One who creats fear can remove it as well. The Lord is Omnipotent. Therefore He knows how to reward the good and punish the bad.

Just An Atom, But Gigantic

The Lord has as many synonyms as antonyms for His attributes which are equally appropriate in both the contexts. This spectacular speciality about the qualities that quality the otherwise unqualified Master of the Universe is the main theme of the following verse:

अणुर्बृहत्कृशः स्थूलो गुणभृन्निर्गुणो महान् ।
अधृतः स्वधृतः स्वास्यः प्राग्वंशो वंशवर्धनः ॥

aṇur-bṛhat-kṛśaḥ sthūlo guṇabhṛn-nigruṇo mahān I
adhṛtaḥ svadhṛtaḥ svāsyaḥ pragvaṁśo vaṁśavardhanaḥ II

There are three sets of antonyms glorifying the auspicious attributes of the Lord. One wonders how the oppposites co-exist in the Supreme with no contradiction or conflict. He is just an atom *aṇu* to look at, but a marvellous giant *bṛhat* in action. The *Kṭhopaniṣad* confirms this contrastive correlation by saying that the Lord is the minutest of the minute *aṇoraṇīyān* but yet greater than the greatest *mahato mahīyān*. The *Upaniśad* adds a significant note saying that He stays in a small cell in the innermost consciousness of the individual self *ātmasya jantor-nihito guhāyām*. But He is not in one isolated cell. He is everywhere wherever there is life. It is mysterious how the Invisible is Omnipresent. But it is a fact visualized by the great seers of inward vision.

The second set of antonyms is *kṛśaḥ* - thin and *sthūlaḥ* - thick, fat, gross, bulky or large. He is as thin as a ray of light but as thick as the milky way crowded with clusters of countless stars. Like the human body which has two forms--the subtle - *sūkṣma* and the gross - *sthūla*, the Lord too has two forms of manifestations--as small as the atom or a cell and as big as the Universe. He is flexible in form, but retains the same essence of existence whether He is visible or invisible.

The last set of antonymns presents the Lord as *Guṇabhṛt,* the bearer of attributes like *sattva, rajas, and tamas:* Creator, Preserever and Destroyer: awakened, asleep and dreamless: past, present, future and so on. One can visualize Him through these attributes which are generated by Him though He transcends them all. When He rises above these descriptions and definitions, He is extolled as *Nirguṇaḥ* devoid of all properties. He is cordless but well-knit with the entire universe. He is a bow without string, but springs a spray of arrows felt only when hurt. Inspite of His being free from all worldly attributes, qualities and properties, He promotes these assets in His devotees so that they too can transcend these temporal accomplishments and attain the Eternal Bliss endless and elevating. Hence, He is hymned as *Nirguṇaḥ*.

It is because of this co-existence of the opposites--minute and marvellous, subtle and gross,with and without attributes-- He is adored and worshipped as 'The Great'- *Mahān.* His greatness lies in His flexibility, adaptability, accessibility and universality which place Him higher than all measured heights. He is higher than the highest *mahato mahīyān.*

About this unique greatness of the Lord, *Āpastamba* says in his *Dharmasūtra* that it is impossible to describe or define His glory,even for the sake of argument, because He is devoid of all such attributes and avoids them so that He can make His presence felt anywhere without depending upon the material devices like sound, body and touch. He is eternally pure and all pervading.

The second line in the verse adds four more names of the Lord to illustrate this point.The first among these names is *Adhṛtaḥ* unsustained. Nothing can sustain Him as everything is sustained by Him. He sustains all the five elements which, in turn, sustain all living beings. He is the Supreme Spirit that needs no support. In *Chāndogya Upaniṣad* [7.24], when the question was raised as to 'How and where does the Excellence *Bhagavān* exist?', the answer comes 'in His own glory'. The most illustrious and the glorious Lord of the Universe needs no external support. He is established in His own glory. Hence, the name *Svadhṛtaḥ,* Self-established.

These two names *Adhṛtaḥ* and *Svadhṛtaḥ* also indicate that it is extremely difficult and almost impossible to 'hold' the Lord even for a second in one's own heart, by one's own efforts, but this impossibility becomes possible in a moment, the moment the Lord chooses to be with His devotees. Thus the inaccessible *Adhṛta* becomes instantly *Svadhṛta* through pure devotion.

The next name *Svāsyaḥ* is a very sweet one because it tells us how sweet the Lord sounds in His dialogue with His devotees. Mostly He speaks through silence which is more eloquent than His speech.His facial complexion, the delightful smile on His face and the marvellous movement of His lips before He starts articulating His heart in the language of the soul speak volumes about His unheard melodies sweeter than those heard. He is, therefore, very fittingly hymned,in this name, as *Svāsya (su + asya) or (sva + āsya)* one with beautiful face or voice and also One who has His own Characteristic way of expressing His thoughts, not necessarily in words, but just by mere looks and facial complexion.

While describing *Gopīs* who address Lord *Kṛṣṇa* in the language of their hesitating shy-ness, the Hindi poet *Ratnākar* says,'they said nothing orally, tried to say a lot through their eyes and whatever is left they conveyed through shyness and hesitation'.

The last two names in the verse *Prāgvaṁśaḥ* and *Vaṁśavardhanaḥ* glorify the Lord as the originator of a primeval race. There was nothing before it came into existence and it expanded without any break in the ages that followed. He is therefore the originator and promoter of the primeval race. Hence, the names *Prāgvaṁśaḥ and Vaṁśavardhanaḥ.*

Extolled For His Excellence

All the *Vedas* , *Upaniṣads* and the holy books like the *Rāmāyaṇa, Mahābhāratā* and the eighteen *Purāṇas* are full of glorification of the Lord. This excellence is explained in the following verse:

भारभृत्कथितो योगी योगीशः सर्वकामदः ।
आश्रमः श्रमणः क्षामः सुपर्णो वायुवाहनः ॥

bhāra-bhṛt-kathito yogī yogīśaḥ sarva-kāmadaḥ |
āśramaḥ śramaṇaḥ kṣāmaḥ suparṇo vāyu-vāhanaḥ ||

Readiness to bear any burden without grudge and take up any challenge with high sense of duty is the most significant aspect of any excellence. Lord excels all in this respect. Day and night, He bears the burden of the whole universe and takes it in a sportive manner. The saint-singer *Tyāgarāja* asks the Lord, 'When the whole Universe is within you and you are the Universe, how can I be a burden to you, my Lord!' (*Brova Bhāramā Rāma Bhuvanamella Nī Vai Yuṇḍaga). He treats the whole *Bhuvana* - world as His *Bhavana* - home. This is the first and the most significant excellence of the Lord which is glorified in this first name *Bhārabhṛt,* the Bearer of all forms of burdens connected with the Universe.

The second name *Kathitaḥ* 'extolled' refers to His glory extolled in all the sacred texts and saintly people who realized Him and His supremacy. *Bhagavān* Himself tells *Arjuna*, 'I alone am to be known by all the *Vedas* because I am the subject matter in all these sacred texts' *[Gītā 15-15]* All celestial deities including *Brahmā* and *Śiva* adore Lord *Viṣṇu*. Hence, He is hymned as *Kathitaḥ*.

In the next two names, the Lord is extolled as *Yogī* and *Yogīśaḥ*. Himself being a *Yogī* in the universal sense of the term. He is accepted by all the *Yogīs* as their ideal. Hence, the name *Yogīśaḥ,* the Lord of all *Yogīs*. They look for Him whenever they have any doubt about anything connected with the yogic science. In the sacred text *Gītā* where the Lord Himself teaches *yoga,* He is presented as *Yogeśvaraḥ*. It is said in the concluding verse of the whole text [ch. 18-78] that where there is *Kṛṣṇa,* the Lord of *yoga* and also *Arjuna - Pārtha* with bow in his hand, there will be grace, victory and glory. The Lord asserts that this is His personal conviction *dhruvā nītirmatirmama*. The entire *Gītā* is described as *Yogaśāstra* (the science of *yoga*).

Gītā the authority on *yoga* as a way of life, defines the term *yoga* in a single word *samatvam* equanimity [ch. 2-50]. The *Yogeśvara* in *Gītā* and *Yogīśaḥ* in the sacred hymn, *Sahasranāma* are one and the same. In *Gītā, Kṛṣṇa* was Himself the exponent of *yoga* and in *Sahasranāma, Bhīṣma* projects Him as the Lord of all *yogīs*. In both the cases, the most significant and characteristic feature of a *yogī* is 'equanimity', and the Lord presents His own example for this saying that He treats all beings alike without any preference or prejudice *samoham srva bhūteṣu na me dveṣyosti na priyaḥ* [Ch. 9-29]

In spite of this Supreme status the Lord holds in the field of *yoga,* He is very generous to His devotees. He assures them that He will certainly fulfil all their wishes. Hence He is hymned, in the name that follows, as *Sarvakāmdaḥ,* the fulfiller of all the desires. He is so generous in this respect that He fulfils the desires not only of His pure-minded devotees, but sometimes of the worst sinners too so that they may improve themselves.As far as His devotees are concerned, He assures them that He will absolve them of all their sins even if they discord all their *dharmas* (religious duties). They should only have full faith in Him and take refuge in Him alone. He tells them 'not to worry' *mā śucaḥ*.

In the next name *Āśramaḥ,* the Lord goes a step forward and offers His home as the hermitage where they can live peacefully leaving all their worries to Him. What is more is that He not only offers His abode of peace as a spiritual resort *āśrama* to His devotees,but he Himself assumes the form of an *āśrama* - hermitage. So generous, compassionate and considerate is the Lord for His devotees who just surrender all their desires, grievances and drawbacks to Him.

Hard-working and simple living are the pre-requisites of an asramite, one who has chosen to lead the life in a hermitage under the guidance of the Head of the *āśrama,* the Lord Himself in this context. For this purpose, the Lord Himself sets an example and inculcates love for labour the characteristic feature of a *śramaṇa,* a spiritual seeker taken to a life of austerity. Hence, the Lord is hymned here as *Śramaṇaḥ,* one who enjoys austere life and promotes the same among His devotees who are the inmates of His hermitage.

The next word *kṣāmaḥ* indicates that an inmate of a hermitage should be prepared to forego most of the luxuries and sometimes even the bare necesssaries of life. These austerities may reduce the physical frame of the devotees but that compensates in the form of spiritual growth. The merit of penance that promotes proximity to the Lord is brought out in this name *Kṣāmaḥ.*

The next name *Suparṇaḥ* has several meanings. The word *suparṇa* means a bird, a leaf and also *Garutmān,* the celestial carrier of Lord *Viṣṇu. Upaniṣad* speaks of two birds *dvāsuparṇa* who sit on the branch of a tree--one enjoying the taste of a fruit and the other one just observing the scene and the event. The word used for the two birds in this context is *suparṇā*. One can easily imagine who these two birds are. The attribute *Suparṇaḥ* means not only the leaves and other vegetation which provides food for the community but also, more significantly, the leaves or the pages of the sacred texts like *Vedas* and other holy scriptures usually written on the palm leaves. The leaves get sanctified by these carvings or writings and hence they become 'leaves adorable' *Suparṇa*. One who is well-versed in the spiritual learning conveyed through these leaves of holy literature are also *Suparṇas* in this context. *Garutmān*, who is also called *Suparṇa* stands for immortality. He brought nectar *amṛta* from heaven to satisfy his mother. His name is a terror for all poisonous creatures. He is always with the Lord serving Him in His visits to the holy places and holy men. Thus the name *Suparṇa* is a highly significant epithet for the Lord who provides food for the hungry, wisdom for the seekers and salvation or immortality to the realized souls.

The last name in the verse is *Vāyuvāhanaḥ*. The word immediately suggests that the Lord uses wind or winds as His vehicle-s.There are seven types of wind each of which are further classified into seven types. Thus the fortynine (7x7) forms of the wind serve as automobiles for the frequent visits of the Lord. In fact, the wind blows because of His fear, as the *Upaniṣad* says - *Bhiṣasmad vātaḥ pavati.*

In His incarnation as *Rāma, Hanumān* the offspring of the wind-God serves as His vehicle in times of urgency. This also supports the sense of the epithet *Vāyuvāhanaḥ*.

The process is reciprocal too, as the Lord makes the wind move and the wind serves Him as an automobile van--eternal and ever present as long as the wind exists.

The Sagittarian

The Lord is as compassionate and considerate to His devotees as hard, sharp and stubborn towards the evil forces. In His incarnation as *Rāma*, He was known as *Kodaṇḍpāṇi* ever ready with a powerful bow in His hands. Starting from His first adventure in protecting the hermitage of *Viśvāmitra* from the onslaught of terrifying demons like *Mārīca* right upto his encounter with *Rāvaṇa,* the Lord presented Himself as a universal figure in wielding His bow and arrows with an enchanting skill in the art of archery. This aspect of divinity manifested by the Lord as *Rāma* is the main theme of the verse that follows:

धनुर्धरो धनुर्वेदो दण्डो दमयिता दमः ।
अपराजितः सर्वसहो नियन्ता नियमो यमः ॥

dhanurdharo dhanurvedo daṇḍo damayitā damaḥ ।
aparājitaḥ sarvasaho niyantā niyamo yamaḥ ॥

The glorifiction of the Lord as an expert in the science of archery starts with two names *Dhanurdharaḥ* and *Dhanurvedaḥ*. He is always ready with His bow in His hands (*dhanurdharaḥ*) with a thorough knowledge (both theoretical and practical) in the intricacies of wielding the bow (*dhanurveda*). Accordingly He is adored and worshipped as *Dhanurdharaḥ* and *Dhanurvedaḥ*. The skill in wielding a bow *Dhanurvidyā* appears to be an inborn trait with *Rāma* who practised it on the lines of Vedic tradition under the guidance of the sage *Viśvāmitra,* the inventor of *Gāyatrī* and several other *astras* (mystic missiles). *Dhaurveda* is one of the four *upa-vedas*, the other three being *Āyurveda* (medicine), *Gāndharva veda* (music) and *Sthāpatya* (architecture). Thus from archery to architecture, *Rāma* was well - versed in all the skills but specialised in *Dhanurveda* as glorified by *Nārada* as *dhanurvede ca niṣṭhitaḥ.*

The word *dhanus* has an astronomical significance too. It stands for the ninth sign of the Zodiac Sagittarius, the residential quarters of Jupiter. According to *Vālmīki*, Moon and Jupiter were on the ascent in the rising Zodiac when *Rāma* was born *Vākpatāvindunā saha.* Jupiter the Lord of Sagittarius, is known for intellectual brilliance and word-culture and Moon stands for the charming personality and the tranquillity of mind. *Rāma* was always admired by one and all as a rare combination of charming personallity *somavat priyadarśanaḥ* and as intellectual of a very high order ranking with or even excelling *Bṛhaspati* (Jupiter). It is therefore no wonder if He is extolled in this hymn as *Dhanurdharaḥ* and *Dhanurvedaḥ.* He can therefore be considered as a Sagittarian in the virtual sense of the term as the key to His success in all the battles He fought was His skill in wielding the bow.

The next three names *Daṇḍaḥ* (shrewd and sure in punishing the wicked), *Damayitā* (subduer) and *Damaḥ* (self restraint) also sing the glory of *Rāma*, the ruler who always kept His foes on their toes. In *Daṇḍaka* forest during His exile, He was a terror to all the evil forces causing harrassment to the sages. He destroyed 14000 demons commisioned by *Khara* in a few minutes. The dreadful demons like *Virādha, Kabandha, Kumbhakarṇa* and finally *Rāvaṇa* were all done to death by Him. But the surprising fact was that they were all admiration for Him. *Vāli* felt thoroughly convinced about the righteousness of *Rāma* in catching him unaware. Even *Rāvaṇa* ultimately accepted in his heart of hearts that *Rāma* was not an ordinary man, but *Nārāyaṇa* (God) in the form of *nara* (man). *Tārā* and *Mandodarī* too admired *Rāma* even though He killed their husbands. This is because all the acts of *Rāma* in His encounters with the evil forces were inspired by His non-compromising commitment to the establishment of justice. That is why He is glorified in these three names as *Daṇḍaḥ* (an instrument of justice), *Damayitā* (bent upon punishing the punishable without any personal prejudice) and *Damaḥ* (always alert, vigilant and restrained in His words, acts and movements inspiring even his opponents to emulate Him).

The next line starts with the name *Aparājitaḥ*, never defeated by any one. This applies to the Lord in all His incarnations and manifestations. He never faced any defeat in any of His encouonters.

The secret behind this guaranteed victory in spite of the serious set backs on the way is His unsurpassable humility and unassuming divinity. He can subdue any one with these two weapons. 'Be humble, but bold' was His motto which He always practised and then preached. Hence, He is hymned as *Sarvasahaḥ*, competent in all His actions.

The last three names are *Niyantā*, one who controls the misdeeds and misconduct of others, *Niyamaḥ*, the law-abiding and *Yamaḥ*, self disciplined as a part of *yoga* or dreadful like the god of death. These are the three aspects of the Lord which He displays when He has to act as a dictator. His only concern in all these matters is to ensure that all His intentions, actions, decisions and directions are balanced and just.

The Abode Of Truth And Righteousness

Natural love for character, strict adherence to truth, righteous conduct, unpolluted intentions and promotion of universal love and cordiality are the essential requirements for peace and harmony in any organizational set up. These qualities are found in abundance in the Lord who presents an example for excellence in organizational and judicial matters. These traits are glorified in the following verse:

सत्त्ववान्सात्त्विकः सत्यः सत्यधर्मपरायणः ।
अभिप्रायः प्रियार्होऽर्हः प्रियकृत्प्रीतिवर्धनः ॥

sattvavān-sāttvikaḥ satyaḥ satya-dharma-parāyaṇaḥ I
abhiprāyaḥ priyārho'rhaḥ priyakṛt-prītivardhanaḥ II

The first name *Sattvavān* presents the Lord as one possessed of *sattva*, the essence of existence, strength, eneregy, courage, goodness, virtue and so on. The characteristic feature of *sat* is *sattva* - *sato bhavaḥ*. *Sat* is also glorified as one of the threefold apellations of the Absolute *Brahman*, the other two being *om* and *tat*. Thus the name *Sattvavān* glorifies the Lord as the most substantial one with immense potentialities of existence, excellence and bliss. The word *sattva* is also the highest of the three *guṇas* - *sattva, rajas* and *tamas*. In this sense also the epithet *Sattvavān* glorifies the Lord as the essence of strength, virtue and righteousness.

The next name *Sātvikaḥ* obviously refers to this supreme *guṇa* which is found predominently in gods and heavenly beings. The Lord being the Supreme head of all celestials is very appropriately adored as *Sāttvikaḥ*.

The name that follows, namely, *Satyaḥ* shifts the focus from *sattva* (essence of excellence) to *Satyaḥ* (truth). Thus this attribute projects the Lord as Truth personified or Truth itself. Strict adherence to truth in day to day life is as good as worshipping God. In fact there is a religious ritual among Hindus where the Lord *Nārāyaṇa* is worshipped as an embodiment of truth *Satya-nārāyaṇa*. It is customary to worship this deity, *Satya-nārāyaṇa* whenever something good or auspicious happens in a family. The idea is to rededicate oneself to the strict adherence to truth. 'Truth and truth alone is God' - is the message conveyed through such rituals.

Sometimes truth and justice may not go together. For instance ,in the *Rāmāyaṇa* itself , *Kaikeyī* demands the exile of *Rāma* on the strength of truth, quoting the two boons granted to her by the King *Daśaratha*. But justice asserts that *Rāma's* exile is not justified from any angle. This conflict resulting in a crisis was however resolved by *Rāma* in a moment by voluntarily proceeding to the forest leaving the Kingdom for his brother *Bharata* on his own free will. Only a supreme soul like *Rāma* can make such a sacrifice. That is why He is admired as *Satya dharma parāyaṇaḥ* (Acme of truth and righteousness). The sage *Nārada* tells the epic poet *Vālmīki* that *Rāma* is *dharma* personified in matters relating to 'truth'. *Satye dharma ivāparaḥ*. He is wholly devoted to both truthfulness and righteousness and prepared to face any consequences. The entire story of the epic *Rāmāyaṇa* (the march of *Rāma*) is a glorious illustration of this judicial combination of truth - *satyam* and righteousness - *dharma*.

The second line starts with a strange epithet *Abhiprāyaḥ* which is an abstract noun meaning intention, import, contention or opinion. But the root-meaning of the word *abhiprāyaḥ* is to go near, approach or reach ultimately. In this sense, this attribute of the Lord indicates that He is the ultimate goal of all walks of life. Whatever way we choose, our ultimate aim is to reach Him and have His grace.

The last four names in this verse, namely, *Priyārhaḥ, Arhaḥ, Priyakṛt* and *Prītivardhanaḥ* are all admiration for the universal love the Lord promotes. In the first place, the entire universe has immense love for Him and worship Him seeking His grace. He deserves all this not merely because of His divinity but more so because of His keen interest in the welfare of each and every soul in the universe and instinctive love for the whole creation which is His own. Hence, He is hymned as *Priyārhaḥ*, worshipped by His beloved devotees. He deserves all this worship inspired by spontaneous love for His glorious personality. Hence He is *Arhaḥ.*

He promotes love among all living beings by making their lives not merely livable, but lovable too. He generates love among the people by presenting His own example and demonstrating the miracle that love can bring about. He is therefore adored as *Priyakṛt* One who does what is pleasing to all. In the process of promoting universal love, the Lord creates a bond of love and affection between the members of family which gradually extends to society, community and ultimately to the global relations. The whole universe is interlinked with this instinctive love which is promoted by the loving God or God of Love. Hence, is hymed as *Prītivardhanaḥ.*

The Sun His Eye

The Omnipresent Lord of the Universe moves in the endless space around, leading the Light of His own creation, spreading the vibrant radiance all around, accepting the auspicious oblations offered on the way and blazing forth through the rays of the sun and the moon to bless His beloved subjects with the sole object of making the life on earth and heaven equally blissful. This is described very picturesquely in the following ten names:

विहायसगतिर्ज्योतिः सुरुचिर्हुतभुग्विभुः ।
रविर्विरोचनः सूर्यः सविता रविलोचनः ॥

vihāyasagatir-jotiḥ surucir-huta-bhug-vibhuḥ I
ravir-virocanaḥ sūryaḥ savitā ravi-locanaḥ II

The sky is said to be the body for the Supreme Spirit. Where there is sky, there is God. So, He is Omnipresent because there is no space without sky. The Lord is both mobile and stable. Where He is mobile, He moves in the celestial path. The wind serves as His vehicle as has already been noticed in His attribute *Vāyu-vāhanaḥ*. It is the wind that makes Him move and the space for His movements is provided by the sky. Hence, He is glorified in the firse name of this verse as *Vihāyasagatiḥ,* One who gathers momentum in the outer space. To see Him, one has to look either at the outer space or the innermost corner of the heart, where there is continuous glow of the Light Eternal *paraṁ jyoti*. Therefore, He is glorified in the second name as *Jyotiḥ*. The *Nārāyaṇa Upaniṣad* equates Lord *Nārāyaṇa* with this eternal light shining within and without *Nārāyaṇa paro jyotiḥ*. It is under His instructions and out of fear for Him, the fire burns and the sun shines, as sung by the sages. It is His light that shines and makes all splendid things radiant.

This radiance transmitted by all celestial luminaries is supposed to be very auspicious as He is the source of all brilliance and radiance *tasya bhāsā sarvamidaṁ vibhāti*. Being the inexhaustible source of this universal radiance that benefits the whole creation, the Lord is adored as *Surucih*, the source of all welcoming effulgence.

The Lord accepts and receives with pleasure the oblations offered to Him through the sacred fire. He is, therefore, adored as *Hutabhuk* consumer of oblations.

It is worth remembering, in this context, that the Lord made it clear to *Arjuna* in *Gītā* that He would gladly accept even the small offerings like a leaf or a flower or a fruit or few drops of water if they are offered with devotion. It is the devotion that matters for the Lord and not the denomination or demonstration.

Then the Lord is glorified as *Vibhuḥ,* a small epithet covering the entire universe. The word *vibhu* means the Omnipresent. He is everywhere. When *Prahlāda,* a great devotee depicted in *Śrīmad-bhāgavatam* was challenged by his father *Hiraṇyakaśipu* if God can be seen in a pillar standing right in front, the Lord honoured the commitment of His devotee and emerged from the piller at the touch of the sword and destroyed the demon. This is how the Lord makes His presence felt and protects His devotees wherever and whenever they think of Him. That is why He is *Vibhuḥ,* the Omnipresent.

All the five names in the second line of the verse refer to Sun, the visible evidence of the Universal light of the Lord that manifests itself in various forms.

The first among these five names is *Raviḥ,* the Sun. He is so called because he extracts the liquids and the essence of the earth through his rays. Here the Lord is identified with Sun in his role as *Ravi.* The Lord also withdraws the whole essence of all existence only to revive it and give it a new form so that His creation may be ever green and always fresh.

The next name is *Virocanaḥ* 'splendid in several ways and forms'. All the luminaries - both celestial and terrestrial - draw their radiance from the same source, the Lord Himself who is glorified in this attribute as *Virocanaḥ.*

The next name *Sūryaḥ* is the most popular name for the sun. The *Vedas* sing His glory saying *Sūrya,* the Sun is the soul of the whole world - mobile or stable - *sūrya ātmā jagatastasthuṣaśca.* The literal meaning of the word *sūrya* is one who brings forth all necessaries of life. He is the life-giver. He generates activity the moment he rises. He provides rest to the tired people in his absence. He is the 'breath of life' *prāṇa* as observed by the sages *ādityo ha vai prāṇaḥ.* Of all the things the *Sūrya* brings forth, the most important is the grace and grandeur of this splendid world we live in. The sages called it *Śrīḥ* which means all forms of splendour including the spiritual radiance. It is *Sūrya* who brings this to us *Sūte Sriyamiti va Sūryaḥ.* The word *sūya* means *yajña* and *sūrya* too performs *yajña* consistently for the welfare of the world - extracting the essence through his rays and returing them in the form of fresh and fragrant showers of rain. He protects the world from starvation by converting waste into wealth.

The next name *Savitā* is also equally significant. The word *savitā* means who produces, generates, yields etc. it is this *Savita* whom we worship while chanting *Gāyatrī.* He sharpens our intellect and thereby promotes our spiritual growth leading to the highest attainment of Absolute Bliss.

The last name *Ravilocanaḥ* declares that Sun or *Ravi* is the eye of the Lord. He looks for us through the Sun. Similarly if we want to have a glimpse of the Lord in His radiant splendour, we have to make our way through the sun *Ravi.* Hence, the name *Ravilocanaḥ.* The famous hymn *Puruṣa Sūkta* tells us that the moon is born of the Lord's mind and sun of His eyes. The *Muṇḍaka* however combines both sun and moon and says that these are the eyes of the Lord. In any case, it is the Lord in the form of *Ravi* who grants us eye-sight and mental blance. The mind is very often reflected in the eyes and the eyes convey the message to the mind.

Thus the whole verse with ten attributes of the Lord gives us a glimpse of the spiritual radiance hidden in the vibrations that these names produce.

The Pedestal Of The World

The world stands on the strong foundation and the sustained support of the Lord who bears the burden of the whole universe like the celestial serpent *Ananta* or *Ādiśeṣa* with thousand hoods. This is explained in the following ten attributes of the Lord :

अनन्तो हुतभुग्भोक्ता सुखदो नैकजोऽग्रजः ।
अनिर्विण्णः सदामर्षी लोकाधिष्ठानमद्भुतः ॥

ananto huta-bhug-bhoktā sukhado naikajo'grajaḥ ।
anirviṇṇaḥ sadāmarṣī lokādhiṣṭhānam-adbhutaḥ ॥

The lord has no beginning and no end. He is therefore glorified as *Anādi* and *Ananta*. The first name of the Lord in this verse is *Anantaḥ*. In this context, this name will have to be interpreted as the divine serpent *Ananta* which supports the earth eternally - as long as the world exists. In *Gītā,* Lord *Kṛṣṇa* says, 'I am Ananta among the *Nāgās* - serpents'- *anantaścāsmi nāgānām*. It can be *Ādi-śeṣa* as well. Or it can be just a general attribute of the Lord extolling His infinite glory. In all respects and aspects, He is *Ananta* the Infinite.

The next name *Hutabhuk* means that the Lord consumes all the oblations offered to the God of Fire in the sacrificial worships. Whatever is put in the fire will ultimately go to the Lord. The God of Fire is just a messenger or carrier.

It is in the same sense and context that the Lord is adored as *Bhokta*. Even in daily life, it is the Lord who virtually consumes what we eat or drink. *Bhagavān* Himself said in *Gītā* that He would help the individuals in digesting food they consume by sitting in them in the form of *Vaiśvānara,* the fire of digestion in the stomach. This name figures in the *Sahasranāma* thrice (Sl. No. 143, 500 and 888). This is the last occurrence of the name. In another context, the Lord was indentified with the'Food' *Bhojanam* (Sl. No. 142) that we eat. He is food, He is the consumer and He is the one who acts as a catalytic agent in digesting all that is consumed. What else can one expect from the Lord when He has taken full charge of our nourishment-in providing food and also offering His assistance in its proper assimilation?

This is the reason why He is glorified in the next name as *Sukhadaḥ* One who confers comfort or happiness. This is immediately followed by another name *Naikadaḥ* which means that the Lord has many things to offer to His devotees. In fact He looks after all our requirements with parental affection. He is also glorified as *Agrajaḥ,* the first born. This is supported by the Vedic observation that the Lord alone existed in the beginning as *Hiraṇyagarbha* who was the master *pati* of all living beings *Bhūtasys jātaḥ patireka āsīt.* In this sense also He is *Agraja.*

As the Lord has no desire unfulfilled, He never feels dejected or depressed and so are His devotees whom He never allows to be in such a state. He keeps them thoroughly happy and satisfied. Hence, He is hymned as *Anirviṇṇaḥ* never depressed.

Even if His devotees commit some mistake sometimes due to circumstances beyond their control, He tries to understand their helplessness sympathetically and forgives them. This is the remarkable greatness of the Lord who is, therefore, admired and adored here as *Sadāmarṣī,* One who always forgives defaulters on merit.

He is always available for any help, support or sympathy, because He is the Lord of the Universe - the basic foundation of all that exists. Hence, He is glorified as *Lokādhiṣṭhānam* the pedastal of the world. He is the standing support to all the problems faced by His devotees or others.

This is really marvellous and magnanimous of the Lord who is the real master sincerely working for the welfare of all living beings. He is therefore extolled as *Adbhutaḥ* the Marvellous.

Blissful Shower Of Blessings

The sacred hymn, *Śrī Viṣṇu Sahasranāma Stotram* is almost coming to an auspicious summing up. The following verse, therefore, strikes a pleasant note of blissful blessings on the devoted aspirants who chant the thousand names of the Lord with rapt attention. In a way, this is *Svastyayanam* (the concluding session) of the holy congregation.

Incidentally, the verse that follows containing names or attributes of the Lord starting with the word *svasti* (benediction) inaugurates the last hundred names of the text. The ten names glorified in the verse are as follows:

सनात्सनातनतमः कपिलः कपिरप्ययः ।
स्वस्तिदः स्वस्तिकृत्स्वस्ति स्वस्तिभुक्स्वस्तिदक्षिणः ॥

sanāt-sanātana-tamaḥ kapilaḥ kapir-apyayaḥ I
svastidaḥ svastikṛt-svasti svastibhuk-svasti-dakṣiṇaḥ II

The first attribute of the Lord *Sanāt* glorifies the antiquity of the Lord who is as ancient as time because He identifies Himself with time eternal. This He told *Arjuna* when he wanted to know the real form of the Lord. He said 'I am Time Eternal' - *Kāló'smi.* In order to glorify this antiquity and also qualify that antiquity, the hymn mentions a supplementary attribute as well and that is *Sanātanatamaḥ* the Most Ancient.

Apart from the sense of antiquity and the eternity of the Lord who is Time personified, these two names *Sanāt* and *Sanātanatamaḥ* sound complimentary conveying the good wishes and blessings of the learned *Ācārya* who has recited the sacred names of the Lord in His own presence (*Śrī Kṛṣṇa* was present when *Bhiṣma* was reciting these names for the benefit of the *Pāṇḍavas*). There is an aura of auspicious articulation, soft, sweet and scintillating in these two words which themselves serve as benediction to the benedictory attributes of the Lord that form the second line of this verse.

The two words *Sanāt* and *Sanātana* are derived from the root *san* which means to love, like, worship, honour, acquire, obtain, receive graciously or bestow with blessings. Based on this connotation, the attribute *Sanāt* conveys the sense 'always', 'forever'. The *Ācārya* seems to be blessing in these words 'May such moments enlighten you forever'. The second attribute *Sanātanatamaḥ* that follows immediately conveys that this exhilarating experience should perpetuate in your minds and hearts.

After these two benedictory attributes, the *Ācārya* articulates three significant words *Kapilaḥ*, *Kapiḥ* and *Apyayaḥ*. *Kapila* is the name of a sage who reduced to ashes 60,000 sons of *Sagara* who accused the sage of having stolen the sacrificial horse of their father. He is also said to have been the founder of the *Sāṅkhya* system of philosophy. This name figured earlier (Sl.No. 531) in this sacred hymn.This is repeated here with a different connotation and purpose. The blessings of the *Maharaṣi* of *Kapilācārya's* stature are invoked here as inaugural words for the benedictory address. The word *Kapila* also means Sun. It also indicates the colour 'orange brown' or 'slightly reddish'. All these things have their own significance.

The second name in this series is *Kapiḥ* which simply means an ape or monkey. It also means *sun*. As a monkey, the image of *Hanumān*, the monarch among monkeys and a close associate and favourite of both *Rāma* and *Sītā* whom he united comes to the fore front. *Hanumān* is noted for his mastery over words and word-culture which wins the admiration of no less a person than *Rāma.* It is therefore relevant to recollect this name in this context.

The last word in this line *apyayaḥ* literaly means to approach or to flow into or dissolve. The *Māṇḍūkya Upaniṣad* uses this word along with the word *bhava-bhavāpyayau hi bhūtānām* (the advent and the merger of all beings). Thus this attribute of the Lord refers to His eternal abode of absolute bliss which serves as the resting place for all the living beings at the time of the dissolution of the universe. This also means the salvation which the Lord grants to His devotees in due recognition of their merit.

Now the five names starting with the word *savasti* commence with the attribute *Svastidaḥ,* One who confers blessings on His devotees in the form *Svasti.* The word-meaning of the word *svasti* is 'may it be well with you' (*su + asti = svasti,* means O.K.). Everything is O.K. when the Lord showers His blissful blessings on the earth and its inhabitants.

He not only grants this boon of *Svasti* but also effects it and makes it available to all. Hence, the attribute *Svastikṛt* which means that the Lord also inspires the well-meaning people to do good things so that they may deserve His grace. So graceful is the Lord.

The next epithet *Svasti* takes us still closer to the Lord who Himself assumes the form of *Svasti* and presents Himself on all auspicious occasions. He does not stop here. He joins His devotees in enjoying these blissful blessings granted by Him to make sure that His blessings have really proved to be blissful for His beloved ones. He actually shares this 'blissful experience' with them. Hence, the Lord is adored as *Svastibhuk* by His devotees with affection and gratitude.

The last name in this benedictory verse is *Svastidakṣiṇaḥ* which highlights the dexterity of the Lord in granting the divine bliss, the essence of all being and becoming to His devotees. He is, no doubt, competent to grant it, but at the same time He is highly objective, sincere, honest and skilful in passing His Verdict. He is always on the right side(*dakṣiṇa* means right in *Saṁskṛt* language). While adopting a sophisticated and straightforward approach in the matter He maintains dignity and decency of the Divinity He stands for so that His decision stands the test of time and the time-honoured standards and norms of Truth, Righteousness, Universal love, abiding peace and harmony.

The word *dakṣiṇā* may also have something to contribute to the attribute *Svastidakṣiṇaḥ*. The word *dakṣiṇā* means a gift or present offered to a scholar or priest who performs a religious rite as a token of reverence and gratitude. In this context, the Lord Himself is the priest besides His being a guest as well as a host. Therefore the question of offering something to Him does not arise when He Himself is confering His blessings on the devotees. A sincere prayer wishing the whole universe to continue to be a blissful abode of the Lord *Svasti* is the *dakṣiṇā* that can be offered to Him. In this respect also He is appropriately extolled as *Svastidakṣiṇāḥ*.

Valiant But Not Violent

The Lord who has the whole universe under His control maintains a marvellous balance between authority and affection. He never loses His temper and never expresses His anger unless He is face to face with villainous violence. Even then He exercises His power and prowess to the extent it is absolutely essential so that the calm He always promotes does not take a violent and villainous trun. This remarkable strategy and statesmanship found in the Lord is explained in the following names:

अरौद्रः कुण्डली चक्री विक्रम्यूर्जितशासनः ।
शब्दातिगः शब्दसहः शिशिरः शर्वरीकरः ॥

araudraḥ kuṇḍalī cakrī vikramyūrjita-śāsanaḥ ।
śabdātigaḥ śabdasahaḥ śiśiraḥ śarvarī-karaḥ ॥

The verse starts with the negation of anything dreadful, terrific, frightful and formidable. All these features are contained in the word *rudra* and therefore one who has these characteristics is called *Raudraḥ*. There are eleven *Rudras* supposed to be inferior mainfestations of Lord *Śiva* who is said to be the head of this group. One who is devoid of these traits or qualities is *Aroudraḥ*. The verse starts with this attribute of the Lord. *Aroudraḥ*, therefore, stands for one who is devoid of wrath, violence or terror. That is to say that the Lord is a fine specimen of refined temperament inspite of His powerful status as the Lord of the Universe.

In the next name, He is glorified as *Kuṇḍalī* which means 'decorated with ear rings' or 'coiling like a serpent' . This may refer to the celestial serpent *Śeṣa*. It certainly points out to the inherent power of the Omnipotent hidden under His stature as the Lord of the Universe. It means that He is all-powerful.

He is then glorified as *Cakrī*, having a discus in His hand. This refers to *Viṣṇu* who always holds His *Sudarśana-cakra* in one of His four arms. This discus is supposed to represent the 'mind' which always wavers. It is also depicted as a symbol of the ever moving cycle of time.

The next name is *Vikramī* which means 'one endowed with prowess'. This particularly extols the swift movement of the Lord. In His incarnation as *Vāmana,* He was known for His great strides occupying the three worlds with His feet.

Though the Lord is very generous by nature, when it comes to tackling evil forces disturbing the peace and harmony, He never spares them. He is very strong in making His rule effective and energetic. He is therefore extolled as *Ūrjitaśāsanaḥ*, strong in strict adherence to the moral code of conduct.

It is very difficult to describe the glory of the Lord in words. Human voice and mind cannot catch Him. He transcends the limitations of speech. Hence the name *Śabdātigaḥ*.

But at the same time, the Vedic seers and spiritual leaders tried to express their experiences in clear terms and the Lord too appreciates their attempts in spite of the limitations. He is, therefore, projected as *Śabdasahaḥ*, extolled by all the *Vedas* in enchanting language. He likes the voice of vision, but will not confine Himself to it. One has to grow beyond these media to experience His real essence and excellence.

He is very cool in temperament and promotes the same in His devotees as well. It is only when the world with five elements and the allied senses and sense-objects cools down, the absolute reality can be understood and appreciated. Hence, the attribute *Śiśiraḥ*. *Śiśira* is one of the six seasons, the last one in the cycle. This is immediately followed by spring *Vasanta*. The year ends with *Śiśira* and starts again with *Vasanta*. The Lord identifies Himself with the entire cycle of seasons as revealed in His earlier attributes, *Ṛtuḥ*, *Sudarśanaḥ*, *Kālaḥ* etc. Here the particular season *Śiśira* has been mentioned to highlight the powerful, purposeful and peaceful governance of the Lord.

The last name *Śarvarīkaraḥ* presents the Lord as the creator or the generator of the night. Day and night are compared to the forms of *Bhagavān Śiva* and *Bhagavatī Pārvatī* in the *Rāmāyaṇa* of *Vālmīki* - *Gatā Bhagavatī rātriḥ, ahas-śivamupasthitam.* Day creates activity and the night provides rest. In *Gītā,* day and night are presented in a different context. *Bhagavān* tells *Arjuna* that what is day for the sages is night for the common man and what is day for the common man is night for the sage. Here the day stands for *Saṁsāra* and the night for *ātman*. In this sense, the epithet *Śarvarīkaraḥ* would mean that God creates the night so that we can relax and allow the *Saṁsāra* to cool down and then realize the excellence of atmic existence.

The Holy Name Will Do

The following verse in the sacred hymn, *Sahasranāma* sings the glory of the Lord who is gentle, handsome, skilful, efficient, considerate, learned, fearless and auspicious in all respects. Even His name will do to elevate the person to the highest attainment of absolute bliss if it is properly cultivated. It is important to understand, in this context, that all the attributes extolled in these names are meant for cultivation by the aspirants of spiritual awareness. *Bhūtātmā*, the material person can rise to the level of *Paramātmā*, the Supreme soul if these qualities are cultivated. It is with this background that the names covered in the following verse have to be studied and recited to get the real benefit.

अक्रूरः पेशलो दक्षो दक्षिणः क्षमिणां वरः ।
विद्वत्तमो वीतभयः पुण्यश्रवणकीर्तनः ॥

akrūraḥ peśalo dakṣo dakṣiṇaḥ kṣamiṇāṁ varaḥ ।
vidvattamo vītabhayaḥ puṇya-śravaṇa-kīrtanaḥ ॥

Where there is divinity, there can be no cruelty. Where there is absolutely no room for curelty, there the Lord dwells. Anger or wrath is the root cause of all forms of curelty. Therefore the Lord never allows these ill-feelings to come anywhere near Him. Hence, He is hymned in the first name of this verse as *Akrūraḥ*. In the previous verse, the first name was *Araudraḥ* meaning free from wrath. Here it is *Akrūraḥ* free from cruelty.

Cruelty can not be hidden. It shows its ugly face on the facial complexion itself. Those who are free from anger and curel intentions look healthy-physically and mentally. That is why the Lord is glorified in the second name as *Peśalaḥ,* beautiful in thought, looks and words. The verbal expression reveals the mind which is reflected in the face. The attribute *Peśalaḥ* therefore indicates this handsomeness in the physical structure and wholesomeness in mental set up and holiness in the spiritual radiance. These are the qualities which an individual has to cultivate in order to have an access to the divine grace of the Lord.

The next epithet is *Dakṣaḥ* which means competent in expression and action. It also means technical skill. *Śaṅkara Bhagavatpāda* considers three qualities essential to make one competent. These are maturity-*pravṛddhi,* capacity-*śakti* and quick execution *śīghrakāritā.* Himself being fully equipped with these qualities, He expects every one entrusted with personnel and material management to imbibe these qualities. Those who are good and capable in their duties have covered half the way to divinity and the rest they can leave for Him.

It is not enough if one is efficient and capable *dakṣa.* He should also be amicable to his fellow-workers. He should be friendly and sympathetic with them. This is the quality indicated in the next attribute *Dakṣiṇaḥ.* In Indian poetics, there is a type of hero called *Dakṣiṇanāyaka* who is friendly with more than one partner in life. Though this is not the amicability that is exactly expected of a devotee of God, one who is devoted to his duty as well as devotion to God with equal dedication and regard, comes under the category of *dakṣiṇa* as used in this epithet of the Lord. The same type of balance in loyalty and devotion is essential for a house-holder who has to discharge his responsibilities as a family-member and at the same time have an eye on his devotional and spiritual activities. The material proseprity *abhyudaya* and spiritual attainment *nisśreyas* should go hand in hand. This is exactly what the Lord expects from His devotees.

Forbearance, patience and forgiveness are also equally important for a sincere, honest and large-hearted worker devoted to God and the world around him. This expectation of the Lord from His devotees is explained in the epithet *Kṣamiṇāṁvaraḥ* the most commendable among those who have these qualities. *Vālmīki* depicts *Rāma* as an ideal character in this respect. He compares him in forbearance with the Mother Earth *Kṣamayā prithivī samaḥ*.

This quality of *Rāma* we find at the best when He entertains *Vibhīṣaṇa* without any hesitation as His own man and tells His friends like *Sugrīva* who were critical and even nervous about this hasty (?) decision of *Rāma* that He was prepared to pardon and accept even *Rāvaṇa* if he approaches Him. This is the height of forbearance which we find in the Lord incarnated as *Rāma*. Similar instances can be quoted from the life of *Kṛṣṇa* too. This is the basic trait of God and godly personalities which is glorified here.

Scholarship, learning and wisdom which are the characteristics of an intellectual engaged in service to humanity are covered in the next epithet of the Lord - *Vidvattamaḥ*, highly learned and well-versed in intellectual and spiritual wisdom. Mere wisdom will not do. The wise man with sharp intellect should be fearless too. He should be prepared to express his sincere opinion before any authority without fear. This fearlessness is a 'must' if 'intellect' has to serve the purpose. This is what is glorified in the attribute *Vītabhayaḥ* 'free from fear'.

The last name in the verse *Puṇyaśravaṇa-kīrtanaḥ* glorifies the miracle that the holy name of the Lord can produce. If God is in your heart and if you really feel that He is guiding you in all your thoughts, words and actions, nothing can go wrong with you. Think of Him and do what He tells you from the innermost layers of your consciousness. This inner voice is the voice of the Lord vibrant towards your feelings. His holy name will do to set you in motion in the proper direction and also ensure that nothing goes wrong anywhere. This is the message that the *Ācārya* conveys to *Yudhiṣṭhira* who has great responsibilities as the Head of a Kingdom. The name of the Lord and His attributes are enough to guide not only kings but also innumerable celestial deities. He is the Supreme. His name is a spell that dispels all fears and paves the way for peace.

The Good That Dispels Bad

If we are good at heart and feel the presence of God in the heart of our hearts, all the evils vanish in a moment and the Good that is God dispels all evil feelings, harsh words and curel acts and purify the heart to make it livable for Him and lovable for the world around us. How this happens is explained in the following nine attributes of the Lord:

उत्तारणो दुष्कृतिहा पुण्यो दुःस्वप्ननाशनः ।
वीरहा रक्षणः सन्तो जीवनः पर्यवस्थितः ॥

uttāraṇo duṣ-kṛtihā puṇyo duḥ-svapna-nāśanaḥ ।
vīrahā rakṣaṇaḥ santo jīvanaḥ paryavasthitaḥ ॥

God-willing all obstacles can be surmounted in a second. One can cross over the ocean of *Saṁsāra* (life-cycles) under the protection of His name. He saves us from all troubles and turmoils of life and lead us to the highest state of Bliss if only we think of Him and remember His name and His glories manifest in all that we see, think, express and experience. This is the purport of his first epithet in this verse: *Uttāraṇaḥ*, deliverer, Savior who takes us across the ocean standing in our way. *Nārada* in His aphorisms glorifying the potentialities of devotion *Bhaktisūtras*, says that a sincere devotee crosses the ocean of worldly life and also helps others in doing so with the blissful blessings of the Lord *sa tarati lokānstārayati.*

Whatever evil deeds one has done in the past, the moment he comes into touch with the Lord and is blessed by Him, all his past with polluted thoughts and criminal deeds undergoes a remarkable change. The only condition is that he should be in a position to confess sincerely form his heart that he has completely surrendered to Him at His feet. This is what *Rāma* tells his friends when *Vibhīṣaṇa* seeks shelter and protection under Him. He says, 'once a person comes and prostrates before me and declares that he is mine and only mine *tavāsmi*, He is prepared to dispel all fears from his heart and this assurance covers all beings in this world' [*Rāmāyaṇa* 6-18-33].

This transformation of the bad into the good, the wicked into the wise and the sinful into the saintly becomes possible because of the holy presence of the Lord. His touch energizes all beings and transforms them into pious souls. In *Gītā*, the Lord assures His devotees saying that even if one is the most sinful of all, he will cross this pond of pollution with the help of the boat of awareness, wisdom and knowledge. That is why the Lord is adored as *Duṣkṛtihā*, He dispels all evil effects of wickedness and crookedness. *Ahalyā* regained her physical form at the mere sight of the Lord. There can be no sin anywhere near when the Lord is with us, in us and around us.

It is enough if we say He is *Puṇyaḥ* purity,holiness or sinlessness personified. The Lord has earlier been glorified as *Śarvarīkaraḥ* (the maker of the night). All that happens during the day gets reflected in the night in our dreams. We speak to ourselves within ourselves and exclusively for ourselves in these dreams. If we think of God, He will appear in our dreams and talk to us, but makes us forget all about it the moment we open our eyes. If we have evil thoughts in our mind, they figure in our dreams and sometimes give us dreadful, terrific and depressing experience. If God is there at the back of our minds even while sleeping, this untoward thing does not happen.That is why the Lord is adored as *Duḥ-svapnanāśanaḥ*,the dispeller of the evil effects of bad dreams, nasty ideas and destructive designs.

The next line starts with the attribute *Vīraḥā*. The word *vīraḥ* normally means a hero, warrior or champion. If this popular meaning is taken, the epithet will mean 'One who keeps or drives away or destroys the vagaries of the valiant people disturbing peace and harmony and restores the basic values of life'.These disturbing forces need not necessarily be external. They can be internal as well. *Śaṅkara Bhagavatpāda* too interprets the meaning of this attribute as 'the destroyer' *ha* of various *vi* wrong paths *ira* pursued bybpeople by granting them salvation. As the theme of this set of epithets is the victory of good over evil, this interpretation also seems to be sound.

The main objective of the Lord, even in this approach to the evil minded people, is to provide protection to the pious section. He is, therefore, glorified as the protector by improvising means of protection. Hence, the name *Rakṣaṇaḥ*. He has to provide protection, not to individuals but to all the beings in the three worlds. His objective is general protection *Rakṣaṇaḥ*.

While He removes the destructive forces from the path of righteousness, He also takes special care to see that the virtuous, well meaning and good people are given full support. The attribute used for the Lord in this context is *Santaḥ*, the Good, those who stick to the right path based on non-violent and peace-loving measures. The Lord stands by them, in them and for them in all such eventualities. Promotion of 'Good' automatically dispels the bad. God favours good people, as He is where good is.

The life-giver has to preserve the life He has given. He is the very breath of life and therefore makes life livable. Hence, He is adored as *Jīvanaḥ*, life in its universal sense.

The last attribute in this verse *Paryavasthitaḥ* extols the Omnipresent form of the Lord. He is present everywhere and therefore looks after all living beings with proper care and compassion so that life in general may be happy. *Sarve janāḥ sukhino bhavantu* (May all people be happy) is the prayer of all His devotees and the Lord pays full attention to this basic requirement of enduring life on earth.

Variety Of Forms And Powers

Infinity is the basic attribute of the Lord as every glory associated with Him is endless, immeasurable and unfathomable. His divinity lies in creating diversity in unity and again re-establishing the basic unity. This multi-dimensional manifestation of the Lord is glorified in the following verse:

अनन्तरूपोऽनन्तश्रीर्जितमन्युर्भयापहः ।
चतुरस्रो गभीरात्मा विदिशो व्यादिशो दिशः ॥

anantarūpo'nanta-śrīrjitamanyur-bhayāpahaḥ ।
caturasro gabhīrātmā vidiśo vyādiśo diśaḥ ॥

He manifests Himself in endless forms starting from a gigantic fish *matsya* to *Rāma*, the son of *Daśaratha, Kṛṣṇa*, the divine off-spsring of *Devakī* and *Buddha* the messenger of peace and non-violence. Besides these landmarks of divine manifestations (incarnations) of the Lord, His transcendental radiance finds a glorious self-expression in all extraordinary genius found in men and women from time to time throughout the world, as proclaimed by the Lord Himself. It is this power of manifestation in endless forms that projects the Lord as *Anantarūpaḥ* and *Anantaśrīḥ*, the infinite variety of forms, powers, glories and grandeur.

Despite the divine powers the Lord exercises for the creation, preservation and dissolution of the universe in accordance with the Law of Nature, He never expresses His anger. Even when he has to punish the wicked, He does it with a balanced mind with no aggresive attitude even towards His avowed enemy. In fact He has no enemy from His side. All are equal for Him. He resorts to annihilation as an inevitable measure to protect the rest without any ill-feeling in His heart. This is illustrated in His killing of *Vāli, Rāvaṇa* and other evil forces.He convinces *Vāli* that He was fully justified in resorting to this step.He advises *Vibhīṣaṇa* not to think ill of his heroic brother *Rāvaṇa* whose wickedness ends with his death. Hence, He is glorified as *Jitamanyuḥ*, conqueror of anger.

Anger creates fear in the minds of both the parties,one who generates it and the one who is subjected to it.Therefore one who conquers anger and keeps it firmly under his control is neither afraid of anyone nor does he make others afraid of him. The Lord who is extolled as *Jitamanyuḥ* (conqueror of anger) in the previous name is adored in the next attribute as *Bhayāpahaḥ*, the remover of all fear. He helps His devotees in overcoming the fear of death also. One who has the divine grace of the Lord is never afraid of anything including death. Where there is faith in God, there can be no fear. Fearlessness *abhayam* is the first quality of a person belonging to divine origin as declared by the Lord Himself [*Gītā*. 16-1]. Absolute fearlessness, perfect purity of mind, deep and undisturbed meditation and straightforwardedness in thought,word and deed are the virtues associated with divine temperament. The basis for all this is fearlessness. God helps His devotees in attaining this state of mind. Hence, the name *Bhayāpahaḥ*.

The next line starts with the attribute *Caturasraḥ* or *Caturaśraḥ* which means a geometrical figure of a quadrilateral with the four sides equal. This is also called a square. In a symbolic way, the Lord is extolled in this name as a square-shaped personality *caturasraḥ*. In other words, He is just and judicious in His response to the prayers of all His devotees. There are four types of devotees who approach the Lord - those who are in distress *ārta*, those who seek to understand the reality *jijñāsu*, those who are interested in material prosperity *arthārthī* and those who have perfect knowledge of the absolute reality *jñānī*. The Lord says that these are all fortunate and blessed; but the *Jñānī* (the real knower) excels the other three as he never deviates from his path of devotion. Nevertheless all are equally dear and near to the Lord as they are all in the right path though there is difference in their proximity to the abode of the Lord. He is therefore very appropriately extolled in this epithet as *Caturasraḥ*.

This epithet also draws our attention to the fourfold glories of the Lord - as a promoter of the four principal aims of life (namely) *dharma, artha, kāma* and *mokṣa,* the four *āśramās* (stages) of life, namely, *brahmacarya, gārhasthya, vānaprastha* and *sannyāsa,* and so on. Some of these fourfold manifestations of the Lord already figured in this sacred hymn while adoring the Lord as *Caturmūrtiḥ, Caturbāhuḥ* and so on. The present attribute *Caturasra* emphasizes the significance of the Lord's equal attention, attachment and patronage for all the four categories. He made it clear more than once in His Song Celestial *Bhagavad Gītā* that He will entertain all types of devotion and approach and He will react and respond in the same tone and in the same tune. He is quite sure that whatever the path we follow, we have ultimately to reach Him. This is what is conveyed in a geometrical way in the glorious tribute *Caturasraḥ*.

The next name *Gabhīrātmā* projects the depth of the Lord's feelings for His devotees. No one can imagine His love for His devotees.

He identifies Himself with them. But at the same time, He subjects them to all tests and ordeals. It is only when they come out of these hardships and cross over the hurdles, they qualify themselves for His grace. That is why He is extolled as *Gabhīrātmā,* unfathomable in His intentions and ways of treating the people accroding to their standing and understanding.

The next three names *Vidiśaḥ, Vyādiśaḥ* and *Diśaḥ* try to focus our attention on the main point that the ways of the Lord may be diverse, but the result of all His trials is the same - to grant the highest bliss to them ultimately. He bestows various things to various people according to their desires, abilities and spiritual advancement. This is what is meant by the attribute *Vidiśaḥ.* The commands He issues to various people of varied stages of attainment are also different. The objective, again, is the same. This is the idea behind the sacred name *Vyādiśaḥ.* Finally, the last name *Diśaḥ* summarises the whole process saying that the Lord does not merely direct, but He gives proper guidance as to how to go about in the spiritual path which is very narrow, delicate and perilous too.

The Being Without Beginning

When we have just started feeling that we are approaching almost the concluding phase of the sacred hymn, the *Ācārya* suddenly takes us back to the beginning of all beings and the Being without a beginning. This refreshing and retrospective thought-wave can be felt in the following attributes of the Lord:

अनादिर्भूर्भुवो लक्ष्मीः सुवीरो रुचिराङ्गदः ।
जननो जनजन्मादिर्भीमो भीमपराक्रमः ।।

anādir-bhūrbhuvo lakṣmīḥ suvīro rucirāṅgadaḥ |
janano janajanmādir-bhīmo bhīma-parākramaḥ ||

Being the most ancient *Sanātanatamaḥ* of all that is ancient *Sanat*, the Supreme Being from whom all the being has emerged, obviously, can not have any beginning of His own. He is therefore glorified in the first attribute in this verse as *Anādiḥ* one without a beginning. He is the root cause of all creation.

The next name *Bhūrbhuvaḥ* is a highly significant name with a mystic shade of meaning. In common parlance, the word *Bhūḥ* means earth, the support and shelter of all living beings. *Bhuvaḥ* means ether, the atmospheric sphere immediately above the earth and below the level of *Svargaḥ* or *Svaḥ*, the mystic name for the third of the three worlds and the three words *Bhūḥ, Bhuvaḥ Svaḥ*. Incidentally, these three words are considered to be three worlds or three planes of inner consiousness which are sacred utterances for an aspirant, usually uttered before performing any worship to the Lord or chanting any *mantra*. Even if we take the common meaning of the terms *bhūḥ* and *bhuvaḥ* for the time being, the epithet *Bhūrbhuvaḥ* would mean the Being *bhūḥ* of all beings *bhuvaḥ* or the supporter of the supporting earth. Earth supports all living beings and the life they live while the Lord supports the earth itself. Thus He is the *Bhūḥ* of *Bhūrbhuvaḥ*, the Grand parental figure for the whole creation. He is *Brahma of Brahma* and the earth of the earth. In *Gītā, Bhagavān* himself says, 'I am the father of the world, and also the mother, the guardian and grandfather' *pitā, mātā, dhātā* and *pitāmahaḥ*. In short, He is 'Be all' of all the being that exists.

Equally significant is the attribute *Lakṣmīḥ*. What is surprising is that this is a feminine name - the name of the goddess of fortune, prosperity and beauty, regarded as the wife of *Viṣṇu* whose thousand names are being glorified in this sacred hymn. She is supposed to have sprung from the ocean of milk *Kṣīra-sāgara* along with moon and nectar. As an independent epithet of Lord *Viṣṇu,* this name suggests how the divine couple are identical with one another. Goddess *Lakṣmī* is supposed to be always gracing the blissful bosom of the Lord. Hence, He is known as *Śrīvatsalāñchanaḥ*. In a series of fourteen names starting or associated with *Śrī,* the Lord was earlier glorified as *Śrīvatsavakṣāḥ,* having *Śrī,* as a mark of His bosom. There are several other points of significance in glorifying the Lord, in this name, as *Lakṣmī* Herself. They are one and the same, inseparable and undistinguishable.

One can link up this attribute *Lakṣmīḥ* with the previous one *Bhūrbhuvaḥ* in which case the epithet would mean the resplendent splendour of the terrestrial and celestial planes which are controlled by

Lord *Viṣṇu*. In fact, in Indian mythology Lord *Viṣṇu* is supposed to be equally endeared to both *Śrīdevī* and *Bhūdevī* representing, in secular terminology, the Earth and the Heaven. The Lord always endeavours to bring about a harmony between earth and heaven. Like the 'poet's frenzy glorified by Shakespeare as a link between the earth and the heaven, the divine link between the same is here extolled by the *Ācārya* in this sacred hymn.

The next name *Suvīraḥ* focusses our attention on the multiple ways, movements or vibrations of the Lord which promote anything that is good - good to all. The expression *su* stands for all that is adorable, acquirable, adaptable and hence, auspicious. The word *Vīraḥ* is not confined to its popular meaning 'hero' here. It means all activity promoting general welfare including refined speech or speech-culture. Where there is sense and sophistication in what we think, express and act in our day to day life, there exists divinity in the form of *Suvīraḥ,* a perfect soul with pious feelings and responses.

In the next attribute *Rucirāṅgadaḥ*, the Lord is presented as handsome, good-looking and well-decorated form of divinity worshipped by His devotees. The word *ruciraḥ* does not mean merely beautiful or attractive, it also indicates the refined taste in appreciating the divinity behind the beauty. Such are the armlets *aṅgadaḥ* which the Lord is adorned with. It is the judicious combination of physical beauty and metaphysical sanctity that takes us closer and closer to the quarters of the divine mansion.

The next line starts with two names, both relating to birth and other allied events in life. The first name is *Jananaḥ* the process of procreation in the worldly sense and creation in the broader sense. The Lord is the creator of creators - Creator General of the entire universe. Hence, He is adored as *Jananaḥ* - a very simple, but highly significant and thought-provoking epithet for the Lord of the Universe.

The same idea is amplified in the next name *Janajanmādiḥ,* the promoter of procreation, creation and other allied activities of all living beings - both terrestrial and celestial. He is as much responsible for birth and growth of civilization and culture as for the death or termination of life and dissolution of the whole universe. It is out of fear for Him that the death performs its duty in time (as the *Upaniṣad* says, *mṛtyur dhāvati pañcamaḥ*).

Hence, the Lord is extolled as *Bhīmaḥ,* the terrific and *Bhīmaparākramaḥ* (of Terrifying strength). He promotes both Love and Fear and ensures their proper utilization so that truth and justice may prevail in the world.

The Smile That Blossoms

Though the Lord is extolled as *Bhīma* (terrific) and *Bhīma-parākramaḥ* (of terrifying strength and valour), He rarely resorts to these measures. He does it only when it is absolutely essential and unavoidable. Normally His strategy is very soft and smooth. A simple and sweet smile from His lips and a sign of alarm in His looks will do to solve the most intricate problems in life. This unique pattern of public handling adopted by the Lord finds a vivid description in the following lines:

आधारनिलयो धाता पुष्पहासः प्रजागरः ।
ऊर्ध्वगः सत्पथाचारः प्राणदः प्रणवः पणः ।।

ādhāranilayo dhātā puṣpahāsaḥ prajāgaraḥ |
ūrdhvagaḥ sat-pathācāraḥ prāṇadaḥ praṇavaḥ paṇaḥ ||

Being the ultimate and eternal abode for all living beings and also for the five elements-earth, water, wind, fire and sky - at the time of deluge, the Lord is glorified as *Ādhāranilayaḥ*. He is not only the final abode or support for all, but also the ultimate for all forms of supports. Hence the attribute.

As He is the support even for those who support others, He Himself does not need any support. He supports those who support others, creates those who create the world and provide nourishment to those who nourish the beings. He is *Dhātā* (caretaker) for *Dhātās* (the caretakers). There is, therefore, none above Him. Hence, He is extolled as *Dhātā* and *Adhātā*. He has no other *dhātā* for His sake. Strictly speaking He, virtually acts as *Dhātā* (creator), *Vidhātā* (ordainer) and *Sandhātā* (coordinator). Hence, real *Dhātā* - three dimensional *Dhātā*. This attribute is real both as *Dhātā* and *Adhātā*. To make it more meaningful we can add the implied epithets like *Vidhātā* and *Sandhātā* as well as mentioned above.

The next name *Puṣpahāsaḥ* which projects the Lord as the full-blossomed flower adding grace and fragrance to the whole universe is a splendid name for the Lord. The smile of a flower is the gift of God as He Himself smiles like a flower. The twinkling starts, the grand galaxies, the generous clouds, the deep waters of the seas, the pleasant and placid flow of the river-water and the whole dynamic movements of the countless atoms glorifying the immense potentialities of the Universe are all living bards singing the sophisticated smile of the Lord which blossoms forth as the Universe.

But this smile of the Lord is very vigilant, wakeful and watchful. It does not allow the universe to be complascent even for a moment. The smile of the Lord keeps a watch over its admirers. He is ever-alert though ever smiling. This unique combination of cheer and caution is what is glorified in the next attribute *Prajāgaraḥ* - ever awake. Though He appears to be relaxing in the deep ocean of milk on the soft bed of the celestial serpent *ananta,* He has His millions of eyes wide open to observe the whole universe.

Then we come to the second line which starts with the epithet *Ūrdhvagaḥ* which means 'One who transcends all and moves in higher planes.' His vision goes beyond all worldly values and it takes His devotees also to the same plane. He is never narrow, ever vigilant but always smiling with a blissful blossom.

He follows the path of *sat* righteousness, straight-forwardness, nobility, virtue, respect and reverence as He is always fond and in favour of the right-minded people *Santaḥ* which attribute firgured earlier in this hymn. He is one with such good people, pious souls and godly persons who follow His path and in reciprocation, the Lord follows their path. Hence, the Lord is admired and adored as *Satpathācāraḥ,* moving in the path of righteousness followed by noble, pious and saintly persons.

Being the most benevolent, bounteous and blissful in nature, the Lord bestows the Best to His nearest and dearest devotees. Even to common people who consciously or unconsciously admire and adore Him in some form or other are blessed by Him with the same bliss. The most precious gift He offers to all living beings in the universe is *prāṇaḥ,* the breath of life. He is, therefore *Prāṇadātā,*the bestower of life. Hence, He is glorified as *Prāṇadaḥ. Prāṇa,* the vital air is the essence of very existence. Hence, this is the most valuable gift the Lord bestows on all without any discrimination.

There are occasions when the Lord not only granted this at the time of birth, but also revived it in case of emergency. He revived *Parīkṣit* and granted him new birth.

The second gift He bestows to the gifted people is the sacred syllable *om* which is called *Praṇavaḥ.* This primordial sound which is the essence of the whole universe and the second name of the Lord is not only the most precious gift but the most auspicious one. As *Kaṭhopaniṣad* points out, one who realizes and visualizes this single sacred and mystic syllable in all its implications can get whatever he desires - *yo yadicchati tasya tat.* This is, therefore, the most cherished and covetable gift that one can expect from the Lord. In a way, this gift is also universal in the ultimate sense, because all the sounds, syllables, words, sentences, rhymes, lyrics, hymns and creative expressions are originated from this single, sacred and primordial sound *om* which is the real name of the Lord, as the sage *Patañjali* says in his *Yogasūtra* that *Praṇava* is what He is known by *tasya vācakaḥ praṇavaḥ*.

The third category of the gifts, the Lord reserves for the deserving people depending upon their good conduct is termed *Paṇaḥ*, a negotiable instrument which the Lord grants as a reward. This is how He deals with people who are material in outlook. He bargains with them, encourages them to do something good and then satisfies them with colourful gifts.

He Knows What He Is

The highest form of knowledge that one can aspire for in life is to visualize the Self (the Supreme Self) within himself and to experience for himself what 'That' exactly is. He and he alone knows 'What' He (the inner one) is. This 'What' is 'He' or 'That' is more important than 'Who' He is. The following verse in the sacred hymn dives deep into this divinity which is an integral part of humanity.

प्रमाणं प्राणनिलयः प्राणभृत्प्राणजीवनः ।
तत्त्वं तत्त्वविदेकात्मा जन्ममृत्युजरातिगः ॥

pramāṇaṁ prāṇa-nilayaḥ prāṇabhṛt-prāṇa-jīvanaḥ I
tattvaṁ tattvavid-ekātmā janma-mṛtyu-jarātigaḥ II

He, the Lord of the Universe is the highest authority *pramāṇam* in assessing how far the aspirant has progressed in his practical experience of the Self seated in him helping him at every step, housing him, sustaining him and virtually living with him, in him and around him. It is this affinity or affection of the Lord, the universal soul for the individual one that is depicted in the first four names or attributes - *Pramāṇam* the highest and the most authentic form of knowledge or awareness; *Prāṇanilayaḥ*, the one who has housed him in his own abode giving him the very breath of life so that he can make full and optimum use of the mortal frame given to him for a stipulated period; *Prāṇabhṛt,* one who provides the required sustenance to enable him to progress in his pursuit and finally *Prāṇajīvanaḥ* staying with him all the time as his life-breath enabling him to breathe as long as he lives.

These four forms of the divine Grace that every individual enjoys unasked are expressed in an elegant and inspiring phraseology which every individual has to assimilate and cultivate to hnow what He or That is - the essence of existence and excellence in life. This is what has been termed *tattvam* the Essence of That and Thou. One who comprehends and cultivates this absolute reality in life becomes a *tattvavid* in the real sense of the term. This is all that 'this' individual soul is expected to do, know and experience with total identification with 'That' universal soul.

Then he becomes *Ekātmā* one with his real self which is no longer individual but becomes one with the universal transcending the transitory stages of life like birth *janma*, death *mṛtyu* and old age *jara*. For him, there is no death. The gradual decay of the mortal frame given to him as a tool or instrument to conduct this experiment is a boon which the Lord grants to him as a reward for his successful conduct in the orientation programme organized not merely for one isolated individual, but for the whole universe, a living laboratory for the aspirants of self-awareness and through that, the awareness of 'That' one reality. All this is a result of the divine grace which enables us to transcend all limitations and landmarks of this life as *Janma-mṛtyu-jarātigaḥ*, the concluding epithet of the Lord in this verse.

Only the blessed few will come to know who He is, what He is and what 'that' *tat* is. It is this 'that' which the sages and seers of this holy land (the universe) have glorified as the Absolute Reality realizing which nothing else remains to be realized.

The Tree With Three That Grows

Having glorified the significance of *tat* as the highest form of knowledge, the *Sahasranāma* now presents the three spheres of spiritual growth of an aspirant -- *Bhūh* the Terrestrial, *Bhuvaḥ* the atmospheric or ethereal and *Svaḥ* the celestial.The Lord of the univerese is projected as a Tree that extends itself across these three spheres. How this spiritual, divine and in a sense mystic Tree enables the aspirant to cross the ocean of life-cycles is explained in the following verse:

भूर्भुवः स्वस्तरुस्तारः सविता प्रपितामहः ।
यज्ञो यज्ञपतिर्यज्वा यज्ञाङ्गो यज्ञवाहनः ॥

bhūrbhuvaḥ svas-tarus-tāraḥ savitā pra-pitāmahaḥ /
yajño yajña-patir-yajvā yajñāṅgo yajña-vāhanaḥ //

The three syllables *bhūḥ bhuvaḥ* and *svaḥ* with which the first attribute starts represent the three spheres or the three worlds --*Bhūloka* (the terrestrial world - or earth), *Bhuvarloka* (the atmosphere immediately above the earth), and *Svarloka* (the heaven). In Vedic terminology, these three syllables have a mystic significance and are called *Vyāhṛtis,* sacred utterances used in chanting *mantras* like *Gāyatrī.* In both the senses, this epithet glorifies the Lord as a resting place for all the inhabitants of the three worlds standing as the Eternal Tree spread over the entire universe. The Lord is therefore, glorified as this symbolic Tree with Three phases, *Bhūrbhuvasvastarūḥ.*

The next name *Tāraḥ* is, in a way, an extension of the previous one. This epithet glorifies the Lord as a ferry which helps His devotees in crossing the ocean of birth and death or the life-cycles.The whole expression *Bhūrbhuvasvastarustāraḥ* can also be considered as a single attribute of the Lord as the sense conveyed in both the names is almost the same.

But what is more significant is the Vedic touch and the mystic interpretation of the sacred syllables whose mere utterance with *Om* preceding *Om Bhūrbhuvasvaḥ* generates vibrations of Vedic hymns. Light and sound are the two basic factors which promote Vedic atmosphere in which the Lord is worshipped with sacred hymns. Before we start any *pūjā* or worship, it is customary to light a lamp and ring a small bell along with chanting of Vedic *mantras*. It is this that makes us feel the presence of the Lord amidst us during the celebration. Thus this lengthy name of the Lord paves the way for more than ten names that are going to follow from the next line -- all extolling the sanctity and significance of *yajña*, a sacrificial ritual.

There are two more names in the same line - *Savitā* and *Prapitāmahaḥ*. *Savitā* means Sun. But literally, the word means 'one who generates, produces or yields'. Being the bestower of all physical splendour, intellectual brilliance and spiritual radiance like the Sun, the Lord is appropriately adored here as *Savitā*. He is also called *Prapitāmahaḥ* as He is the Creator of the Creator *Brahmā*. *Brahmā* is adored as *Pitāmaha* (grandfather) and so, the Lord is extolled as great grand father of the universe.

Now start a series of attributes of the Lord--all starting and dealing with the religious ritual called *yajña*. The first in the series is *Yajña*, the sacrificial rite itself where oblations are offered to the God of Fire. 'Sacrifice' is not a happy equivalent of *yajña*. The word *yajña* is very

very wide in its canvas and covers almost all forms of worship offered with a sense of dedication coupled with a spirit of sacrifice.Every householder, particularly a *Brāhmaṇa*, is supposed to perform five sacrificial acts every day which are called 'the five *yajñas*'. *Bhūta-yajña* (service to fellow beings), *Manuṣya-yajña* (entertainment of guests), *Pitṛ-yajña* (remembering the ancestors, particularly parents), *Deva-yajña* (worshipping a deity of one's choice) and *Brahma-yajña* (Vedic studies and dissemination of knowledge). The word *yajña* can be split into two parts *yat* and *jña* in which case *yajña* would mean to investigate and find out for oneself the source of of all resources in the world, wherefrom all the beings are born, how they are sustained and where they merge ultimately. These are some of the areas where *yajña* comes into picture.

It is therefore appropriate to understand the attribute *Yajña* appropriated for the Lord from this broad perspective. In the first attribute, He is identified with the ritual *yajña* itself. He is called *Yajñaḥ*.Then He is glorified as *Yajñapatiḥ*, the Lord of all sacrificialrites. He presides over these acts. The next attribute *Yajvā* presents Him as the performer of these rites.This is followed by the attribute *Yajñāṅgaḥ*. He is a part of the sacrifice.This is also interpreted as sacrifice-limbed having the sacrifices as His limbs.

Śaṅkara Bhagavatpāda quotes a long passage from *Harivaṁśa* to illustrate how the various components of the *yajña* form the various limbs of the Lord who is worshipped as *Yajñapuruṣa* (*yajña* personified).

The last name in this line is *Yajñavāhanaḥ*, the carrier of sacrifices. This can also be interpreted as a vehicle to reach the Lord.

We shall have more to know about *yajña* in the next verse too.

He Is Food, He Is God

Food plays an important role in all forms of *yajña*. Food is freely distributed to all--poor and rich, the learned and the ignorant, friends and enemies, good and bad in all such rituals. Food is the basic requirement for the existence of all beings. There is a natural link between food and God as explained by the Lord Himself in *Gītā*. He said, 'All beings are evolved from food, production of food is dependent on rain, rain ensues from the performance of rituals like *yajña*, *yajña* or worship is rooted in righteous mind and action, the action contemplated takes its origin in the knowledge of *Brahman* as laid down in the *Vedas* and the highest form of knowledge is the awareness of God' (Ch. 3-14, 15). This is how God and Food are interlinked and it is *yajña* that promotes this link and it is a part of the daily routine--consciously or unconsciously followed by all including God because God is food and food is God.

The following verse will tell us more about this:

यज्ञभृद्यज्ञकृद्यज्ञी यज्ञभुग्यज्ञसाधनः ।
यज्ञान्तकृद्यज्ञगुह्यमन्नमन्नाद एव च ।।

yajñabhṛd-yajñakṛd-yajñī yajñabhug-yajñasādhanaḥ /
yajñāntakṛd-yajñaguhyam-annam-annāda eva ca //

The last five attributes in the previous verse were entirely based on *yajña* or ritualistic and community worship.This series is continued in the present verse also.

The first name in this verse is *Yajñabhṛt*, patron and protector of the ritualistic form of worship *yajña*. Then He is extolled as *Yajñakṛt*. He is an active participant in these religious rites--particularly in the beginning of a *yuga* (aeon) as a creator and at the end as a destroyer.The next attribute *Yajñī* presents the Lord as the Chief Executive of a *yajña* while the other persons and agencies form a part of it. He is the whole, everything else is a part like the body *aṅgī* and the limbs *aṅga*. He is the organiser and others are organs. He is then adored as *Yajñabhuk*, One who enjoys and appreciates the ritual and the devotion behind it. Feeling behind such acts of devotion and austerity is what matters more than the mechanical process. Hence, the Lord is extolled as *Yajñabhuk*. What pleases Him is the devotion or dedication behind it and the inward pleasure or the divine bliss that emerges out of it. Delight is His food. If He is delighted, He blesses the participants with the everlasting and immeasurable bliss that knows no bounds and finds no exprssion.

That is why He is eulogized in the next epithet as *Yajñasādhanaḥ*. The ritual or *yajña* is just a means (one of the means) to reach Him. He is, therefore, the goal of all such enterprises. If everything goes well, He will ensure that the fruits of such love and labour go to the right people though they neither expect any return nor do they enter into such activities with personal interests. Salvation, the ultimate goal of life, automatically follows such selfless serevice. Any action or duty performed with genuine love for the act and for the betterment of all living beings in general will be rewarded by the Lord in an appropriate manner. That is why He is adored as *Yajñāntakṛt*, One who fulfils the desire of His devotees by leading the ritual to a meaningful, fruitful and blissful completion.

The last attribute associated with such a sacrificial rite *yajña* is *Yajñaguhyam*. The secret or the sacred objective behind such sacrifices is the Lord Himself. If one becomes really aware of the divinity within him and presence of the Lord in all beings in the universe including his own self, he has really achieved what is the most sacred and unique achievement of such selfless sacrifices. Any sacrifice never seeks any favour from any one. It is a positive effort to identify himself with the universe and the universal soul. This is the most significant merit underlined in *yajña*. One who knows *yat* where from he is, he knows who he is and what he is and how he is equated or identified with ' that' Absolute Reality.

Having extolled the glories of the Lord in terms of a remarkable act of righteousness , namely, *yajña*, the *Ācārya* presents two more attributes of the Lord in the end-- *Annam* (the food) and *Annādaḥ* (one who eats or consumes or enjoys it). God is identified here, very surprisingly indeed, with both the consumed and the consumer. He is both *Bhojanam* food and *Bhoktā*, the intaker. In fact these two expressions *Bhojanam* and *Bhoktā* had earlier figured in this sacred hymn (142 and 143). These two attributes of the Lord were also preceded by another equally significant one *Bhrājiṣṇuḥ*, the Radiant. The spiritual radiance of the Lord is mainly due to His identification with both the food proper and its consumption. It is a natural phenomenon that what is consumed, in return, consumes the consumer too. This is the secret of the whole deliberation on the subject of *yajña* leading to food. God gives us food and expects us to understand the secret behind the process of consumption. Nothing is virtually consumed. It is only transformation or conservation of energy.

With this concluding note, the *Ācārya* turns back to the *Ātman*, the Soul of all souls and pays a glorious tribute to the Lord personally present when these names were being recited by the *Ācārya*.

The Song That Sings For Him

While glorifying the unique role of the Lord in promoting righteousness in the whole universe citing His close association with *yajña*, the *Ācārya* suddenly saw *Śrī Kṛṣṇa* sitting right in front of Him listening to him with an attentive mind. In the last sixteen attributes of the sacred hymn he was about to recite, he must have thought it appropriate to pay his personal homage and humble *praṇām* to Him as it was He who conducted the *Mahāyajña* in the battle field. Suddenly he was reminded of so many events and started narrating his personal appreciation keeping those memorable thoughts, words and deeds.

This peresonal note can easily be found in the last two verses containing 16 names of the Lord. The first phase of this 'sweet' sixteen can be seen in the following verse:

आत्मयोनिः स्वयंजातो वैखानः सामगायनः ।
देवकीनन्दनः स्रष्टा क्षितीशः पापनाशनः ॥

ātma-yoniḥ svayaṁ-jāto vaikhānaḥ sāma-gāyanaḥ ।
devakī-nandanaḥ sraṣṭā kṣitīśaḥ pāpa-nāśanaḥ ॥

The first attribute is *Ātmayoniḥ*. He Himself is the cause of His advent. There cannot be any other cause for the ascent or descent of the Lord except *ātman*. As the *Aitereya Upanṣad* says, 'In the beginning there was *ātman* and *ātman* alone'. So the material cause of any creative process can only be *ātman*. Hence, the Lord is glorified as *Ātmayoniḥ* the Self as the sole source.

The next epithet *Svayañjātaḥ* shows that not only the material cause, but even the instrumental cause for His advent is He Himself. In other words, He is self-born *Svayañjātaḥ*.

Then the *Ācārya* gives an instance when the Lord had to assume the form of *Varāha* to find His way to the nether world and kill the demon *Hiraṇyākṣa*. Hence, He is extolled as *Vaikhānaḥ* Deep Burrower or Divine Digger. He was prepared to take any step to revive righteousness and root out evil tendencies. The word *vaikhānaḥ* also suggests that the Lord is a mine of physical, mental and spiritual potentialities. He is Omnipotent, Omnipresent and Omniscient. The entire knowledge of the self is generated from Him. The mere thought of His glorious face, looks, voice and actions fills the heart with blissful ideas and transforms the individual soul into a realized soul, a man with divine potentialities. In this sense also the attribute *Vaikhānaḥ* fits in marvellously.

Inspite of His universal occupations, He takes things very easy and finds time to sing and dance on the banks of the river *Yamunā*. He dances to the tune of His play-mates just to please them and give them a feel of the divine touch-- the touch of the Absolute. His melodious tunes played on His flute attract the whole village including maids and married women to the lovely river-bed at midnight. Actually He does not sing Himself. The songs themselves sing for Him. Like men and women, boys and girls, cattle and birds, the waves of the river also come to hear Him and feel thrilled to realize in the end that their eyes (not the ears) were hearing Him and ears (not the eyes) were seeing Him. This is the height of total absorption of their mind, heart and soul in the soul-ful music of their master. This was His *Sāmagāna*, the melodies of *Sāma veda*. In fact the melodious hymns of the *Sāmaveda* get echoed in His presence and nobody knows whether His flute is playing for Him or He is playing His flute. This is the music that can be heard in the celestial sphere inspired by the unheard *anāhata* melodies of the Master.

Now the *Ācārya* comes back to his normal state of mind and tells *Yudhiṣṭhira*, 'Look here, it was about this visible God, *Devakīnandana* that I have been talking to you all the time. He is the born son of *Devakī*. But in reality, He is *Sraṣṭā*, the Creator of the whole universe. He is *Kṣitīśaḥ* , the Lord of the whole globe, the three worlds. The mere casual utterance of His name can dispel all sins because He is *Pāpanāśanaḥ*. No sin can touch Him. He makes His devotees also free from all sins'.

This is the celebrity who has been with us in the battle field and fought for neither of the parties but for establishing the basic norms of righteousness *dharma* in the world.

The *Ācārya* has many more things to say. This will continue in the remaining eight names glorifying the Lord in the coming verse.

The Great Grand Guardian

The concluding verse of the sacred hymn, *Śrī Viṣṇu Sahasranāma Stotram* pays Homage to the Lord present in the selected audience as an august personality. He was glorified in the previous verse as the promoter of bliss to Mother *Devakī - Devakīnandana*, the Creator *sraṣṭā*, the Lord of the Universe *Kṣitīsaḥ* and Destroyer of all sins by His mere thought *Pāpanāśanaḥ*. In the present verse which is presented to the Lord present in the audience as *Śrī Kṛṣṇa*, the spirit behind the entire battle of *Mahābhārata*, the main focus is on the various weapons and arms at His command which He uses solely to protect the 'Right' and promote 'Righteousness' *dharma*. The whole verse consisting of eight excellences of the Lord glorifies Him as the Great Grand Guardian of peace and harmony in the whole universe.

शंखभृन्नन्दकी चक्री शार्ङ्गधन्वा गदाधरः ।
रथाङ्गपाणिरक्षोभ्यः सर्वप्रहरणायुधः ॥

śaṅkhabhṛn-nandakī cakrī śārṅga-dhanvā gadādharaḥ I
rathāṅga-pāṇir-akṣobhyaḥ sarva-praharaṇāyudhaḥ II

The *Ācārya* first mentions the Conch which the Lord holds in His hands as an auspicious symbol of the primordial sound *Om*. This is the Conch *Śaṅkha Śrī Kṛṣṇa* blew on the first day of the battle immediately after the grand old man of the *Kaurava* race *Bhīṣma* blew his conch roaring terribly like a lion. Naturally, the *Ācārya* was reminded of that thrill, cheer and terror all combined. That is why he starts his citation of the arms and weapons held and wielded by the Lord on that memorable day. The conch also stands for the ego because the warrior blows it to proclaim his readiness to face the battle. But the conch the Lord blew was an auspicious one with a significant name *Pāñcajanyaḥ* symbolizing the five life- winds *prāṇās*, the five sacred fires maintained by a house-holder, the five rivers *Śatadru, Vipāṣā, Irāvatī, Candrabhāgā* and *Vitastā* flowing in the area around *Kurukṣetra* where the battle of *Mahābhārata* was fought, the five elements - earth, water, fire, wind and space and five senses (motor and sensory) and *pañcāyatan*, the abode of the senses, the body.

Thus by mentioning the conch *śaṅkha* as the first symbol of valour, resolve and articulation of Lord *Kṛṣṇa, Bhīṣma* conveyed a comprehensive account of the battle of *Mahābhārata* and also the one we daily fight in life. By the way, *Śaṅkha* or conch is not an arm, it is just a symbol of heroism with a bit of ego behind it.

The second attribute in this verese *Nandakī* indicates the sword (of knowledge) which the Lord holds in His hand and uses to destroy ignorance and generate awareness even in the battle field. In fact this is what He did while preaching *Gītā* to *Arjuna* without using the sword. That was pure *Nandaka* which promotes bliss through blessings and preaching.

Then comes the discus or the wheel called *Sudarśanaḥ* which is the most powerful weapon of the Lord. It was probably a monopoly of the *Muralīdhara* to have flute on His lips to entertain the masses and the dreadful discus *Sudarśanacakra* on the fingers of the other hand. He can work wonders with it. He used this to save His devotees like *Gajendra, Ambarīṣa* and severeal others. He twirls the wheel of life-cycles also with this. Being the most fascinating and powerful weapon the Lord wields, this is rightly named *Sudarśana*, nice to look at. The word *sudarśanaḥ* also figured as an attribute of the Lord in the context of the cycle of seasons ṛtuḥ and the time *kālaḥ* -- *Ṛtuḥ Sudarśanaḥ Kālaḥ* (Sl.Nos. 416-18). Here the name *Sudarśana* is not mentioned. The Lord is just glorified as *Cakrī*. *Śaṅkara Bhagavatpāda* comments on this attribute saying that He has the discuss called *Sudarśana* in His hand which represents the mind-principle. He also adds that the Lord uses this to set the wheel of *Saṁsāra* in motion.

After gloryfying the conch *Śaṅkha* the sword *Nandakī* and the discus *Cakra*, the *Ācārya* mentions the bow called *Śārṅga* which, according to *Śaṅkara*, represents the senses and egotism *ahaṅkāra*. The Lord with this bow called *Śārṅga* in His hand is extolled as *Śārṅgadhanvā*. A similar attribute *Sudhanvā* (Sl. No. 567) figured earlier. While commenting on this epithet *Śaṅkara* mentions *Śārṅga* and says that this bow symbolizes senses (eyes, etc.). The *Upaniṣads* often compare the primordial sound *praṇavaḥ* with a bow and *ātman* with an arrow. In the present context, however, the name of the bow *Śārṅga* is clearly specified. The word is derived from *śṛṅga* which means the peak or a horn or the supreme. This seems to be a multidimensional attribute of the Lord projecting Him as an all-round archer.

The next attribute *Gadādharaḥ* clearly refers to the mace or club held by the Lord. This club or *gadā* is said to be symbolic of intelligence *prajñā* or the principle of intellect *Buddhi* . The name associated with this celebrated mace or club is *Kaumodakī*. The author of *Śiśupāla vadha*, an epic poem in *Saṁskṛt* mentioned this mace *Kaumodakī* and depicted it as thr promoter of blissful consciousness *modayati-sma cetaḥ*.

Almost the last weapon of the Lord mentioned in this series of attributes pertaining to His martial equipment is *Rathāṅgapāṇiḥ*. This presents the Lord as One having the wheel of a chariot in His hand. This is, obviously, different from the earlier attribute *Cakrī* though the purport of both is almost the same. This latter one (also perhaps the last one in the list) does not refer to the wheel called *Sudarśana* which has a very broad canvas of comprehension and interpretation. The epithet *Rathāṅgapāṇiḥ* clearly refers to the wheel of a chariot which Lord *Kṛṣṇa* carried in His hand and rushed to *Bhīṣma* in a spirit of attack and *Bhīṣma* still remembers that unique scene when the Lord Himself approaches him to grant him the highest bliss. Recollecting this scene all of a sudden, the *Ācārya* glorifies the Lord in that posture of *Rathāṅgapāṇiḥ* which he can never forget. In *Śrīmad Bhāgavatam, Bhīṣma* is said to have glorified the facial complexion of the Lord in that posture as *Tribhuvana kamanam* (fascinating for all the three worlds).

The glorification of the weapons of the Lord almost concludes with this attribute. Then follows the citation of the transcendental tranquility and equanimity that *Śrī Kṛṣṇa* maintained throughout the period of the great war. In one word, he describes this superb quality of the Lord as *Akṣobhyaḥ*, unshakable, unperturbable because He is unassailable. In fact He agreed to help *Arjuna* in this great battle on one condition that He will not use any weapons. That is why He rushed to *Bhīṣma* with the wheel of a chariot in His hand and not with *Sudarśanacakra*. It should be noted with care that only four arms or weapons of the Lord are mentioned in this context-- *Nandakī* (the sword), *Sudarśana* (the discus or *cakra*), *Śārṅgadhanvā* (the bow called *Śārṅga*) and *Kaumodakī* (the mace or the club). The other two-- the conch-shell *Śaṅkha* and *Rathāṅga* (the wheel of the chariot) are not virtually weapons.

Now we come to the last and the most comprehensive attribute which projects the Lord as Omnipotent with multi-dimensional equipment of arms and weapons (known and unknown, visible and invisible, hostile and healing) which cover all eventualities of offence and defence. The Lord is adored and admired towards the end of the celebrated hymn, as *Sarvapraharaṇāyudhaḥ*, He who is armed with all kinds of weapons to protect those dedicated to the basic values of life, promoting peace and harmony in all the worlds and punish those who tried to destroy them so that truth succeeds in the end and righteousness rules over other forces and survives.

There are instances where the Lord had to invent new weapons to do this work for which He had to incarnate Himself in various forms. For instance, He had to use His finger-nails to kill *Hiraṅyakaśipu* because he was granted a boon that he cannot be killed by any one with or without life. The Lord discovered that nails grow but do not have life.

In His incarnation as *Rāma*, the Lord acquired many mystic missiles with the help of the sage *Viśvāmitra* and utilized the services of *Hanumān*, the gigantic monkey-chief who used trees, stones, mountains, horses, elephants, chariots, and even warriors in destroying the forces of the enemies striking one against the other taking both from their side. Nothing can be more resourceful than this. Similarly *Rāma* organized the construction of a bridge across the sea without any external devices and walked across the sea as a pleasant voyage. Such instances are many in Indian mythology and classical compositions by epic poets.

There is a strange and striking beauty in this concluding attribute of the Lord *Sarvapraharaṇāyudhaḥ*. The word *praharaṇam* means striking, beating, attacking, assailing and so on. Hence, the expression *praharaṇāyudha* has come to mean striking with deadly weapons. But the word *praharī* which is also derived from the same root *prahṛ* means a guard who keeps a constant watch and vigil over the area entrusted to him. That is how the word *praharaḥ* has come to mean the eighth part of a whole day, roughly three hours. This was the period of shifts of watchmen engaged in this work of striking the hours with a bell and keeping the watch fully awake. Taking this etymology into account, our sacred epithet of the Lord *Sarvapraharaṇāyudhaḥ* lends itself to this additional interpretation that the Lord not only protects His devotees and other innocent and right-minded people, but keeps a watch over any untoward incidents that may disturb peace and harmony in general. If there is any such contingency, He foresees it in advance and takes preventive and corrective measures to nullify or rectify them. In this sense, the Lord as *Sarvapraharaṇāyudhaḥ* acts as the Great Grand Guardian of all living beings in all the three worlds.

This, being the concluding and the most auspicious attribute in the thousand names *Sahasranāma* of Lord *Viṣṇu*, is recited once again to give it an auspicious completion. The name is also followed by the sacred syllable *Om* to invoke the blessings of the Lord. Moreover the recitation of the thousand names of the Lord starts with *Om Viśvaṁ Viṣṇuḥ* ...... and therefore it concludes also with a similar phraseology:

सर्वप्रहरणायुध ॐ नम इति

sarvapraharaṇāyudhaḥ om nama iti

The utterance of the word *namaḥ* is also an auspicious one as the *Taittirīya Upaniṣad* says :

तन्नम इत्युपासीत नम्यन्तेऽस्मै कामाः

tannama ityupāsīta namyaṅte' smai kāmāḥ

(worship Him as *Namaḥ* , all the desires will bow before you).

इति शम्

Iti Śam

The Epilogue

Having narrated the thousand epithets of the Lord as promised to the King *Yudhiṣṭhira, Bhīṣma* explains to him the significance of the recitation of these divine glories in detail. He says:

इतीदं कीर्तनीयस्य केशवस्य महात्मनः ।
नाम्नां सहस्रं दिव्यानामशेषेण प्रकीर्तितम् ॥

itīdaṁ kīrtanīyasya keśavasya mahātmanaḥ ।
nāmnāṁ sahasraṁ divyānāmaśeṣeṇa prakīrtitam ॥

The thousand divine attributes of the Great Being *Keśava,* worthy of all glorification, have thus been recounted without any modification (additions or omissions).

य इदं शृणुयान्नित्यं यश्चापि परिकीर्तयेत् ।
नाशुभं प्राप्नुयात्किञ्चित्सोऽमुत्रेह च मानवः ॥

ya idaṁ śṛṇuyānnityaṁ yaścāpi parikīrtayet ।
nāśubhaṁ prāpnuyātkiñcitso'mutreha ca mānavaḥ ॥

He who listens to this hymn every day regularly or recites this with understanding never faces anything untoward either in this life or in the life hereafter.

वेदान्तगो ब्राह्मणः स्यात्क्षत्रियो विजयी भवेत्।
वैश्यो धनसमृद्धः स्याच्छूद्रः सुखमवाप्नुयात्॥

vedāntago brāhmaṇaḥ syātkṣatriyo vijayī bhavet |
vaiśyo dhanasamṛddhaḥ syācchūdraḥ sukhamavāpnuyāt ||

By reciting this, a Brahmin acquires Vedic knowledge and wisdom, a *Kṣatriya* becomes Victorious, a *Vaiśya* flourishes in business and becomes rich and a *Śūdra* enjoys comfort and happiness.

धर्मार्थी प्राप्नुयाद्धर्ममर्थार्थी चार्थमाप्नुयात्।
कामानवाप्नुयात्कामी प्रजार्थी प्राप्नुयात्प्रजाम्॥

dharmārthī prāpnuyāddharmamarthārthī cārthamāpnuyāt |
kāmānavāpnuyātkāmī prajārthī prāpnuyātprajām ||

He who wants to be righteous will become righteous, He who wants wealth will become wealthy. He who has desires will get his desires fulfilled. He who wants children will be blessed accordingly.

भक्तिमान्यः सदोत्थाय शुचिस्तद्गत मानसः।
सहस्रं वासुदेवस्य नाम्नामेतत्प्रकीर्तयेत्॥

bhaktimānyaḥ sadotthāya śucistadgata mānasaḥ |
sahasraṁ vāsudevasya nāmnāmetatprakīrtayet ||

यशः प्राप्नोति विपुलं ज्ञातिप्राधान्यमेव च।
अचलां श्रियमाप्नोति श्रेयः प्राप्नोत्यनुत्तमम्॥

yaśaḥ prāpnoti vipulaṁ jñātiprādhānyameva ca |
acalāṁ śṛīyamāpnoti śreyaḥ prāpnotyanuttamam ||

If a devotee gets up early in the morning, cleanses himself and recites these names of *Vāsudeva* with undivided attention, he will attain immense glory, gets a name in his circle of friends and relatives, acquires material wealth and highest bliss in the end.

न भयं क्वचिदाप्नोति वीर्यं तेजश्च विन्दति।
भवत्यरोगो द्युतिमान्बलरूपगुणान्वितः॥

na bhayaṁ kvacidāpnoti vīryaṁ tejaśca vindati |
bhavatyarogo dyutimān-balarūpaguṇānvitaḥ ||

Such a man will never be a victim to any type of fear, but rather progresses in prowess and brilliance. He will be hale and healthy, brilliant, strong, good-looking and virtuous.

रोगार्तो मुच्यते रोगाद्बद्धो मुच्येत बन्धनात्।
भयान्मुच्येत भीतस्तु मुच्येतापन्न आपदः॥

rogārto mucyate rogādbaddho mucyeta bandhanāt |
bhayānmucyeta bhītastu mucyetāpanna āpadaḥ ||

दुर्गाण्यतितरत्याशु पुरुषः पुरुषोत्तमम्।
स्तुवन्नामसहस्रेण नित्यं भक्ति समन्वितः॥

durgāṇyatitaratyāśu puruṣaḥ puruṣottamam |
stuvannāma-sahasreṇa nityaṁ bhakti samanvitaḥ ||

One who worships the Supreme Soul by reciting these thousand names daily with devotion will be free from ailment if he is sick, will be released from prison if he is victimised, will be free from fear if he is frightened and comes out of danger if he is in danger. He will surmount all difficulties in no time if he is distressed.

वासुदेवाश्रयो मर्त्यो वासुदेव परायणः।
सर्वपापविशुद्धात्मा याति ब्रह्म सनातनम्॥

vāsudevāśrayo martyo vāsudeva parāyaṇaḥ |
sarvapāpa-viśuddhātmā yāti brahma sanātanaṁ ||

Any mortal being who entrusts his care to the Lord *Vāsudeva* and trusts in Him with full faith will be freed from all sins, gets purified and ultimately attains eternal bliss.

न वासुदेव भक्तानामशुभं विद्यते क्वचित्।
जन्म मृत्यु जरा व्याधि भयं नैवोपजायते॥

na vāsudeva bhaktānāmaśubhaṁ vidyate kvacit |
janma mṛtyu jarā vyādhi bhayaṁ naivopajāyate ||

इमं स्तवमधीयानः श्रद्धा भक्तिसमन्वितः।
युज्येतात्मसुखक्षान्ति श्रीधृतिस्मृतिकीर्तिभिः॥

imaṁ stavamadhīyānaḥ śraddhā-bhakti-samanvitaḥ |
yujyetātmasukhakṣānti śrīdhṛtismṛti-kīrtibhiḥ ||

The devotees of *Vāsudeva* have nothing to fear any time or anywhere. Birth,death, old age, illness or any other fear will not touch them.

One who recites this hymn with faith and devotion will enjoy personal happiness, peace, prosperity, stability, retentive power and fame.

न क्रोधो न च मात्सर्यं न लोभो नाशुभामतिः।
भवन्ति कृतपुण्यानां भक्तानां पुरुषोत्तमे॥

na krodho na ca mātsaryaṁ na lobho nāśubhāmatiḥ |
bhavanti kṛtapuṇyānāṁ bhaktānāṁ puruṣottame ||

Blessed are the devotees of the Lord *Puruṣottama* whom anger, malice, greed or hatred can never approach.

द्यौः सचन्द्रार्क नक्षत्रा खं दिशो भूर्महोदधिः ।
वासुदेवस्य वीर्येण विधृतानि महात्मनः ॥

dyouḥ sacandrārka nakṣatrā khaṁ diśo bhūrmahodadhiḥ ।
vāsudevasya vīryeṇa vidhṛtāni mahātmanaḥ ॥

The firmament with the moon, the sun, the stars, the sky, the quarters, the earth and the ocean are held in position by the might of the Great Being *Vāsudeva*.

ससुरासुरगंधर्वं सयक्षोरगराक्षसम् ।
जगद्वशे वर्ततेदं कृष्णस्य सचराचरम् ॥

sasurāsura gandharvaṁ sayakṣoragarākṣasam ।
jagadvaśe vartatedaṁ kṛṣṇasya sacarācaram ॥

The universe mobile and immobile, with the celestials, demons and fairies, elfs, serpents and giants is completely under the sway of *Kṛṣṇa*.

इन्द्रियाणि मनो बुद्धिः सत्त्वं तेजो बलं धृतिः ।
वासुदेवात्मकान्याहुः क्षेत्रं क्षेत्रज्ञ एव च ॥

indriyāṇi mano buddhiḥ sattvaṁ tejo balaṁ dhṛtiḥ ।
vāsudevātmakānyāhuḥ kṣetraṁ kṣetrajña eva ca ॥

The senses, the mind and intellect, stamina, splendour, strength and mobility, the individual souls and the one Supreme Soul are all of *Vāsudeva* as pronounced by the learned.

सर्वागमानामाचारः प्रथमं परिकल्पते।
आचारप्रभवो धर्मो धर्मस्य प्रभुरच्युतः ॥

sarvāgamānāmācāraḥ prathamaṁ parikalpate I
ācāraprabhavo dharmo dharmasya prabhuracyutaḥ II

Right conduct has precedence over all the sciences of morality. The ethical way of life emanates from right conduct. *Acyuta* is the Lord of the ethical way of life.

ऋषयः पितरो देवा महाभूतानि धातवः।
जङ्गमाजङ्गमं चेदं जगन्नारायणोद्भवम् ॥

ṛṣayaḥ pitaro devā mahābhūtāni dhātavaḥ I
jaṅgamājaṅgamaṁ cedaṁ jagannārāyaṇodbhavam II

The seers, the manes, the celestials, the five elements, the great components, and the whole universe mobile and immobile emanate from *Nārāyaṇa.*

योगो ज्ञानं तथा सांख्यं विद्याः शिल्पादि कर्म च।
वेदाः शास्त्रणि विज्ञानमेतत्सर्वं जनार्दनात् ॥

yogo jñānaṁ tathā sāṅkhyaṁ vidyāḥ śilpādi karma ca I
vedāḥ śāstrāṇi vijñānametatsarvaṁ janārdanāt II

Yogic science, philosophical knowledge including *Sāṅkhya* philosophy, all sciences, arts, crafts, the *vedas,* all branches of science-pure and applied are all from *Janārdana.*

एको विष्णुर्महद्भूतं पृथग्भूतान्यनेकशः ।
त्रींल्लोकान्व्याप्य भूतात्मा भुङ्क्ते विश्वभुगव्ययः ॥

eko viṣṇurmahadbhūtaṁ pṛthagbhūtānyanekaśaḥ |
trīnllokānvyāpya bhūtātmā bhuṅkte viśvabhugavyayaḥ ||

The one Great Being is *Viṣṇu* and the individual beings are innumerable. The undecaying enjoyer of the Universe who is the Universe itself enjoys the three worlds completely entwining it.

इमं स्तवं भगवतो विष्णोर्व्यासेन कीर्तितम् ।
पठेद्य इच्छेत्पुरुषः श्रेयः प्राप्तुं सुखानि च ॥

imaṁ stavaṁ bhagavato viṣṇorvyāsena kīrtitam |
paṭhedya icchetpuruṣaḥ śreyaḥ prāptuṁ sukhāni ca ||

Those who aspire for prosperity and happiness are advised to make it a point to recite this hymn glorifying Lord *Viṣṇu* sung by *Vyāsa.*

विश्वेश्वरमजं देवं जगतः प्रभवाप्ययम् ।
भजन्ति ये पुष्कराक्षं न ते यान्ति पराभवम् ॥

viśveśvaramajaṁ devaṁ jagataḥ prabhavāpyayam |
bhajanti ye puṣkarākṣaṁ na te yānti parābhavam ||

Those who worship the Lord whose eyes are like the lotus flower and who is the Lord of the Universe will never encounter any reverses.

The Text

श्रीविष्णु सहस्रनाम स्तोत्रम्

SRĪ VIṢṆU SAHASRANĀMA STOTRAṀ

ॐ विश्वं विष्णुर्वषट्कारो भूतभव्यभवत्प्रभुः ।
भूतकृद्भूतभृद्भावो भूतात्मा भूतभावनः ॥१॥

om viśvaṁ viṣṇurvaṣaṭkāro bhūta-bhavya-bhavatprabhuḥ |
bhūtakṛd-bhūtabhṛd-bhāvo bhūtātmā bhūtabhāvanaḥ ||1||

पूतात्मा परमात्मा च मुक्तानां परमा गतिः ।
अव्ययः पुरुषः साक्षी क्षेत्रज्ञोऽक्षर एव च ॥२॥

pūtātmā paramātmā ca muktānāṁ paramā gatiḥ |
avyayaḥ puruṣaḥ sākṣī kṣetrajño'kṣara eva ca ||2||

योगो योगविदां नेता प्रधानपुरुषेश्वरः ।
नारसिंहवपुः श्रीमान् केशवः पुरुषोत्तमः ॥३॥

yogo yogavidāṁ netā pradhāna-puruṣeśvaraḥ |
nārasiṁhavapuḥ śrīmān keśavaḥ puruṣottamaḥ ||3||

सर्वः शर्वः शिवः स्थाणुर्भूतादिर्निधिरव्ययः ।
संभवो भावनो भर्ता प्रभवः प्रभुरीश्वरः ।।४।।

sarvaḥ śarvaḥ śivaḥ sthāṇur-bhūtādir-nidhir-avyayaḥ I
saṁbhavo bhāvano bhartā prabhavaḥ prabhur-īśvaraḥ II4II

स्वयंभूः शंभुरादित्यः पुष्कराक्षो महास्वनः ।
अनादिनिधनो धाता विधाता धातुरुत्तमः ।।५।।

svayaṁbhūḥ śaṁbhur-ādityaḥ puṣkarākṣo mahā-svanaḥ I
anādi-nidhano dhātā vidhātā dhātur-uttamaḥ II5II

अप्रमेयो हृषीकेशः पद्मनाभोऽमरप्रभुः ।
विश्वकर्मा मनुस्त्वष्टा स्थविष्ठः स्थविरो ध्रुवः ।।६।।

aprameyo hṛṣīkeśaḥ padma-nābho'mara-prabhuḥ I
viśva-karmā manus-tvaṣṭā sthaviṣṭhaḥ sthaviro dhruvaḥ II6II

अग्राह्यः शाश्वतः कृष्णो लोहिताक्षः प्रतर्दनः ।
प्रभूतस्त्रिककुब्धाम पवित्रं मङ्गलं परम् ।।७।।

agrāhyaḥ śāśvataḥ kṛṣṇo lohitākṣaḥ pratardanaḥ I
prabhūtas-trikakubdhāma pavitraṁ maṅgalaṁ paraṁ II7II

ईशानः प्राणदः प्राणो ज्येष्ठः श्रेष्ठः प्रजापतिः ।
हिरण्यगर्भो भूगर्भो माधवो मधुसूदनः ।।८।।

īśānaḥ prāṇadaḥ prāṇo jyeṣṭhaḥ śreṣṭhaḥ prajāpatiḥ I
hiraṇyagarbho bhūgarbho mādhavo madhu-sūdanaḥ II8II

ईश्वरो विक्रमी धन्वी मेधावी विक्रमः क्रमः।
अनुत्तमो दुराधर्षः कृतज्ञः कृतिरात्मवान्॥९॥

īśvaro vikramī dhanvī medhāvī vikramaḥ kramaḥ |
anuttamo durādharṣaḥ kṛtajñaḥ kṛtir-ātmavān ||9||

सुरेशः शरणं शर्म विश्वरेताः प्रजाभवः।
अहः संवत्सरो व्यालः प्रत्ययः सर्वदर्शनः॥१०॥

sureśaḥ śaraṇaṁ śarma viśva-retāḥ prajā-bhavaḥ |
ahaḥ saṁvatsaro vyālaḥ pratyayaḥ sarva-darśanaḥ ||10||

अजः सर्वेश्वरः सिद्धः सिद्धिः सर्वादिरच्युतः।
वृषाकपिरमेयात्मा सर्वयोगविनिःसृतः॥११॥

ajaḥ sarveśvaraḥ siddhaḥ siddhiḥ sarvādir-acyutaḥ |
vṛṣākapir-ameyātmā sarva-yoga-viniḥsṛtaḥ ||11||

वसुर्वसुमनाः सत्यः समात्मा सम्मितः समः।
अमोघः पुण्डरीकाक्षो वृषकर्मा वृषाकृतिः॥१२॥

vasur-vasumanāḥ satyaḥ samātmā sammitaḥ samaḥ |
amoghaḥ puṇḍarīkākṣo vṛṣa-karmā vṛṣākṛtiḥ ||12||

रुद्रो बहुशिरा बभ्रुर्विश्वयोनिः शुचिश्रवाः।
अमृतः शाश्वतस्थाणुर्वरारोहो महातपाः॥१३॥

rudro bahuśirā babhrur viśva-yoniḥ śuciśravāḥ |
amṛtaḥ śāśvata-sthāṇur-varāroho mahā-tapāḥ ||13||

सर्वगः सर्वविद्भानुर्विष्वक्सेनो जनार्दनः ।
वेदो वेदविदव्यङ्गो वेदाङ्गो वेदवित्कविः ॥१४॥

sarvagaḥ sarva-vid-bhānur-viṣvakseno janārdanaḥ ।
vedo vedavid-avyaṅgo vedāṅgo vedavit-kaviḥ ॥14॥

लोकाध्यक्षः सुराध्यक्षो धर्माध्यक्षः कृताकृतः ।
चतुरात्मा चतुर्व्यूहश्चतुर्दंष्ट्रश्चतुर्भुजः ॥१५॥

lokādhyakṣaḥ surādhyakṣo dharmādhyakṣaḥ kṛtākṛtaḥ ।
caturātmā catur-vyūhaś-catur-daṁṣṭraś-catur-bhujaḥ ॥15॥

भ्राजिष्णुर्भोजनं भोक्ता सहिष्णुर्जगदादिजः ।
अनघो विजयो जेता विश्वयोनिः पुनर्वसुः ॥१६॥

bhrājiṣṇur-bhojanaṁ bhoktā sahiṣṇur-jagad-ādijaḥ ।
anagho vijayo jetā viśva-yoniḥ punar-vasuḥ ॥16॥

उपेन्द्रो वामनः प्रांशुरमोघः शुचिरूर्जितः ।
अतीन्द्रः संग्रहः सर्गो धृतात्मा नियमो यमः ॥१७॥

upendro vāmanaḥ prāṁśur-amoghaḥ śucir-ūrjitaḥ ।
atīndraḥ saṅgrahaḥ sargo dhṛtātmā niyamo yamaḥ ॥17॥

वेद्यो वैद्यः सदायोगी वीरहा माधवो मधुः ।
अतीन्द्रियो महामायो महोत्साहो महाबलः ॥१८॥

vedyo vaidyaḥ sadā-yogī vīrahā mādhavo madhuḥ ।
atīndriyo mahāmāyo mahotsāho mahābalaḥ ॥18॥

महाबुद्धिर्महावीर्यो महाशक्तिर्महाद्युतिः ।
अनिर्देश्यवपुः श्रीमानमेयात्मा महाद्रिधृक् ॥१९॥

mahābuddhir-mahāvīryo mahāśaktir-mahādyutiḥ ।
anirdeśyavapuḥ śrīmān-ameyātmā mahādridhṛk ॥19॥

महेष्वासो महीभर्ता श्रीनिवासः सतां गतिः ।
अनिरुद्धः सुरानन्दो गोविन्दो गोविदांपतिः ॥२०॥

maheṣvāso mahībhartā śrīnivāsaḥ satāṁ gatiḥ ।
aniruddhaḥ surānando govindo govidāṁ-patiḥ ॥20॥

मरीचिर्दमनो हंसः सुपर्णो भुजगोत्तमः ।
हिरण्यनाभः सुतपाः पद्मनाभः प्रजापतिः ॥२१॥

marīcir-damano haṁsaḥ suparṇo bhujagottamaḥ ।
hiraṇya-nābhaḥ sutapāḥ padmanābhaḥ prajāpatiḥ ॥21॥

अमृत्युः सर्वदृक् सिंहः सन्धाता सन्धिमान् स्थिरः ।
अजो दुर्मर्षणः शास्ता विश्रुतात्मा सुरारिहा ॥२२॥

amṛtyuḥ sarva-dṛk siṁhaḥ sandhātā sandhimān sthiraḥ ।
ajo durmarṣaṇaḥ śāstā viśrutātmā surārihā ॥22॥

गुरुर्गुरुतमो धाम सत्यः सत्यपराक्रमः ।
निमिषोऽनिमिषः स्रग्वी वाचस्पतिरुदारधीः ॥२३॥

gurur-gurutamo dhāma satyaḥ satya-parākramaḥ ।
nimiṣo'nimiṣaḥ sragvī vācaspatir-udāradhīḥ ॥23॥

अग्रणीर्ग्रामणीः श्रीमान् न्यायो नेता समीरणः।
सहस्रमूर्धा विश्वात्मा सहस्राक्षः सहस्रपात् ॥२४॥

agraṇīr-grāmaṇīḥ śrīmān nyāyo netā samīraṇaḥ |
sahasra-mūrdhā viśvātmā sahasrākṣaḥ sahasrapāt ||24||

आवर्तनो निवृत्तात्मा संवृतः सम्प्रमर्दनः।
अहः संवर्तको वह्निरनिलो धरणीधरः ॥२५॥

āvartano nivṛttāmā saṁvṛtaḥ sampramardanaḥ |
ahaḥ saṁvartako vahnir-anilo dharaṇī-dharaḥ ||25||

सुप्रसादः प्रसन्नात्मा विश्वधृग्विश्वभुग्विभुः।
सत्कर्ता सत्कृतः साधुर्जह्नुर्नारायणो नरः ॥२६॥

suprasādaḥ prasannātmā viśva-dhṛg-viśva-bhug-vibhuḥ |
sat-kartā sat-kṛtaḥ sādhur-jahnur-nārāyaṇo naraḥ ||26||

असंख्येयोऽप्रमेयात्मा विशिष्टः शिष्टकृच्छुचिः।
सिद्धार्थः सिद्धसंकल्पः सिद्धिदः सिद्धिसाधनः ॥२७॥

asaṅkhyeyo'-prameyātmā viśiṣṭaḥ śiṣṭakṛc-chuciḥ |
siddhārthaḥ siddha-saṅkalpaḥ siddhidaḥ siddhisādhanaḥ ||27||

वृषाही वृषभो विष्णुर्वृषपर्वा वृषोदरः।
वर्धनो वर्धमानश्च विविक्तः श्रुतिसागरः ॥२८॥

vṛṣāhī vṛṣabho viṣṇur-vṛṣaparvā vṛṣodaraḥ |
vardhano vardhamānaś-ca viviktaḥ śruti-sāgaraḥ ||28||

सुभुजो दुर्धरो वाग्मी महेन्द्रो वसुदो वसुः ।
नैकरूपो बृहद्रूपः शिपिविष्टः प्रकाशनः ॥२९॥

subhujo durdharo vāgmī mahendro vasudo vasuḥ |
naikarūpo bṛhad-rūpaḥ śipiviṣṭaḥ prakāśanaḥ ||29||

ओजस्तेजोद्युतिधरः प्रकाशात्मा प्रतापनः ।
ऋद्धः स्पष्टाक्षरो मन्त्रश्चन्द्रांशुर्भास्करद्युतिः ॥३०॥

ojas-tejo-dyuti-dharaḥ prakāśātmā pratāpanaḥ |
ṛddhaḥ spaṣṭākṣaro mantraś-candrāṁśur-bhāskara-utiḥ ||30||

अमृतांशूद्भवो भानुः शशबिन्दुः सुरेश्वरः ।
औषधं जगतः सेतुः सत्यधर्मपराक्रमः ॥३१॥

amṛtāṁśūdbhavo bhānuḥ śaśabinduḥ sureśvaraḥ |
auṣadhaṁ jagataḥ setuḥ satya-dharma-parākramaḥ ||31||

भूतभव्यभवन्नाथः पवनः पावनोऽनलः ।
कामहा कामकृत्कान्तः कामः कामप्रदः प्रभुः ॥३२॥

bhūta-bhavya-bhavan-nāthaḥ pavanaḥ pāvano'nalaḥ |
kāmahā kāmakṛt-kāntaḥ kāmaḥ kāmapradaḥ prabhuḥ ||32||

युगादिकृद्युगावर्तो नैकमायो महाशनः ।
अदृश्यो व्यक्तरूपश्च सहस्रजिदनन्तजित् ॥३३॥

yugādikṛd-yugāvarto naikamāyo mahāśanaḥ |
adṛśyo vyakta-rūpaś-ca sahasrajid-anantajit ||33||

इष्टोऽविशिष्टः शिष्टेष्टः शिखण्डी नहुषो वृषः।
क्रोधहा क्रोधकृत्कर्ता विश्वबाहुर्महीधरः ॥३४॥

iṣṭo'viśiṣṭaḥ śiṣṭeṣṭaḥ śikhaṇḍī nahuṣo vṛṣaḥ ।
krodhahā krodhakṛt-kartā viśva-bāhur-mahīdharaḥ ॥34॥

अच्युतः प्रथितः प्राणः प्राणदो वासवानुजः।
अपां निधिरधिष्ठानमप्रमत्तः प्रतिष्ठितः ॥३५॥

acyutaḥ prathitaḥ prāṇaḥ prāṇado vāsavānujaḥ ।
apāṁ nidhir-adhiṣṭhānaṁ apramattaḥ pratiṣṭhitaḥ ॥35॥

स्कन्दः स्कन्दधरो धुर्यो वरदो वायुवाहनः।
वासुदेवो बृहद्भानुरादिदेवः पुरन्दर ॥३६॥

skandaḥ skanda-dharo dhuryo varado vāyuvāhanaḥ ।
vāsudevo bṛhad-bhānur-ādidevaḥ purandaraḥ ॥36॥

अशोकस्तारणस्तारः शूरः शौरिर्जनेश्वरः।
अनुकूलः शतावर्तः पद्मी पद्मनिभेक्षणः ॥३७॥

aśokas-tāraṇas-tāraḥ śūraḥ śaurir-janeśvaraḥ ।
anukūlaḥ śatāvartaḥ padmī padma-nibhekṣaṇaḥ ॥37॥

पद्मनाभोऽरविन्दाक्षः पद्मगर्भः शरीरभृत्।
महर्द्धिर्ऋद्धो वृद्धात्मा महाक्षो गरुडध्वजः ॥३८॥

padmanābho'ravindākṣaḥ padmagarbhaḥ śarīrabhṛt ।
maharddhir-ṛddho vṛddhātmā mahākṣo garuḍa-dhvajaḥ ॥38॥

अतुलः शरभो भीमः समयज्ञो हविर्हरिः ।
सर्वलक्षणलक्षण्यो लक्ष्मीवान्समितिञ्जयः ।।३९।।

atulaḥ śarabho bhīmaḥ samayajño havirhariḥ I
sarvalakṣaṇa-lakṣaṇyo lakṣmīvān-samitiñjayaḥ II39II

विक्षरो रोहितो मार्गो हेतुर्दामोदरः सहः ।
महीधरो महाभागो वेगवानमिताशनः ।।४०।।

vikṣaro rohito mārgo hetur-dāmodaraḥ sahaḥ I
mahīdharo mahābhāgo vegavan-amitāśanaḥ II40II

उद्भवः क्षोभणो देवः श्रीगर्भः परमेश्वरः ।
करणं कारणं कर्ता विकर्ता गहनो गुहः ।।४१।।

udbhavaḥ kṣobhaṇo devaḥ śrīgarbhaḥ parameśvaraḥ I
karaṇaṁ kāraṇaṁ kartā vikartā gahano guhaḥ II41II

व्यवसायो व्यवस्थानः संस्थानः स्थानदो ध्रुवः ।
परर्द्धिः परमस्पष्टस्तुष्टः पुष्टः शुभेक्षणः ।।४२।।

vyavasāyo vayavasthānaḥ saṁsthānaḥ sthānado dhruvaḥ I
pararddhiḥ parama-spaṣṭas-tuṣṭaḥ puṣṭaḥ śubhekṣaṇaḥ II42II

रामो विरामो विरजो मार्गो नेयो नयोऽनयः ।
वीरः शक्तिमतां श्रेष्ठो धर्मो धर्मविदुत्तमः ।।४३।।

rāmo virāmo virajo mārgo neyo-nayo'nayaḥ I
vīraḥ śaktimatāṁ śreṣṭho dharmo dharma-vid-uttamaḥ II43II

वैकुण्ठः पुरुषः प्राणः प्राणदः प्रणवः पृथुः ।
हिरण्यगर्भः शत्रुघ्नो व्याप्तो वायुरधोक्षजः ॥४४॥

vaikuṇṭhaḥ puruṣaḥ prāṇaḥ prāṇadaḥ praṇavaḥ pṛthuḥ I
hiraṇya-garbhaḥ śatrughno vyāpto vāyur-adhokṣajaḥ II44II

ऋतुः सुदर्शनः कालः परमेष्ठी परिग्रहः ।
उग्रः संवत्सरो दक्षो विश्रामो विश्वदक्षिणः ॥४५॥

ṛtuḥ sudarśanaḥ kālaḥ parameṣṭhī parigrahaḥ I
ugraḥ saṁvatsaro dakṣo viśrāmo viśva-dakṣiṇaḥ II45II

विस्तारः स्थावरस्थाणुः प्रमाणं बीजमव्ययम् ।
अर्थोऽनर्थो महाकोशो महाभोगो महाधनः ॥४६॥

vistāraḥ sthāvara-sthāṇuḥ pramāṇaṁ bījam-avyayaṁ I
artho'nartho mahākośo mahābhogo mahādhanaḥ II46II

अनिर्विण्णः स्थविष्ठोऽभूर्धर्मयूपो महामखः ।
नक्षत्रनेमिर्नक्षत्री क्षमः क्षामः समीहनः ॥४७॥

anirviṇṇaḥ sthaviṣṭho'bhūr-dharma-yūpo mahā-makhaḥ I
nakṣatra-nemir-nakṣatrī kṣamaḥ kṣāmaḥ samīhanaḥ II47II

यज्ञ इज्यो महेज्यश्च क्रतुः सत्रं सतां गतिः ।
सर्वदर्शी विमुक्तात्मा सर्वज्ञो ज्ञानमुत्तमम् ॥४८॥

yajña ijyo mahejyaś-ca kratuḥ satraṁ satāṁ gatiḥ I
sarvadarśī vimuktātmā sarvajño jñānam-uttamaṁ II48II

सुव्रतः सुमुखः सूक्ष्मः सुघोषः सुखदः सुहृत्।
मनोहरो जितक्रोधो वीरबाहुर्विदारणः ॥४९॥

suvrataḥ sumukhaḥ sūkṣmaḥ sughoṣaḥ sukhadaḥ suhṛt I
manoharo jita-krodho vīrabāhur-vidāraṇaḥ II49II

स्वापनः स्ववशो व्यापी नैकात्मा नैककर्मकृत्।
वत्सरो वत्सलो वत्सी रत्नगर्भो धनेश्वरः ॥५०॥

svāpanaḥ svavaśo vyāpī naikātmā naika-karma-kṛt I
vatsaro vatsalo vatsī ratna-garbho dhaneśvaraḥ II50II

धर्मगुब्धर्मकृद्धर्मी सदसत्क्षरमक्षरम्।
अविज्ञाता सहस्रांशुर्विधाता कृतलक्षणः ॥५१॥

dharmagub-dharmakṛd-dharmī sad-asat-kṣaram-akṣaraṁ I
avijñātā sahasrāṁśur-vidhātā kṛta-lakṣaṇaḥ II51II

गभस्तिनेमिः सत्त्वस्थः सिंहो भूतमहेश्वरः।
आदिदेवो महादेवो देवेशो देवभृद्गुरुः ॥५२॥

gabhasti-nemiḥ sattvasthaḥ siṁho bhūta-maheśvaraḥ I
ādidevo mahādevo deveśo devabhṛd-guruḥ II52II

उत्तरो गोपतिर्गोप्ता ज्ञानगम्यः पुरातनः।
शरीरभूतभृद्भोक्ता कपीन्द्रो भूरिदक्षिणः ॥५३॥

uttaro gopatir-goptā jñānagamyaḥ purātanaḥ I
śarīra-bhūta-bhṛd-bhoktā kapīndro bhūridakṣiṇaḥ II53II

सोमपोऽमृतपः सोमः पुरुजित्पुरुसत्तमः ।
विनयो जयः सत्यसंधो दाशार्हः सात्वतां पतिः ॥५४॥

somapo'mṛtapaḥ somaḥ purujit-purusattamaḥ ।
vinayo jayaḥ satyasandho dāśārhaḥ sātvatāṁ patiḥ ॥54॥

जीवो विनयितासाक्षी मुकुन्दोऽमितविक्रमः ।
अम्भोनिधिरनन्तात्मा महोदधिशयोऽन्तकः ॥५५॥

jīvo vinayitā-sākṣī mukundo'mitavikramaḥ ।
ambhonidhir-anant-ātmā mahodadhi-śayo'ntakaḥ ॥55॥

अजो महार्हः स्वाभाव्यो जितामित्रः प्रमोदनः ।
आनन्दो नन्दनो नन्दः सत्यधर्मा त्रिविक्रमः ॥५६॥

ajo mahārhaḥ svābhāvyo jitāmitraḥ pramodanaḥ ।
ānando nandano nandaḥ satya-dharmā trivikramaḥ ॥56॥

महर्षिः कपिलाचार्यः कृतज्ञो मेदिनीपतिः ।
त्रिपदस्त्रिदशाध्यक्षो महाशृङ्गः कृतान्तकृत् ॥५७॥

maharṣiḥ kapilācāryaḥ kṛtajño medinī-patiḥ ।
tripadas-tridaśādhyakṣo mahāśṛṅgaḥ kṛtāntakṛt ॥57॥

महावराहो गोविन्दः सुषेणः कनकाङ्गदी ।
गुह्यो गभीरो गहनो गुप्तश्चक्रगदाधरः ॥५८॥

mahāvarāho govindaḥ suṣeṇaḥ kanakāṅgadī ।
guhyo gabhīro gahano guptaś-cakra-gadādharaḥ ॥58॥

वेधाः स्वाङ्गोऽजितः कृष्णो दृढः संकर्षणोऽच्युतः ।
वरुणो वारुणो वृक्षः पुष्कराक्षो महामनाः ॥५९॥

vedhāḥ svāṅgo'jitaḥ kṛṣṇo dṛḍhaḥ saṅkarṣaṇo'cyutaḥ ।
varuṇo vāruṇo vṛkṣaḥ puṣkarākṣo mahā-manāḥ ॥59॥

भगवान् भगहानन्दी वनमाली हलायुधः ।
आदित्यो ज्योतिरादित्यः सहिष्णुर्गतिसत्तमः ॥६०॥

bhagavān bhagahā-nandī vanamālī halāyudhaḥ ।
ādityo jyotir-ādityaḥ sahiṣṇur-gati-sattamaḥ ॥60॥

सुधन्वा खण्डपरशुर्दारुणो द्रविणप्रदः ।
दिविस्पृक्सर्वदृग्व्यासो वाचस्पतिरयोनिजः ॥६१॥

sudhanvā khaṇḍa-paraśur-dāruṇo draviṇa-pradaḥ ।
divi-spṛk-sarva-dṛg-vyāso vācaspatir-ayonijaḥ ॥61॥

त्रिसामा सामगः साम निर्वाणं भेषजं भिषक् ।
सन्यासकृच्छमः शान्तो निष्ठा शान्तिः परायणम् ॥६२॥

trisāmā sāmagaḥ sāma nirvāṇaṁ bheṣajaṁ bhiṣak ।
sanyāsa-kṛcchamaḥ śānto niṣṭhā śāntiḥ parāyaṇaṁ ॥62॥

शुभाङ्गः शान्तिदः स्रष्टा कुमुदः कुवलेशयः ।
गोहितो गोपतिर्गोप्ता वृषभाक्षो वृषप्रियः ॥६३॥

śubhāṅgaḥ śāntidaḥ sraṣṭā kumudaḥ kuvaleśayaḥ ।
gohito gopatir-goptā vṛṣabhākṣo vṛṣapriyaḥ ॥63॥

अनिवर्ती निवृत्तात्मा संक्षेप्ता क्षेमकृच्छिवः ।
श्रीवत्सवक्षाः श्रीवासः श्रीपतिः श्रीमतांवरः ॥६४॥

anivartī nivṛttātmā saṅkṣeptā kṣema-kṛcchivaḥ |
śrīvatsa-vakṣāḥ śrīvāsaḥ śrīpatiḥ śrīmatāṁ-varaḥ ||64||

श्रीदः श्रीशः श्रीनिवासः श्रीनिधिः श्रीविभावनः ।
श्रीधरः श्रीकरः श्रेयः श्रीमाँल्लोकत्रयाश्रयः ॥६५॥

śrīdaḥ śrīśaḥ śrīnivāsaḥ śrīnidhiḥ śrīvibhāvanaḥ |
śrīdharaḥ śrīkaraḥ śreyaḥ śrimānlloka-trayāśrayaḥ ||65||

स्वक्षः स्वङ्गः शतानन्दो नन्दिर्ज्योतिर्गणेश्वरः ।
विजितात्माविधेयात्मा सत्कीर्तिश्छिन्नसंशयः ॥६६॥

svakṣaḥ svaṅgaḥ śatānando nandir-jyotir-gaṇeśvaraḥ |
vijitātmā-vidheyātmā satkīrtiś-chinnasaṁśayaḥ ||66||

उदीर्णः सर्वतश्चक्षुरनीशः शाश्वतस्थिरः ।
भूशयो भूषणो भूतिर्विशोकः शोकनाशनः ॥६७॥

udīrṇaḥ sarvataś-cakṣur-anīśaḥ śāśvata-sthiraḥ |
bhūśayo bhūṣaṇo bhūtir-viśokaḥ śoka-nāśanaḥ ||67||

अर्चिष्मानर्चितः कुम्भो विशुद्धात्मा विशोधनः ।
अनिरुद्धोऽप्रतिरथः प्रद्युम्नोऽमितविक्रमः ॥६८॥

arciṣmān-arcitaḥ kumbho viśuddhātmā viśodhanaḥ |
aniruddho'prati-rathaḥ pradyumno'mita-vikramaḥ ||68||

कालनेमिनिहा वीरः शौरिः शूरजनेश्वरः ।
त्रिलोकात्मा त्रिलोकेशः केशवः केशिहा हरिः ॥६९॥

kāla-nemi-nihā vīraḥ śauriḥ śūra-janeśvaraḥ ।
trilokātmā trilokeśaḥ keśavaḥ keśihā hariḥ ॥69॥

कामदेवः कामपालः कामी कान्तः कृतागमः ।
अनिर्देश्यवपुर्विष्णुर्वीरोऽनन्तो धनञ्जयः ॥७०॥

kāmadevaḥ kāmapālaḥ kāmī kāntaḥ kṛtāgamaḥ ।
anirdeśya-vapur-viṣṇur-vīro'nanto dhanañjayaḥ ॥70॥

ब्रह्मण्यो ब्रह्मकृद्ब्रह्मा ब्रह्म ब्रह्मविवर्धनः ।
ब्रह्मविद्ब्राह्मणो ब्रह्मी ब्रह्मज्ञो ब्राह्मणप्रियः ॥७१॥

brahmaṇyo brahmakṛd-brahmā brahma brahma-vivardhanaḥ ।
brahmavid-brāhmaṇo brahmī brahmajño brāhmaṇa-priyaḥ ॥71॥

महाक्रमो महाकर्मा महातेजा महोरगः ।
महाक्रतुर्महायज्वा महायज्ञो महाहविः ॥७२॥

mahākramo mahākarmā mahātejā mahoragaḥ ।
mahākratur-mahāyajvā mahā-yajño mahā-haviḥ ॥72॥

स्तव्यः स्तवप्रियः स्तोत्रं स्तुतिः स्तोता रणप्रियः ।
पूर्णः पूरयिता पुण्यः पुण्यकीर्तिरनामयः ॥७३॥

stavyaḥ stavapriyaḥ stotraṁ stutiḥ stotā raṇapriyaḥ ।
pūrṇaḥ pūrayitā puṇyaḥ puṇya-kīrtir-anāmayaḥ ॥73॥

मनोजवस्तीर्थकरो वसुरेता वसुप्रदः ।
वसुप्रदो वासुदेवो वसुर्वसुमना हविः ॥७४॥

manojavas-tīrthakaro vasuretā vasupradaḥ ।
vasuprado vāsudevo vasur-vasumanā haviḥ ॥74॥

सद्गतिः सत्कृतिः सत्ता सद्भूतिः सत्परायणः ।
शूरसेनो यदुश्रेष्ठः सन्निवासः सुयामुनः ॥७५॥

sad-gatiḥ sat-kṛtiḥ sattā sad-bhūtiḥ sat-parāyaṇaḥ ।
śūraseno yaduśreṣṭhaḥ san-nivāsaḥ suyāmunaḥ ॥75॥

भूतावासो वासुदेवः सर्वासुनिलयोऽनलः ।
दर्पहा दर्पदो दृप्तो दुर्धरोऽथापराजितः ॥७६॥

bhūtāvāso vāsudevaḥ sarvāsu-nilayo'nalaḥ ।
darpahā darpado dṛpto durdharo'thāparājitaḥ ॥76॥

विश्वमूर्तिर्महामूर्तिर्दीप्तमूर्तिरमूर्तिमान् ।
अनेकमूर्तिरव्यक्तः शतमूर्तिः शताननः ॥७७॥

viśvamūrtir-mahāmūrtir-dīptamūrtir-amūrtimān ।
aneka-mūrtir-avyaktaḥ śata-mūrtiḥ śatānanaḥ ॥77॥

एको नैकः सवः कः किं यत्तत्पदमनुत्तमम् ।
लोकबन्धुर्लोकनाथो माधवो भक्तवत्सलः ॥७८॥

eko naikaḥ savaḥ kaḥ kiṁ yat-tat-padam-anuttamam ।
loka-bandhur-loka-nātho mādhavo bhakta-vatsalaḥ ॥78॥

सुवर्णवर्णो हेमाङ्गो वराङ्गश्चन्दनाङ्गदी।
वीरहा विषमः शून्यो घृताशीरचलश्चलः ॥७९॥

suvarṇa-varṇo hemāṅgo varāṅgaś-candanāṅgadī ।
vīrahā viṣamaḥ śūnyo ghṛtāśīr-acalaś-calaḥ ॥79॥

अमानी मानदो मान्यो लोकस्वामी त्रिलोकधृक् ॥
सुमेधा मेधजो धन्यः सत्यमेधा धराधरः ॥८०॥

amānī mānado mānyo loka-svāmī triloka-dhṛk ।
sumedhā medhajo dhanyaḥ satya-medhā dharādharaḥ ॥80॥

तेजोवृषो द्युतिधरः सर्वशस्त्रभृतां वरः।
प्रग्रहो निग्रहो व्यग्रो नैकशृङ्गो गदाग्रजः ॥८१॥

tejo-vṛṣo dyuti-dharaḥ sarva-śastra-bhṛtāṁ varaḥ ।
pragraho nigraho vyagro naikaśṛṅgo gadāgrajaḥ ॥81॥

चतुर्मूर्तिश्चतुर्बाहुश्चतुर्व्यूहश्चतुर्गतिः।
चतुरात्मा चतुर्भावश्चतुर्वेदविदेकपात् ॥८२॥

catur-mūrtiś-catur-bāhuś-catur-vyūhaś-catur-gatiḥ ।
catur-ātmā catur-bhāvaś-catur-veda-vid-ekapāt ॥82॥

समावर्तोऽनिवृत्तात्मा दुर्जयो दुरतिक्रमः।
दुर्लभो दुर्गमो दुर्गो दुरावासो दुरारिहा ॥८३॥

samāvarto'nivṛttātmā durjayo duratikramaḥ ।
durlabho durgamo durgo durāvāso durāriha ॥83॥

शुभाङ्गो लोकसारङ्गः सुतन्तुस्तन्तुवर्धनः ।
इन्द्रकर्मा महाकर्मा कृतकर्मा कृतागमः ॥८४॥

śubhāṅgo loka-sāraṅgaḥ sutantus-tantu-vardhanaḥ ।
indra-karmā mahā-karmā kṛta-karmā kṛtāgamaḥ ॥84॥

उद्भवः सुन्दरः सुन्दो रत्ननाभः सुलोचनः ।
अर्को वाजसनः शृङ्गी जयन्तः सर्वविज्जयी ॥८५॥

udbhavaḥ sundaraḥ sundo ratna-nābhaḥ sulocanaḥ ।
arko vājasanaḥ śṛṅgī jayantaḥ sarva-vijjayī ॥85॥

सुवर्णबिन्दुरक्षोभ्यः सर्ववागीश्वरेश्वरः ।
महाह्रदो महागर्तो महाभूतो महानिधिः ॥८६॥

suvarṇa-bindur-akṣobhyaḥ sarva-vāgīśvareśvaraḥ ।
mahāhrado mahā-garto mahā-bhūto mahā-nidhiḥ ॥86॥

कुमुदः कुन्दरः कुन्दः पर्जन्यः पावनोऽनिलः ।
अमृताशोऽमृतवपुः सर्वज्ञः सर्वतोमुखः ॥८७॥

kumudaḥ kundaraḥ kundaḥ parjanyaḥ pāvano'nilaḥ ।
amṛtāśo'mṛta-vapuḥ sarvajñaḥ sarvato-mukhaḥ ॥87॥

सुलभः सुव्रतः सिद्धः शत्रुजिच्छत्रुतापनः ।
न्यग्रोधोदुम्बरोऽश्वत्थश्चाणूरान्ध्रनिषूदनः ॥८८॥

sulabhaḥ suvrataḥ siddhaḥ śatru-jic-chatru-tāpanaḥ ।
nyagrodho-dumbaro'śvatthaś-cāṇūrāndhra-niṣūdanaḥ ॥88॥

सहस्रार्चिः सप्तजिह्वः सप्तैधाः सप्तवाहनः ।
अमूर्तिरनघोऽचिन्त्यो भयकृद्भयनाशनः ॥८९॥

sahasrārciḥ sapta-jihvaḥ saptaidhāḥ sapta-vāhanaḥ ।
amūrtir-anagho'cintyo bhayakṛdbhaya-nāśanaḥ ॥89॥

अणुर्बृहत्कृशः स्थूलो गुणभृन्निर्गुणो महान् ।
अधृतः स्वधृतः स्वास्यः प्राग्वंशो वंशवर्धनः ॥९०॥

aṇur-bṛhat-kṛśaḥ sthūlo guṇabhṛn-nigruṇo mahān ।
adhṛtaḥ svadhṛtaḥ svāsyaḥ prāgvaṁśo vaṁśavardhanaḥ ॥90॥

भारभृत्कथितो योगी योगीशः सर्वकामदः ।
आश्रमः श्रमणः क्षामः सुपर्णो वायुवाहनः ॥९१॥

bhāra-bhṛt-kathito yogī yogīśaḥ sarva-kāmadaḥ ।
āśramaḥ śramaṇaḥ kṣāmaḥ suparṇo vāyu-vāhanaḥ ॥91॥

धनुर्धरो धनुर्वेदो दण्डो दमयिता दमः ।
अपराजितः सर्वसहो नियन्ता नियमो यमः ॥९२॥

dhanurdharo dhanurvedo daṇḍo damayitā damaḥ ।
aparājitaḥ sarvasaho niyantā niyamo yamaḥ ॥92॥

सत्त्ववान्सात्त्विकः सत्यः सत्यधर्मपरायणः ।
अभिप्रायः प्रियार्होऽर्हः प्रियकृत्प्रीतिवर्धनः ॥९३॥

sattvavān-sāttvikaḥ satyaḥ satya-dharma-parāyaṇaḥ ।
abhiprāyaḥ priyārho'rhaḥ priyakṛt-prītivardhanaḥ ॥93॥

विहायसगतिर्ज्योतिः सुरुचिर्हुतभुग्विभुः ।
रविर्विरोचनः सूर्यः सविता रविलोचनः ॥९४॥

vihāyasagatir-jotiḥ surucir-huta-bhug-vibhuḥ ।
ravir-virocanaḥ sūryaḥ savitā ravi-locanaḥ ॥94॥

अनन्तो हुतभुग्भोक्ता सुखदो नैकजोऽग्रजः ।
अनिर्विण्णः सदामर्षी लोकाधिष्ठानमद्भुतः ॥९५॥

ananto huta-bhug-bhoktā sukhado naikajo'grajaḥ ।
anirviṇṇaḥ sadāmarṣī lokādhiṣṭhānam-adbhutaḥ ॥95॥

सनात्सनातनतमः कपिलः कपिरप्ययः ।
स्वस्तिदः स्वस्तिकृत्स्वस्ति स्वस्तिभुक्स्वस्तिदक्षिणः ॥९६॥

sanāt-sanātana-tamaḥ kapilaḥ kapir-apyayaḥ ।
svastidaḥ svastikṛt-svasti svastibhuk-svasti-dakṣiṇaḥ ॥96॥

अरौद्रः कुण्डली चक्री विक्रम्यूर्जितशासनः ।
शब्दातिगः शब्दसहः शिशिरः शर्वरीकरः ॥९७॥

araudraḥ kuṇḍalī cakrī vikramyūrjita-śāsanaḥ ।
śabdātigaḥ śabdasahaḥ śiśiraḥ śarvarī-karaḥ ॥97॥

अक्रूरः पेशलो दक्षो दक्षिणः क्षमिणां वरः ।
विद्वत्तमो वीतभयः पुण्यश्रवणकीर्तनः ॥९८॥

akrūraḥ peśalo dakṣo dakṣiṇaḥ kṣamiṇāṁ varaḥ ।
vidvattamo vītabhayaḥ puṇya-śravaṇa-kīrtanaḥ ॥98॥

उत्तारणो दुष्कृतिहा पुण्यो दुःस्वप्ननाशनः।
वीरहा रक्षणः सन्तो जीवनः पर्यवस्थितः ॥९९॥

uttāraṇo duṣ-kṛtihā puṇyo duḥ-svapna-nāśanaḥ ।
vīrahā rakṣaṇaḥ santo jīvanaḥ paryavasthitaḥ ॥99॥

अनन्तरूपोऽनन्तश्रीर्जितमन्युर्भयापहः।
चतुरस्रो गभीरात्मा विदिशो व्यादिशो दिशः ॥१००॥

anantarūpo'nanta-śrīrjitamanyur-bhayāpahaḥ ।
caturasro gabhīrātmā vidiśo vyādiśo diśaḥ ॥100॥

अनादिर्भूर्भुवो लक्ष्मीः सुवीरो रुचिराङ्गदः।
जननो जनजन्मादिर्भीमो भीमपराक्रमः ॥१०१॥

anādir-bhūrbhuvo lakṣmīḥ suvīro rucirāṅgadaḥ ।
janano janajanmādir-bhīmo bhīma-parākramaḥ ॥101॥

आधारनिलयो धाता पुष्पहासः प्रजागरः।
ऊर्ध्वगः सत्पथाचारः प्राणदः प्रणवः पणः ॥१०२॥

ādhāranilayo dhātā puṣpahāsaḥ prajāgaraḥ ।
ūrdhvagaḥ sat-pathācāraḥ prāṇadaḥ praṇavaḥ paṇaḥ ॥102॥

प्रमाणं प्राणनिलयः प्राणभृत्प्राणजीवनः।
तत्त्वं तत्त्वविदेकात्मा जन्ममृत्युजरातिगः ॥१०३॥

pramāṇaṁ prāṇa-nilayaḥ prāṇabhṛt-prāṇa-jīvanaḥ ।
tattvaṁ tattvavid-ekātmā janma-mṛtyu-jarātigaḥ ॥103॥

भूर्भुवः स्वस्तरुस्तारः सविता प्रपितामहः ।
यज्ञो यज्ञपतिर्यज्वा यज्ञाङ्गो यज्ञवाहनः ॥१०४॥

bhūrbhuvaḥ svas-tarus-tāraḥ savitā pra-pitāmahaḥ I
yajño yajña-patir-yajvā yajñāṅgo yajña-vāhanaḥ II104II

यज्ञभृद्यज्ञकृद्यज्ञी यज्ञभुग्यज्ञसाधनः ।
यज्ञान्तकृद्यज्ञगुह्यमन्नमन्नाद एव च ॥१०५॥

yajñabhṛd-yajñakṛd-yajñī yajñabhug-yajñasādhanaḥ I
yajñāntakṛd-yajñaguhyam annam-annāda eva ca II105II

आत्मयोनिः स्वयंजातो वैखानः सामगायनः ।
देवकीनन्दनः स्रष्टा क्षितीशः पापनाशनः ॥१०६॥

ātma-yoniḥ svayaṁ-jāto vaikhānaḥ sāma-gāyanaḥ I
devakī-nandanaḥ sraṣṭā kṣitīśaḥ pāpa-nāśanaḥ II106II

शंखभृन्नन्दकी चक्री शार्ङ्गधन्वा गदाधरः ।
रथाङ्गपाणिरक्षोभ्यः सर्वप्रहरणायुधः ॥१०७॥

śaṅkhabhṛn-nandakī cakrī śārṅga-dhanvā gadādharaḥ I
rathāṅga-pāṇir-akṣobhyaḥ sarva-praharaṇāyudhaḥ II107II

सर्वप्रहरणायुध ॐ नम इति ॥

sarva-praharaṇāyudha om nama iti II

Śrī Viṣṇu Sahasranāmāvaliḥ

1.	ॐ विश्वस्मै नमः	om viśvasmai namaḥ
2.	ॐ विष्णवे नमः	om viśṇave namaḥ
3.	ॐ वषट्काराय नमः	om vaṣaṭkārāya namaḥ
4.	ॐ भूतभव्यभवत्प्रभवे नमः	om bhūtabhavyabhavatprabhave namaḥ
5.	ॐ भूतकृते नमः	om bhūtakṛte namaḥ
6.	ॐ भूतभृते नमः	om bhūtabhṛte namaḥ
7.	ॐ भावाय नमः	om bhāvāya namaḥ
8.	ॐ भूतात्मने नमः	om bhūtātmane namaḥ
9.	ॐ भूतभावनाय नमः	om bhūtabhāvanāya namaḥ
10.	ॐ पूतात्मने नमः	om pūtātmane namaḥ
11.	ॐ परमात्मने नमः	om paramātmane namaḥ
12.	ॐ मुक्तानांपरमायैगतये नमः	om muktānāṁparamāyaigataye namaḥ
13.	ॐ अव्ययाय नमः	om avyayāya namaḥ
14.	ॐ पुरुषायनमः	om puruṣāya namaḥ
15.	ॐ साक्षिणे नमः	om sākṣiṇe namaḥ
16.	ॐ क्षेत्रज्ञाय नमः	om kṣetrajñāya namaḥ
17.	ॐ अक्षराय नमः	om akṣarāya namaḥ
18.	ॐ योगाय नमः	om yogāya namaḥ
19.	ॐ योगविदामं नेत्रे नमः	om yogavidāṁ netre namaḥ
20.	ॐ प्रधानपुरुषेश्वराय नमः	om pradhānapuruṣeśvarāya namaḥ
21.	ॐ नारसिंहवपुषे नमः	om nārasiṁhavapuṣe namaḥ
22.	ॐ श्रीमते नमः	om śrīmate namaḥ
23.	ॐ केशवाय नमः	om keśavāya namaḥ

24.	ॐ पुरुषोत्तमाय नमः	*om puruṣottamāya namaḥ*
25.	ॐ सर्वस्मै नमः	*om sarvasmai namaḥ*
26.	ॐ शर्वाय नमः	*om śarvāya namaḥ*
27.	ॐ शिवाय नमः	*om śivāya namaḥ*
28.	ॐ स्थाणवे नमः	*om sthāṇave namaḥ*
29.	ॐ भूतादये नमः	*om bhūtādaye namaḥ*
30.	ॐ निधये नमः	*om nidhaye namaḥ*
31.	ॐ अव्ययाय नमः	*om avyayāya namaḥ*
32.	ॐ सम्भवाय नमः	*om saṁbhavāya namaḥ*
33.	ॐ भावनाय नमः	*om bhāvanāya namaḥ*
34.	ॐ भर्त्रे नमः	*om bhartre namaḥ*
35.	ॐ प्रभवाय नमः	*om prabhavāya namaḥ*
36.	ॐ प्रभवे नमः	*om prabhave namaḥ*
37.	ॐ ईश्वराय नमः	*om īśvarāya namaḥ*
38.	ॐ स्वयम्भुवे नमः	*om svayaṁbhuve namaḥ*
39.	ॐ शम्भवे नमः	*om śaṁbhave namaḥ*
40.	ॐ आदित्याय नमः	*om ādityāya namaḥ*
41.	ॐ पुष्कराक्षाय नमः	*om puṣkarākṣāya namaḥ*
42.	ॐ महास्वनाय नमः	*om mahāsvanāya namaḥ*
43.	ॐ अनादिनिधनाय नमः	*om anādinidhanāya namaḥ*
44.	ॐ धात्रे नमः	*om dhātre namaḥ*
45.	ॐ विधात्रे नमः	*om vidhātre namaḥ*
46.	ॐ धातव उत्तमाय नमः	*om dhātava uttamāya namaḥ*
47.	ॐ अप्रमेयाय नमः	*om aprameyāya namaḥ*
48.	ॐ हृषीकेशाय नमः	*om hṛṣīkeśāya namaḥ*
49.	ॐ पद्मनाभाय नमः	*om padmanābhāya namaḥ*
50.	ॐ अमरप्रभवे नमः	*om amaraprabhave namaḥ*
51.	ॐ विश्वकर्मणे नमः	*om viśvakarmaṇe namaḥ*
52.	ॐ मनवे नमः	*om manave namaḥ*
53.	ॐ त्वष्ट्रे नमः	*om tvaṣṭre namaḥ*

54. ॐ स्थविष्ठाय नमः | om sthaviṣṭhāya namaḥ
55. ॐ स्थविराय ध्रुवाय नमः | om sthavirāya dhruvāya namaḥ
56. ॐ अग्राह्याय नमः | om agrāhyāya namaḥ
57. ॐ शाश्वताय नमः | om śāśvatāya namaḥ
58. ॐ कृष्णाय नमः | om kṛṣṇāya namaḥ
59. ॐ लोहिताक्षाय नमः | om lohitākṣāya namaḥ
60. ॐ प्रतर्दनाय नमः | om pratardanâya namaḥ
61. ॐ प्रभूताय नमः | om prabhūtāya namaḥ
62. ॐ त्रिककुब्धाम्ने नमः | om trikakubdhāmne namaḥ
63. ॐ पवित्राय नमः | om pavitrāya namaḥ
64. ॐ मङ्गलायपरस्मै नमः | om maṅgalāyaparasmai namaḥ
65. ॐ ईशानाय नमः | om īśānāya namaḥ
66. ॐ प्राणदाय नमः | om prāṇadāya namaḥ
67. ॐ प्राणाय नमः | om prāṇāya namaḥ
68. ॐ ज्येष्ठाय नमः | om jyeṣṭhāya namaḥ
69. ॐ श्रेष्ठाय नमः | om śreṣṭhāya namaḥ
70. ॐ प्रजापतये नमः | om prajāpataye namaḥ
71. ॐ हिरण्यगर्भाय नमः | om hiraṇyagarbhāya namaḥ
72. ॐ भूगर्भाय नमः | om bhūgarbhāya namaḥ
73. ॐ माधवाय नमः | om mādhavāya namaḥ
74. ॐ मधुसूदनाय नमः | om madhusūdanāya namaḥ
75. ॐ ईश्वराय नमः | om īśvarāya namaḥ
76. ॐ विक्रमिणे नमः | om vikramiṇe namaḥ
77. ॐ धन्विने नमः | om dhanvine namaḥ
78. ॐ मेधाविने नमः | om medhāvine namaḥ
79. ॐ विक्रमाय नमः | om vikramāya namaḥ
80. ॐ क्रमाय नमः | om kramāya namaḥ
81. ॐ अनुत्तमाय नमः | om anuttamāya namaḥ
82. ॐ दुराधर्षाय नमः | om durādharṣāya namaḥ
83. ॐ कृतज्ञाय नमः | om kṛtajñāya namaḥ

84. ॐ कृतिरात्मवते नमः	*om kṛtirātmavate namaḥ*
85. ॐ सुरेशाय नमः	*om sureśāya namaḥ*
86. ॐ शरणाय नमः	*om śaraṇāya namaḥ*
87. ॐ शर्मणे नमः	*om śarmaṇe namaḥ*
88. ॐ विश्वरेतसे नमः	*om viśvaretase namaḥ*
89. ॐ प्रजाभवाय नमः	*om prajābhavāya namaḥ*
90. ॐ अह्ने नमः	*om ahre namaḥ*
91. ॐ संवत्सराय नमः	*om saṁvatsarāya namaḥ*
92. ॐ व्यालाय नमः	*om vyālāya namaḥ*
93. ॐ प्रत्ययाय नमः	*om pratyayāya namaḥ*
94. ॐ सर्वदर्शनाय नमः	*om sarvadarṣanāya namaḥ*
95. ॐ अजाय नमः	*om ajāya namaḥ*
96. ॐ सर्वेश्वराय नमः	*om sarveśvarāya namaḥ*
97. ॐ सिद्धाय नमः	*om siddhāya namaḥ*
98. ॐ सिद्धये नमः	*om siddhaye namaḥ*
99. ॐ सर्वादये नमः	*om sarvādaye namaḥ*
100. ॐ अच्युताय नमः	*om acyutāya namaḥ*
101. ॐ वृषाकपये नमः	*om vṛṣākapaye namaḥ*
102. ॐ अमेयात्मने नमः	*om ameyātmane namaḥ*
103. ॐ सर्वयोगविनिसृताय नमः	*om sarvayogavinisṛtāya namaḥ*
104. ॐ वसवे नमः	*om vasave namaḥ*
105. ॐ वसुमनसे नमः	*om vasumanase namaḥ*
106. ॐ सत्याय नमः	*om satyāya namaḥ*
107. ॐ समात्मने नमः	*om samātmane namaḥ*
108. ॐ असम्मिताय नमः	*om asammitāya namaḥ*
109. ॐ समाय नमः	*om samāya namaḥ*
110. ॐ अमोघाय नमः	*om amoghāya namaḥ*
111. ॐ पुण्डरीकाक्षाय नमः	*om puṇḍarīkākṣāya namaḥ*
112. ॐ वृषकर्मणे नमः	*om vṛṣakarmaṇe namaḥ*
113. ॐ वृषाकृतये नमः	*om vṛṣākṛtaye namaḥ*

114. ॐ रुद्राय नमः om rudrāya namaḥ
115. ॐ बहुशिरसे नमः om bahuśirase namaḥ
116. ॐ बभ्रवे नमः om babhrave namaḥ
117. ॐ विश्वयोनये नमः om viśvayonaye namaḥ
118. ॐ शुचिश्रवसे नमः om śuciśravase namaḥ
119. ॐ अमृताय नमः om amṛtāya namaḥ
120. ॐ शाश्वतस्थाणवे नमः om śāśvatasthāṇave namaḥ
121. ॐ वरारोहाय नमः om varārohāya namaḥ
122. ॐ महातपसे नमः om mahātapase namaḥ
123. ॐ सर्वगाय नमः om sarvagāya namaḥ
124. ॐ सर्वविद्भानवे नमः om sarvavidbhānave namaḥ
125. ॐ विष्वक्सेनाय नमः om viṣvaksenāya namaḥ
126. ॐ जनार्दनाय नमः om janārdanāya namaḥ
127. ॐ वेदाय नमः om vedāya namaḥ
128. ॐ वेदविदे नमः om vedavide namaḥ
129. ॐ अव्यङ्गाय नमः om avyṅgāya namaḥ
130. ॐ वेदाङ्गाय नमः om vedāṅgāya namaḥ
131. ॐ वेदविदे नमः om vedavide namaḥ
132. ॐ कवये नमः om kavaye namaḥ
133. ॐ लोकाध्यक्षाय नमः om lokādhyakṣāya namaḥ
134. ॐ सुराध्यक्षाय नमः om surādhyakṣāya namaḥ
135. ॐ धर्माध्यक्षाय नमः om dharmādhyakṣāya namaḥ
136. ॐ कृताकृताय नमः om kṛtākṛtāya namaḥ
137. ॐ चतुरात्मने नमः om caturātmane namaḥ
138. ॐ चतुर्व्यूहाय नमः om caturvyūhāya namaḥ
139. ॐ चतुर्दंष्ट्राय नमः om caturdaṁṣṭrāya namaḥ
140. ॐ चतुर्भुजाय नमः om caturbhujāya namaḥ
141. ॐ भ्राजिष्णवे नमः om bhrājiṣṇave namaḥ
142. ॐ भोजनाय नमः om bhojanāya namaḥ
143. ॐ भोक्त्रे नमः om bhoktre namaḥ

144.	ॐ सहिष्णवे नमः	*om sahiṣṇave namaḥ*
145.	ॐ जगदादिजाय नमः	*om jagadādijāya namaḥ*
146.	ॐ अनघाय नमः	*om anaghāya namaḥ*
147.	ॐ विजयाय नमः	*om vijayāya namaḥ*
148.	ॐ जेत्रे नमः	*om jetre namaḥ*
149.	ॐ विश्वयोनये नमः	*om viśvayonaye namaḥ*
150.	ॐ पुनर्वसवे नमः	*om punarvasave namaḥ*
151.	ॐ उपेन्द्राय नमः	*om upendrāya namaḥ*
152.	ॐ वामनाय नमः	*om vāmanāya namaḥ*
153.	ॐ प्रांशवे नमः	*om prāṁśave namaḥ*
154.	ॐ अमोघाय नमः	*om amoghāya namaḥ*
155.	ॐ शुचये नमः	*om śucaye namaḥ*
156.	ॐ ऊर्जिताय नमः	*om ūrjitāya namaḥ*
157.	ॐ अतीन्द्राय नमः	*om atīndrāya namaḥ*
158.	ॐ संग्रहाय नमः	*om saṅgrahāya namaḥ*
159.	ॐ सर्गाय नमः	*om sargāya namaḥ*
160.	ॐ धृतात्मने नमः	*om dhṛtātmane namaḥ*
161.	ॐ नियमाय नमः	*om niyamāya namaḥ*
162.	ॐ यमाय नमः	*om yamāya namaḥ*
163.	ॐ वेद्याय नमः	*om vedyāya namaḥ*
164.	ॐ वैद्याय नमः	*om vaidyāy namaḥ*
165.	ॐ सदायोगिने नमः	*om sadāyogine namaḥ*
166.	ॐ वीरघ्ने नमः	*om vīraghne namaḥ*
167.	ॐ माधवाय नमः	*om mādhavāya namaḥ*
168.	ॐ मधवे नमः	*om madhave namaḥ*
169.	ॐ अतीन्द्रियाय नमः	*om atīndriyāya namaḥ*
170.	ॐ महामायाय नमः	*om mahāmāyāya namaḥ*
171.	ॐ महोत्साहाय नमः	*om mahotsāhāya namaḥ*
172.	ॐ महाबलाय नमः	*om mahābalāya namaḥ*
173.	ॐ महाबुद्धये नमः	*om mahābuddhaye namaḥ*

174. ॐ महावीर्याय नमः om mahāvīryāya namaḥ
175. ॐ महाशक्तये नमः om mahāśaktaye namaḥ
176. ॐ महाद्युतये नमः om mahādyutaye namaḥ
177. ॐ अनिर्देश्यवपुषे नमः om anirdeśyavapuṣe namaḥ
178. ॐ श्रीमते नमः om śrīmate namaḥ
179. ॐ अमेयात्मने नमः om ameyātmane namaḥ
180. ॐ महाद्रिधृषे नमः om mahādridhṛṣe namaḥ
181. ॐ महेष्वासाय नमः om maheṣvāsāya namaḥ
182. ॐ महीभर्त्रे नमः om mahībhartre namaḥ
183. ॐ श्रीनिवासाय नमः om śrīnivāsāya namaḥ
184. ॐ सतांगतये नमः om satāṁgataye namaḥ
185. ॐ अनिरुद्धाय नमः om aniruddhāya namaḥ
186. ॐ सुरानन्दाय नमः om surānandāya namaḥ
187. ॐ गोविन्दाय नमः om govindāya namaḥ
186. ॐ गोविदांपतये नमः om govidāṁpataye namaḥ
189. ॐ मरीचये नमः om marīcaye namaḥ
190. ॐ दमनाय नमः om damanāya namaḥ
191. ॐ हंसाय नमः om haṁsāya namaḥ
192. ॐ सुपर्णाय नमः om suparṇāya namaḥ
193. ॐ भुजगोत्तमाय नमः om bujagottamāya namaḥ
194. ॐ हिरण्यनाभाय नमः om hiraṇyanābhāya namaḥ
195. ॐ सुतपसे नमः om sutapase namaḥ
196. ॐ पद्मनाभाय नमः om padmanābhāya namaḥ
197. ॐ प्रजापतये नमः om prajāpataye namaḥ
198. ॐ अमृत्यवे नमः om amṛtyave namaḥ
199. ॐ सर्वदृशे नमः om sarvadṛśe namaḥ
200. ॐ सिंहाय नमः om siṁhāya namaḥ
201. ॐ सन्धात्रे नमः om sandhātre namaḥ
202. ॐ सन्धिमते नमः om sandhimate namaḥ
203. ॐ स्थिराय नमः om sthirāya namaḥ

204. ॐ अजाय नमः — *om ajāya namaḥ*
205. ॐ दुर्मर्षणाय नमः — *om durmarṣaṇāya namaḥ*
206. ॐ शास्त्रे नमः — *om śāstre namaḥ*
207. ॐ विश्रुतात्मने नमः — *om viśrutātmane namaḥ*
208. ॐ सुरारिघ्ने नमः — *om surārighne namaḥ*
209. ॐ गुरवे नमः — *om gurave namaḥ*
210. ॐ गुरुतमाय नमः — *om gurutamāya namaḥ*
211. ॐ धाम्ने नमः — *om dhāmne namaḥ*
212. ॐ सत्याय नमः — *om satyāya namaḥ*
213. ॐ सत्यपराक्रमाय नमः — *om satyaparākramāya namaḥ*
214. ॐ निमिषाय नमः — *om nimiṣāya namaḥ*
215. ॐ अनिमिषाय नमः — *om animiṣāya namaḥ*
216. ॐ स्रग्विणे नमः — *om sragviṇe namaḥ*
217. ॐ वाचस्पतय उदारधिये नमः — *om vācaspataya udāradhiye namaḥ*
218. ॐ अग्रण्ये नमः — *om agraṇye namaḥ*
219. ॐ ग्रामण्ये नमः — *om grāmaṇye namaḥ*
220. ॐ श्रीमते नमः — *om śrīmate namaḥ*
221. ॐ न्यायाय नमः — *om nyāyāya namaḥ*
222. ॐ नेत्रे नमः — *om netre namaḥ*
223. ॐ समीरणाय नमः — *om samīraṇāya namaḥ*
224. ॐ सहस्रमूर्ध्ने नमः — *om sahasramūrdhne namaḥ*
225. ॐ विश्वात्मने नमः — *om viśvātmane namaḥ*
226. ॐ सहस्राक्षाय नमः — *om sahasrākṣāya namaḥ*
227. ॐ सहस्रपदे नमः — *om sahasrapade namaḥ*
228. ॐ आवर्तनाय नमः — *om āvartanāya namaḥ*
229. ॐ निवृत्तात्मने नमः — *om nivṛttātmane namaḥ*
230. ॐ संवृताय नमः — *om saṁvṛtāya namaḥ*
231. ॐ सम्प्रमर्दनाय नमः — *om sampramardanāya namaḥ*
232. ॐ अहः संवर्तकाय नमः — *om ahaḥ saṁvartakāya namaḥ*
233. ॐ वह्नये नमः — *om vahnaye namaḥ*

234.	ॐ अनिलाय नमः	*om anilāya namaḥ*
235.	ॐ धरणीधराय नमः	*om dharaṇīdharāya namaḥ*
236.	ॐ सुप्रसादाय नमः	*om suprasādāya namaḥ*
237.	ॐ प्रसन्नात्मने नमः	*om prasannātmane namaḥ*
238.	ॐ विश्वधृषे नमः	*om viśvadhṛṣe namaḥ*
239.	ॐ विश्वभुजे नमः	*om viśvabhuje namaḥ*
240.	ॐ विभवे नमः	*om vibhave namaḥ*
241.	ॐ सत्कर्त्रे नमः	*om satkartre namaḥ*
242.	ॐ सत्कृताय नमः	*om satkṛtāya namaḥ*
243.	ॐ साधवे नमः	*om sādhave namaḥ*
244.	ॐ जह्नवे नमः	*om jahnave namaḥ*
245.	ॐ नारायणाय नमः	*om nārāyaṇāya namaḥ*
246.	ॐ नराय नमः	*om narāya namaḥ*
247.	ॐ असंख्येयाय नमः	*om asaṅkhyeyāya namaḥ*
248.	ॐ अप्रमेयात्मने नमः	*om aprameyātmane namaḥ*
249.	ॐ विशिष्टाय नमः	*om viśiṣṭāya namaḥ*
250.	ॐ शिष्टकृते नमः	*om śiṣṭakṛte namaḥ*
251.	ॐ शुचये नमः	*om śucaye namaḥ*
252.	ॐ सिद्धार्थाय नमः	*om siddhārthāya namaḥ*
253.	ॐ सिद्धसंकल्पाय नमः	*om siddhasaṅkalpāya namaḥ*
254.	ॐ सिद्धिदाय नमः	*om siddhidāya namaḥ*
255.	ॐ सिद्धिसाधनाय नमः	*om siddhisādhanāya namaḥ*
256.	ॐ वृषाहिणे नमः	*om vṛṣāhiṇe namaḥ*
257.	ॐ वृषभाय नमः	*om vṛṣabhāya namaḥ*
258.	ॐ विष्णवे नमः	*om viṣṇave namaḥ*
259.	ॐ वृषपर्वणे नमः	*om vṛṣaparvaṇe namaḥ*
260.	ॐ वृषोदराय नमः	*om vṛṣodarāya namaḥ*
261.	ॐ वर्धनाय नमः	*om vardhanāya namaḥ*
262.	ॐ वर्धमानाय नमः	*om vardhamānāya namaḥ*
263.	ॐ विविक्ताय नमः	*om viviktāya namaḥ*

264. ॐ श्रुतिसागराय नमः — *om śrutisāgarāya namaḥ*
265. ॐ सुभुजाय नमः — *om subhujāya namaḥ*
266. ॐ दुर्धराय नमः — *om durdharāya namaḥ*
267. ॐ वाग्मिने नमः — *om vāgmine namaḥ*
268. ॐ महेन्द्राय नमः — *om mahendrāya namaḥ*
269. ॐ वसुदाय नमः — *om vasudāya namaḥ*
270. ॐ वसवे नमः — *om vasave namaḥ*
271. ॐ नैकरूपाय नमः — *om naikarūpāya namaḥ*
272. ॐ बृहद्रूपाय नमः — *om bṛhadrūpāya namaḥ*
273. ॐ शिपिविष्टाय नमः — *om śipiviṣṭāya namaḥ*
274. ॐ प्रकाशनाय नमः — *om prakāśanāya namaḥ*
275. ॐ ओजस्तेजोद्युतिधराय नमः — *om ojastejodyutidharāya namaḥ*
276. ॐ प्रकाशात्मने नमः — *om prakāśātmane namaḥ*
277. ॐ प्रतापनाय नमः — *om pratāpanāya namaḥ*
278. ॐ ऋद्धाय नमः — *om ṛddhāya namaḥ*
279. ॐ स्पष्टाक्षराय नमः — *om spaṣṭākṣarāya namaḥ*
280. ॐ मन्त्राय नमः — *om mantrāya namaḥ*
281. ॐ चन्द्रांशवे नमः — *om candrāṁśave namaḥ*
282. ॐ भास्करद्युतये नमः — *om bhāskaradyutaye namaḥ*
283. ॐ अमृतांशूद्भवाय नमः — *om amṛtāṁśūdbhavāya namaḥ*
284. ॐ भानवे नमः — *om bhānave namaḥ*
285. ॐ शशबिन्दवे नमः — *om śaśabindave namaḥ*
286. ॐ सुरेश्वराय नमः — *om sureśvarāya namaḥ*
287. ॐ औषधाय नमः — *om auṣadhāya namaḥ*
288. ॐ जगतः सेतवे नमः — *om jagataḥ setave namaḥ*
289. ॐ सत्यधर्मपराक्रमाय नमः — *om satyadharmaparākramāya namaḥ*
290. ॐ भूतभव्यभवन्नाथाय नमः — *om bhūtabhavyabhavannāthāya namaḥ*
291. ॐ पवनाय नमः — *om pavanāya namaḥ*
292. ॐ पावनाय नमः — *om pāvanāya namaḥ*
293. ॐ अनलाय नमः — *om analāya namaḥ*

294. ॐ कामघ्ने नमः om kāmaghne namaḥ
295. ॐ कामकृते नमः om kāmakṛte namaḥ
296. ॐ कान्ताय नमः om kāntāya namaḥ
297. ॐ कामाय नमः om kāmāya namaḥ
298. ॐ कामप्रदाय नमः om kāmapradāya namaḥ
299. ॐ प्रभवे नमः om prabhave namaḥ
300. ॐ युगादिकृते नमः om yugādikṛte namaḥ
301. ॐ युगावर्ताय नमः om yugāvartāya namaḥ
302. ॐ नैकमायाय नमः om naikamāyāya namaḥ
303. ॐ महाशनाय नमः om mahāśanāya namaḥ
304. ॐ अदृश्याय नमः om adṛśyāya namaḥ
305. ॐ व्यक्तरूपाय नमः om vyaktarūpāya namaḥ
306. ॐ सहस्रजिते नमः om sahasrajite namaḥ
307. ॐ अनन्तजिते नमः om anantajite namaḥ
308. ॐ इष्टाय नमः om iṣṭāya namaḥ
309. ॐ अविशिष्टाय नमः om aviśiṣṭāya namaḥ
310. ॐ शिष्टेष्टाय नमः om śiṣṭeṣṭāya namaḥ
311. ॐ शिखण्डिने नमः om śikhaṇḍine namaḥ
312. ॐ नहुषाय नमः om nahuṣāya namaḥ
313. ॐ वृषाय नमः om vṛṣāya namaḥ
314. ॐ क्रोधघ्ने नमः om krodhaghne namaḥ
315. ॐ क्रोधकृत्कर्त्रे नमः om krodhakṛtkartre namaḥ
316. ॐ विश्वबाहवे नमः om viśvabāhave namaḥ
317. ॐ महीधराय नमः om mahīdharāya namaḥ
318. ॐ अच्युताय नमः om acyutāya namaḥ
319. ॐ प्रथिताय नमः om prathitāya namaḥ
320. ॐ प्राणाय नमः om prāṇāya namaḥ
321. ॐ प्राणदाय नमः om prāṇadāya namaḥ
322. ॐ वासवानुजाय नमः om vāsavānujāya namaḥ
323. ॐ अपांनिधये नमः om apāṁnidhaye namaḥ

324.	ॐ अधिष्ठानाय नमः	*om adhiṣṭhānāya namaḥ*
325.	ॐ अप्रमत्ताय नमः	*om apramattāya namaḥ*
326.	ॐ प्रतिष्ठिताय नमः	*om pratiṣṭhitāya namaḥ*
327.	ॐ स्कन्दाय नमः	*om skandāya namaḥ*
328.	ॐ स्कन्दधराय नमः	*om skandadharāya namaḥ*
329.	ॐ धुर्याय नमः	*om dhuryāya namaḥ*
330.	ॐ वरदाय नमः	*om varadāya namaḥ*
331.	ॐ वायुवाहनाय नमः	*om vāyuvāhanāya namaḥ*
332.	ॐ वासुदेवाय नमः	*om vāsudevāya namaḥ*
333.	ॐ बृहद्भानवे नमः	*om bṛhadbhānave namaḥ*
334.	ॐ आदिदेवाय नमः	*om ādidevāya namaḥ*
335.	ॐ पुरन्दराय नमः	*om purandarāya namaḥ*
336.	ॐ अशोकाय नमः	*om aśokāya namaḥ*
337.	ॐ तारणाय नमः	*om tāraṇāya namaḥ*
338.	ॐ ताराय नमः	*om tārāya namaḥ*
339.	ॐ शूराय नमः	*om śūrāya namaḥ*
340.	ॐ शौरये नमः	*om śauraye namaḥ*
341.	ॐ जनेश्वराय नमः	*om janeśvarāya namaḥ*
342.	ॐ अनुकूलाय नमः	*om anukūlāya namaḥ*
343.	ॐ शतावर्ताय नमः	*om śatāvartāya namaḥ*
344.	ॐ पद्मिने नमः	*om padmine namaḥ*
345.	ॐ पद्मनिभेक्षणाय नमः	*om padmanibhekṣaṇāya namaḥ*
346.	ॐ पद्मनाभाय नमः	*om padmanābhāya namaḥ*
347.	ॐ अरविन्दाक्षाय नमः	*om aravindākṣāya namaḥ*
348.	ॐ पद्मगर्भाय नमः	*om padmagarbhāya namaḥ*
349.	ॐ शरीरभृते नमः	*om śarīrabhṛte namaḥ*
350.	ॐ महर्द्धये नमः	*om maharddhaye namaḥ*
351.	ॐ ऋद्धाय नमः	*om ṛddhāya namaḥ*
352.	ॐ वृद्धात्मने नमः	*om vṛddhātmane namaḥ*
353.	ॐ महाक्षाय नमः	*om mahākṣāya namaḥ*

354. ॐ गरुडध्वजाय नमः om garuḍadhvajāya namaḥ
355. ॐ अतुलाय नमः om atulāya namaḥ
356. ॐ शरभाय नमः om śarabhāya namaḥ
357. ॐ भीमाय नमः om bhīmāya namaḥ
358. ॐ समयज्ञाय नमः om samayajñāya namaḥ
359. ॐ हविर्हरये नमः om havirharaye namaḥ
360. ॐ सर्वलक्षणलक्षण्याय नमः om sarvalakṣaṇalakṣaṇyāya namaḥ
361. ॐ लक्ष्मीवते नमः om lakṣmīvate namaḥ
362. ॐ समितिञ्जयाय नमः om samitiñjayāya namaḥ
363. ॐ विक्षराय नमः om vikṣarāya namaḥ
364. ॐ रोहिताय नमः om rohitāya namaḥ
365. ॐ मार्गाय नमः om mārgāya namaḥ
366. ॐ हेतवे नमः om hetave namaḥ
367. ॐ दामोदराय नमः om dāmodarāya namaḥ
368. ॐ सहाय नमः om sahāya namaḥ
369. ॐ महीधराय नमः om mahīdharāya namaḥ
370. ॐ महाभागाय नमः om mahābhāgāya namaḥ
371. ॐ वेगवते नमः om vegavate namaḥ
372. ॐ अमिताशनाय नमः om amitāśanāya namaḥ
373. ॐ उद्भवाय नमः om udbhavāya namaḥ
374. ॐ क्षोभणाय नमः om kṣobhaṇāya namaḥ
375. ॐ देवाय नमः om devāya namaḥ
376. ॐ श्रीगर्भाय नमः om śrīgarbhāya namaḥ
377. ॐ परमेश्वराय नमः om parameśvarāya namaḥ
378. ॐ करणाय नमः om karaṇāya namaḥ
379. ॐ कारणाय नमः om kāraṇāya namaḥ
380. ॐ कर्त्रे नमः om kartre namaḥ
381. ॐ विकर्त्रे नमः om vikartre namaḥ
382. ॐ गहनाय नमः om gahanāya namaḥ
383. ॐ गुहाय नमः om guhāya namaḥ

384.	ॐ व्यवसायाय नमः	*om vyavasāyāya namaḥ*
385.	ॐ व्यवस्थानाय नमः	*om vyavasthānāya namaḥ*
386.	ॐ संस्थानाय नमः	*om saṁsthānāya namaḥ*
387.	ॐ स्थानदाय नमः	*om sthānadāya namaḥ*
388.	ॐ ध्रुवाय नमः	*om dhruvāya namaḥ*
389.	ॐ परर्द्धये नमः	*om pararddhaye namaḥ*
390.	ॐ परमस्पष्टाय नमः	*om paramaspaṣṭāya namaḥ*
391.	ॐ तुष्टाय नमः	*om tuṣṭāya namaḥ*
392.	ॐ पुष्टाय नमः	*om puṣṭāya namaḥ*
393.	ॐ शुभेक्षणाय नमः	*om śubhekṣaṇāya namaḥ*
394.	ॐ रामाय नमः	*om rāmāya namaḥ*
395.	ॐ विरामाय नमः	*om virāmāya namaḥ*
396.	ॐ विरताय नमः	*om viratāya namaḥ*
397.	ॐ मार्गाय नमः	*om mārgāya namaḥ*
398.	ॐ नेयाय नमः	*om neyāya namaḥ*
399.	ॐ नयाय नमः	*om nayāya namaḥ*
400.	ॐ अनयाय नमः	*om anayāya namaḥ*
401.	ॐ वीराय नमः	*om vīrāya namaḥ*
402.	ॐ शक्तिमतां श्रेष्ठाय नमः	*om śaktimatāṁ śreṣṭhāya namaḥ*
403.	ॐ धर्माय नमः	*om dharmāya namaḥ*
404.	ॐ धर्मविदुत्तमाय नमः	*om dharmaviduttamāya namaḥ*
405.	ॐ वैकुण्ठाय नमः	*om vaikuṇṭhāya namaḥ*
406.	ॐ पुरुषाय नमः	*om puruṣāya namaḥ*
407.	ॐ प्राणाय नमः	*om prāṇāya namaḥ*
408.	ॐ प्राणदाय नमः	*om prāṇadāya namaḥ*
409.	ॐ प्रणवाय नमः	*om praṇavāya namaḥ*
410.	ॐ पृथवे नमः	*om pṛthave namaḥ*
411.	ॐ हिरण्यगर्भाय नमः	*om hiraṇyagarbhāya namaḥ*
412.	ॐ शत्रुघ्नाय नमः	*om śatrughnāya namaḥ*
413.	ॐ व्याप्ताय नमः	*om vyāptāya namaḥ*

414. ॐ वायवे नमः *om vāyave namaḥ*
415. ॐ अधोक्षजाय नमः *om adhokṣajāya namaḥ*
416. ॐ ऋतवे नमः *om ṛtave namaḥ*
417. ॐ सुदर्शनाय नमः *om sudarśanāya namaḥ*
418. ॐ कालाय नमः *om kālāya namaḥ*
419. ॐ परमेष्ठिने नमः *om parameṣṭhine namaḥ*
420. ॐ परिग्रहाय नमः *om parigrahāya namaḥ*
421. ॐ उग्राय नमः *om ugrāya namaḥ*
422. ॐ संवत्सराय नमः *om saṁvatsarāya namaḥ*
423. ॐ दक्षाय नमः *om dakṣāya namaḥ*
424. ॐ विश्रामाय नमः *om viśrāmāya namaḥ*
425. ॐ विश्वदक्षिणाय नमः *om viśvadakṣiṇāya namaḥ*
426. ॐ विस्ताराय नमः *om vistārāya namaḥ*
427. ॐ स्थावरस्थाणवे नमः *om sthāvarasthāṇave namaḥ*
428. ॐ प्रमाणाय नमः *om pramāṇāya namaḥ*
429. ॐ बीजमव्ययाय नमः *om bījamavyayāya namaḥ*
430. ॐ अर्थाय नमः *om arthāya namaḥ*
431. ॐ अनर्थाय नमः *om anarthāya namaḥ*
432. ॐ महाकोशाय नमः *om mahākośāya namaḥ*
433. ॐ महाभोगाय नमः *om mahābhogāya namaḥ*
434. ॐ महाधनाय नमः *om mahādhanāya namaḥ*
435. ॐ अनिर्विण्णाय नमः *om anirviṇṇāya namaḥ*
436. ॐ स्थविष्ठाय नमः *om sthaviṣṭhāya namaḥ*
437. ॐ अभुवे नमः *om abhuve namaḥ*
438. ॐ धर्मयूपाय नमः *om dharmayūpāya namaḥ*
439. ॐ महामखाय नमः *om mahāmakhāya namaḥ*
440. ॐ नक्षत्रनेमये नमः *om nakṣatranemaye namaḥ*
441. ॐ नक्षत्रिणे नमः *om nakṣatriṇe namaḥ*
442. ॐ क्षमाय नमः *om kṣamāya namaḥ*
443. ॐ क्षामाय नमः *om kṣāmāya namaḥ*

444.	ॐ समीहनाय नमः	*om samīhanāya namaḥ*
445.	ॐ यज्ञाय नमः	*om yajñāya namaḥ*
446.	ॐ इज्याय नमः	*om ijyāya namaḥ*
447.	ॐ महेज्याय नमः	*om mahejyāya namaḥ*
448.	ॐ क्रतवे नमः	*om kratave namaḥ*
449.	ॐ सत्राय नमः	*om satrāya namaḥ*
450.	ॐ सतांगतये नमः	*om satāṁgataye namaḥ*
451.	ॐ सर्वदर्शिने नमः	*om sarvadarśine namaḥ*
452.	ॐ विमुक्तात्मने नमः	*om vimuktātmane namaḥ*
453.	ॐ सर्वज्ञाय नमः	*om sarvajñāya namaḥ*
454.	ॐ ज्ञानायोत्तमाय नमः	*om jñānāyottamāya namaḥ*
455.	ॐ सुव्रताय नमः	*om suvratāya namaḥ*
456.	ॐ सुमुखाय नमः	*om sumukhāya namaḥ*
457.	ॐ सूक्ष्माय नमः	*om sūkṣmāya namaḥ*
458.	ॐ सुघोषाय नमः	*om sughoṣāya namaḥ*
459.	ॐ सुखदाय नमः	*om sukhadāya namaḥ*
460.	ॐ सुहृदे नमः	*om suhṛde namaḥ*
461.	ॐ मनोहराय नमः	*om manoharāya namaḥ*
462.	ॐ जितक्रोधाय नमः	*om jitakrodhāya namaḥ*
463.	ॐ वीरबाहवे नमः	*om vīrabāhave namaḥ*
464.	ॐ विदारणाय नमः	*om vidāraṇāya namaḥ*
465.	ॐ स्वापनाय नमः	*om svāpanāya namaḥ*
466.	ॐ स्ववशाय नमः	*om svavaśāya namaḥ*
467.	ॐ व्यापिने नमः	*om vyāpine namaḥ*
468.	ॐ नैकात्मने नमः	*om naikātmane namaḥ*
469.	ॐ नैककर्मकृते नमः	*om naikakarmakṛte namaḥ*
470.	ॐ वत्सराय नमः	*om vatsarāya namaḥ*
471.	ॐ वत्सलाय नमः	*om vatsalāya namaḥ*
472.	ॐ वत्सिने नमः	*om vatsine namaḥ*
473.	ॐ रत्नगर्भाय नमः	*om ratnagarbhāya namaḥ*

474.	ॐ धनेश्वराय नमः	*om dhaneśvarāya namaḥ*
475.	ॐ धर्मगुपे नमः	*om dharmagupe namaḥ*
476.	ॐ धर्मकृते नमः	*om dharmakṛte namaḥ*
477.	ॐ धर्मिणे नमः	*om dharmiṇe namaḥ*
478.	ॐ सते नमः	*om sate namaḥ*
479.	ॐ असते नमः	*om asate namaḥ*
480.	ॐ क्षराय नमः	*om kṣarāya namaḥ*
481.	ॐ अक्षराय नमः	*om akṣarāya namaḥ*
482.	ॐ अविज्ञात्रे नमः	*om avijñātre namaḥ*
483.	ॐ सहस्रांशवे नमः	*om sahasrāṁśave namaḥ*
484.	ॐ विधात्रे नमः	*om vidhātre namaḥ*
485.	ॐ कृतलक्षणाय नमः	*om kṛtalakṣaṇāya namaḥ*
486.	ॐ गभस्तिनेमये नमः	*om gabhastinemaye namaḥ*
487.	ॐ सत्त्वस्थाय नमः	*om sattvasthāya namaḥ*
488.	ॐ सिंहाय नमः	*om siṁhāya namaḥ*
489.	ॐ भूतमहेश्वराय नमः	*om bhūtamaheśvarāya namaḥ*
490.	ॐ आदिदेवाय नमः	*om ādidevāya namaḥ*
491.	ॐ महादेवाय नमः	*om mahādevāya namaḥ*
492.	ॐ देवेशाय नमः	*om deveśāya namaḥ*
493.	ॐ देवभृद्गुरवे नमः	*om devabhṛdgurave namaḥ*
494.	ॐ उत्तराय नमः	*om uttarāya namaḥ*
495.	ॐ गोपतये नमः	*om gopataye namaḥ*
496.	ॐ गोप्त्रे नमः	*om goptre namaḥ*
497.	ॐ ज्ञानगम्याय नमः	*om jñānagamyāya namaḥ*
498.	ॐ पुरातनाय नमः	*om purātanāya namaḥ*
499.	ॐ शरीरभूतभृते नमः	*om śarīrabhūtabhṛte namaḥ*
500.	ॐ भोक्त्रे नमः	*om bhoktre namaḥ*
501.	ॐ कपीन्द्राय नमः	*om kapīndrāya namaḥ*
502.	ॐ भूरिदक्षिणाय नमः	*om bhūridakṣiṇāya namaḥ*
503.	ॐ सोमपाय नमः	*om somapāya namaḥ*

504. ॐ अमृतपाय नमः | *om amṛtapāya namaḥ*
505. ॐ सोमाय नमः | *om somāya namaḥ*
506. ॐ पुरुजिते नमः | *om purujite namaḥ*
507. ॐ पुरुसत्तमाय नमः | *om purusattamāya namaḥ*
508. ॐ विनयाय नमः | *om vinayāya namaḥ*
509. ॐ जयाय नमः | *om jayāya namaḥ*
510. ॐ सत्यसंधाय नमः | *om satyasandhāya namaḥ*
511. ॐ दाशार्हाय नमः | *om dāśārhāya namaḥ*
512. ॐ सात्वतांपतये नमः | *om sātvatāṁpataye namaḥ*
513. ॐ जीवाय नमः | *om jīvāya namaḥ*
514. ॐ विनयितासाक्षिणे नमः | *om vinayitāsākṣiṇe namaḥ*
515. ॐ मुकुन्दाय नमः | *om mukundāya namaḥ*
516. ॐ अमितविक्रमाय नमः | *om amitavikramāya namaḥ*
517. ॐ अम्भोनिधये नमः | *om ambhonidhaye namaḥ*
518. ॐ अनन्तात्मने नमः | *om anantātmane namaḥ*
519. ॐ महोदधिशयाय नमः | *om mahodadhiśayāya namaḥ*
520. ॐ अन्तकाय नमः | *om antakāya namaḥ*
521. ॐ अजाय नमः | *om ajāya namaḥ*
522. ॐ महार्हाय नमः | *om mahārhāya namaḥ*
523. ॐ स्वाभाव्याय नमः | *om svābhāvyāya namaḥ*
524. ॐ जितामित्राय नमः | *om jitāmitrāya namaḥ*
525. ॐ प्रमोदनाय नमः | *om pramodanāya namaḥ*
526. ॐ आनन्दाय नमः | *om ānandāya namaḥ*
527. ॐ नन्दनाय नमः | *om nandanāya namaḥ*
528. ॐ नन्दाय नमः | *om nandāya namaḥ*
529. ॐ सत्यधर्मणे नमः | *om satyadharmaṇe namaḥ*
530. ॐ त्रिविक्रमाय नमः | *om trivikramāya namaḥ*
531. ॐ महर्षये कपिलाचार्याय नमः | *om maharṣaye kapilācāryāya namaḥ*
532. ॐ कृतज्ञाय नमः | *om kṛtajñāya namaḥ*
533. ॐ मेदिनीपतये नमः | *om medinīpataye namaḥ*

534. ॐ त्रिपदाय नमः | *om tripadāya namaḥ*
535. ॐ त्रिदशाध्यक्षाय नमः | *om tridaśādhyakṣāya namaḥ*
536. ॐ महाशृङ्गाय नमः | *om mahāśṛṅgāya namaḥ*
537. ॐ कृतान्तकृते नमः | *om kṛtāntakṛte namaḥ*
538. ॐ महावराहाय नमः | *om mahāvarāhāya namaḥ*
539. ॐ गोविन्दाय नमः | *om govindāya namaḥ*
540. ॐ सुषेणाय नमः | *om suṣeṇāya namaḥ*
541. ॐ कनकाङ्गदिने नमः | *om kanakāṅgadine namaḥ*
542. ॐ गुह्याय नमः | *om guhyāya namaḥ*
543. ॐ गभीराय नमः | *om gabhīrāya namaḥ*
544. ॐ गहनाय नमः | *om gahanāya namaḥ*
545. ॐ गुप्ताय नमः | *om guptāya namaḥ*
546. ॐ चक्रगदाधराय नमः | *om cakragadādharāya namaḥ*
547. ॐ वेधसे नमः | *om vedhase namaḥ*
548. ॐ स्वाङ्गाय नमः | *om svāṅgāya namaḥ*
549. ॐ अजिताय नमः | *om ajitāya namaḥ*
550. ॐ कृष्णाय नमः | *om kṛṣṇāya namaḥ*
551. ॐ दृढाय नमः | *om dṛḍhāya namaḥ*
552. ॐ संकर्षणायाच्युताय नमः | *om saṅkarṣaṇāyācyutāya namaḥ*
553. ॐ वरुणाय नमः | *om varuṇāya namaḥ*
554. ॐ वारुणाय नमः | *om vāruṇāya namaḥ*
555. ॐ वृक्षाय नमः | *om vṛkṣāya namaḥ*
556. ॐ पुष्कराक्षाय नमः | *om puṣkarākṣāya namaḥ*
557. ॐ महामनसे नमः | *om mahāmanase namaḥ*
558. ॐ भगवते नमः | *om bhagavate namaḥ*
559. ॐ भगघ्ने नमः | *om bhagaghne namaḥ*
560. ॐ आनन्दिने नमः | *om ānandine namaḥ*
561. ॐ वनमालिने नमः | *om vanamāline namaḥ*
562. ॐ हलायुधाय नमः | *om halāyudhāya namaḥ*
563. ॐ आदित्याय नमः | *om ādityāya namaḥ*

564. ॐ ज्योतिरादित्याय नमः om jyotirādityāya namaḥ
565. ॐ सहिष्णवे नमः om sahiṣṇave namaḥ
566. ॐ गतिसत्तमाय नमः om gatisattamāya namaḥ
567. ॐ सुधन्वने नमः om sudhanvane namaḥ
568. ॐ खण्डपरशवे नमः om khaṇḍaparaśave namaḥ
569. ॐ दारुणाय नमः om dāruṇāya namaḥ
570. ॐ द्रविणप्रदाय नमः om draviṇapradāya namaḥ
571. ॐ दिवःस्पृशे नमः om divaḥ spṛśe namaḥ
572. ॐ सर्वदृग्व्यासाय नमः om sarvadṛgvyāsāya namaḥ
573. ॐ वाचस्पतयेऽयोनिजाय नमः om vācaspataye'yonijāya namaḥ
574. ॐ त्रिसाम्ने नमः om trisāmne namaḥ
575. ॐ सामगाय नमः om sāmagāya namaḥ
576. ॐ साम्ने नमः om sāmne namaḥ
577. ॐ निर्वाणाय नमः om nirvāṇāya namaḥ
578. ॐ भेषजाय नमः om bheṣajāya namaḥ
579. ॐ भिषजे नमः om bhiṣaje namaḥ
580. ॐ सन्यासकृते नमः om saṁnyāsakṛte namaḥ
581. ॐ शमाय नमः om śamāya namaḥ
582. ॐ शान्ताय नमः om śāntāya namaḥ
583. ॐ निष्ठायै नमः om niṣṭhāyai namaḥ
584. ॐ शान्त्यै नमः om śāntyai namaḥ
585. ॐ परायणाय नमः om parāyaṇāya namaḥ
586. ॐ शुभाङ्गाय नमः om śubhāṅgāya namaḥ
587. ॐ शान्तिदाय नमः om śāntidāya namaḥ
588. ॐ स्रष्ट्रे नमः om sraṣṭre namaḥ
589. ॐ कुमुदाय नमः om kumudāya namaḥ
590. ॐ कुवलेशयाय नमः om kuvaleśayāya namaḥ
591. ॐ गोहिताय नमः om gohitāya namaḥ
592. ॐ गोपतये नमः om gopataye namaḥ
593. ॐ गोप्त्रे नमः om goptre namaḥ

594.	ॐ वृषभाक्षाय नमः	*om vṛṣabhākṣāya namaḥ*
595.	ॐ वृषप्रियाय नमः	*om vṛṣapriyāya namaḥ*
596.	ॐ अनिवर्तिने नमः	*om anivartine namaḥ*
597.	ॐ निवृत्तात्मने नमः	*om nivṛttātmane namaḥ*
598.	ॐ संक्षेप्त्रे नमः	*om saṅkṣeptre namaḥ*
599.	ॐ क्षेमकृते नमः	*om kṣemakṛte namaḥ*
600.	ॐ शिवाय नमः	*om śivāya namaḥ*
601.	ॐ श्रीवत्सवक्षसे नमः	*om śrīvatsavakṣase namaḥ*
602.	ॐ श्रीवासाय नमः	*om śrīvāsāya namaḥ*
603.	ॐ श्रीपतये नमः	*om śrīpataye namaḥ*
604.	ॐ श्रीमतांवराय नमः	*om śrīmatāṁvarāya namaḥ*
605.	ॐ श्रीदाय नमः	*om śrīdāya namaḥ*
606.	ॐ श्रीशाय नमः	*om śrīśāya namaḥ*
607.	ॐ श्रीनिवासाय नमः	*om śrīnivāsāya namaḥ*
608.	ॐ श्रीनिधये नमः	*om śrīnidhaye namaḥ*
609.	ॐ श्रीविभावनाय नमः	*om śrīvibhāvanāya namaḥ*
610.	ॐ श्रीधराय नमः	*om śrīdharāya namaḥ*
611.	ॐ श्रीकराय नमः	*om śrīkarāya namaḥ*
612.	ॐ श्रेयसे नमः	*om śreyase namaḥ*
613.	ॐ श्रीमते नमः	*om śrīmate namaḥ*
614.	ॐ लोकत्रयाश्रयाय नमः	*om lokatrayāśrayāya namaḥ*
615.	ॐ स्वक्षाय नमः	*om svakṣāya namaḥ*
616.	ॐ स्वङ्गाय नमः	*om svaṅgāya namaḥ*
617.	ॐ शतानन्दाय नमः	*om śatānandāya namaḥ*
618.	ॐ नन्दये नमः	*om nandaye namaḥ*
619.	ॐ ज्योतिर्गणेश्वराय नमः	*om jyotirgaṇeśvarāya namaḥ*
620.	ॐ विजितात्मने नमः	*om vijitātmane namaḥ*
621.	ॐ अविधेयात्मने नमः	*om avidheyātmane namaḥ*
622.	ॐ सत्कीर्तये नमः	*om satkīrtaye namaḥ*
623.	ॐ छिन्नसंशयाय नमः	*om chinnasaṁśayāya namaḥ*

624.	ॐ उदीर्णाय नमः	*om udīrṇāya namaḥ*
625.	ॐ सर्वतश्चक्षुषे नमः	*om sarvataścakṣuṣe namaḥ*
626.	ॐ अनीशाय नमः	*om anīśāya namaḥ*
627.	ॐ शाश्वतस्थिराय नमः	*om śāśvatasthirāya namaḥ*
628.	ॐ भूशयाय नमः	*om bhūśayāya namaḥ*
629.	ॐ भूषणाय नमः	*om bhūṣaṇāya namaḥ*
630.	ॐ भूतये नमः	*om bhūtaye namaḥ*
631.	ॐ विशोकाय नमः	*om viśokāya namaḥ*
632.	ॐ शोकनाशनाय नमः	*om śokanāśanāya namaḥ*
633.	ॐ अर्चिष्मते नमः	*om arciṣmate namaḥ*
634.	ॐ अर्चिताय नमः	*om arcitāya namaḥ*
635.	ॐ कुम्भाय नमः	*om kumbhāya namaḥ*
636.	ॐ विशुद्धात्मने नमः	*om viśuddhātmane namaḥ*
637.	ॐ विशोधनाय नमः	*om viśodhanāya namaḥ*
638.	ॐ अनिरुद्धाय नमः	*om aniruddhāya namaḥ*
639.	ॐ अप्रतिरथाय नमः	*om apratirathāya namaḥ*
640.	ॐ प्रद्युम्नाय नमः	*om pradyumnāya namaḥ*
641.	ॐ अमितविक्रमाय नमः	*om amitavikramāya namaḥ*
642.	ॐ कालनेमिनिघ्ने नमः	*om kālaneminighne namaḥ*
643.	ॐ वीराय नमः	*om vīrāya namaḥ*
644.	ॐ शौरये नमः	*om śauraye namaḥ*
645.	ॐ शूरजनेश्वराय नमः	*om śūrajaneśvarāya namaḥ*
646.	ॐ त्रिलोकात्मने नमः	*om trilokātmane namaḥ*
647.	ॐ त्रिलोकेशाय नमः	*om trilokeśāya namaḥ*
648.	ॐ केशवाय नमः	*om keśavāya namaḥ*
649.	ॐ केशिघ्ने नमः	*om keśighne namaḥ*
650.	ॐ हरये नमः	*om haraye namaḥ*
651.	ॐ कामदेवाय नमः	*om kāmadevāya namaḥ*
652.	ॐ कामपालाय नमः	*om kāmapālāya namaḥ*
653.	ॐ कामिने नमः	*om kāmine namaḥ*

654. ॐ कान्ताय नमः — *om kāntāya namaḥ*
655. ॐ कृतागमाय नमः — *om kṛtāgamāya namaḥ*
656. ॐ अनिर्देश्यवपुषे नमः — *om anirdeśyavapuṣe namaḥ*
657. ॐ विष्णवे नमः — *om viṣṇave namaḥ*
658. ॐ वीराय नमः — *om vīrāya namaḥ*
659. ॐ अनन्ताय नमः — *om anantāya namaḥ*
660. ॐ धनञ्जयाय — *om dhanañjayāya namaḥ*
661. ॐ ब्रह्मण्याय नमः — *om brahmaṇyāya namaḥ*
662. ॐ ब्रह्मकृते नमः — *om brahmakṛte namaḥ*
663. ॐ ब्रह्मणे नमः — *om brahmaṇe namaḥ*
664. ॐ ब्रह्मणे नमः — *om brahmaṇe namaḥ*
665. ॐ ब्रह्मविवर्धनाय नमः — *om brahmavivardhanāya namaḥ*
666. ॐ ब्रह्मविदे नमः — *om brahmavide namaḥ*
667. ॐ ब्राह्मणाय नमः — *om brāhmaṇāya namaḥ*
668. ॐ ब्रह्मिणे नमः — *om brahmiṇe namaḥ*
669. ॐ ब्रह्मज्ञाय नमः — *om brahmajñāya namaḥ*
670. ॐ ब्राह्मणप्रियाय नमः — *om brāhmaṇapriyāya namaḥ*
671. ॐ महाक्रमाय नमः — *om mahākramāya namaḥ*
672. ॐ महाकर्मणे नमः — *om mahākarmaṇe namaḥ*
673. ॐ महातेजसे नमः — *om mahātejase namaḥ*
674. ॐ महोरगाय नमः — *om mahoragāya namaḥ*
675. ॐ महाक्रतवे नमः — *om mahākratave namaḥ*
676. ॐ महायज्वने नमः — *om mahāyajvane namaḥ*
677. ॐ महायज्ञाय नमः — *om mahāyajñāya namaḥ*
678. ॐ महाहविषे नमः — *om mahāhaviṣe namaḥ*
679. ॐ स्तव्याय नमः — *om stavyāya namaḥ*
680. ॐ स्तवप्रियाय नमः — *om stavapriyāya namaḥ*
681. ॐ स्तोत्राय नमः — *om stotrāya namaḥ*
682. ॐ स्तुतये नमः — *om stutaye namaḥ*
683. ॐ स्तोत्रे नमः — *om stotre namaḥ*

684.	ॐ रणप्रियाय नमः	*om raṇapriyāya namaḥ*
685.	ॐ पूर्णाय नमः	*om pūrṇāya namaḥ*
686.	ॐ पूरयित्रे नमः	*om pūrayitre namaḥ*
687.	ॐ पुण्याय नमः	*om puṇyāya namaḥ*
688.	ॐ पुण्यकीर्तये नमः	*om puṇyakīrtaye namaḥ*
689.	ॐ अनामयाय नमः	*om anāmayāya namaḥ*
690.	ॐ मनोजवाय नमः	*om manojavāya namaḥ*
691.	ॐ तीर्थकराय नमः	*om tīrthakarāya namaḥ*
692.	ॐ वसुरेतसे नमः	*om vasuretase namaḥ*
693.	ॐ वसुप्रदाय नमः	*om vasupradāya namaḥ*
694.	ॐ वसुप्रदाय नमः	*om vasupradāya namaḥ*
695.	ॐ वासुदेवाय नमः	*om vāsudevāya namaḥ*
696.	ॐ वसवे नमः	*om vasave namaḥ*
697.	ॐ वसुमनसे नमः	*om vasumanase namaḥ*
698.	ॐ हविषे नमः	*om haviṣe namaḥ*
699.	ॐ सद्गतये नमः	*om sadgataye namaḥ*
700.	ॐ सत्कृतये नमः	*om satkṛtaye namaḥ*
701.	ॐ सत्तायै नमः	*om sattāyai namaḥ*
702.	ॐ सद्भूतये नमः	*om sadbhūtaye namaḥ*
703.	ॐ सत्परायणाय नमः	*om satparāyaṇāya namaḥ*
704.	ॐ शूरसेनाय नमः	*om śūrasenāya namaḥ*
705.	ॐ यदुश्रेष्ठाय नमः	*om yaduśreṣṭhāya namaḥ*
706.	ॐ सन्निवासाय नमः	*om sannivāsāya namaḥ*
707.	ॐ सुयामुनाय नमः	*om suyāmunāya namaḥ*
708.	ॐ भूतावासाय नमः	*om bhūtāvāsāya namaḥ*
709.	ॐ वासुदेवाय नमः	*om vāsudevāya namaḥ*
710.	ॐ सर्वासुनिलयाय नमः	*om sarvāsunilayāya namaḥ*
711.	ॐ अनलाय नमः	*om analāya namaḥ*
712.	ॐ दर्पघ्ने नमः	*om darpaghne namaḥ*
713.	ॐ दर्पदाय नमः	*om darpadāya namaḥ*

714. ॐ दृप्ताय नमः — om dṛptāya namaḥ
715. ॐ दुर्धराय नमः — om durdharāya namaḥ
716. ॐ अपराजिताय नमः — om aparājitāya namaḥ
717. ॐ विश्वमूर्तये नमः — om viśvamūrtaye namaḥ
718. ॐ महामूर्तये नमः — om mahāmūrtaye namaḥ
719. ॐ दीप्तमूर्तये नमः — om dīptamūrtaye namaḥ
720. ॐ अमूर्तिमते नमः — om amūrtimate namaḥ
721. ॐ अनेकमूर्तये नमः — om anekamūrtaye namaḥ
722. ॐ अव्यक्ताय नमः — om avyaktāya namaḥ
723. ॐ शतमूर्तये नमः — om śatamūrtaye namaḥ
724. ॐ शताननाय नमः — om śatānanāya namaḥ
725. ॐ एकस्मै नमः — om ekasmai namaḥ
726. ॐ नैकस्मै नमः — om naikasmai namaḥ
727. ॐ सवाय नमः — om savāya namaḥ
728. ॐ काय नमः — om kāya namaḥ
729. ॐ कस्मै नमः — om kasmai namaḥ
730. ॐ यस्मै नमः — om yasmai namaḥ
731. ॐ तस्मै नमः — om tasmai namaḥ
732. ॐ पदमनुत्तमाय नमः — om padamanuttamāya namaḥ
733. ॐ लोकबन्धवे नमः — om lokabandhave namaḥ
734. ॐ लोकनाथाय नमः — om lokanāthāya namaḥ
735. ॐ माधवाय नमः — om mādhavāya namaḥ
736. ॐ भक्तवत्सलाय नमः — om bhaktavatsalāya namaḥ
737. ॐ सुवर्णवर्णाय नमः — om suvarṇavarṇāya namaḥ
738. ॐ हेमाङ्गाय नमः — om hemāṅgāya namaḥ
739. ॐ वराङ्गाय नमः — om varāṅgāya namaḥ
740. ॐ चन्दनाङ्गदिने नमः — om candanāṅgadine namaḥ
741. ॐ वीरघ्ने नमः — om vīraghne namaḥ
742. ॐ विषमाय नमः — om viṣamāya namaḥ
743. ॐ शून्याय नमः — om śūnyāya namaḥ

744. ॐ घृताशिषे नमः	*om ghṛtāśiṣe namaḥ*
745. ॐ अचलाय नमः	*om acalāya namaḥ*
746. ॐ चलाय नमः	*om calāya namaḥ*
747. ॐ अमानिने नमः	*om amānine namaḥ*
748. ॐ मानदाय नमः	*om mānadāya namaḥ*
749. ॐ मान्याय नमः	*om mānyāya namaḥ*
750. ॐ लोकस्वामिने नमः	*om lokasvāmine namaḥ*
751. ॐ त्रिलोकधृषे नमः	*om trilokadhṛṣc namaḥ*
752. ॐ सुमेधसे नमः	*om sumedhase namaḥ*
753. ॐ मेधजाय नमः	*om medhajāya namaḥ*
754. ॐ धन्याय नमः	*om dhanyāya namaḥ*
755. ॐ सत्यमेधसे नमः	*om satyamedhase namaḥ*
756. ॐ धराधराय नमः	*om dharādharāya namaḥ*
757. ॐ तेजोवृषाय नमः	*om tejovṛṣāya namaḥ*
758. ॐ द्युतिधराय नमः	*om dyutidharāya namaḥ*
759. ॐ सर्वशस्त्रभृतांवराय नमः	*om sarvaśastrabhṛtāṁvarāya namaḥ*
760. ॐ प्रग्रहाय नमः	*om pragrahāya namaḥ*
761. ॐ निग्रहाय नमः	*om nigrahāya namaḥ*
762. ॐ व्यग्राय नमः	*om vyagrāya namaḥ*
763. ॐ नैकश्रृङ्गाय नमः	*om naikaśṛṅgāya namaḥ*
764. ॐ गदाग्रजाय नमः	*om gadāgrajāya namaḥ*
765. ॐ चतुर्मूर्तये नमः	*om caturmūrtaye namaḥ*
766. ॐ चतुर्बाहवे नमः	*om caturbāhave namaḥ*
767. ॐ चतुर्व्यूहाय नमः	*om caturvyūhāya namaḥ*
768. ॐ चतुर्गतये नमः	*om caturgataye namaḥ*
769. ॐ चतुरात्मने नमः	*om caturātmane namaḥ*
770. ॐ चतुर्भावाय नमः	*om caturbhāvāya namaḥ*
771. ॐ चतुर्वेदविदे नमः	*om caturvedavide namaḥ*
772. ॐ एकपदे नमः	*om ekapade namaḥ*
773. ॐ समावर्ताय नमः	*om smāvartāya namaḥ*

774. ॐ अनिवृत्तात्मने नमः om anivṛttātmane namaḥ
775. ॐ दुर्जयाय नमः om durjayāya namaḥ
776. ॐ दुरतिक्रमाय नमः om duratikramāya namaḥ
777. ॐ दुर्लभाय नमः om durlabhāya namaḥ
778. ॐ दुर्गमाय नमः om durgamāya namaḥ
779. ॐ दुर्गाय नमः om durgāya namaḥ
780. ॐ दुरावासाय नमः om durāvāsāya namaḥ
781. ॐ दुरारिघ्ने नमः om durārighne namaḥ
782. ॐ शुभाङ्गाय नमः om śubhāṅgāya namaḥ
783. ॐ लोकसारङ्गाय नमः om lokasāraṅgāya namaḥ
784. ॐ सुतन्तवे नमः om sutantave namaḥ
785. ॐ तन्तुवर्धनाय नमः om tantuvardhanāya namaḥ
786. ॐ इन्द्रकर्मणे नमः om indrakarmaṇe namaḥ
787. ॐ महाकर्मणे नमः om mahākarmaṇe namaḥ
788. ॐ कृतकर्मणे नमः om kṛtakarmaṇe namaḥ
789. ॐ कृतागमाय नमः om kṛtāgamāya namaḥ
790. ॐ उद्भवाय नमः om udbhavāya namaḥ
791. ॐ सुन्दराय नमः om sundarāya namaḥ
792. ॐ सुन्दाय नमः om sundāya namaḥ
793. ॐ रत्ननाभाय नमः om ratnanābhāya namaḥ
794. ॐ सुलोचनाय नमः om sulocanāya namaḥ
795. ॐ अर्काय नमः om arkāya namaḥ
796. ॐ वाजसनाय नमः om vājasanāya namaḥ
797. ॐ शृङ्गिणे नमः om śṛṅgiṇe namaḥ
798. ॐ जयन्ताय नमः om jayantāya namaḥ
799. ॐ सर्वविज्जयिने नमः om sarvavijjayine namaḥ
800. ॐ सुवर्णबिन्दवे नमः om suvarṇabindave namaḥ
801. ॐ अक्षोभ्याय नमः om akṣobhyāya namaḥ
802. ॐ सर्ववागीश्वरेश्वराय नमः om sarvavāgīśvareśvarāya namaḥ
803. ॐ महाह्रदाय नमः om mahāhradāya namaḥ

804.	ॐ महागर्ताय नमः	*om mahāgartāya namaḥ*
805.	ॐ महाभूताय नमः	*om mahābhūtāya namaḥ*
806.	ॐ महानिधये नमः	*om mahānidhaye namaḥ*
807.	ॐ कुमुदाय नमः	*om kumudāya namaḥ*
808.	ॐ कुन्दराय नमः	*om kundarāya namaḥ*
809.	ॐ कुन्दाय नमः	*om kundāya namaḥ*
810.	ॐ पर्जन्याय नमः	*om parjanyāya namaḥ*
811.	ॐ पावनाय नमः	*om pāvanāya namaḥ*
812.	ॐ अनिलाय नमः	*om anilāya namaḥ*
813.	ॐ अमृताशाय नमः	*om amṛtāśāya namaḥ*
814.	ॐ अमृतवपुषे नमः	*om amṛtavapuṣe namaḥ*
815.	ॐ सर्वज्ञाय नमः	*om sarvajñāya namaḥ*
816.	ॐ सर्वतोमुखाय नमः	*om sarvatomukhāya namaḥ*
817.	ॐ सुलभाय नमः	*om sulabhāya namaḥ*
818.	ॐ सुव्रताय नमः	*om suvratāya namaḥ*
819.	ॐ सिद्धाय नमः	*om siddhāya namaḥ*
820.	ॐ शत्रुजिते नमः	*om śatrujite namaḥ*
821.	ॐ शत्रुतापनाय नमः	*om śatrutāpanāya namaḥ*
822.	ॐ न्यग्रोधाय नमः	*om nyagrodhāya namaḥ*
823.	ॐ उदुम्बराय नमः	*om uduṁbarāya namaḥ*
824.	ॐ अश्वत्थाय नमः	*om aśvatthāya namaḥ*
825.	ॐ चाणूरान्ध्रनिषूदनाय नमः	*om cāṇūrāndhraniṣūdanāya namaḥ*
826.	ॐ सहस्रार्चिषे नमः	*om sahasrārciṣe namaḥ*
827.	ॐ सप्तजिह्वाय नमः	*om saptajihvāya namaḥ*
828.	ॐ सप्तैधसे नमः	*om saptaidhase namaḥ*
829.	ॐ सप्तवाहनाय नमः	*om saptavāhanāya namaḥ*
830.	ॐ अमूर्तये नमः	*om amūrtaye namaḥ*
831.	ॐ अनघाय नमः	*om anaghāya namaḥ*
832.	ॐ अचिन्त्याय नमः	*om acintyāya namaḥ*
833.	ॐ भयकृते नमः	*om bhayakṛte namaḥ*

834. ॐ भयनाशनाय नमः — *om bhayanāśanāya namaḥ*
835. ॐ अणवे नमः — *om aṇave namaḥ*
836. ॐ बृहते नमः — *om bṛhate namaḥ*
837. ॐ कृशाय नमः — *om kṛśāya namaḥ*
838. ॐ स्थूलाय नमः — *om sthūlāya namaḥ*
839. ॐ गुणभृते नमः — *om guṇabhṛte namaḥ*
840. ॐ निर्गुणाय नमः — *om nirguṇāya namaḥ*
841. ॐ महते नमः — *om mahate namaḥ*
842. ॐ अधृताय नमः — *om adhṛtāya namaḥ*
843. ॐ स्वधृताय नमः — *om svadhṛtāya namaḥ*
844. ॐ स्वास्याय नमः — *om svāsyāya namaḥ*
845. ॐ प्राग्वंशाय नमः — *om prāgvaṁśāya namaḥ*
846. ॐ वंशवर्धनाय नमः — *om vaṁśavardhanāya namaḥ*
847. ॐ भारभृते नमः — *om bhārabhṛte namaḥ*
848. ॐ कथिताय नमः — *om kathitāya namaḥ*
849. ॐ योगिने नमः — *om yogine namaḥ*
850. ॐ योगीशाय नमः — *om yogīśāya namaḥ*
851. ॐ सर्वकामदाय नमः — *om sarvakāmadāya namaḥ*
852. ॐ आश्रमाय नमः — *om āśramāya namaḥ*
853. ॐ श्रमणाय नमः — *om śramaṇāya namaḥ*
854. ॐ क्षामाय नमः — *om kṣāmāya namaḥ*
855. ॐ सुपर्णाय नमः — *om suparṇāya namaḥ*
856. ॐ वायुवाहनाय नमः — *om vāyuvāhanāya namaḥ*
857. ॐ धनुर्धराय नमः — *om dhanurdharāya namaḥ*
858. ॐ धनुर्वेदाय नमः — *om dhanurvedāya namaḥ*
859. ॐ दण्डाय नमः — *om daṇḍāya namaḥ*
860. ॐ दमयित्रे नमः — *om damayitre namaḥ*
861. ॐ दमाय नमः — *om damāya namaḥ*
862. ॐ अपराजिताय नमः — *om aparājitāya namaḥ*
863. ॐ सर्वसहाय नमः — *om sarvasahāya namaḥ*

864. ॐ नियन्त्रे नमः	*om niyantre namaḥ*
865. ॐ अनियमाय नमः	*om aniyamāya namaḥ*
866. ॐ अयमाय नमः	*om ayamāya namaḥ*
867. ॐ सत्त्ववते नमः	*om sattvavate namaḥ*
868. ॐ सात्त्विकाय नमः	*om sāttvikāya namaḥ*
869. ॐ सत्याय नमः	*om satyāya namaḥ*
870. ॐ सत्यधर्मपरायणाय नमः	*om satyadharmaparāyaṇāya namaḥ*
871. ॐ अभिप्रायाय नमः	*om abhiprāyāya namaḥ*
872. ॐ प्रियार्हाय नमः	*om priyārhāya namaḥ*
873. ॐ अर्हाय नमः	*om arhāya namaḥ*
874. ॐ प्रियकृते नमः	*om priyakṛte namaḥ*
875. ॐ प्रीतिवर्धनाय नमः	*om prītivardhanāya namaḥ*
876. ॐ विहायसगतये नमः	*om vihāyasagataye namaḥ*
877. ॐ ज्योतिषे नमः	*om jyotiṣe namaḥ*
878. ॐ सुरुचये नमः	*om surucaye namaḥ*
879. ॐ हुत्भुजे नमः	*om hutbhuje namaḥ*
880. ॐ विभवे नमः	*om vibhave namaḥ*
881. ॐ रवये नमः	*om ravaye namaḥ*
882. ॐ विरोचनाय नमः	*om virocanāya namaḥ*
883. ॐ सूर्याय नमः	*om sūryāya namaḥ*
884. ॐ सवित्रे नमः	*om savitre namaḥ*
885. ॐ रविलोचनाय नमः	*om ravilocanāya namaḥ*
886. ॐ अनन्ताय नमः	*om anantāya namaḥ*
887. ॐ हुतभुजे नमः	*om hutbhuje namaḥ*
888. ॐ भोक्त्रे नमः	*om bhoktre namaḥ*
889. ॐ सुखदाय नमः	*om sukhadāya namaḥ*
890. ॐ नैकजाय नमः	*om naikajāya namaḥ*
891. ॐ अग्रजाय नमः	*om agrajāya namaḥ*
892. ॐ अनिर्विण्णाय नमः	*om anirviṇṇāya namaḥ*
893. ॐ सदामर्षिणे नमः	*om sadāmarṣiṇe namaḥ*

894. ॐ लोकाधिष्ठानाय नमः | *om lokādhiṣṭhānāya namaḥ*
895. ॐ अद्भुताय नमः | *om adbhutāya namaḥ*
896. ॐ सनान् नमः | *om sanān namaḥ*
897. ॐ सनातनतमाय नमः | *om sanātanatamāya namaḥ*
898. ॐ कपिलाय नमः | *om kapilāya namaḥ*
899. ॐ कपये नमः | *om kapaye namaḥ*
900. ॐ अप्ययाय नमः | *om apyayāya namaḥ*
901. ॐ स्वस्तिदाय नमः | *om svastidāya namaḥ*
902. ॐ स्वस्तिकृते नमः | *om svastikṛte namaḥ*
903. ॐ स्वस्तये नमः | *om svastaye namaḥ*
904. ॐ स्वस्तिभुजे नमः | *om svastibhuje namaḥ*
905. ॐ स्वस्तिदक्षिणाय नमः | *om svastidakṣiṇāya namaḥ*
906. ॐ अरौद्राय नमः | *om araudrāya namaḥ*
907. ॐ कुण्डलिने नमः | *om kuṇḍaline namaḥ*
908. ॐ चक्रिणे नमः | *om cakriṇe namaḥ*
909. ॐ विक्रमिणे नमः | *om vikramiṇe namaḥ*
910. ॐ ऊर्जितशासनाय नमः | *om ūrjitaśāsanāya namaḥ*
911. ॐ शब्दातिगाय नमः | *om śabdātigāya namaḥ*
912. ॐ शब्दसहाय नमः | *om śabdasahāya namaḥ*
913. ॐ शिशिराय नमः | *om śiśirāya namaḥ*
914. ॐ शर्वरीकराय नमः | *om śarvarīkarāya namaḥ*
915. ॐ अक्रूराय नमः | *om akrūrāya namaḥ*
916. ॐ पेशलाय नमः | *om peśalāya namaḥ*
917. ॐ दक्षाय नमः | *om dakṣāya namaḥ*
918. ॐ दक्षिणाय नमः | *om dakṣiṇāya namaḥ*
919. ॐ क्षमिणांवराय नमः | *om kṣamiṇāṁvarāya namaḥ*
920. ॐ विद्वत्तमाय नमः | *om vidvattamāya namaḥ*
921. ॐ वीतभयाय नमः | *om vītabhayāya namaḥ*
922. ॐ पुण्यश्रवणकीर्तनाय नमः | *om puṇyaśravaṇakīrtanāya namaḥ*
923. ॐ उत्तारणाय नमः | *om uttāraṇāya namaḥ*

924.	ॐ दुष्कृतिघ्ने नमः	*om duṣkṛtighne namaḥ*
925.	ॐ पुण्याय नमः	*om puṇyāya namaḥ*
926.	ॐ दुःस्वप्ननाशनाय नमः	*om duḥsvapnanāśanāya namaḥ*
927.	ॐ वीरघ्ने नमः	*om vīraghne namaḥ*
928.	ॐ रक्षणाय नमः	*om rakṣaṇāya namaḥ*
929.	ॐ सद्भ्यो नमः	*om sadbhyo namaḥ*
930.	ॐ जीवनाय नमः	*om jīvanāya namaḥ*
931.	ॐ पर्यवस्थिताय नमः	*om paryavasthitāya namaḥ*
932.	ॐ अनन्तरूपाय नमः	*om anantarūpāya namaḥ*
933.	ॐ अनन्तश्रिये नमः	*om anantaśriye namaḥ*
934.	ॐ जितमन्यवे नमः	*om jitamanyave namaḥ*
935.	ॐ भयापहाय नमः	*om bhayāpahāya namaḥ*
936.	ॐ चतुरश्राय नमः	*om caturaśrāya namaḥ*
937.	ॐ गभीरात्मने नमः	*om gabhīrātmane namaḥ*
938.	ॐ विदिशाय नमः	*om vidiśāya namaḥ*
939.	ॐ व्यादिशाय नमः	*om vyādiśāya namaḥ*
940.	ॐ दिशाय नमः	*om diśāya namaḥ*
941.	ॐ अनादये नमः	*om anādaye namaḥ*
942.	ॐ भुवो भुवे नमः	*om bhuvo bhuve namaḥ*
943.	ॐ लक्ष्म्यै नमः	*om lakṣmyai namaḥ*
944.	ॐ सुवीराय नमः	*om suvīrāya namaḥ*
945.	ॐ रुचिराङ्गदाय नमः	*om rucirāṅgadāya namaḥ*
946.	ॐ जननाय नमः	*om jananāya namaḥ*
947.	ॐ जनजन्मादये नमः	*om janajanmādaye namaḥ*
948.	ॐ भीमाय नमः	*om bhīmāya namaḥ*
949.	ॐ भीमपराक्रमाय नमः	*om bhīmaparākramāya namaḥ*
950.	ॐ आधारनिलयाय नमः	*om ādhāranilayāya namaḥ*
951.	ॐ अधात्रे नमः	*om adhātre namaḥ*
952.	ॐ पुष्पहासाय नमः	*om puṣpahāsāya namaḥ*
953.	ॐ प्रजागराय नमः	*om prajāgarāya namaḥ*

954. ॐ ऊर्ध्वगाय नमः *om ūrdhvagāya namaḥ*
955. ॐ सत्पथाचाराय नमः *om satpathācārāya namaḥ*
956. ॐ प्राणदाय नमः *om prāṇadāya namaḥ*
957. ॐ प्रणवाय नमः *om praṇavāya namaḥ*
958. ॐ पणाय नमः *om paṇāya namaḥ*
959. ॐ प्रमाणाय नमः *om pramāṇāya namaḥ*
960. ॐ प्राणनिलयाय नमः *om prāṇanilayāya namaḥ*
961. ॐ प्राणभृते नमः *om prāṇabhṛte namaḥ*
962. ॐ प्राणजीवनाय नमः *om prāṇajīvanāya namaḥ*
963. ॐ तत्त्वाय नमः *om tattvāya namaḥ*
964. ॐ तत्त्वविदे नमः *om tattvavide namaḥ*
965. ॐ एकात्मने नमः *om ekātmane namaḥ*
966. ॐ जन्ममृत्युजरातिगाय नमः *om janmamṛtyujarātigāya namaḥ*
967. ॐ भूर्भुवःस्वस्तरवे नमः *om bhūrbhuvaḥsvastarave namaḥ*
968. ॐ ताराय नमः *om tārāya namaḥ*
969. ॐ सवित्रे नमः *om savitre namaḥ*
970. ॐ प्रपितामहाय नमः *om prapitāmahāya namaḥ*
971. ॐ यज्ञाय नमः *om yajñāya namaḥ*
972. ॐ यज्ञपतये नमः *om yajñapataye namaḥ*
973. ॐ यज्वने नमः *om yajvane namaḥ*
974. ॐ यज्ञाङ्गाय नमः *om yajñāṅgāya namaḥ*
975. ॐ यज्ञवाहनाय नमः *om yajñavāhanāya namaḥ*
976. ॐ यज्ञभृते नमः *om yajñabhṛte namaḥ*
977. ॐ यज्ञकृते नमः *om yajñakṛte namaḥ*
978. ॐ यज्ञिने नमः *om yajñine namaḥ*
979. ॐ यज्ञभुजे नमः *om yajñabhuje namaḥ*
980. ॐ यज्ञसाधनाय नमः *om yajñasādhanāya namaḥ*
981. ॐ यज्ञान्तकृते नमः *om yajñāntakṛte namaḥ*
982. ॐ यज्ञगुह्याय नमः *om yajñaguhyāya namaḥ*
983. ॐ अन्नाय नमः *om om annāya namaḥ*

984.	ॐ अन्नादाय नमः	*om annādāya namaḥ*
985.	ॐ आत्मयोनये नमः	*om ātmayonaye namaḥ*
986.	ॐ स्वयंजाताय नमः	*om svayañjātāya namaḥ*
987.	ॐ वैखानाय नमः	*om vaikhānāya namaḥ*
988.	ॐ सामगायनाय नमः	*om sāmagāyanāya namaḥ*
989.	ॐ देवकीनन्दनाय नमः	*om devakīnandanāya namaḥ*
990.	ॐ स्रष्ट्रे नमः	*om sraṣṭre namaḥ*
991.	ॐ क्षितीशाय नमः	*om kṣitīśāya namaḥ*
992.	ॐ पापनाशनाय नमः	*om pāpanāśanāya namaḥ*
993.	ॐ शङ्खभृते नमः	*om śaṅkhabhṛte namaḥ*
994.	ॐ नन्दकिने नमः	*om nandakine namaḥ*
995.	ॐ चक्रिणे नमः	*om cakriṇe namaḥ*
996.	ॐ शार्ङ्गधन्वने नमः	*om śārṅgadhanvane namaḥ*
997.	ॐ गदाधराय नमः	*om gadādharāya namaḥ*
998.	ॐ रथाङ्गपाणये नमः	*om rathāṅgapāṇaye namaḥ*
999.	ॐ अक्षोभ्याय नमः	*om akṣobhyāya namaḥ*
1000.	ॐ सर्वप्रहरणायुधाय नमः	*om sarvapraharaṇāyudhāya namaḥ*

Sanskrit Pronunciation Guide

Vowels

अ a आ ā इ i ई ī उ u ऊ ū ऋ ṛ ॠ ṝ

ऌ ḷ ए e ऐ ai ओ o औ au

ं ṁ (*anusvara*) : ḥ (*visarga*)

Consonants

Gutturals :	क ka	ख kha	ग ga	घ gha	ङ ṅa
Palatals :	च ca	छ cha	ज ja	झ jha	ञ ña
Cerebrals :	ट ṭa	ठ ṭha	ड ḍa	ढ ḍha	ण ṇa
Dentals :	त ta	थ tha	द da	ध dha	न na
Labials:	प pa	फ pha	ब ba	भ bha	म ma
Semivowels :	य ya	र ra	ल la	व va	
Sibilants :	श śa	ष ṣa	स sa		
Aspirate :	ह ha	ऽ = ' *(avagraha) - the apostrophe*			
	क्ष kṣa	ज्ञ jña			

Some Other Works By The Author

Telugu

Anudina Rāmāyaṇaṁ
Gītāmṛtaṁ
Upaniṣatsudhā
Ādi-Anādi
Caturviṁśati
Ihaṁ-Paraṁ
Rāmāyaṇa Paramārthaṁ

Hindi

Āndhra - Hindī Rūpaka
Śrī Kāmākṣī Vilāsa
Santa Tyāgarāja
Sahasradhārā
Śrī Sahasrikā
Satya Śatī
Rāmakathā Navanīta

English

Women In Vālmīki
Thoughts On Rāmāyaṇa
Voice Of Vision
Vālmīki
Songs Of Rāmadāsa